IF YOU'RE SECOND YOU ARE NOTHING

Oliver Holt is the chief sports writer for the *Daily Mirror* and was named the British Press Gazette Sports Writer of the Year in 2005 and 2006. This is his first book.

OLIVER HOLT

IF YOU'RE SECOND YOU ARE NOTHING

FERGUSON AND SHANKLY

PAN BOOKS

First published 2006 by Macmillan

First published in paperback 2007 by Pan Books
an imprint of Pan Macmillan Ltd
Pan Macmillan, 20 New Wharf Road, London N1 9RR
Basingstoke and Oxford
Associated companies throughout the world
www.panmacmillan.com

ISBN 978-0-330-44314-2

Copyright © Oliver Holt 2006

The right of Oliver Holt to be identified as the
author of this work has been asserted by him in accordance
with the Copyright, Designs and Patents Act 1988.

All rights reserved. No part of this publication may be
reproduced, stored in or introduced into a retrieval system, or
transmitted, in any form, or by any means (electronic, mechanical,
photocopying, recording or otherwise) without the prior written
permission of the publisher. Any person who does any unauthorized
act in relation to this publication may be liable to criminal
prosecution and civil claims for damages.

9 8 7 6 5 4 3 2 1

A CIP catalogue record for this book is available from
the British Library.

Typeset by Set Systems Ltd, Saffron Walden, Essex
Printed and bound in Great Britain by
Mackays of Chatham plc, Chatham, Kent

This book is sold subject to the condition that it shall not,
by way of trade or otherwise, be lent, re-sold, hired out,
or otherwise circulated without the publisher's prior consent
in any form of binding or cover other than that in which
it is published and without a similar condition including this
condition being imposed on the subsequent purchaser.

Visit www.panmacmillan.com to read more about all our books
and to buy them. You will also find features, author interviews and
news of any author events, and you can sign up for e-newsletters
so that you're always first to hear about our new releases.

For Alice and Edie

Thanks to Sir Tom Finney, Ian Callaghan,
Brian Hall, Phil Thompson, Ronnie Moran,
Ian Cotton, Ray Clemence, Peter Robinson,
Shelley Rohde, Tim Park, Paul Jewell,
Martin O'Neill, Gary Pallister, Mark McGhee,
David Beckham, Terry Byrne, Simon Oliveira
and Liverpool Football Club.

Contents

Introduction: A Glow Like Fire / 1

1: Shankly Adrift / 13

2: Ferguson's Childhood — A River Ran Through It / 31

3: Shankly and the Horror of the Leaving of Liverpool / 41

4: Ferguson, the Man with the Casting Vote / 56

5: Shankly and a Show of Red Strength / 64

6: Ferguson, Rangers and their Mixed Marriage / 86

7: Shankly and the New Breed / 98

8: Ferguson — A Frightening Bastard from the Start / 113

9: Shankly and a Vision of Hell / 122

10: Ferguson and a Case Dismissed / 132

11: Shankly's Greatest Day / 142

12: Ferguson and his Father's Eyes / 155

13: Shankly and Napoleon Bonaparte's Big Idea / 169

14: Ferguson and the Glory of Gothenburg / 186

15: Shankly and the Building of the Boot Room / 199

16: Ferguson and the Death of his Hero / 221

17: Shankly, Huddersfield and the Gateway to Immortality / 228

18: Ferguson and the Great Purge of Old Trafford / 236

19: Shankly and the New Creed at Workington / 254

20: Ferguson Breaks the Dam / 264

21: Shankly at the Outposts / 282

22: Ferguson at the Peak of his Powers / 289

23: Shankly, Tom Finney and the War / 304

24: Ferguson and the Wonder of Barcelona / 319

25: Shankly and the Escape from Underground / 336

26: Ferguson – The Rock and a Hard Place / 342

27: Shankly – Man from a Dead Town / 371

28: Ferguson, Beckham and Things that End in Tears / 377

Bibliography / 401

Index / 403

Introduction:
A Glow Like Fire

Bill Shankly spoke in a rasp but his words were like poetry. His voice was rough but to his players it seemed like balm. Now and then, on the long coach journeys that took the Aberdeen team to away matches in the early 1980s, Alex Ferguson would slip a tape into the machine and listen to Shankly talking, his big ideas and his observations on the human condition filling the bus as Ferguson and his team travelled to the strongholds of Scottish football and laid them waste.

Shankly died in 1981 but Ferguson still listened to the voice. He listened to the recording of Shankly talking to a journalist. He listened to him talking about how team spirit was a form of socialism. He listened to Shankly's tales of growing up in Ayrshire in a family of ten children and how his father would give him a 'sock on the jaw' if he misbehaved. He listened to him talking about how he tried to cope with defeat by cleaning the cooker or mowing the lawn, forgetting the pain in the drudgery of a simple task.

He drank in the story of how Shankly had introduced an all-red strip at Liverpool in 1965. He heard Shankly burn with pride when he talked about it. 'There was a glow like a fire,' Shankly said on the tape. 'I felt a glow that night at Anfield. I thought "Christ, there must be a fire."' He heard Shankly say he believed players should be banned from laughing for a week after every lost game.

And even though Ferguson was just at the start of his brilliant career then, even though his future pre-eminence and everything he was to achieve could only be guessed at, he listened to Shankly talking about how hard it was when he retired as Liverpool manager in the summer of 1974 and found the days stretching out before him, filled only with the emptiness of a life on football's outside.

'I train every morning,' Shankly said on the tapes, which were recorded a year after he quit, 'and I see the players. I don't talk to them very much. From there, I get my bearings. It has been difficult for me, who has been in the game all my life and football's the only thing I know. From the training session, I get my bearings and I go and have lunch with my wife and then I know where I am. If I didn't have the training session in the morning, I would be a little bit lost. The morning is the only time I find difficult and when that's past, the rest of the day is more or less the same as it was.'

Shankly did not offer the old smooth prizes. He did not make glib remarks about how he had no regrets. In the months after he retired, he came to realize he had made a terrible mistake. He found the pain of no longer being Liverpool manager hard to bear. He had taken over in December 1959 and won three league titles, two FA Cups and the Uefa Cup. But his second great Anfield side was on the cusp of greatness when he left and he had to watch as his former assistant, Bob Paisley, guided what was still essentially Shankly's team to victory in the 1977 European Cup Final in Rome.

Ferguson learned a lesson from that. He stepped back from the brink when he was poised to retire in the summer of 2002 at the age of sixty. He heard speculation that Sven-Goran Eriksson was going to replace him and he couldn't stand it. He said his wife, Cathy, had persuaded him to stay on but nobody was buying that. The truth was, he knew that a life without football would be a slow torture for him. He knew that being on the outside would eat at him the way it ate at Shankly. He knew it would probably kill him the way it killed Shankly.

There's a twist, though. If Shankly plunged himself into

unhappiness by leaving Liverpool when he did, his premature retirement ensured his unblemished immortality. He did not have time to grow old in the spotlight. Neither he nor his team sank into decline while he was at the helm. Instead, he laid the foundations for Liverpool's greatness, he is recognized as the father of the club and the Kop still sings his name. His image is still everywhere at Anfield. There is a statue of him outside the superstore with a simple message at its base: 'He Made the People Happy.'

It hasn't been the same for Ferguson. He saved himself when he postponed his retirement but it could be argued that his legacy is suffering. Has he stayed too long and presided over the beginning of United's decline after the decade of domestic domination that he created? In the years since 2002, some would argue that he has made a series of bad decisions, on and off the pitch, that have undermined his reputation. A string of seemingly personal vendettas with players, the Irish racehorse owners John Magnier and J. P. McManus and, of course, journalists, have become part of his life. If Shankly left too soon, maybe Ferguson has stayed too long.

If Shankly is remembered almost exclusively with warmth and affection, if his aphorisms fill the pages of a thousand books of quotations, the appreciation of Ferguson's greatness is for some being polluted by his unchecked bellicosity and his accumulation of enemies.

In the last line of his enthralling autobiography *Managing My Life*, published in 1999, Ferguson mentioned the values he had learned growing up in the tight-knit Clydeside shipbuilding community of Govan. 'Loyalty has been the anchor of my life,' he said. The trouble is that in football, loyalty and strong leadership do not always go hand in hand. What kind of loyalty was it to allow David Beckham to leave Old Trafford after he had been at the club for more than a decade as man and boy? What kind of loyalty was it to launch a character assassination of his long-term assistant, Brian Kidd? What kind of loyalty to rid himself of Roy Keane so peremptorily? In football hard decisions have to be made, and people who were once indispensable discarded, but what kind of loyalty was it to sue his friend John Magnier for upwards of £50 million when Magnier had showered favours and privileges upon him that Ferguson would never have glimpsed without him?

Mark McGhee, the former Aberdeen striker who shared Ferguson's greatest triumphs north of the border and was adopted by him as a protégé for a time when he was manager at Reading, Leicester and Wolves, has tasted his brand of loyalty, too. A week after McGhee was sacked at Molineux and at a low ebb, he bumped into Ferguson in the directors' room at Ewood Park where both men had gone to scout a game. Ferguson blanked him.

'It seems to be a trait of his that he has this ability to dispose of people,' McGhee, now manager of Brighton and Hove Albion, said. 'It is because they are no longer of any use to him. He doesn't need them. He has moved on. He needs change. He has become something ... I suppose it was the same with Beckham. It's not so much a ruthlessness. It's more of a selfishness. It's like when he's finished with you, he loses interest.

'At Blackburn, I was standing by the door and he came walking out and he walked right past me. He had been very keen for me to go to Wolves and I'm sure that when the chairman, Jonathan Hayward, phoned him, he would have praised me. He perhaps felt he had put his reputation on the line and then with me not getting them promoted he perhaps felt that was a slight on him. I can live with that but I know he's wrong.

'As a manager, he was more of an influence on me than anyone else. The biggest influence he had on me was that I realized from him that it doesn't come easy. You have to be prepared to sacrifice. You have to be prepared to fall out with people. You have got to be prepared to make decisions.

'When I left Leicester and went to Wolves, it was because it was what he would have done. I think there is a connection between Fergie and Shankly. I think I looked at Fergie and realized it could be done and I think it's a little bit like that with Fergie and Shankly: he saw this guy from the same sort of background who was now a god. He used to make us listen to the tapes on the bus. Some of what Shanks says is bollocks but some of it is way ahead, like preparation and eating and warm-downs.

'One of the things that linked them was that they were both proud of where they came from. I think part of their drive is to prove that people from their background can do well, and when Fergie looked at Shankly that's what he saw: a man who in any other life would just be a wee miner.

'I think it's unfair to say that Fergie's players didn't regard him with affection as well as respect. He's probably his own worst enemy because he's always had this side to him where he . . . you know . . . moves on. But I think people like Beckham and Ryan Giggs and these boys, even Gordon Strachan and people who maybe don't speak to him any more as friends, would put him top of the list of influences on their careers. Perhaps with Shankly, it has become a bit more romantic with the passing of the years. I don't know whether it was as real as that.'

Strachan's relationship with Ferguson grew strained when Ferguson twice accused him of being deceitful when he moved away from him both at Aberdeen and United. Strachan made a joke of it. 'Fergie used to play tapes of Bill Shankly talking,' he said. 'I remember that and a singer he liked. I don't know who it was but it was crap. He played it on the team bus, too, and all the boys hated it. Until one night it got chucked away. If he's still wondering who threw that tape off the bus, it was me. So maybe he was right and I'm not to be trusted.'

As a man, Shankly was easier to like. He lived a simple life. He did not covet material gain. He lived in the same semi-detached suburban house his whole career at Liverpool. He lived in a simpler time, before agents and the ravenous demands of the media. He never compromised his beliefs. He was never seduced by the worlds that football might have opened up to him. He loved the game for the game's sake. He was entranced by football until the end. There was a purity about him that few in the game could claim now, and which has slipped further and further away from Ferguson now that he is in the winter of his reign.

As a manager, Ferguson has been more successful. There are many who feel that for the sake of his legacy, he should have quit in 2002. If he had, he would not have embroiled Manchester United in his row with Magnier over Rock of Gibraltar, which led to pages of adverse publicity. A line can be drawn straight from that row, and Magnier's steady acquisition of shares in United, to the takeover of the club by Malcolm Glazer and his family.

If he had quit in 2002, Ferguson would not have indulged Rio Ferdinand and made a mockery of the principles of personal responsibility and hard work he had once taught his young players. If he had quit in 2002, he would not have had to alienate so many United fans and compromise his principles by accepting the takeover of the club by Malcolm Glazer in the spring of 2005.

There have been some high points in the past three seasons, even if there has been no league trophy. United won the Carling Cup in the spring of 2006 and celebrated the capture of such a cheap trinket with an enthusiasm that merely confirmed how far they had demoted their ambitions.

Ferguson deserves credit, too, for helping United to exert mild pressure on Chelsea at the end of the 2005–06 season. They were 17 points behind the champions at one point and closed the gap to 7 points. Then they drew at home to Sunderland on Good Friday and the title was Chelsea's again. United really only got close because Chelsea had started to relax.

So much of the last four years seems to have been about contradicting what Ferguson used to say. Once, he gave the impression that the club did not care about the Carling Cup.

Then, when United won it in 2006 and it was all they had left, he said they had always considered it an important trophy. Once, he said he could never be a boss's man. Then he seemed to cosy up to the Glazers and sided against thousands of fans disillusioned by the takeover.

In the 1972–73 season, when his playing career was winding down at Falkirk, Ferguson was the spokesman for what he called 'a mutinous crew' of players who threatened a strike in an argument with the club's manager. 'For my part,' Ferguson said, 'perhaps I should have been stronger in arguing against the strike but I would not ever have wanted to be known as a boss's man. To someone with my upbringing, that would have been a heinous crime.'

And yet as the Glazers prepared their takeover of the club from their base in Palm Beach, Florida, prepared to load United with debt, prepared to raise the ticket prices for the fans, Ferguson stayed silent. In fact, on 3 July 2005, just five days after Glazer had won total control of the club, Ferguson met with Glazer's sons, Joel, Avi and Bryan, and seemed to support them. 'The meeting was very positive and relaxed and they made it clear they would back the team,' Ferguson said. 'This has been a difficult time for all involved but the most important thing now is to get back to football.'

Some United fans confronted him at Budapest airport when United arrived to play the second leg of their Champions League qualifying tie against Debrecen. A couple of fans rounded on Ferguson and chief executive David Gill and accused Ferguson of selling out. Ferguson said he considered his prime responsibility was to his staff, some of whom had been working with him for fifteen years. When the supporters persisted with their criticisms, Ferguson cut them short. 'If you don't like it,' he said, 'go and watch Chelsea.'

It is hard to imagine Shankly ever being caught in a situation where he might be out of tune with the supporters. Shankly lived and worked for the supporters. He constantly reminded his players of their responsibilities to the fans. Most of his former players talk of the times they saw him paying the train fare from Liverpool to London or London to Liverpool for fans who had run out of money.

Think of one overriding image from Ferguson's time in charge at Old Trafford and it is probably an impression of him standing on the touchline at the stadium gesturing at his watch and gesticulating at the referee. Think of an abiding image of Shankly and it is of him walking round Anfield after a title triumph with a supporter's scarf tied around his neck, saluting the fans with a clenched fist.

Shankly felt a communion with the Liverpool supporters that runs deeper than any bond Ferguson has established in his nineteen years at Old Trafford. Of course, he is admired and respected by most of the United faithful for the astonishing consistency of the success he has achieved. But, for some, there is something missing. Maybe it's a lack of charm. Maybe a lack of grace. And, unfortunately, the fact that Ferguson is perceived by some as a bully. You can possibly admire the bully as a manager but you can't admire the bully as a man. The point of comparing Ferguson with Shankly is that in many ways Shankly shines a light on Ferguson's shortcomings and on his limitations. That's why even though Shankly did not win as many trophies as Ferguson, even though he did not win the European Cup like Ferguson, he will always be revered in a way that Ferguson will never know. Shankly, more than Jock Stein or Bob Paisley or Brian Clough, was a man of humour and dynamism grounded in the working classes that were his audience.

There will never be any problem with acclaiming Ferguson as one of the greatest managers in British football history, but something will always be withheld by some when he is appraised as a man. Many look at Ferguson and see a man consumed by his anger and his pain and his hostility. Just how far does a man have to go to see that he has won? Just how much money does he have to earn before he realizes he's not being screwed by the system like his father was? How far does he have to travel before he can rest and tell himself he's made it, that he can stop scrabbling and scraping and whingeing and complaining and protesting? That he can stop being angry and resentful?

The tragedy of Ferguson as he thrashes around in his bitterness and his angst is that he is a fiercely intelligent man. He is capable of great charm, too. And of humour. Certainly, most journalists who have ever been granted an individual interview with him will say readily that it was the most rewarding and fascinating hour they have spent in their professional lives.

It is harder to present his redeeming features, because so many of his associates are scared to talk about him for fear of offending him. Ferguson himself refused to shine a light on the issues that have dominated his life since his autobiography was published in 1999.

Mark McGhee is right, too: many of Ferguson's players continue to regard him purely as an influence for good in their lives. Players like Ryan Giggs, Gary Neville and Nicky Butt have spoken often about the enormous debt of gratitude they owe him. And before their schism, Roy Keane talked about the respect he felt for Ferguson as they approached the climax of their Treble season in the spring of 1999 and prepared for the last league game of the campaign against Spurs.

'The manager is the only Man in here,' Keane said. 'Yes, he's hard. He radiates purpose. He's intense, focused, driven. His commitment, his insatiable hunger, never cease to amaze me. He sets the tone, especially on a day like this when the carnival atmosphere around the place can cause you to forget the objective, a result. Remember who you are, remember that you are Manchester United players. Remember what you did to get here, now go and do it one more time. And you'll win.'

Glimpses of the humorous, jocular, gently chiding Ferguson are still memories to be cherished. Late in 2005, a couple of days before United played Chelsea in the league at Old Trafford and sports journalists were queuing up again to dance on his grave, the United manager gave one of his last Friday press conferences dedicated to print journalists at the club's Carrington training headquarters. A few weeks later there was one final conflagration and the last personal connection with the daily newspaper beat reporters disappeared.

But on that Friday in early November, Ferguson was all bonhomie and levity. He greeted a couple of the writers who had travelled up from London with knowing remarks that made it plain they had made the journey north because they scented his blood. Then, he got stuck into the banter.

Somebody asked him about Jose Mourinho's recent jibes about Arsène Wenger. Mourinho had accused Wenger of being a voyeur. He had said Wenger talked so often about Chelsea that he imagined the Arsenal boss training a telescope on the Chelsea training ground. There is no love lost between Ferguson and Wenger, the man who has been the United manager's greatest rival over the last decade. 'I'll tell you what Wenger is,' Ferguson said with a glint in his eye, 'and it's got nothing to do with vision.'

Then, he talked about the brotherhood of managers and how much he valued the occasional contact between bosses. One of the things that turned him against Wenger was his early refusal to join him in his office for a post-match glass of red wine. Ferguson considered that unforgivable. He talked about how much he loved the company at the League Managers' Association dinner and how he regretted the gradual loss of the time managers used to share at the end of a game, time eroded now by media commitments and the rush to get on a waiting coach and head for the airport.

His eyes lit up when he casually asked the score or so of journalists crammed into the small room at Carrington how many games Chelsea had gone unbeaten. He was met by a sea of blank faces. He was beside himself with joy. 'What, you don't know?' he said. 'Some journalists youse are. And you've got the cheek to criticize me. You can't do your job. Research is the most important thing a journalist should have. And you're sitting there, not a fucking clue any of you. That'll do me.'

United beat Chelsea the following Sunday. A fortnight later, they beat Charlton at The Valley. Ferguson spent much of the hour before the game alone in the office of the Charlton manager, Alan Curbishley, watching the horse-racing on the television. When he walked along the touchline before the game, the United fans, who had been booing him a few weeks earlier, applauded him raucously. And Ferguson, suddenly looking a little frail and every day of his sixty-three years old, stood applauding them back, looking like Brezhnev or Khrushchev standing on the podium and clapping the General Assembly.

What he seems never to have grasped, as he has circled the wagons around him and his teams throughout his career, is that people want to like him. They want to match his achievements as a manager with a man with a character they can admire. They want him to be more like Shankly, more approachable, more human, less defensive, less angry.

But that is not Ferguson's way. He seems to need conflict. He always has done. He thrives on it. 'If you're second, you are nothing,' Shankly once said. Ferguson believes that too. Perhaps he would have been a mediocrity if he had not driven himself so hard and sought confrontation so energetically. At the end of that Friday press conference, he smirked when somebody mentioned it would be his nineteenth anniversary in charge of Manchester United two days later. 'Are you bringing me a present, you miserable so and sos?' he said.

As he got up to leave, someone asked him if he had suffered through times like this before when people were busily predicting his imminent demise and telling him that his reign was over. 'Yes,' he said, 'plenty of them. And I've had to face you lot after it. So nothing changes. I'm ready for youse.'

1: Shankly Adrift

In the declining years of his life, when he was dying slowly from redundancy and irrelevance and the great grief of being unwanted, Bill Shankly took his holidays in Blackpool on the Lancashire coast. He and his wife, Nessie, always stayed at the Norbreck Castle Hotel, an outcast from Las Vegas Boulevard with its concrete façade bookended by two turrets doused in purple rinse. But it stands on the Queen's Promenade in Bispham on the northern edge of town, where Edwardian holidaymakers once came to take the air, and Shankly loved it for the bracing winds and the views of the churning Irish Sea.

He still played football. Even there. He was in his late sixties and age had started to pinch his face but there is a patch of grass that isn't quite a lawn sandwiched between the hotel and the car park. Shankly organized a daily two-a-side challenge match with two hotel waiters and his old friend Jock Dodds, the former Blackpool and Sheffield United centre forward. They hurtled around on that grass, the two old men and the pair of Greek waiters, as parties of pensioners clambered off their coaches and shuffled past towards the hotel foyer.

When the others left, Shankly headed for the promenade with his wife. They crossed the tracks that took the trams from Fleetwood in the north to Stargate in the south, through the special little gate reserved for hotel guests. Sometimes they sat in the fine red Victorian shelters that dotted the seafront every hundred yards or so; lovely, ornate buildings with wrought-iron finery cascading down from the roof. Sometimes, on sunny days, they would take deckchairs with them and sit gazing out towards the Isle of Man in the distance.

After a few days away, Shankly always grew bored. He craved talk about the glory days. He craved football talk. So he phoned friends and urged them to come and visit him for the afternoon. Every year, it was the same routine. It got to the point where Peter Robinson, the Liverpool chief executive who had worked closely with Shankly for the last decade of his Anfield reign, came to expect the call. For a few minutes, he would resist, pleading pressure of work. But Shankly told him it would do him good to get away from the office. He always persuaded him in the end.

They sat out in their deckchairs for hours. When the wind began to howl, Nessie fled back across the road to the Norbreck Castle. Robinson looked up and down the seafront as the promenade gradually emptied. But Shankly never budged. 'He just wanted someone to talk to,' Robinson said. 'We would be the only people sitting on the promenade in those gale-force winds and there was no way Bill was going to move. He told me sitting out there in that weather would set me up for the winter and how well I would be, but I always seemed to come down with a terrible cold that would be with me for about a month.'

At the start of the 1970s, Shankly had been in his pomp. He had rebuilt his first great Liverpool side that had won the league in 1963–64 and 1965–66, the FA Cup in 1965 and reached the semi-finals of the European Cup in 1965. He created a new side that won the league for a third time under his management in 1972–73 and then captured the FA Cup playing champagne football inspired by Kevin Keegan, Steve Heighway, Tommy Smith and Emlyn Hughes in 1974.

And then, even though everyone begged him not to, even though they told him he would regret it, he quit. In the summer of 1974, he walked away from the Liverpool job. Soon, just as everybody had told him, he wished he hadn't, but by then it was too late, and to his keen dismay he found there was no way back in. By the end of the 1970s, one of England's greatest managers and one of its most fascinating, charismatic characters was sitting alone on the Blackpool promenade like King Lear on the heath, inviting the elements to do their worst, urging the winds to rage and the rain to spout.

His isolation and his belief that the game he loved had turned its back on him make up one of the great tragedies of modern football. He was football's version of one that loved not wisely but too well. If ever a man deserved to be cloaked in adoration by a sport he had ennobled, it was Shankly. If ever a football man deserved to die happy, secure in the mutual admiration that should have existed between him and the club he created, it was Shankly. But football seems not to be designed to supply happy endings for managers and their football clubs, and Shankly was consigned to a fretful existence. For him, life without football was purgatory.

Professional football had always been his refuge from the world. When he signed for Carlisle United in 1932 it brought him escape from the dying mining community of Glenbuck, a life down the pit and the Depression. Some miners drank to dull the hardship but Shankly was teetotal. Football was his sanctuary. 'He had a fetish for fresh air,' one of his friends remarked. Shankly never lost the feeling that football was his salvation right through his life. 'It's great to be alive, lads,' he told his players. 'All you need is the green grass and the ball.'

Football was his escape and he wanted it to be the same for the supporters who came to watch Liverpool. That was his mission, his socialism: to give the fans who came to watch Liverpool on their day off from the docks or the shipyards or the factories some relief from the drudgery of their daily lives. Football allowed Shankly to be a fugitive from life, and when he resigned as Liverpool manager he suddenly found that life had caught up with him and now he was in chains.

He still played, of course. Five-a-sides with friends at a

leisure centre in Stanley Park, that kind of thing. He still watched, too. Nothing would keep him away from that. 'If there was no football on at Liverpool, he'd go to Everton,' his former captain, Tommy Smith, said. 'If there was nothing on at Everton, he'd go to Manchester. If there was nothing on at Manchester, he'd go to Newcastle. If there was nothing on at all, he'd go to a park and watch a few kids kick a ball around. If there was no games on, he'd organize one. He was one of them fellas.'

But retirement crushed him. Separation from Liverpool destroyed him. As he watched the club he had built and nurtured as if it was a cherished child flourish and prosper under his former assistant, Bob Paisley, Shankly withered. He was hit by the slamming realization that he had quit too soon, and the last seven years in the life of one of the most passionate, charismatic and likable figures English football has ever known were played out as a poignant anticlimax tinged with bitterness and crowded with regret.

He raged against the idea that he had somehow come to the end of his meaningful life. He seethed with resentment at the notion that he had been put out to grass after a forty-year career in football that had begun as a player with Carlisle United and had brought him an FA Cup winner's medal with Preston North End in 1938 and seven trophies as Liverpool boss. One of five brothers who played professional football, Shankly abhorred the suggestion that leaving Liverpool had robbed him of a purpose in life.

'Retirement is when you get in a coffin and they put the lid down and your name is on the top,' he said a few years after he left Anfield. 'It is the stupidest word I have ever heard in all my life. Nobody can retire. Look at what's happened in Russia. The president's just died at seventy-eight and the man who's replaced him is seventy-one. In China, they don't start until they are seventy. People when they get to a certain age here, it's "Oh they should retire." What a word. Stricken from the record, "retirement". I object to it. I'm retired from Anfield, yeah. Retired from football and from life, no.'

Shankly had given his life to Liverpool. Between 1959 and 1974 he had transformed it from a dour, underfunded Second Division backwater living in the shadow of Everton into the best team in the country. He had devoted himself utterly to the club and to the job. He took his wife out twice socially in fifteen years in Liverpool, once to a garden party, once to the theatre. One time, when he checked in at a hotel on a Liverpool trip abroad, he wrote 'Anfield' in the space where the form asked for place of residence. Somebody pointed out it meant the place where he lived. 'That is where I live,' Shankly said.

That was part of what made him such a revered figure. He was brutally honest about how football meant everything to him. He liked boxing and he fed his players steak because he had read that Joe Louis existed on it. And he enjoyed gangster movies. If John Wayne was Sir Alex Ferguson's hero, James Cagney was Shankly's. But boxing and gangster films didn't amount to hobbies for Shankly. They were just something to fill the time when there was no football to watch. Shankly was a tough little man from an Ayrshire mining village destined for ruin, but like Cagney's most famous characters, there was vulnerability just below the surface.

And, really, when he left Liverpool, he had nothing. Because football had been everything. He had no other hobbies. He was not a golfer or a tennis player. He didn't fish or hunt. He wasn't a great reader. He wasn't a gambler or a drinker. He didn't like horse-racing, like Paisley or Sir Alex Ferguson. He didn't go on foreign holidays. He went to Palma in Majorca once but his wife was scared of flying so Blackpool became their staple. He even lived in a house in the Liverpool suburb of West Derby that was surrounded on three sides by football pitches. On one side was the Everton training ground, Bellefield. On another, some school playing fields that have now been renamed in his honour. And on the third, the pitches belonging to St Edward's College on Sandfield Park.

But suddenly, football didn't seem to want him. He was never offered another real job after he left Anfield, even though he was only sixty. He would have liked to manage Scotland, but there was never an approach. He would have welcomed involvement with another leading First Division side but the call never came. When he did an interview with Shelley Rohde on Granada's *Live From Two* programme a few months before his death in July 1981, she asked him about his current football work.

'You've not been resting in your retirement, have you?' she said happily. 'I understand you've been involved in some consultancy work with Altrincham.' Shankly did not blush but he stuttered a little. It wasn't Rohde's fault – in fact, it was a superb interview – but there was something about the brightness with which she referred to a job that was so terribly inconsequential, so ill-fitting for a man of Shankly's stature, that its poignancy was almost unbearable. But she was right. All Shankly got were a few consultancies at places like Wrexham and Tranmere Rovers, where his former Liverpool skipper, Ron Yeats, was in charge, and calls for advice from old friends.

Liverpool had had to tell him to stay away from their Melwood training ground in the mornings after he kept turning up there the season after he had retired as if nothing had changed. The players were delighted to see him because most of them worshipped him. When he turned up, they still called him 'boss'. Eventually, the Liverpool chairman, John Smith, told Shankly that he was no longer welcome there when the players were training because it was undermining the authority of Paisley as he tried to establish himself. Shankly was deeply hurt. He wrote in his autobiography.

'I still wanted to help Liverpool because the club had become my life, but I wasn't given the chance. I was willing to work for the club for nothing more than my pension. I was willing to help in any capacity, just to advise, if necessary, so that there would be no disruption at all while Bob got run in. Everything would have been clear with the club. I would have taken my cards. But I would have been in touch and if anybody had had any problems, I could have helped. Maybe the problems didn't crop up. Maybe they didn't need my advice.

'I went to the training ground at Melwood for a while. It is only down the road from where I live. But then I got the impression it would perhaps be better if I stopped going. I felt there was some resentment – "What the hell is he doing here?" So I changed my life . . . I packed up going to Melwood and I also stopped going to the directors' box at Anfield. I would have loved to have been invited to away matches but I waited and waited until I became tired of waiting.

'Finally, after 20 months and after Liverpool had won the league championship again, I was invited to travel with the club to Bruges for the second leg of the Uefa Cup Final. I accepted because I didn't want anyone to think I was petty but it came too late for my peace of mind. I couldn't help wondering why it had taken them so long. And I was not impressed with the arrangements they made for me in Bruges where I was put into a different hotel to the one used by the official party. I found that quite insulting.

'I might add that I count Everton amongst the clubs who have welcomed me over the last few seasons. I have been received more warmly by Everton than I have been by Liverpool. It is scandalous and outrageous that I should have to write these things about the club I helped to build into what it is today because if the situation had been reversed, I would have invited people to games. It would have been a wonderful honour to have been made a director of Liverpool Football Club but I don't go round saying "I would like to be this and that". That's begging and I'm not a beggar.

'It was never my intention to have a complete break with

Liverpool but at the same time I wasn't going to put my nose in where it wasn't wanted. Maybe I was an embarrassment to some people. Maybe they thought I should have asked them if I wanted to go to away matches. Maybe they didn't even think about it. That's their business. Nothing to do with me.'

There was a clear desperation about Shankly's desire to stay involved. It was made worse by the fact that opportunities to stay in football were more limited than they are now. If Sky's *Soccer Saturday* programme had existed in the late Seventies, Shankly would have been a stalwart just like his protégé Phil Thompson is now. He was, after all, the first king of the football sound bite, a genius with the spoken word, a master orator and communicator. He would have been on chat shows all the time. He would have been acclaimed wherever he went as a football legend, knighted by the Queen and bathed in the same kind of affection that covers Sir Bobby Robson in his old age. But the legends business wasn't what it is now.

So all that was left for Shankly was to fret at the margins. For a while, he hosted a chat show on Radio City, the local Liverpool station. The producers tore their hair out because he talked about his hero and former Preston teammate Tom Finney so much. He did some charity work. He popped up at various matches. Martin O'Neill, the former Celtic manager who won a European Cup winner's medal with Nottingham Forest, remembers him wandering into the Forest dressing room at the City ground before a match against Liverpool. Shankly had grown friendly with Brian Clough by then.

He turned up at the soccer school run by Ian St John, one of the foundation stones of the first Liverpool side Shankly built in the early sixties. St John had been signed at the same time as Ron Yeats in the summer of 1961, but he had fallen out with Shankly when Shankly began to squeeze him out of the side towards the end of the decade. There is still bitterness in those memories for St John but he finished his recent autobiography by recalling that visit from Shankly:

'Ronnie Yeats and I were organising a session of penalty kicks. Shankly loved nothing more than taking a penalty. A nine-year-old was keeping goal. Shankly tore in and blasted home his kick. If it had hit the boy on the head, it could have decapitated him. Shankly glowed and said to the youngster "don't worry, son, Ray Clemence wouldn't have stopped that". By then, Bill Shankly was an old and rather saddened man but something inside him still blazed. Like Liverpool Football Club, I guess I still feel the benefit.'

Shankly was Liverpool's Zelig in that no man's land of his between retirement and death. Watch footage of the celebrations after the 1977 European Cup Final triumph and there is Shankly with Kevin Keegan, cautioning him against over-exuberance on the open-top bus. And the first thing Kenny Dalglish remembers after signing for Liverpool is being ushered to a table to have a cup of tea with Shankly and his wife. 'Don't over-eat at the hotel,' Shankly told him, 'and don't lose your accent.' He spent more time with Nessie and his family. And he attended a succession of sportsman's dinners where he would often be the guest speaker.

Clemence, the great goalkeeper that Shankly signed from Scunthorpe United in 1967, sensed the growing sadness of Shankly's exclusion. 'I bumped into him a number of times after he left,' Clemence said. 'The longer it went on, the more . . . I don't know if "sorry" is the word to say but . . . When he was the manager of Liverpool Football Club and we had him on a daily basis, you would be invited to dinners and Shanks would be speaking and he could get up and speak for an hour and although we had him every day of the week he would still be fantastic to listen to with all his stories and quips.

'When he retired from football, a major part of his life was taken away and I heard him speak at two or three dinners after he had retired and certainly you could tell that a major part of his life had gone. He started talking about his other loves, boxing and gangsters in New York and all that sort of stuff, and it wasn't what people wanted to hear. And I just felt a bit sorry that he was starting to go into areas he didn't need to go to. Like so many people in football, when people have been in the game as long as he has, it makes up so much of your life. It has to in order for someone to be successful. Then, when you walk away from that, it leaves a big void. It leaves a massive void and I'm sure it did with Shanks.

'Shanks was such a great man. He influenced my life on the field and the way I lived my life off the field. He set you such high standards in terms of how to behave, how to give the best you can whatever you are doing. It might not finish up being good enough but if you have given everything you can then no one can have a go at you and you haven't cheated yourself. In life, if you do that, if you have respect for people on and off the field, you won't go too far wrong at the end of it.'

Shankly's obsession was not cheating the people. He wanted that to be his epitaph: that he had never cheated anyone, that he had always done his best. He drummed it into his players that they had a duty to the fans, a duty to the working classes who parted with their hard-earned wages to come and watch the team play. Whenever he heard tales of hardship among the supporters, Shankly tried to help, either by procuring match tickets or, more typically, by paying for train fares for Liverpool fans marooned at Euston after an away game in London with no money to pay for the journey back north.

Countless former players bear witness to acts of generosity like that. Shankly felt a genuine empathy with the supporters that stemmed from his own harsh upbringing as the ninth child of a family of ten in Glenbuck. When he resigned as manager, he made a point of going to watch one match against Coventry City from the Kop. 'I am a working man and I went among my own kind,' he said. Another of his heroes was Robert Burns, the Scottish poet. Shankly acclaimed him a socialist. But the first socialist, he said, was Jesus Christ.

'I am a socialist although I do not have any great faith in

any of the political parties,' he said. 'The socialism I believe in is not really politics. It is a way of living. It is humanity. I believe the only way to live and to be truly successful is by collective effort with everyone working for each other, everyone helping each other and everyone having a share of the rewards at the end of the day. That might be asking a lot but it's the way I see football and the way I see life.'

It was his passion for the people, his skill as a demagogue, his fierce respect for the working man that has helped to elevate him above the ranks of so many other successful managers. Even though Paisley won more trophies than Shankly, Shankly's force of character, his principles and his sheer dynamism meant that Paisley's achievements were destined to be overshadowed by the deeds of his predecessor and the affection in which Shankly was held.

Shankly harboured a lasting suspicion of the club's directors and of the patrician classes in general. 'In our language,' he said, 'there are words that mean the same thing but some are short words and some are long words. The big men use the big words knowing full well that only ten per cent of the viewers will understand. Well, we don't. We use words that everybody understands. So instead of saying somebody was "avaricious", I would say he was "bloody greedy".'

Shankly's time at Liverpool was about far more than just winning trophies. It was about something much bigger and more important than that. 'Bill Shankly was a three-dimensional man; disciplined, determined and dedicated,' Canon Arnold Myers, the rector of St Mary's Church in West Derby, said at Shankly's funeral. 'He refined civic pride and lifted us to a loyalty and unity greater than ourselves. Bill Shankly did not do this all for himself, but for a team, a vast family, for a city, and for an ideal.'

That is why the supporters on the Kop still sing his name today. That is why they will always sing it. That's why, in the magnificent din that preceded Liverpool's Champions League semi-final second-leg victory over Chelsea in May 2005, the supporters on the Kop held up banners bearing Shankly's name and sang about his memory. 'Outside the Shankly gates,' the Anfield choir sang that night, 'I heard a Kopite calling, "Shankly, they have taken you away", but you left a great eleven, before you went to heaven, now it's glory round the Fields of Anfield Road.'

And it's why, a few years ago, the brilliant firebrand *Daily Mirror* columnist Brian Reade, the last of the great left-wing newspaper polemicists, wrote about the criteria for being a hero and the men and women who qualified to be his idols. 'People worth idolising are passionate, generous, gutsy souls who see through life's bullshit and battle for the underdog,' Reade wrote. 'It's why, if I'd been in charge of the BBC's 100 Greatest Britons, the nation would be voting on this top 10: Dennis Skinner, Bill Shankly, Robin Hood, Barbara Castle, Spike Milligan, Wilfred Owen, Jack Jones, The Tolpuddle Martyrs, Pat Phoenix and Keir Hardie.'

Shankly would have liked that. He was proud of his socialism and happy that he could call himself an acquaintance of the former Labour prime minister Sir Harold Wilson, who was the MP for the Merseyside constituency of Huyton, more recently the home of the current Liverpool captain, Steven Gerrard. A few months before his death, Shankly appeared with Wilson, who had also been his first guest on the Radio City show, on *Live from Two* with Shelley Rohde. Wilson was interviewed first and spoke at length about the hardships his own father, an industrial chemist, had suffered when he was made redundant.

Soon after, Shankly was brought into the conversation, and it turned back to his own childhood in Glenbuck in the 1920s when the coal industry there was in decline. Shankly, who looked as smart and as dapper as ever, every inch the tailor's son, grew animated and emotional when he began to talk about redundancy. He felt the hardships of the working man fiercely anyway, but now his words were infused with the distress of his own fading usefulness.

'The cruellest thing in the world is unemployment,' Shankly said. 'You feel as if you are unwanted. It is a long time ago when I was in Glenbuck but I can still see the faces of the unemployed now. It is coming back now that I talk about that word "redundancy" and it is a terrible word. It affects people's minds. It is a terrible thing. You have to fight back against it. If you cannot fight back, there is nothing for you.'

As Wilson slumped back on the couch on the set at the Granada studios in Manchester, puffing on his pipe, Shankly perched right on the edge of his seat. He got more and more expressive the longer the conversation went on. It was as if he had been longing for a stage again and this was his chance to unleash everything he had been wanting to say and pour out all his frustrations about the way his life was ending.

'Everything I have got, I owe to football,' he said, holding his arms out wide. 'You only get out of the game what you put into it, Shelley. I put everything into it that I could and I still do. For the people that I was playing for and the players that I managed. I did not cheat them out of anything. I put all my heart and soul into it to the extent that my family suffered. I regret that very much. But you know, somebody said: "Football is a matter of life and death to you" and I said: "Listen, it's more important than that."'

Of all Shankly's memorable sayings, it was that line about football and life and death that came to be remembered more than any other. It has been bastardized, too, and taken out of its context. Because in its context there is a sadness about what Shankly said. The Hillsborough Disaster of 1989, where so many Liverpool fans lost their lives, exposed the emptiness of that line of Shankly's. But his words also spoke of a man who loved football too much, a man who neglected everything else in the service of the game.

Like many other great men, he had a drive and an ambition, a messianic zeal, that enabled him to put his work ahead of his family. His wife and his two daughters, Barbara and Jeanette, were submerged in Shankly's quest to make Liverpool the greatest football team in the world. Once, when he was asked if he had had a good Christmas, he said: 'Aye, no bad, four points out of six.' In his obsession to avoid cheating the public, he neglected those who were closest to him. He is far from alone in that. But when his active involvement in football was gone, all he had left was the wait for death.

Sometimes, his story feels like reading an Edward Thomas poem. It feels like a lament for a time gone by, for the passing of something that we will never be able to recapture, a time when a man like Shankly with his childishly fierce enthusiasm for the game could rise to its summit without his zeal being compromised or emasculated by megalomaniac chairmen or grasping agents.

His story is a mourning for a golden age when titans like Harry Catterick, Don Revie, Matt Busby, Tommy Docherty and Shankly duelled with each other on muddy pitches at packed stadiums up and down the country. Most of all, there was a purity about Shankly's love of the game that was utterly un-adulterated. His rule was not tainted by media allegations of nepotism and bullying, as Ferguson's has been.

One of the great differences between them is that some feel Shankly quit too soon and Ferguson stayed too long. Shankly paid for his decision in life, but perhaps he has been vindicated posthumously by the regard in which he is now held by Liverpool supporters. It never turned sour for Shankly at Liverpool in the way that some feel it has started to for Ferguson at Old Trafford. Shankly quit while he was at the top. Ferguson is clinging on for dear life as Chelsea have harried United into a decline. Shankly's legacy is secure. It will never be touched. Ferguson's is uncertain.

As the *Live from Two* interview neared its end, Shankly told

Shelley Rohde that he would like to be buried at Anfield. The studio audience tittered. They thought he was joking. But Shankly was serious. He talked about a casket of ashes that was already buried behind the goal-line at the Kop end and launched another tirade against retirement. 'I will be buried in spirit there,' he said. 'Even if my body does not go there. Because Anfield was the greatest thing that happened to me.'

Shankly clenched his fist towards the end of his speech and held it tight by his chest, but even now Rohde's abiding memory of the man she interviewed is of someone fighting for an identity. 'He gave the impression of being totally honest,' Rohde said. 'He didn't seem like one of those people who had rehearsed his answers. But he did seem a bit lost. It was almost as if he did not quite know what to do with himself. He and Harold Wilson both gave off the air of men who had outlived their useful lives. They had done it all and now they were looking back more in sorrow than in anger.'

Shankly died in Liverpool's Broadgreen Hospital on 29 September 1981. He had had a heart attack three days earlier but his condition had stabilized and he appeared to be recovering. Then he had a second heart attack and this time he could not be saved. Nessie was by his side. At the Labour Party annual conference in Brighton, delegates stood in silence to pay their respects and tributes flooded in from around the world.

'I believe Bill Shankly died of a broken heart after he stopped managing Liverpool and saw them go on to even greater success without him,' the Leeds midfielder and accomplished newspaper columnist Johnny Giles wrote. 'Giving your whole life to a football club is a sad mistake.'

At his funeral, a couple of days later, Keegan, who Shankly had also signed from Scunthorpe, in 1971, and turned into a superstar, took his place in the funeral cortège as it left Shankly's home. A few hundred yards away, the Everton players had walked down the path from Bellefield out to the street so they could pay their respects as Shankly's coffin passed by. 'The players, still in their muddy kit, had stopped training and had all lined up, their heads bowed in respect,' Keegan said. 'It was one of the loveliest things I have ever seen in football.'

Keegan and some of the other outstanding players of Shankly's years at Anfield had been chosen as the pall-bearers. Yeats, the captain of the 1965 FA Cup-winning side, Emlyn Hughes, the skipper of the team that won the trophy in 1974, John Toshack, Keegan's strike partner, Ian Callaghan, the man who still holds the club's record for most appearances, Tommy Smith, the fearsome Anfield Iron, Ian St John, who scored the winner in the 1965 final, and Keegan all gathered in the front room of Shankly's modest house at 30 Bellefield Avenue.

The undertaker came into the room as they stood talking quietly and looking at Shankly's coffin. He told them not to pick it up by the handles as they were only made of plastic. Shankly hated things that were fake and when the undertaker left the room, Yeats did a quick impersonation. 'Jesus Christ,' he said, in Shankly's Scottish growl, 'a plastic job.' Shankly's former players laughed until the tears ran down their cheeks.

Keegan has never forgotten what Shankly did for him. Even though he liked Paisley, he wrote in his autobiography that 'the club died a little when Shanks left'. He dedicated the book to Shankly. 'He was like a father to me,' he wrote.

'He taught me more about football than anyone, lessons that have stood me in good stead ever since. He believed in me far more than I believed in myself. He made me a better player because I thought that if he believed in me then I must be good.

'He told me after three games with Liverpool that I would play for England within a year and a half. Everything I achieved in football was down to him. He always seemed to say the right thing at the right time. We had a very, very special relationship. I felt I got as close to him as any player could. We were both miners' sons and I think he saw some of his younger self in me. We related to each other. And in a football sense, he adopted me. He said very little to me on how I should play, preferring to give me my head, although one day as I prepared to run out he said: "Eh, son, just go out there and drop hand grenades." '

Keegan remembered those words. In June 1999 he told Paul Scholes the same thing before an England match against Sweden against Wembley. No one realized at the time that he was quoting Shankly, and Scholes was sent off after taking the advice rather too literally by implanting his studs in the thigh of Stefan Schwarz. But a myriad other memories of Shankly still float back down the years, and his legacy to Liverpool Football Club is still tangible.

Melwood is unrecognizable now from the basic training ground Shankly inherited. At the turn of the century, Gérard Houllier oversaw the building of a new state-of-the-art facility with an indoor swimming pool, gym, weights room and a sophisticated set of treatment rooms. But one of the last survivors of the Boot Room, the brains trust that used to gather in Shankly's day in the Anfield room where the apprentices cleaned the boots, is still a regular at Melwood. Ronnie Moran, who was club captain when Shankly arrived in December 1959 and joined stalwarts like Paisley, Joe Fagan and Reuben Bennett in the Boot Room in the mid-Sixties, still drives down from his house in Crosby twice a week and strolls around the fields of Melwood to be with his memories of Shankly and all the triumphs they enjoyed together.

Moran goes in every Tuesday and Friday. He wanders into the referee's room and changes alone into the set of kit the club still give him at the start of each season. He doesn't want to get in the way so he waits in there until he hears the first team trotting outside towards the pitches. Then he wanders out into the fresh air.

A few of the club's old servants used to go to Melwood together and chat as they walked the perimeter, their route hugging the concrete fences that keep unwanted visitors out. They liked to refer to it as 'walking round the prison exercise yard'. But Tom Saunders, who was in charge of Liverpool's schoolboy teams, died a few years ago and another pal had to stop coming when his wife fell ill. So now Moran walks the walk by himself.

Sometimes he retrieves a few stray balls for the first team and kicks them back towards the pitch they're training on. But mostly he knows to keep himself to himself. He stopped working for the club in 1999 after forty-seven years as a player and a coach and he does not want to give anyone a reason to object to his visits. Football clubs can be suspicious, paranoid places. Managers sometimes imagine plots where there are none. So Moran keeps his head down.

The club's good to him. They still give him a pair of season tickets to go with his match-day parking space on Stanley Park and he's still got the run of Anfield. Most of all, he treasures the regular visits to Melwood where the fields dance with happy memories of young footballers who were carrying all before them. Moran takes care not to overstep the mark on his walks by making himself too visible. He watched Shankly retire and try to pretend that he was still on the inside. Moran saw how tragically that ended. He doesn't want it happening to him.

In a way, Moran has what Shankly craved but could not have. He's still part of the family. He still belongs. And he commands respect. Partly because of what he achieved in his own right and the guidance he gave to several generations of players. Partly because people still associate him with the name of Bill Shankly.

One day last year, Moran was sitting in the one of the Melwood anterooms with a journalist when Steven Gerrard walked through.

'I'm not talking about you, son,' Moran said, with a smile.

'It's okay,' Gerrard said, 'you're allowed.'

2: Ferguson's Childhood
– A River Ran Through It

When he remembers how it was in his childhood, Sir Alex Ferguson thinks of a young Robert de Niro and the New York neighbourhood that Vito Corleone inhabited as he made his way in the world in *The Godfather: Part II*. When Ferguson was growing up, the Clydeside community of Govan seemed to him to have the working-class vibrancy, energy and honour he saw in Francis Ford Coppola's depiction of Hell's Kitchen in the 1920s.

When he watched that film, he saw a place of tenements, madding crowds and character forged in adversity. He saw people making happiness out of hardship. He saw saloons, just like the bars that crowded the Govan Road where he spent his childhood in the 1940s. On Friday and Saturday nights, he and his younger brother Martin gazed out of their bedroom window to the street below to watch the fist fights spilling out of the pubs on to the pavement.

There was the noise, too. The hum. The buzz. The clanging. The drilling. The hammering. The industry. Ferguson lived with his parents and his brother and their Irish lodgers, Frank and Madge McKeever, in a two-bedroom first-floor flat in a tenement building at 667 Govan Road. It had an inside toilet, which was considered a luxury, but space was in short supply. The boys had one bedroom, the McKeevers had the other, and Ferguson's parents slept on a fold-down bed in the kitchen.

The flat was directly above a bar called Dick Welsh's, just along from another pub called The Victoria Bar, and Ferguson was fascinated by the sight of the beer barrels being unloaded at Dick Welsh's. There were about fifty bars on the Govan Road. Heavy drinking was a big social problem among the shipyard workers and dockers. For them it was a momentary escape from the grind and the relentless poverty. One of Ferguson's childhood friends, Bernard McNally, lived in a street known as Wine Alley. It was not a happy place.

The Govan Road was one of the community's main arteries and followed the contours of the south bank of the Clyde for a couple of miles. The Fergusons' flat was near the junction with Neptune Street, better known as the Irish Channel. From his window, Ferguson could see all the business of Govan conducted below him. He liked to listen to the raucous cries of Fletcher the coal merchant doing his rounds in his horse-drawn cart.

Govan teemed with life then. There were organ-grinders, fruit sellers, bookies' runners, religious processions and shipyard workers. Shipyard workers in their thousands. Ferguson's home was a few hundred yards from the south bank of the Clyde, and as he tried to get to sleep, he could hear the din of the riveters and the panel-beaters working the night shift as they made the big ships take shape at the Harland and Wolff yard where the giant cranes rose high into the sky.

Ferguson's father, also called Alex, worked at the Fairfield shipyard a few hundred yards the other side of Govan Cross from the tenement where the family lived. He was well respected, both by his workmates and by his sons. He was a disciplinarian who was quick to anger and slow to praise but his fierce work ethic and his understated nobility shaped Ferguson's character.

He loved his boys deeply, too. When the Ibrox Stadium Disaster unfolded on 2 January 1971, Ferguson and his father launched a frantic search for Martin, who had been at the game, and scoured all his usual post-match Govan haunts. His father grew more and more anguished, and they were on the point of going to the Orkney Street police station to see if his name was among the dead when Martin was finally tracked down. His father was so overcome with relief that he hit out at his younger son.

Ferguson wrote at the start of his autobiography:

'No matter what kind of journey we make of life, where we started out will always be part of us. The greatest piece of fortune any of us can enjoy in this world is to be born into a loving family, and it is a double blessing when the surrounding community also gives us warmth and a sense of belonging. My gratitude to my parents is endless and so is my affection for Govan.

'Nobody could have had a better home than I had. Martin and I were never without the precious reassurance that came from knowing that our mother and father invariably put our interests ahead of theirs, that they felt nothing was too good for us.'

Ferguson made that affection for Govan and his upbringing obvious to anyone who ever went into his office at The Cliff, Manchester United's old training ground in Salford, the precursor to Carrington. In pride of place on a wall next to his desk was a white sign with what looked at first sight like a jumble of black letters printed on it. 'HACUMFIGOVIN,' it said. Polite enquiry revealed that it was 'I come from Govan' with a local pronunciation.

Other tributes to his childhood and his heritage surround him, too. The house where he lives in the affluent south Manchester suburb of Wilmslow, the new base of the fiercely aspirational Cheshire set, is called Fairfields. It sounds like the kind of trite, bucolic name someone from the city might give to his country home until you remember where Ferguson's father worked.

The allusions to his past do not stop there, either. When Ferguson was fifteen, the Fairfield yard completed work on a cargo liner called the *Queensland Star*. Ferguson named the first racehorse he owned after the ship, and Queensland Star brought him his first-ever winner in 1998. The ship itself had been broken up by then. Its last voyage, in November 1979, took it from Newhaven in Sussex to a breaker's yard in Kaohsiung, Taiwan.

For much of Ferguson's youth, his father worked as a timekeeper at Fairfield. The timekeeper's job usually made a man unpopular, but the man who was known as Big Fergie by his pals retained their camaraderie because he was scrupulously straight. When Martin Ferguson applied for a job at the yard, the interviewer gave him quite a grilling up to the point when he realized who his father was. 'You're Fergie's boy?' he said. 'Start Monday.'

Shipbuilding on the Clyde was booming again in the Forties, and when Ferguson was a toddler his father was working on the building of the aircraft carrier *Theseus*, which was launched in July 1944 and was part of the British fleet involved in the Suez Crisis of 1956. His father earned £7 a week – not a bad wage. But for that, he had to work Tuesday and Thursday night, Saturday morning and all day Sunday on top of his regular hours.

Theirs was a traditional working-class household in many ways. His father expected his evening meal to be waiting for him on the table when he came home from work, so Ferguson would crane his neck out of the bedroom window to try to spot him approaching down the Govan Road. It was difficult. Most of the men wore bunnets or cloth caps that made them almost indistinguishable from one another, but Ferguson was an expert at recognizing his father's gait. The bunnets were the trademark of the Glasgow shipyard worker. Disputes between management and men were known as Bowlers v. Bunnets.

There were other things that set Ferguson's father apart. He was a Celtic supporter in an area that was regarded as a Rangers stronghold. Rangers' Ibrox ground was only about a third of a mile away, at the other end of the Broomloan Road. Sectarianism was rife in postwar Glasgow, but Ferguson's father stayed above it. He was the chairman of the local branch of the Celtic Supporters Club in Epsom Street and organized buses to take members to Parkhead, 4 miles away, on match days. But he refused to allow the singing of IRA songs on the premises.

It was unusual for a Protestant to follow Celtic but Ferguson's father did not feel constrained by the prejudices that ruled so many others on Clydeside. He had married his wife, Elizabeth, without any real thought for the fact that she was a Catholic. Perhaps that explains why, unlike many managers of his generation, Ferguson has never succumbed to racial stereotyping when it comes to judging players. He is many things but he is not a bigot. He was brought up in a fair man's house.

Ferguson's father knew he was bringing his children up in a hard environment where it would be easy for them to slip away into a life of meaninglessness and despair. Govan provided the opposite of a cosseted existence, but that is one of the many reasons why Ferguson has always made a point of getting to the Manchester United training ground at 8 a.m. most days. Hard work and redemption were twinned in his mind from an early age.

'Many of the boys from Govan who were brought up with me ended up in jail or took to drink,' Ferguson said. 'The temptation to slide into that dead-end existence was all around us but most families had a working-class ethic founded on the parents' determination to give their kids a chance. A majority of my friends responded to the encouragement they were given but, inevitably, there were others who did not have the strength to resist the influences that were always threatening to drag them down.'

It helped Ferguson that there was another strong and positive influence in his childhood, his primary school teacher, Elizabeth Thomson. Ferguson went to Broomloan Road Primary School, a few hundred yards from the tenement where he lived. It had a reputation as one of the toughest schools in the area. Ferguson was more than capable of looking after himself, but

but Elizabeth Thomson helped him through a couple of difficult years at the end of his time there.

For a boy with a robust attitude, a boy who was feared by many of his classmates, Ferguson was surprisingly susceptible to illness. He missed long periods of school with a kidney problem and another set of lessons recovering from two hernia operations. He missed so much schooling, in fact, that he failed the qualifying examination he had to pass to gain entry to Govan High School and had to remain behind at Broomloan Road for an extra year.

It was at that stage that Elizabeth Thomson took personal responsibility for Ferguson, so earning his undying gratitude. With her help, he passed the 'qually' at the second attempt with such good marks that he was put in the top stream at Govan High. But he had already missed a year and had to wait another six months before he could be settled into a new class. He felt mortified to be a thirteen-year-old among a class of boys and girls two years his junior.

In fact, Ferguson rated that experience and the way he was treated at Rangers as the two most traumatic times of his life. His school trials even elicited a rare admission of vulnerability from him in his autobiography. 'The embarrassment I felt, especially in relation to the girls,' he said, 'was so deep that I never overcame it and the rest of my time at school was torture, at least as far as the lessons were concerned.

'Ultimately, I was able to use the bad times to fuel the drive that carried me forward in later years but that didn't seem likely while I was going through them. Sometimes, the feeling of vulnerability I had then can come back to remind me that nobody is ever totally safe from the demons of insecurity.'

Ferguson's refuge, his way of restoring his pride, was football. He had started going to watch Rangers in the late Forties. Ibrox wasn't as secure then as it is now and Ferguson perfected a way of sneaking in for free. He got into scrapes, too. Club stewards chased him once when they spotted him trying to vault a wall and he was caught when he fell into a pothole full of water.

By then, his father had started to take him and Martin to kick a ball around in Pirie Park in West Drumoyne, near where Ferguson was born at 357 Shieldhall Road on New Year's Eve 1941. He played a few games for a local junior team called Govan Rovers, but there was no official school football team at Broomloan Road and Ferguson and his pals organized friendlies against the best primary school team in the area, St Saviour's.

From the age of nine, Ferguson also began to play for the Life Boys, the junior section of the 129th Company of the local Boys' Brigade, an overwhelmingly Protestant institution similar to the Scouts. Ferguson only joined to play football, but it did mean he had to attend church twice on Sundays. The highlight of his time there was winning the Glasgow and District Cup by beating the Polmadie Company.

The Life Boys sealed their victory with a 4–2 victory in Polmadie, 7 or 8 miles away from Govan on the south side of Glasgow and the furthest Ferguson and his teammates had ever travelled for a match. 'What we felt was more than pleasure,' Ferguson said, 'it was joy. Our team manager, Johnny Boreland, bought us all ice creams with double nougat wafers and eating them walking down the Polmadie Road, with our boots tied at the laces and dangling round our necks, was the most exhilarating experience of my young life.'

Ferguson found everything about Govan exhilarating in those days. The community was his cradle and the times he enjoyed there he found rich beyond compare. But the community has not prospered as he has prospered. By the late 1960s it had fallen into economic decline and the shipbuilding yards began to close down. Most of the shipyards have gone now. After many different incarnations, Fairfield still exists as a branch of BAE Systems, although not in the same splendour or with nearly the same amount of employees as when Ferguson's father worked there.

The immediate area around where Ferguson lived has suffered particularly grievously. Parts of it are so deserted and desolate, it feels as if tumbleweeds should be blowing through them. A few of the buildings in Neptune Street and Broomloan Road have survived slum clearance but the community is as dead now as Shankly's old Glenbuck. Other areas of Glasgow have enjoyed a shimmering regeneration, but not Govan. The buzz and the hum have gone, even if a few houses remain.

Harland and Wolff is no more. There are no longer cranes towering above that part of the Clyde. Ferguson's tenement at 667 Broomloan Road has gone, too. There's a low-slung concrete fire station there now, and nothing to mark the spot where one of Britain's greatest managers grew up.

A few hundred yards down the Govan Road, tall fences topped with barbed wire and signs boasting that the premises are protected by Braveheart Security stop unwanted visitors from wandering round the remains of Prince's Dock and the quays where rows of ships used to wait to be loaded and unloaded. Now, flotsam and jetsam floats in the stagnant, filthy water and grass grows over the stone quays once worn smooth by the footsteps of working men.

There is some regeneration. A mile or so further upriver, the beautiful curves of Glasgow Science Centre grace the south bank of the Clyde like Sydney Opera House transported to Scotland. Pacific Drive wanders through the park around it and roads filter off it, filled with arc after arc of smart new houses.

But back in Ferguson's part of Govan, all is quiet and still. A growing number of asylum seekers are trying to eke out an existence there. It seems sad that the deracinated should be forced into an area whose own roots have been ripped out. Some of the new arrivals trundle down the empty streets, sometimes pushing prams, heading for the forbidding tower blocks that replaced the tenements where Ferguson and his contemporaries lived.

The saddest sight of all is Ferguson's old school on the corner of Broomloan Road and Summertown Road. Sad, because such a fine old building has been abandoned and left to provide amusement for passing vandals. There are spiked tips to the fence that surrounds it. The windows have been boarded up with black plywood and then covered with metal grilles so that nothing is left to chance. It seems depressing that so much energy has been devoted to keeping people out when once people like Sir Alex Ferguson were invited in to spend an important part of their lives learning in the school's high-ceilinged classrooms.

Ferguson has done his best to keep places like one of his boyhood clubs, Harmony Row, alive. He has supported them with public appearances and donations. But even though he has kept in regular touch with Elizabeth Thomson and welcomed her as his guest for several weekends at his Fairfields home, his old school is beyond help. He went back there in 1996 as part of a documentary about his life and stood in front of the ruined building covered in graffiti that has been sprayed and scrawled on the fences and the walls.

At one point, his eyes lit up. 'I wonder if it's still there,' he said, gazing eagerly past the camera to a point in the play-ground. He was looking for a hole in the school wall that he had discovered he could squeeze through as a young boy. He used it to his advantage if he got into a fight with a kid who was bigger than him. It happened quite often, apparently.

Ferguson's tactic was to belt his opponent and then, if he sensed the fight might not go his way, to turn tail and run for that hole in the wall. He could force his way through it, knowing that a bigger lad would get stuck and be forced to give up the pursuit.

To many his ideas of conflict resolution have remained largely unrefined since then, but his need to flee from a foe diminished as his power within British football grew and grew. Now, as old age beckons him, the foe is Time itself. There is no hole in any wall anywhere that will rescue him from that.

3: Shankly and the Horror of the Leaving of Liverpool

Peter Robinson and the Liverpool board of directors had grown so used to Bill Shankly threatening to resign that they had become blasé about it. Once, it happened in the middle of the season, prompted by Liverpool's failure to beat Everton to the signing of Howard Kendall from Preston in 1967. Shankly was furious and said he was quitting. He didn't turn up for work for two days. The board kept it from the press and after a couple of soothing telephone calls, Shankly relented and returned.

Mostly, though, Shankly's flirtations with resignation came during the summer months when he began to worry about whether he could replicate the success of the previous season. 'It was partly fear of failure,' Robinson said. 'If you lost during the season, there was another game within three or four days or seven days at the most. So you could do something about it.

'In the summer, I think Bill always worried about being unsuccessful. A number of times, he talked about how he was going to finish and we would just brush it aside and when the players came back, he was fine again. The time with the Kendall incident, we spoke to him and he huffed and he puffed but then he reappeared again.'

When Shankly said he wanted to resign in the summer of 1974, just a couple of months after he had guided Liverpool to an emphatic and swashbuckling triumph over Newcastle United in the FA Cup Final, the Liverpool board assumed he was crying wolf again. They let it ride. Shankly persisted. Still they let it ride. Shankly was adamant. The board began to get concerned.

Robinson, who had taken over as Liverpool secretary in 1965 and whose job title had changed to chief executive, was the most powerful man at the club. He and Shankly had forged a close friendship in the nine years they had worked together. Professionally, they were the best team in the business too. Shankly identified the players he wanted and left Robinson to seal the deals. Robinson knew him as well as anyone. He thought he could persuade him to change his mind and stay on as manager.

He knew he could be certain it was not a negotiating tactic to try to earn a fatter contract. Shankly didn't go in for that kind of thing. 'Salary was never an issue for him,' Robinson said. 'He was the most honest man I ever met. If you gave him sixpence too much he would give it you back. There was never any question of tough negotiations over his wages. He got good bonuses. But they weren't contractual bonuses. I think in those days, former professional players were just happy to manage clubs.'

One day in the first week of July, Robinson walked down to Shankly's airless, windowless office underneath the Main Stand at Anfield and talked to him for most of the afternoon. It has often been suggested that the Liverpool board was reluctant to offer Shankly the post of general manager or director of football because they had seen the chaos that kind of elevation had wrought at Old Trafford when Matt Busby had become general manager of Manchester United in 1969 and gradually destroyed the authority of the new manager, Wilf McGuinness. But that was not the case.

'I was offering him anything to stay because the thought of him leaving, well, it was unthinkable,' Robinson said. 'I told him he could stay in any capacity he wanted. He could be general manager. He could work one day a week or five days a week. Whatever role he wanted, whatever he wanted to do, just to stay and be there. Liverpool had just won the Cup, the Cup was very important then, and so he thought he was going out at the top.

'I was just trying to explore a means of retaining him in whatever capacity he wanted. That was done without me talking to the board. I would have put that to the board if he had said he would stay. I was absolutely distraught at the thought of him leaving because we had a friendship as well. But Bill was unmovable in that meeting. He didn't go into his reasons.

'The idea that the board was petrified of a carbon copy of what happened with Matt Busby just isn't true. I talked with Bill for two hours and I offered him the post of general manager. A couple of directors weren't too concerned about him going, that is true, because he didn't have the best of relationships with all of them. He didn't have respect for them. But he could have nominated what he wanted to do. I don't think he could have been a director because Bill hated meetings. He would do anything to avoid coming to board meetings. He just didn't like that side. He wouldn't have been suited to that. But he was at the height of his powers when he decided to retire.'

Robinson failed to sway Shankly. The manager didn't even want to hold a farewell press conference, but Robinson told him that was an impossible request. 'You can't just disappear, Bill,' he told him. 'You're Bill Shankly, the great Bill Shankly.' A press conference was convened for Friday 12 July at 12.15. Robinson rang around the newspaper sports editors. He would not tell them what the conference was about but he did say it would be front-page news. Some still thought the club was going to announce the signing of Ray Kennedy.

Shankly walked into the VIP lounge at Anfield wearing a grey suit, an orange shirt, a red tie flecked with black and a red handkerchief tucked into his top pocket. He put his neat little hat on the window ledge behind him and sat down next to the Liverpool chairman, John Smith. Smith looked like an undertaker with his slicked-back hair and his thick black-rimmed glasses, and as he began to read out his statement, the newspapermen present felt dismay mingling with the excitement of witnessing the breaking of a massive story.

'It is with great regret that I, as chairman of Liverpool Football Club, have to inform you that Mr Shankly has intimated that he wishes to retire from active participation in league football,' Smith said. 'The board has, with extreme reluctance, accepted his decision. I would like at this stage to place on record the board's great appreciation of Mr Shankly's magnificent achievements over the period of his managership. Meanwhile, Mr Shankly has agreed to give every assistance to the club for as long as necessary.'

And that was it. Bill Shankly was no longer the manager of Liverpool football club. He sat and talked with the reporters for a while. 'There won't be many days like this, boys,' he said. They felt he was close to tears. It was the most difficult decision ever made, he said. He likened his walk to Smith's office to tell him he was resigning to going to the electric chair. 'I was the best manager in the game,' he said as he eulogized himself. 'I should have won more but I didn't do anything in devious ways. I would break my wife's legs if I played against her but I wouldn't cheat her.'

No one has been able to say definitively why Shankly quit. Initially, Robinson said, Shankly was 'buoyant' about the fact he had retired. A couple of years later, Shankly blamed it on an accumulation of weariness after forty years in the game. He wrote that he only ever intended to take a couple of months off and had then hoped he would be allowed to return to advise the new manager and renew his contribution to the club.

'A series of things went into my decision,' he wrote.

'I had been in the game for more than 40 years as a player and a manager and it had been hard work. I had been to outposts like Carlisle, Grimsby, Workington and Huddersfield where there had been a lot of good players but no real ambition. Then I had been to Liverpool where I had achieved most of the things I wanted to achieve. I would have liked to have won the European Cup, of course, but I had won most other things.

'I had been around a long time and I thought I would like to have a rest, spend more time with my family and maybe get a bit more fun out of life. Whilst you love football, it is a hard, relentless task which goes on and on like a river. There is no time for stopping and resting. So I had to say I was retiring. That's the only word for it, though I believe you retire when you are in your coffin and the lid is nailed down and your name is on it.'

Shankly said that if his great rival, Don Revie, who had just quit at Leeds to become England manager, had moved to Everton as some thought he might, he would have stayed on at Anfield to fight him. But he wanted a rest. Not to retire. Not to leave for ever. Just a rest. But, like Shankly said, football doesn't go in for sabbaticals. You work until you drop or you quit.

'I might have been better saying "look, I'm going to have three or four months off, then I'll start all over again",' he wrote in his autobiography. 'But I didn't. I thought that would have been unfair to the club. That would just have been using them. Making the decision final was like being on a jury and having to say "right, we'll hang him".

'There is no respite for a football manager. Even through the summer, and when he is on holiday, he is still bubbling. It is difficult to relax, no matter how tough and strong he is. I wasn't feeling ill or anything like that but I thought that if I was away from the pressures of Anfield for a while, and rested, it would make me fitter and rejuvenate me. I felt I could contribute more later on.'

Shankly's explanation, though, smacks a little of post-rationalization. For a start, he was the least weary man most people had ever met. He was always humming with a love of life and especially of football. Robinson had told him he could remain on whatever terms he wished. That included taking some time off and returning as director of football, or in another advisory role. Shankly could have had whatever he wanted, but he would not entertain any offer from the club. Not until it was too late, anyway.

Shankly could have had three months off without any eyebrows being raised. The 1974 FA Cup Final was held on 4 May. The next season did not start until the end of August. The Liverpool hierarchy functioned so smoothly that Shankly could have identified the players he wanted and then let Robinson try to secure them. On the pitch, his trusted lieutenants, Paisley, Bennett, Fagan and Moran, could have taken care of pre-season training.

Apart from that, Shankly had always seemed to have a horror of being separated from football, even for the briefest period. 'The close season was always too long for him,' Tommy Smith said in dismay when he heard Shankly had resigned. Even Shankly admitted he wasn't ill. This wasn't a situation like the ones that faced the later Liverpool managers Graeme Souness and Gérard Houllier, who had to take time off to recover from serious heart operations.

As for needing to get fitter, Moran said Shankly was the fittest man he knew. 'Was he fit?' Moran said. 'Oh, fit. That's all he done. He didn't go out. He didn't like going to functions. He must have turned down hundreds of dinner speaking jobs. And he used to enjoy the press, too. If he was here now with the television and all the reporters, you would never have got away from the ground with him.'

Shankly's simple explanation didn't quite ring true. Robinson thought fear of failure was at the root of his decision. His wife Nessie said Shankly had done it for her because she had begun to dread the spotlight that came with being the partner of such a public figure. She had been ill for much of the previous year, in and out of hospital, and Shankly may have felt he finally owed her some of his time.

Brian Hall, the pocket midfielder who played for Shankly in that Cup Final against Newcastle United, had another theory.

'By 1974,' Hall said, 'he had this awesome reputation but the reality was even bigger than the myth. When he walked in, everything in the room stopped. He could not walk into a room without the whole focus of attention shifting on to him.

'He had an aura about him and a personality and a character that was quite spellbinding at times. He was a very, very powerful man because of that charisma he had. When he eventually retired, I wonder if it wasn't just the pressure of being a football manager. It was also the pressure of having to speak in public and have those classic one-line responses ready and firing.

'People expected those one-liners. Maybe he had just had enough. I am fifty-nine and the older I get, the more time I want to spend with my family and do things I enjoy. My outside interests are now beginning to come into my life much more because I want them, too. Maybe that was what was happening to Shanks. He wanted to spend more time with his missus and his grandchildren. Who knows what was whirring round in his mind.

'His public persona was quite simplistic. His football philosophy was quite simplistic. His one-liners were wonderfully simple. His philosophy hit nails on heads. He just got the point. I think he was far more complex a character than he is often assumed to have been. He was quite an intelligent man. He came out of school at fourteen but there was far more to his intellect than met the eye.

'I think it takes a certain genius to be able to come out with the right words at the right time. He would have heated debates and slanging matches with Tommy Smith, whereas with me it would be a far more measured approach, and I would come out of the meeting with him and think: "He's done me again."

'Once, I went in to ask for a rise and he began by saying: "Well, you see son it's the government" and started on a conversation about politics. And when I came out of the meeting, I thought: "He's done me again." I hadn't got my rise. I hadn't even talked about my rise after that initial foray. He had completely switched the conversation around. There was a lot more to this man than the public image and persona. When people speak to journalists, they have a certain façade that they present. What's really inside them doesn't necessarily come out that often. You reach a point when you think: "Maybe I just want to be myself more." '

Disbelief spread on the streets of Liverpool when the news began to seep out. Granada sent its reporter, Tony Wilson, later a presenter, manager of the Manchester band The Happy Mondays and part-owner of Factory Records, into the city to interview fans. The footage is still arresting for the anguished shock on the faces of the supporters. Everybody who has loved Liverpool remembers where they were when they heard the news.

It even seared into the memories of the players. Ian Callaghan was about to set off for a trip to the Lake District. Ray Clemence was in a restaurant with his parents in his home town of Skegness. Ronnie Moran was shopping in Liverpool with his wife when she pointed to the headlines on *Liverpool Echo* billboards. He thought it was a gimmick, a ruse to sell a few more papers. None of them had seen it coming.

Shankly had told Paisley, his loyal assistant, about his decision. Paisley had done everything he could to talk him out of it. He begged him to go away on a cruise with Nessie, and recharge his batteries. It was the right advice but Shankly wouldn't listen. Paisley was convinced Shankly would think differently once he had had a rest. Paisley didn't want the job himself. Not really. He was shy and inarticulate compared to Shankly. He wasn't suited to the increasing demands made by the media. He didn't seek the limelight like Shankly. He was desperate for his boss to stay.

It is easy to assume now, knowing that Paisley went on to win three European Cups and six league titles as Liverpool manager, that he was the automatic choice to succeed Shankly. But he wasn't. It can be revealed now for the first time that when the board asked Shankly who his choice would be, he recommended Jack Charlton, then the manager of Middlesbrough.

Shankly had always been an admirer of Charlton as a player and as a man. He had tried to sign him in 1960, soon after he arrived at Anfield, but the Liverpool board would not sanction the transfer fee. Charlton went on to win a World Cup winners' medal with England in 1966 and played his entire club career with Leeds. He retired from playing at the end of the 1972–73 season and took over at Ayresome Park after Middlesbrough parted company with Stan Anderson.

Charlton made an instant success of management. In Shankly's last season at Anfield, he won Middlesbrough promotion from the old Second Division to the top flight with seven games to spare. They won the division by 15 points. Charlton's impact was such that he was named Manager of the Year, an accolade usually the preserve of a First Division boss.

Shankly was impressed, and as he mulled over his own retirement he began to feel that Charlton would be the best man to whom he could entrust his legacy at Anfield. He liked his forthright style and his honesty and he knew from talking to his rival, Don Revie, how much the Leeds manager valued Charlton's contribution to the strength and spirit of his side.

In his autobiography, published two years after he left Anfield, Shankly rewrote history when he suggested that Paisley had been his choice all along. In fact, when the board told Shankly they were appointing his assistant as manager, Shankly was surprised. Charlton would have been his choice but the board decided not to make an approach to him and settled for continuity instead.

It was the shrewdest decision any football club has ever made. Charlton might or might not have been able to tread in Shankly's footsteps at Anfield, but it is likely that he would have disbanded the Boot Room quartet of Paisley, Fagan, Bennett and Moran and brought in assistants of his own. And whatever success he brought, it could never have matched what Paisley achieved. Shankly's successor is still the only man in football history to have led a club to three European Cup victories.

If Liverpool had gone with Charlton, they might never have played in the European Cup Final that magical night in Rome in 1977. They might never have signed Kenny Dalglish, might never have beaten FC Bruges at Wembley a year later or sealed their third win against Real Madrid three years after that. One of the main strands of English football history would have been stripped away.

Other candidates were considered by Liverpool, too. Former players Gordon Milne, Ron Yeats and Ian St John were all mentioned, but the board decided that Paisley represented the best chance of continued success. But they soon began to realize that they were also being put in an invidious position by Shankly's inability to fade into the background.

Shankly was allowed to take charge of the Liverpool team that faced Leeds in the ill-tempered Charity Shield at Wembley on 10 August that saw Keegan and Billy Bremner sent off. He also led the team into a full-blooded pre-season testimonial match for Billy McNeill at Parkhead. His involvement in both matches hardly encouraged him to make a clean break with the club.

In his excellent 1996 biography of Shankly, Stephen F. Kelly claimed Shankly regretted his decision to quit so bitterly that he begged John Smith for his job back within six weeks. Kelly admitted that even Shankly's wife was sceptical about the claim and Robinson says it never happened. 'I can categorically say that Bill never went to John Smith and asked for his job back,' Robinson said. 'That isn't true. Bill had far too much pride to do that. I would have known about that. Bill would never have done that.'

What is true is that Shankly began to haunt the Liverpool training ground at Melwood. He found it hard to cope with the loss of his rigid daily routine and he missed the camaraderie of the players and the staff more than he had ever imagined. His inability to embrace another life plunged Liverpool into one of the most awkward and saddest dilemmas of their long history.

Those were difficult days for everybody at Liverpool. Difficult, awkward and desperately sad. Moran and former club captain Phil Thompson are both haunted by the same memory, the sight that greeted them each day at the beginning of the 1974–75 season when Paisley had taken over and was supposed to be carving out his role as the new boss.

The players reported to Anfield for pre-season training and climbed on a coach that took them the few miles to Melwood, out in West Derby. 'Bill only lived up the road from Melwood,' Moran said. 'He was two minutes away. He came in every morning after he had retired. He would always be there waiting. Already changed. Always already changed. And soon it began to get a bit awkward.

'The players who had worked with him would be greeting him and it was difficult for Bob. I learnt from that. I don't think Bill was influencing anybody against Bob or anything but he couldn't get out of the way he had worked all his life. He still wanted to be among the players. But my philosophy is that once you finish, you finish. I still come here but I just say hello to the players now and again. That's all. I don't want them to talk to me about football. I don't want to get involved in anything to do with the running of the club.'

The story of Shankly's leaving of Liverpool, his dismay when he found himself with his nose pressed up against the glass of the life that had brought him so much joy, is one of the most poignant episodes in the history of English football. Shankly loved football with a childlike intensity. He loved it utterly and absolutely. It was his religion and his balm.

And a tragedy began to unfold. One of the greatest characters the game in this country has ever known suddenly started to panic because he had turned his back on his past and now there was no way back in. When he kept turning up at Melwood day after day, everyone could sense that Shankly was clinging by his fingertips to the game he had given his life, too, but that the game was shaking him free.

'I was a young lad of twenty when Shankly retired,' Thompson said. 'I had just won the FA Cup. I was absolutely devastated when the guy who gave me my chance said he was packing it in. I'd had absolutely no idea. I have heard stories that Shanks had said nine times that he wanted to resign and the board had always knocked him back. But this time, they accepted it. I think he was a bit surprised.

'We came back to pre-season training and we got off the coach and there is Shanks's car on the car park and who is leaning over the rails of the veranda outside the changing rooms but Shanks. So we all came in. "Morning, boss," says everybody. "Morning boys," says Shanks, "great day, great to see you." It was great to see him, too. I was absolutely thrilled. But as the days wore on and he was there every day and he was walking round every day and he would have his bath down there, I started to feel this was not right.

'I could hear all the more experienced lads talking about it and it began to feel very difficult. We ended up calling Paisley "Bob" and Shanks "Boss". I wanted that to continue but I knew it was wrong. Bob had to fail or succeed in his own right. I could feel it happening. Then one day, Shanks wasn't there. Bob hadn't been happy. How could he do his job with the presence of Shanks hanging over him? And he was right. As young as I was, I knew it was the right thing.

'Shanks started going to Everton's training ground at Bellefield after that. His house actually overlooked Bellefield. He could see Everton training every day. A few months after he retired, he went on the Kop for one of the games. He wanted to feel that togetherness but he got mobbed and it frightened him. People were clamouring round him and he had to come out. I think he wanted to feel the love of the crowd again.

'When I left Liverpool after I'd been part of Gérard Houllier's management team, I wanted to give the new manager some breathing space before I returned to Anfield. They asked me back but imagine if I'm in there at the start of Rafa's first season when things weren't going so well and I'm talking to the chairman and Rafa sees me. He's going to be thinking: "What's that bastard talking about?"

'The decision that Shanks made, well you couldn't have your cake and eat it. Not then, never mind now. Football's like that. You get very touchy about what people say. It's the nature of the game. To have Shanks hovering over you, such a great person as Bill Shankly, was just unworkable for Bob Paisley. Bob knew that Shanks would be talking to the players when the team was picked and saying: "He's got it wrong there" and that is not right. Bob knew that and he had to make his stand early. It was a big call when it came. It was a sad parting of the ways. Shanks still rang me up. I always had the feeling from him that I was his protégé. I felt that I was his legacy after he had gone. A lot of other people probably felt that, too.'

Liverpool have been heavily criticized over the years for the way they handled Shankly's departure. They have been accused of being callous and uncaring. 'They didn't get it wrong very often but they did that time,' Keegan said. He believed Shankly should have been offered a post on the board, something to keep him 'in the family'. He was also disgusted that the club only named some ceremonial gates after Shankly. Keegan thought Anfield should have been renamed The Shankly Stadium. He probably has a point. 'It was the saddest, saddest thing that ever happened at Liverpool,' he said of Shankly's exit.

But apart from naming Anfield after him, it is hard to see what else Liverpool could have done. The idea of making Shankly a director was unworkable. Shankly's attitude to some of the board members was one of open contempt. 'At a football club,' Shankly said, 'there's a holy trinity – the players, the manager and the supporters. Directors don't come into it. They are only there to sign the cheques.' His presence would have thrown board meetings into anarchy. He had turned down the various posts that Robinson had offered him. He had turned down the chance to work part-time. Football directors are not usually sentimental people, but on this occasion they had done their utmost to persuade Shankly to stay inside the fold in whatever capacity he wanted.

John Smith and Robinson were mortified when they realized that Shankly had taken to turning up to training as usual. They hoped for a while that the problem would go away. They did not want to tackle it head on. The last thing they wanted to do was to cause a rift with the man who had brought them so much. But Paisley was growing unsettled and made it plain to the directors that the situation was undermining his authority with the players.

A couple of months earlier, he would have been happy to accept Shankly in some sort of senior role, but it was too late for that now and Shankly's continued presence was beginning to cause confusion. Shankly was an extrovert. Paisley was an introvert. So Shankly was bound to be the more dominant personality. Eventually, Smith told Shankly that it would be best if he stayed away from Melwood in the mornings when the players were there. He did it as gently as he could but Shankly was still deeply hurt. He never went back.

He continued to attend matches at Anfield for a while. 'The only reason he would come to Anfield would be on match days,' Robinson said. 'He came to the majority of the games and everyone made a fuss of him. I continued with him as though he was still there. He would phone me night after night to talk about things concerning the club and other clubs. Just to talk.

'If I had to be very honest and blunt, I think he probably did regret resigning. He began to appear somewhat lost. He was made very welcome everywhere at all the other clubs he used to visit but I think he missed the day-to-day role with the players. I would ring him and we would talk about how George Best had played in a game on television. But I felt he became quite sad. He would talk about who we should sign and who wasn't playing well in the side.'

Shankly's relationship with Paisley soured, too. Paisley felt Shankly was jealous of his immediate success and resented the fact that Liverpool's results didn't suffer obviously in his absence. 'When I got away too well for him,' Paisley said, 'he became a bit jealous and we didn't see much of him.'

Shankly went to Rome for Liverpool's first European Cup Final. He was accompanied by John Keith, a *Daily Express* journalist who knew him well. Keith watched Shankly as Liverpool beat Borussia Moenchengladbach to win the trophy for the first time. Shankly had come close when he took the club to the semi-finals in 1965, only to lose a two-goal first-leg lead in a bitterly controversial second-leg defeat to Inter Milan in the San Siro. By 1977, the European Cup was regarded as the pinnacle of achievement in European club football. 'You could sense his feelings that night,' Keith said. 'Not jealousy, perhaps, but certainly frustration.'

Seven of the players who beat the German champions in Rome's Olympic Stadium were Shankly's players. Clemence, Tommy Smith, Ray Kennedy, whose signing he had organized before he resigned, Emlyn Hughes, Keegan, Steve Heighway and Ian Callaghan, the veteran who had been with Shankly right from the start, the man who had been little more than a boy when Shankly went to visit his parents in their Toxteth tenement in 1960 to persuade them that their lad had a future in the game.

Callaghan thought about Shankly that night in Rome. So did Keegan. And the rest of them. Even amidst their elation, they felt a pang of regret that the architect of it all was only watching from high in the stands. They owed him everything. Liverpool owed him everything. But now Shankly was on the outside looking in. The dance had moved on and it was almost more than he could bear. He could see the delight on his players' faces. He was so close. And yet he was so far away.

4: Ferguson, the Man with the Casting Vote

Alex Ferguson stood in one of the corridors at the Millennium Stadium in February 2006 and listened as the television interviewer inquired after the well-being of Ruud Van Nistelrooy. The interviewer mentioned Van Nistelrooy's sulky countenance as he left the pitch at the end of that day's Carling Cup Final victory over Wigan Athletic. Ferguson began to grin.

Van Nistelrooy had, unexpectedly, been left out of the final which was the highlight of the club's mediocre 2005–06 season. Ferguson had picked Louis Saha as the focal point of his attack instead, and overlooked the Dutchman even when he made his full quota of three substitutions. Van Nistelrooy spent the match looking deeply unhappy on the bench, although he kept his dignity and made a brief show of joining in the celebrations.

When Ferguson was asked about his star striker, he said it was just one of the vicissitudes of a football life. Van Nistelrooy had been all right about it, he said. Then he got to the point. What was the big deal, he said. It had happened to him, too, once. Told he was being left out of a final at ten past two, he said. The interviewer didn't know enough about his previous life to ask Ferguson what happened next.

A couple of newspapers told the story later in the week. It was the 1965 Scottish Cup Final at Hampden Park and Ferguson's Dunfermline side were favoured to beat their opponents, Celtic. Dunfermline were one of the best sides in Scotland that year and missed out on the league title by one point. Ferguson's three years there made up the most successful period of his playing career.

He had arrived at East End Park in the summer of 1964. He gave up his job as a toolmaker at Remington Rand, an American firm famous for its typewriters and electric shavers and which had a factory on the Hillington Estate, on the western edge of Glasgow. He had worked there for six years and helped to lead an apprentices' strike in 1960. As the apprentices' shop steward at Remington Rand, he was keen to come out in support of other apprentices who were striking for improved pay across the country.

He called a meeting in the lavatory at the factory and asked the dozen men there for a show of hands to decide their course of action. They were evenly split so Ferguson thrust his hand into the air and shouted: 'Casting vote.' He led them out on strike with the rest of the apprentices, even though he knew that Amalgamated Engineering Union rules stipulated a two-thirds majority for a strike mandate. At one point, over a thousand workers walked out in support of Ferguson and his dozen colleagues. The strike was successful. The apprentices' wages were increased.

In March 1964, a few months before he joined Dunfermline, Ferguson was in the thick of another labour dispute. He had served his five-year apprenticeship by now but when Remington Rand sacked the firm's Communist union convener, Calum Mackay, Ferguson helped to lead a protest strike, although research in Michael Crick's Ferguson biography, *The Boss*, suggested that Ferguson's role was a small one. The Remington men staged two strikes in support of Mackay, but when the union called for a third, the workers rebelled and the fight for Mackay's reinstatement was abandoned. Soon after, Ferguson left Remington Rand and devoted himself to football.

Jock Stein, the previous Dunfermline manager, had wanted to sign him but had left to go to Celtic before the deal could be done. His successor, Willie Cunningham, pursued Stein's initial interest and signed Ferguson, who was a jagged, abrasive centre forward from St Johnstone. Dunfermline, known as the Pars because in their early days they performed so poorly it looked as if the players were paralytic, joined an unprecedented assault on the domination of the Old Firm.

That season turned into a fierce three-way fight for the title between Dunfermline, Kilmarnock and Hearts. Dunfermline seemed to have the advantage when their last four games of the season were all at home and they were level with their rivals at the top. They beat Rangers and Celtic but they lost to Dundee United and drew with St Johnstone. Ferguson missed a string of chances against his former club. The lost point cost Dunfermline the title which was won by Kilmarnock on goal difference.

Ferguson hoped that the 1965 Cup Final would bring him consolation, but rumours began to circulate that his place was in jeopardy because of the misses against St Johnstone and what Cunningham perceived as a dip in form. The tension grew as the match drew closer. 'It was tearing at my insides,' Ferguson said. Cunningham did not tell anyone the team on the evening before the game, contrary to his usual custom. Nor did he pull Ferguson aside to tell him what the line-up was. Ferguson sensed Cunningham had lost his courage and dare not face him. Only after the players had arrived at Hampden Park and were sitting in the dressing room 50 minutes before kick-off did Cunningham make his announcement.

Ferguson realized the omens were bad when the manager made sure he was flanked by the club chairman and secretary before he started reading out the names, from one to eleven. Ferguson waited and waited. 'The pain in my chest deepened as each name was read out,' he recalled. His name did not come. But because he had been used in several different positions in attack that season, he was only really sure he had been dropped when Cunningham read out the final name, outside left Jacky Sinclair. Ferguson went berserk. 'You bastard,' he yelled at

Cunningham, and even after the chairman had tried to quieten him, Ferguson continued to berate his manager.

'Looking back,' he said, 'I make no apology for the way I reacted. My view is that when the manager is not prepared to give a dropped player his place by telling him the bad news in advance, then there can be no complaint if, when the axe falls without warning 50 minutes before kick off, there is an emotional response. This was a Cup Final. Every player's dream. It is now basic to my philosophy of management to deal personally with players who might have expected to be picked for a game but are not.'

Ferguson had to go back to the players' entrance and tell his father and Cathy Holding, then still his girlfriend, that he was not playing. He felt as disappointed for his father as he did for himself. He wasn't even substitute. There weren't any substitutes then. So he sat in his civilian clothes with his father and his girlfriend in the stand. He watched as Dunfermline lost 3–2. The two forwards chosen ahead of Ferguson, Harry Melrose and John McLaughlin, scored Dunfermline's goals but Ferguson was not appeased. 'I felt we were handicapped by the absence of the determination I could have brought to the game and I think a few of the other players shared that view,' Ferguson said.

Ferguson asked for a transfer but his request was refused. He did not sulk. He used the rage he felt to drive him on the following season. He scored 45 goals in 51 appearances and sensed that suddenly his football career was taking off. He was beginning to feel the benefits of turning his back on Remington Rand and the extra time he now had to devote to his fitness and improving his technique were reflected in his play.

Ferguson got married during that season. The ceremony took place on 12 March 1966 at Martha Street Registry Office in Glasgow. Ferguson came from Protestant stock and Cathy Holding was a Catholic. Neither of them wanted to change religion. They didn't have a honeymoon. After the photographs, Ferguson drove to East End Park to play for Dunfermline against Hamilton. At the end of the season, he slapped in another transfer request. This time he was adamant he would not play for Dunfermline again. In late summer, the club offered to raise his wages from £28 a week to £40 a week. Ferguson decided to stay.

He spent one final season at East End Park. It was not as successful as the other two. But when Berwick Rangers pulled off the greatest shock in Scottish football history by beating Rangers in the first round of the Scottish Cup late in 1966, Rangers transfer-listed their strikers and began to turn their attention to Ferguson. In March 1967 he was also chosen to play for the Scottish League against the Football League. 'He was hardly in the game,' the Everton centre half, Brian Labone said. But then it was Labone who marked him. Anyway, Ferguson's team lost 3–0.

Ferguson thought he had an outside chance of being selected for the full Scotland side that played England at Wembley three weeks later. He booked a plane ticket for his father and got him a seat. But there was little chance of him playing. Denis Law shook off a minor knee injury and the Celtic players Bobby Lennox and Willie Wallace were picked alongside him. Ferguson watched from the stand.

That summer, Ferguson was selected for a Scotland squad that toured Israel, Hong Kong, Australia, New Zealand and Canada. The honour of being selected for the party was devalued when Celtic, Rangers, Leeds and Manchester United withdrew their players. Ferguson scored ten goals in seven appearances for the touring eleven, but the opposition was mediocre at best and the matches were downgraded to B-internationals before they were played.

Ferguson still grows indignant when it is suggested to him, as tactfully as possible, that he never played for his country. But there is no escaping the facts. Yes, he played for a representative XI on several occasions, but he never won a Scotland cap.

It would be wrong, though, to withhold from Ferguson the credit he deserved for achieving so much in his playing career. Even though his time at Rangers turned into such a bitter experience, the margins between success and failure for Ferguson the player were barely distinguishable. But time and again, he seemed to fall just the wrong side of the line. Whether it was being dropped for the 1965 Cup Final, missing a couple of chances that might have won Dunfermline the league the same year, losing his man, Billy McNeill, to concede the opening goal in the 1969 Cup Final, or leaving Rangers a few days before his nemesis, Davie White, was fired, Ferguson always seemed to fall short.

His career was a catalogue of near-misses. He was the ultimate nearly man, the guy who never got the break he deserved, condemned to be remembered as an ungainly player who couldn't quite make it to the very top. He was such an aggressive, awkward forward, such a handful for centre halves, that even his teammates joked that he used to sit in the changing rooms sharpening his elbows before every game.

But Ferguson worked incredibly hard to get where he did. Once or twice, in the early days before Dunfermline, when he was going nowhere at St Johnstone, he thought about giving up. He called his move to St Johnstone from Queen's Park in the summer of 1960 'a blunder that turned into a nightmare'. He considered becoming a customs and excise official. He was a sad loss to that profession. Imagine Ferguson interrogating a nervous traveller about bringing an extra case of Beaujolais back from Dieppe. He would have turned the most poker-faced of amateur smugglers into a wreck.

Ferguson even thought about emigrating to Canada for a while. Skilled toolmakers like him were in demand on the other side of the Atlantic and he was tempted. In the 1963–64 season, he spent more time in the reserves at St Johnstone than he did in the first team. In October he fractured a cheekbone and broke his nose in a reserve game against Airdrie. When he returned to the side at the beginning of December, he was part of a reserve team that lost 10–1 and 11–2 in successive matches. The next game was against Rangers reserves and he had become so disheartened he did something it's hard to imagine him ever doing: he got his brother's girlfriend to phone the St Johnstone manager, Bobby Brown, and pretend that he had flu and could not play.

Ferguson's parents were disgusted with him when they found out what he had done. Brown didn't fall for the trick anyway and the next day a telegram arrived asking Ferguson to phone him. Ferguson did it with a heavy heart but it turned out Brown had tried and failed to sign forward reinforcements and the team had been hit by a legitimate flu outbreak. Brown needed Ferguson to play in the first team's game against Rangers at Ibrox the next day.

'What happened to me at Ibrox that day can only come under the category of miracles,' Ferguson said. He broke out of his scoring drought in style. He scored a hat-trick and became the first opposition player to score three times against Rangers at their own ground. 'I do honestly believe that some power somewhere gave me a break,' Ferguson said, 'and that it was a signal for me to grasp this opportunity and not ever to forget the responsibilities that came with it.'

He got his move to Dunfermline at the end of that season and a career in Canadian toolmaking was never considered again. Even if he was not an international-calibre player, he had a far more distinguished career than some of the men who have come to challenge him as a manager. Neither Jose Mourinho nor Arsène Wenger nor Rafa Benitez had a playing career that even got close to what Ferguson achieved.

He did not have a pampered playing career. He fought his way to the top. He had started his league career at the amateur club Queen's Park, playing in the wide, empty expanses of

Hampden Park for the famous old side. He made his debut when he was still sixteen. Before that, he'd represented Drumchapel Amateurs, a team that became a formidable production line of Scottish excellence, rolling out players like Asa Hartford, Mo Johnston, Archie Gemmill, David Moyes and John Wark. He also played for several national representative sides including Scottish Schoolboys.

And before all of that, right at the start, he turned out for a team called Harmony Row, a boys' club that took its name from a street a few hundred yards away from the Ferguson family's flat in the Govan Road. It was part social club, a way of keeping local lads out of mischief. Ferguson used to play snooker there too. It gave him some of the happiest memories of his youth and he still takes a keen interest in its welfare.

What a sweet, sweet irony it is that one of the formative experiences of Alex Ferguson's football life should have been playing for a team called Harmony Row. It's as funny as the idea of Jose Mourinho turning out for Modesty Drive, Roy Keane representing Tranquillity Boulevard or Shankly taking charge of Apathy Avenue. But there it is: Harmony Row cradled the career of the man with one of the most famously foul tempers in football and launched him on a career of a thousand conflagrations.

5: Shankly and a Show of Red Strength

In the golden years at the end of his reign, Bill Shankly asked the Liverpool maintenance foreman, Bert Johnson, to nail a sign to the wall over the stairs that took the players from their dressing rooms out on to the pitch. Johnson painted white letters on a red background. The words read simply: This is Anfield. The Liverpool players used to touch it for luck on their way out. Some of them still do. But Shankly liked to think of it as an intimidating indication of impending doom for visiting teams.

Now and again, the opposition made fun of it as a way of calming their nerves. One Saturday afternoon in March 1972, an hour or so before kick-off, Shankly overheard Newcastle striker Malcolm Macdonald, a man never low on confidence, joking with his manager, Joe Harvey. 'Looks like we've come to the right ground,' Macdonald said as he looked up at the sign. Shankly fixed him with a glare. 'Listen, son,' he said, 'you'll soon bloody find out.' Liverpool won 5–0.

Sometimes, Shankly's life in the early Seventies can seem like one long anecdote. Maybe it was because by then he was a man almost out of his time. He stood out because he was an anachronism. Part of it was because he straddled two television eras, black and white and colour. The change had come in 1968 when the BBC broadcast its first game live in colour, and Shankly's legend somehow grew because the change split his career in the big time right down the middle.

Suddenly, the armchair public could appreciate the vivid

streaks of his personality in the bright red shirt he wore underneath his jacket. They could see the loyalty and the passion that beat within him when he tied a red Liverpool scarf around his neck as he celebrated his third championship victory in 1972–73. Colour gave the black and white managers of the early Sixties vibrancy and life but it did not strip away the gravitas they had earned in the days of grey.

By the time he was approaching the end of his Anfield mastery, Shankly's stand-up style and correct bearing were still redolent of the era of Stanley Matthews and Tommy Finney. He was the personification of a period of football that was fast disappearing. Colour television, the abolition of the maximum wage back in 1961 and the advent of George Best as football's first pop star all combined to help the public sense that momentous changes were about to alter football for ever. The reverence for Shankly increased because of that. He was the last of the Mohicans.

Fans at grounds up and down the country paid homage to him, indirectly anyway, with a terrace chant that was popular at the time, whose final line could be adapted to suit the supporters of most clubs:

> Bertie Mee said to Bill Shankly
> 'Have you heard of the North Bank Highbury?'
> 'No', said Shanks, 'I don't think so,
> but I've heard of the Pompey boot boys.'

Shankly was still a brilliant manager. In fact, in many ways he was in his prime at the start of the Seventies. No one ever imagined he might be nearing retirement. Manchester United's period of achievement had run its course by then and they were in sharp decline. Busby had gone. George Best had hit the skids. Bobby Charlton was getting old. They would not win another title until 1993. Shankly, though, had laid the foundations for two further decades of success at Liverpool.

He had served a long and thorough apprenticeship in the

lower leagues and had built Liverpool up from a dilapidated, dour, complacent Second Division club into one of the power-houses of the game. Liverpool hadn't won a trophy since the league title in 1966, but the club was functioning more smoothly than it ever had and Shankly had a system in place that was bound to cultivate new success.

In Paisley, Fagan, Moran and Bennett he had a backroom staff who knew how to motivate the first team and how to stave off rebellion from players fighting to get out of the reserves. He had a scouting system that was second to none, headed by former player Geoff Twentyman and including Shankly's old boss at Huddersfield, Andy Beattie. And most of all, Shankly had an eye for a player, an eye honed by a lifetime of loving football and its protagonists.

Martin O'Neill, the great Celtic manager, who has the same kind of infectious enthusiasm for the game as Shankly, never played for Nottingham Forest against Liverpool at Anfield while Shankly was in charge. But a story he was told by a friend at Forest, a former journeyman footballer called Jim McCann, made a big impression on him. McCann had had a two-day trial at Anfield in the late Sixties. He didn't remember meeting Shankly and the trial was not a success. He moved on to Forest.

A couple of seasons later, Shankly brought his Liverpool side to the City Ground and McCann stood in a group of other apprentices watching their visitors stride down the corridor that led to the dressing rooms. McCann was buried somewhere in the crowd but Shankly caught his eye as he marched past. 'Afternoon, James,' he said. McCann felt 10 feet tall because the legend had remembered him and spoken to him. 'That tells me a lot about Bill Shankly,' O'Neill said.

Shankly loved footballers. Just like Ferguson does. Just like Martin O'Neill does. He studied them, knew them, understood them, muttered in their ears like a horse whisperer. Kicked some, patted others. Encouraged some, scolded others. Nurtured some, exiled others. He devoted himself to them. Which is why he was such a good judge of them and why he was able to do what so few managers ever achieve and build not one, but two, great sides at Anfield.

His record in the transfer market was not perfect but it was good. When he was building his first championship-winning team in the early Sixties, the signings of Ian St John from Motherwell and Ron Yeats from Dundee United in the summer of 1961 were phenomenally successful pieces of business. The capture of midfielder Willie Stevenson from Rangers a year later and winger Peter Thompson from Preston sealed Shankly's first title win with the club in 1963–64.

Second time around, he bought brilliantly again. Emlyn Hughes, Alec Lindsay, Larry Lloyd, Ray Clemence and John Toshack were all outstanding successes. Tony Hateley, who cost £96,000, was a relative failure but Shankly didn't allow that to fester within the club. After one season he shipped him out to Coventry, recouped most of his money and began to look elsewhere. And that was when he found the player who would come to epitomize his last years at Liverpool, another product of a mining community, a shy lad from north Yorkshire called Kevin Keegan.

Keegan grew to be as close to Shankly as any Liverpool player with the possible exception of Hughes. Keegan was a reserved boy when he arrived at Anfield but he was also an incredibly hard worker, a player who would give everything for the team. There were plenty of others like that at Liverpool but the pit heritage that Keegan and Shankly shared gave them a close bond. Shankly liked everything about Keegan's attitude and his fierce desire to succeed.

Keegan had been recommended to Shankly by Beattie, who had seen him playing for Scunthorpe United. Beattie pestered Shankly about him until eventually Liverpool signed him for £35,000 near the end of the 1970–71 season, a couple of weeks before they were due to play Arsenal in the FA Cup Final. 'It turned out to be robbery with violence,' Shankly said about the transfer fee.

When Liverpool lost the final, Shankly was also struck by how downcast Keegan appeared to be even though he had only been watching from the stands. 'When we lost, he looked broken-hearted,' Shankly said, 'and I thought "Christ, here is a real character – and he is not even playing. He probably thinks that if he had been playing, we would have won." And we would have done.'

Keegan was twenty when he signed for Liverpool and he went on to become the first Liverpool superstar. The team ethic had always been dominant at Anfield, and even though there had been great individualists like Peter Thompson and Kop heroes like Ian St John, none of them made the impact that Keegan did. This was a new age.

The hero worship of Best had taken football celebrity to a new level, but Keegan never fell victim to the temptations Best succumbed to. There was a happy charisma about him and fans everywhere loved him for his underdog's determination and the refusal to let anyone quell his spirit. His character was summed up by the nickname he was given when he moved to SV Hamburg in 1977. Mighty Mouse they called him there, but when he arrived at Anfield he soon became Liverpool's talisman.

The other reason there had never been a real star player at Liverpool before was that Shankly himself was such a dominant character. His dictates, sayings and personality infused everything Liverpool did and seeped into the bones of the club. He stressed the subjugation of the individual to the team ethic. His being still seemed rooted in the Fifties. He was about as far removed from the spirit of the Swinging Sixties as it was possible to be, which was ironic given that his influence on Liverpool culture in that decade had rivalled that of The Beatles and the musical movement known as Merseybeat.

His character was formed from a poverty-stricken childhood

and a maturity dominated by war and austerity. He was never going to morph into some sort of libertine as he approached his sixtieth birthday. The fact that he stayed ramrod-straight and utterly devoted to the game in an age when maverick hedonists like Malcolm Allison were taking centre stage marked Shankly out as an object of curious admiration. Allison smoked cigars and wore a ten-gallon hat. He was the anti-Shankly.

Shankly was an eccentric. And he was also a clever, quick and sharp-witted man. Some of his one-liners he rehearsed beforehand. Some he stole from his long-suffering assistant, Bob Paisley. But many of them were his spontaneous inventions. He was a master of repartee, a man not to be outdone in a verbal exchange. And he had a flair for the dramatic which suggested that in another life he might have emulated one of his great heroes, James Cagney. Shankly was so obsessed with Cagney that his solitary concession to excess was a penchant for buying a Cagney-style raincoat in almost every city he visited. He was a great modeller of the touchline coat when Jose Mourinho was still in short pants in Setubal.

His management style was full of idiosyncrasies. How many other managers loitered in the corridor at their ground to try and sow seeds of doubt in the minds of the opposition as they wandered in off their coach? 'I would look up the Rothmans book or the News of the World football annual to refresh my mind on their first names,' he said, 'though I knew most of them, of course. I would be ready for them when they arrived. I'd say things like: "Hello, Jimmy, it's a little bit heavy but it's not a bad ground. In actual fact, it's the kind of ground that suits us." If it was heavy, if it was dry, if it was frosty, it made no difference. I'd say: "Just a touch of frost. I remember the last time we played on a frosty pitch – oh, we didn't half play well".'

It sounds almost amateurish now. It certainly sounds comic. But maybe that's partly because of the way the Shankly legend has grown in the years since he retired. Anfield was a forbidding place to go in the early Seventies. Shankly had made it that way, and when the man himself was there to greet you when you arrived, his zealotry and his intensity burning underneath all that false bonhomie and cod camaraderie, it was unsettling for an opponent. Shankly thought it worked anyway. He also used to report his observations on the appearance of the visiting team to his own players. Those observations were not without embellishment.

In November 1971, in the early months of Keegan's first season at Anfield, Shankly was concerned his young striker might be nervous about facing West Ham and, in particular, England's World Cup-winning captain, Bobby Moore. When he walked back in from casting his eye over Moore and his colleagues, who had recently been reprimanded for enjoying an evening on the tiles in a Blackpool nightclub, Shankly made straight for where Keegan was sitting. 'Christ, son,' he said, 'I've just seen that Bobby Moore. What a wreck. He's got bags under his eyes, he's limping and he's got dandruff. He's been out to a nightclub again, son.' Suddenly, Keegan didn't feel quite so awestruck at the thought of playing against the golden-haired god who had lifted the World Cup in 1966.

Some of the more experienced players knew they were looking at a piece of inspired oratory from a man who loved to perform. But even at that level, Shankly's theatrics helped to ease any tension in the dressing room. He hammered away so long and so often about how good Liverpool were and how decrepit and decadent their opponents would be that even the veterans and intelligent, perceptive men like Brian Hall found themselves believing the creed of Liverpool invincibility that Shankly preached incessantly.

'We always had Friday morning team meetings at Melwood,' Hall said. 'We all gathered in this tiny little room with a green board speckled with white dominoes and red dominoes to signify the players. There'd be sixteen people crammed in there and then the analysis of the opposition would start. One of Shanks's assistants, Reuben Bennett or whoever, would talk for

a while about some team in Eastern Europe he'd been to watch
and it might have taken him three days to get back. After two
or three minutes, Shanks just dismissed it.

'He would set off either destroying the opposition if he knew
them or just saying how great we were if he didn't. It would be
stuff like: "And him he cannot play, and him he drinks too
much." Well, when you've heard that half a dozen times, quite
frankly it doesn't register to the same extent. It is one of those
subliminal things. Week in, week out, week in, week out, you
get told you are the best and it drips away and you end up
believing it. It doesn't have the impact on a weekly basis that it
did when you first went into these meetings and saw this man
perform in front of you. After a while, it's the norm. As far as
motivation was concerned, I think Shanks had a wonderful gift.
When he got you at the club and on the training ground, he
could look you in the eye and see that you were a self-motivator,
that you wanted to win as much as he did.'

These were the men of Shankly's second great Liverpool
team. Many of the first Shankly side that had conquered England and gone right to the brink of being the first British side to
win the European Cup were swept away in the aftermath of an
FA Cup defeat to Watford in February 1970 that capped several
years of underachievement. Ron Yeats, the captain, St John, the
dynamo, Roger Hunt, the goalscorer, and Tommy Lawrence,
the goalkeeper, were all discarded by Shankly. Willie Stevenson
and Gordon Milne had already been sold. Gerry Byrne had
retired and Bobby Graham would never recover his place after
breaking his leg. The survivors were Chris Lawler, Tommy
Smith and Ian Callaghan, and now they were bolstered by a
new group of hungry young recruits.

A new team rose quickly from the ashes of the old one.
Clemence was the new goalkeeper. Lawler was right back. Larry
Lloyd partnered Smith in central defence, Alec Lindsay came in
at left back. Callaghan, who had already been at the club for
a decade, played in midfield with Emlyn Hughes and Steve

Heighway ousted Peter Thompson on the left. Hall, Keegan and John Toshack were all brought in to supplement a faltering attack.

Hall was regarded as something of a curiosity because he had been to Liverpool University. 'That degree won't do you any good today, Hally,' Smith warned him as Hall prepared to face the Leeds United centre backs Norman Hunter and Jack Charlton for the first time. As for Keegan and Toshack, they became one of the most feared forward partnerships in English history.

The training methods remained from the Sixties. The emphasis was still on five-a-sides and Shankly was determined that the staff side would always win their match against the apprentices. 'The staff v kids game always took place on the pitch they called Little Wembley,' Phil Thompson said. 'They would play over there and some of the games between the first-teamers used to end in farce.

'You would have attack v defence and people like Smithy and Larry Lloyd would just dominate the game against Heighway, Keegan and Brian Hall. It could be 14–1 and the staff would still be playing on the other side of the ground. It was more important for them to beat the young lads. Sometimes, it would go past 12 o'clock but we never stopped until the staff got the odd goal in front. Then Shanks would say: "Bob, it's time we finished." The kids would be sick.'

Liverpool finished fifth in the league in 1969–70 and fifth again the next season when the rebuilding had begun. These were transitional years, the phrase managers love to hate but which they resort to sooner or later when things are not going well. Ferguson started to use it after the defeat to Benfica in December 2005 that knocked Manchester United out of the Champions League. He mentioned it again when United drew at home to Everton the following Sunday. Everton were Shankly's tormentors, too, in the first of those transitional seasons, winning the title by nine points ahead of Don Revie's

Leeds, Dave Sexton's Chelsea and Brian Clough's Derby County. In '70–'71, Bertie Mee's Arsenal won the title and a few days later, Arsenal faced Liverpool in the FA Cup Final.

It was the first time Liverpool had been back to Wembley since that emotional 1965 May Day when they won the trophy for the first time. Back then, winning the Cup had been an end in itself, and victory against Leeds had brought a great outpouring of joy on Merseyside, a show of popular emotion and adulation that trumped any homecoming The Beatles enjoyed. Six years later, things had changed. The Beatles had split and Liverpool's priorities were different. Making it back to Wembley was merely a sign that after five years of drought, they were on the road back.

They beat Everton in the semi-final at Maine Road. Brian Hall scored the winner. It fell to him 10 yards out, he controlled it and hooked it across the line. He still glows with the memory of it today as he sits in his office across the road from Anfield. It was his first goal for the club. 'The difference between Everton and the *Queen Mary*,' Shankly said some time after the game, 'is that Everton carry more passengers.' Hall played in the final, too, raiding down the right as Heighway raced down the left. Alun Evans, who was about to be supplanted by Keegan, was up front with Toshack.

But Liverpool weren't good enough to deny Arsenal the Double. The players were gripped by tension on the way to Wembley. This was a young team and they were in unfamiliar territory. Alec Lindsay broke the mood by starting a sing-song with a rendition of Bye-Bye Blackbird, but the tension came back when they walked out before the game. Heighway scored the opener when he drilled a cross shot from the left through a gaping hole at Bob Wilson's near post. But Eddie Kelly equalized and then Charlie George scored a cracker for the winner, lying down on his back, his arms stretched out above his head, so his teammates could mob him. Up in the stands, Keegan, who had been invited down to the Waldorf Hotel on Aldwych to stay with the team and share their preparations, felt the disappointment as keenly as if he had been playing.

Shankly still salvaged something from that Cup Final defeat, though. When the team returned to Liverpool the next day, tens of thousands turned out to greet them at a civic reception even though they had lost. The players were overwhelmed by the display of support and as the open-top bus made its way towards the Town Hall, Shankly tapped Hall on the shoulder.

'Son,' he said, 'you know about these things. What's the name of the Chinaman? Red book. Lots of sayings?'

'Do you mean Chairman Mao, boss?' Hall said.

'He's the fella,' Shankly said.

Hall thought Shankly was going mad, but when the bus arrived at the Town Hall, Shankly made his way to the balcony with the rest of them and began an impassioned speech with his arms outstretched. 'Even Chairman Mao,' he roared through the microphone, 'has never seen a greater show of red strength.' The masses let out a bellowing cheer of approval. Hall looked at Shankly in awe. 'You're not just a clever so and so, you're a genius, you are,' he thought.

Keegan joined the first team on an end-of-season tour to Scandinavia and scored two goals in three games. He was left behind when the squad travelled to Germany a couple of months later for their pre-season tour but that worked in Keegan's favour, too. Shankly was concerned that his attack of Toshack and Alun Evans was misfiring, and when he came back early from Germany, he watched Keegan score twice in a friendly against Southport. He picked him for the first team in the traditional eve-of-season match against the reserves and Keegan's side won 7–1. 'He wanted to be bloody first in everything in training,' Shankly said. 'Whether it was sprinting, jumping over the hurdles, playing five-a-sides, everything. He ran his guts out. Boy, was he keen to be fit.'

There were some, though, who felt that Keegan wasn't ready

for the first team and the First Division. His energy was limitless, but when Brian Hall watched him in the first-team match against the reserves, he thought Keegan was destined for a long spell in the reserves. 'Kevin was a strange case,' Hall said. 'He ran around for fun. He was all over the place. He was like a headless chicken. He never stopped running. We had a Probables v Possibles pre-season match at Anfield and Kevin ran around like a blue-arsed fly. Those of us that had been at the club for a while thought he was never going to make a Liverpool player because he looked brainless.

'But he learned so quickly you had to admire the guy. Physically and mentally, he worked very hard. He never rocked the boat. All the way through his career, he learned. He seemed to be able to adapt himself to whatever environment he was in. He became close to Shanks. Shanks loved him from day one because of his sheer energy. Kevin was living away from home, his father wasn't very well and he was a retired miner so there was an empathy there straight away. There was a stability in Kevin's life that Shanks liked. Kevin wasn't a drinker. He wasn't one for nightclubs. He fitted the mould perfectly for Shanks. There was perhaps a need for Kevin and Emlyn to have a father figure because Emlyn's father died when he was young, too.'

Keegan made his Liverpool debut in the first game of the season against Nottingham Forest and scored in a 3–1 win. He scored ten more in the next eight months but Liverpool lost the title by a hair's breadth to Derby County. It was one of the closest title races in English history. Just one point separated the top four teams. It was so tight that when Derby played City, Shankly said to the City boss Joe Mercer: 'I hope you both lose.'

The title slipped away from Liverpool when they lost to Derby at the Baseball Ground on the penultimate Saturday of the season. They needed to beat Arsenal the following weekend to retain a chance of the Championship. They thought they had snatched victory when Keegan squared a pass to Toshack in the dying minutes of a goalless game at Highbury. Toshack slotted the ball over the line but was judged to be offside. Derby won the title by a point, Leeds were second, Liverpool third. But the days of them being cut adrift of the championship leaders were over.

The way Shankly responded to the shattering blow of losing the title by such a close margin set Liverpool up for the successes of the following season. 'We weren't on Cloud Nine when we thought Toshy had scored at Highbury, we were on Cloud Twenty-Seven,' Hall said. 'There was this explosion of joy from the Liverpool fans and then we realized the referee had disallowed it. So we went from Cloud Twenty-Seven to somewhere below the floor. When we trooped back into the dressing room, we had gone. Some of the lads were in tears.

'I half expected a rollocking because we had come so close, but it was exactly the opposite. Shanks told us well done and what a fantastic performance it had been and what a swine the ref was. You see, Shanks and Bob Paisley and Joe Fagan, they were real football people. They understood where we had been and what had happened. I thought they all showed a lot of compassion. They must have been screaming inside and yet they were professional enough to understand where we were as players. Great management, that.'

Shankly's shining consolation was the realization that his new team was ready. He was already acclaiming Clemence as the best goalkeeper in the world and dreaming of what they could have achieved if he had been between the posts in the Sixties. Tommy Smith, grizzled and fearsome, relished his reputation as the Anfield Iron, a man with whom you most definitely did not mess. 'Tommy Smith was never a boy,' Shankly said. 'He was born a man.'

Phil Thompson was breaking through. Emlyn Hughes was the driving force. And Keegan and Toshack were established as an attacking partnership that still stands as the most potent in Liverpool's history, rivalled only by the clinical beauty created later by Ian Rush and Kenny Dalglish. Keegan and Toshack developed an understanding that was telepathic. Toshack had been struggling to make an impact until Keegan arrived but Keegan was his perfect foil. The next season, they were to sweep all before them.

They scored 26 goals between them as Liverpool beat Arsenal to the title by 3 points. Revie's Leeds were 4 points further back. They clinched the championship at Anfield with a goalless draw against Leicester City in the last game of the season. The players took the plaudits at first and then Shankly strode out on to the pitch, that red shirt and red tie beneath his suit. There was one small indication of the esteem and affection in which Shankly was held when Keith Weller, the Leicester right-winger, walked over to Shankly as he made his way towards the centre circle and made a point of shaking his hand.

Shankly felt incredibly proud. 'My biggest thrill as a player was winning the FA Cup with Preston,' he wrote in his autobiography. 'My greatest day in football was when Liverpool won the FA Cup for the first time. But winning the League Championship for the third time, and with a brand new team, possibly gave me more satisfaction than anything.' Only Matt Busby had won more titles since the war, and the triumph drew Liverpool level with Arsenal as the only winners of eight championships.

Shankly walked to the Kop, who had been roaring out his name over and over again. Supporters threw scarves and flags towards him. When a policeman tried to kick one of the scarves out of Shankly's way, Shankly reprimanded him. 'Don't do that,' he said. 'That's someone's life.' He picked it up and tied it round his neck. That image of him in his suit and red scarf, his arms held out and his fists clenched, is one of the iconic sports pictures of our time. The essence of Shankly was captured in that picture, his togetherness with the fans, his innate socialism, his pride, his showmanship and his charisma.

This was the man his players adored. This was the man who inspired them and seemed larger than life. Most of them still refer to him now, as their hair greys and their eyesight begins to fade, simply as the Great Man. Many of them continue to regard him as the most important influence there has ever been on the successful lives they believe they owe to him. Part of his gift was making them feel important. He did not call himself The Special One. He made his players feel as if they were remarkable instead.

'My relationship with Shankly was uncomplicated,' said Thompson, who made his debut in April 1972. 'It was special. I was a skinny kid who tossed up with a sparrow for his legs and lost. I don't think anybody had ever seen anybody as thin as me playing professional football at the top level. But he believed in me because he knew I had the heart and the commitment and the passion and the skill to make it.

'So he played me in the team, first of all when Emlyn got injured. I did the business so he believed in me. I can remember my first appearance when John Toshack came off with a head injury and it was at Old Trafford and there must have been 60,000 people in there. He told me to play behind Kevin and slot in behind him. I was clever enough to carry that off. I could take orders.

'I went on one run and hit this shot towards where all the Liverpool fans were and Alec Stepney went full-length and turned it round the post. We beat them 3–0 with them having George Best and all. And then the next day, Shanks talked about me to the press. He said he wasn't even sure what my best position was yet. He said I could play in midfield, then again I might be a defender and the way I'd played I could be an attacker. He was asking the press lads if they'd seen my shot. I was reading this and I was thinking: "Oh my goodness, this fella thinks I can play anywhere." That was my first compliment from him and I felt a million dollars.

'I was in and out of the side for a while and the next season, we were playing Arsenal in February, he left me out and Arsenal beat us 2–0. I thought I could have done a job. After the game, Ronnie Moran, who had been my mentor coming through the ranks, gave me some advice. "Do yourself a favour and go in and have a word with him on Monday morning," Ronnie said. I wasn't sure. But he said Shanks would think more of me if I did it.

'I talked it over with my mum over the weekend and she said that if Ronnie said it was the right thing to do, I should do it. I didn't know what to say. On the Monday, I was walking down the corridor towards his office which was at the end. He was coming towards me. I said: "Can I have a word, boss," and he said: "Of course, son, come in and sit down." I told him I wanted to know why I hadn't played on Saturday.

' "Jesus Christ son," he said, "you want to know from me why you didn't play? Did you see that load of shite out there on Saturday? They were crap. Callaghan and Lawler, they are finished, they are has-beens. You son, you're a fantastic player. You should be in here on your bended knees thanking me for not playing you. My God, you are going to play for this club for many years to come. You are going to captain this team and you are going to play for your country. My goodness, you should be thanking me. I saved you from something."

'I walked out of his office and I'm surprised I didn't bump my head on the top of the door frame, I felt that big and that confident. This was Shankly building me up. The problem, of course, was he didn't play me the next fucking week. But there was something in his voice that made him special. It was the Scottish way of how he spoke and his words. They had that comforting sound to them even though he was gruff and it made you feel good.'

The title was clinched on 28 April. Three days earlier, Liverpool had forced their way through to the two-leg Uefa Cup Final. They beat one West German side – Eintracht Frankfurt – and two East German teams – Dynamo Berlin and Dynamo Dresden – in the early rounds and then squeezed past Spurs, the holders, on away goals in the semi-finals.

In the final, another West German side awaited them. The

great Borussia Moenchengladbach team of Berti Vogts, Günter Netzer, who had just destroyed England at Wembley, Rainer Bonhof and Jupp Heynckes began the first leg at Anfield as though they were going to cope comfortably with Liverpool's threat. But the game was played in a downpour, and after half an hour the referee called the game off. Prompted by Paisley, Shankly made a difficult decision. He had left John Toshack out of the original line-up and played Brian Hall instead. Toshack was disgusted and he and Shankly had a furious row. But later that night, after the abandonment and sensing how vulnerable the Germans might be to a more direct approach, Shankly telephoned Toshack at home and told him he was likely to be playing the following night when the game was scheduled to be replayed. Hall was devastated. But Toshack played.

The change worked beautifully. Toshack was utterly dominant in the air. Liverpool's first goal was a Toshack–Keegan classic. The big man nodded it down and Keegan launched himself at the ball as it dropped and sent a bullet header hurtling past the Moenchengladbach keeper. Keegan got another, Larry Lloyd headed a third from a corner and it seemed the trophy was as good as won. But in West Germany a fortnight later, Borussia played like men inspired in the first half and scored two early goals.

'About half an hour before the game, a terrible storm came on,' Shankly said. 'The rain put more pace into the pitch and, boy, did the Germans give us a going-over for 20 minutes. I thought "Oh, dear God, we'll get beaten 15–0 here." The way they were playing was untrue but they had spent themselves a quarter of an hour before half time. A few minutes from the final whistle, I got up and started to walk along the touchline. As I walked, I talked to our players saying "It's all right boys, it's over." Big John Toshack was too shattered to be elated.'

That was the sixty-sixth game of Liverpool's season. It was the first time an English team had won the league title and a cup in Europe. Shankly's wife suggested then that it might be a good time to retire. But Shankly was not ready. He wanted one more crack at the European Cup in the 1973–74 season. But that dream ended with a whimper. Liverpool went out in the second round to Red Star Belgrade, beaten both away and at home by the Yugoslavs. Revie's Leeds would not be denied the league this time either as Liverpool struggled for goals. Keegan top-scored with 12. Toshack only got 5. All that was left was the FA Cup.

There were tensions in the team at the time that taxed Shankly. There was some resentment towards Hughes, who some of his teammates felt worked too hard at being teacher's pet. It was no different to many other football dressing rooms. Most successful teams had strong characters who were not afraid to voice their opinions and Shankly's second great Liverpool side was no different. Still, it took skilful handling to stop the friction damaging team morale.

'I saw all the things going on when I was younger with Tommy Smith and Emlyn at each other's throats,' Thompson said. 'There was a lot of ill-feeling in the dressing room and Shanks had to handle that situation. Tommy was captain in 1972–73 when we won the Uefa Cup and then Emlyn took the captaincy off him. It was extremely difficult in the dressing room.

'I just wondered what was going on. I was the fetcher of the team. If Emlyn or Tommy wanted a couple of drinks, I would jump and do it. Emlyn and Tommy were two powerful people and Shanks had to make sure their disagreements didn't detract from what was happening on the pitch. Shanks got that right. Insults were flying across the dressing room and somehow that had to be handled. Shanks did most of that because Bob Paisley's communication skills were not the best.'

But when they made it to the FA Cup Final again for the second time in four years, this time there was no nervousness among the players. This time, they were confident and relaxed. On the eve of the game, the BBC set up a video link between

Shankly and Joe Harvey from the respective team hotels. When the conversation was coming to an end, Shankly, who sensed apprehension in Harvey's demeanour, took off his headphones a couple of seconds early and turned to someone in the room while the cameras were still rolling. 'Jesus Christ,' he said, 'Joe's beaten already and the game hasn't even started.' Harvey heard what Shankly said. Keegan felt Shankly made sure Harvey heard.

Newcastle had made mistakes in the build-up. Macdonald had done a whole series of interviews talking about how he was going to terrorize the Liverpool defence and young Phil Thompson in particular. He said he was going to expose Thompson's inexperience and make him wish he had never taken up the game. 'Malcolm was the big star up in Newcastle,' Thompson said, 'and he seemed to be in every paper right up until the weekend talking about what he was going to do and how many he was going to score.'

But Shankly had shown great faith in Thompson and Thompson was determined to repay him. He was the last of the young Liverpool-born lads that Shankly brought through into the first team and Thompson felt he owed him a great debt of gratitude. 'Everybody has heard the stories about him not wanting to talk to you when you were injured,' Thompson said. 'But one day when I was injured and I was seventeen and I was worried about whether I was going to be signing professional, he sidled up to me. When you were injured at Liverpool, you just took care of yourself around the training pitches. You didn't have any rehabilitation programme or any member of staff assigned to look after you. You jogged when you were able to jog. You sprinted when you were able to sprint and then it was up to you to say when you were fit and ready to play.

'I had been jogging round and I was walking and he came to me between the A-team pitch and the B-team pitch and he asked me how I was. Normal thing. "Are you sleeping well?" and "Are you eating well?" I used to go home telling my mum the same stories every day about how the great man had spoken to me. This time, I thought he was going to give me a bollocking about when I was going to be fit. But he asked how the injury was. I said I thought I'd be ready for the weekend.

' "You're seventeen in January, aren't you, son?" he said. This was November. "I just want to put your mind at ease, son, we've been very, very pleased with you, all the staff are happy with you and you will be signing a professional contract on your birthday." I wanted to grab him by the ears and give him a kiss. I was absolutely thrilled. He said not to tell any of the other apprentices. But that was his way. The boy's injured, he's proved he has got what it takes, he is doing his best. And he gave me that couple of months' grace knowing I was going to sign. It was a great thought, great man-management. It was just his way.'

Shankly pinned some of Macdonald's newspaper articles up on the noticeboard in the Wembley dressing room. Thompson borrowed the tactic when he was Gérard Houllier's number two at Anfield. Only he had hostile press cuttings laminated and took them away on foreign trips. Thompson had seen how it worked that day of the Cup Final. It had brought out the best in him.

Thompson was the man of the match. He man-marked Macdonald out of the game. 'I'm going to take him home and put him on the mantelpiece for our kid to play with,' Thompson said later. And with the Newcastle attack emasculated, Liverpool played an expansive game, full of verve and energy and skill and confidence. Keegan got the first after Hall had ducked under a cross from Smith. He took one touch to control it on the edge of the area and then volleyed it past Willie McFaul. The second was a beauty. Toshack leapt and flicked a long ball forward and Heighway raced on to it. He pushed it on to his right foot and then hit a clean, crisp, fizzing shot past McFaul's despairing dive and into the bottom corner of the Newcastle net.

The third goal, the last competitive goal ever scored by a team managed by Bill Shankly, was a fitting farewell. It was Liverpool at their formidable best, Liverpool taking the art of pass and move to its apogee. It was exhibition stuff, total football, played with an accomplishment that bemused Newcastle and left them powerless.

It was fitting that Ian Callaghan, Shankly's old faithful, should start the move. He nicked the ball by the halfway line and played a short pass to Hall. Hall moved it wide to Toshack, who checked and played it back to Smith. Smith played a cross-field ball to Alec Lindsay, Lindsay played it down the left touchline to Keegan. Keegan took it back inside, showboating a little bit as he ran and then floating a long, high pass back to Smith on the right.

Smith nonchalantly volleyed the ball on to Hall with the outside of his right foot and then went for the return. Then Smith played a one-two with Heighway that took him surging into the area. He got to the byline and then drove the ball low and hard to the back post where Keegan was waiting to stick out a boot and guide the ball into the empty net. It was simplicity taken to the level of football genius. Eleven unanswered passes and the opposition hadn't even got close to getting a sniff of the ball. It was perfection.

That was the way Shankly looked at it, too. The FA Cup was still an important trophy then, not a consolation prize like it is now, a trophy that managers like Ferguson aggrandize only when they have failed in the Premiership or the Champions League. Shankly felt it would be a good way to go out, his team playing beautiful winning football and the club in rude health. He let his players take the acclaim and strode towards the Wembley tunnel. A couple of Liverpool supporters ran on the pitch and prostrated themselves at his feet so they could kiss his shoes. They looked like men bowing down before their god.

Perhaps that was part of the reason Shankly quit, too. The pressure of being regarded as a deity who could do no wrong was intense. Shankly must have had a horror of the adoration of the Liverpool fans beginning to wane if results began to fade. Even as they bowed down before him, he was steeling himself to walk away.

'After the FA Cup Final,' Shankly wrote in his autobiography, 'I went into the dressing room and I felt tired from all the years. I said to a bloke who was looking after the dressing room: "Get me a cup of tea and a couple of pies for Christ's sake." When I sat down with my tea and my pies, my mind was made up. If we had lost the Final, I would have carried on, but I thought, "Well we've won the Cup now and maybe it's a good time to go." I knew I was going to finish.'

He knew he was going to finish, but even Shankly, the football god, had no idea of the toll his decision was going to take.

6: Ferguson, Rangers and their Mixed Marriage

The outpourings of Alex Ferguson have been visited upon many unfortunate souls but never has his fury been lavished on a victim with quite the vehemence and disgust that infused his verbal and written denunciations of Willie Allison. Allison was the public relations man at Rangers when Ferguson walked wide-eyed through the doors of Ibrox in the summer of 1967, full of dreams about the glories he would achieve as centre forward at the club that had dominated all his boyhood ambitions. Ferguson came to blame Allison for the way the dreams died.

Ferguson has spent the rest of his life trying to recover from the wound that was inflicted upon him when he was forced out of Rangers after two and a half desperately unhappy and barren years. His disappointment was so fierce that it has been blamed for, or credited with, instilling in him the hunger for redemption that drove his insatiably relentless desire to succeed in management. 'No other experience in 40 years as a professional player and manager has created a scar comparable with that left by the treatment I received at Rangers,' Ferguson wrote in his autobiography.

In his despair, Ferguson turned on Allison with particular venom because he was convinced the ex-newspaper man was spreading the poison of sectarianism to damn him before his Rangers career had had a chance to take root. Ferguson's wife Cathy was Catholic and his mother came from a Catholic family, and at a staunchly Protestant club like Rangers where there was a block on signing Catholics, Ferguson believed that provided a man like Allison with enough ammunition to make life uncomfortable for the club's new striker.

Ferguson had grown up in the shadow of Ibrox. The tenement flat where his family lived was sandwiched between the River Clyde and the Rangers stadium, only a few hundred yards from each. Ferguson was a Govan kid. Born and bred. He was entitled to think he would be accorded the special status of a local hero at Ibrox and worshipped in the way that Alan Smith was adored at Leeds United and Robbie Fowler deified at Liverpool. But that never happened to Ferguson at Ibrox.

He was mobbed by happy fans on the day he signed because he was one of Scotland's most highly rated forwards when Rangers snatched him away from Dunfermline Athletic for £65,000, then a record fee between Scottish clubs. He was seen as quite a capture. But a more vivid memory for him was dashing to a friend's car outside Ibrox to try to make a hasty escape after Rangers had handed the title to Celtic in May 1968, pursued by an enraged supporter who gave him a hefty kick on the back of the leg as he fled.

That kind of treatment at the hands of men who worked in the shipyards where his father worked, drank in the pubs where he drank and toiled in the factory where he once toiled, mortified Ferguson. The bond he felt with the tough working-class community he grew up in meant everything to him, and when things began to go wrong at Rangers there was a danger that he would be ostracized by the people he most wanted to please. So Ferguson cast around for scapegoats and Allison headed the queue.

Ferguson was sensitive about the sectarian issue because he knew that by bigotry's exacting and unforgiving standards he was vulnerable to attack. On the day he signed for Rangers one of the directors, Ian McLaren, asked him about his wife's religion. Next, he wanted to know where they had been married. When Ferguson told him it was a registry office, not a Catholic

church, McLaren was relieved. Ferguson was furious with himself for not telling McLaren what he thought of his questions.

'I don't know where my tongue was,' Ferguson said. 'How
could I, who consider myself a strong character, have refrained
from delivering a furious blast in response to such offensive
questions? But that's what happens when you desire something
as badly as I wanted to join Rangers. You are willing to dilute
your personality to make the dream come true.'

Ferguson's passivity that day was not an isolated occurrence.
He knew that sectarianism was endemic in Glasgow and that it
was more entrenched than ever in the late Sixties because it
mirrored the Troubles across the sea in Northern Ireland. And
so, occasionally, he danced with the devil. Even though he had
a Catholic wife, he sang Orange songs in the pub he co-owned
in the Bridgeton district of the city once his playing days were
done.

On 12 July, the anniversary of the Battle of the Boyne,
Ferguson would open the doors of Shaws at 7.30 a.m. and
watch the marchers file in, fold away their sashes and their
Lodge colours and start drinking. When they urged Ferguson to
join in their tribal singing he did not demur. He said it was a
matter of common sense and self-preservation but it cut the high
ground out from under his feet when he attempted to portray
himself as a hapless victim of Allison's hard-line Protestantism.

Ferguson was convinced from the start of his time at Ibrox
that Allison influenced the thinking of the club's doddering
chairman, John Lawrence, against him. There is no real evidence
of that, although there is plenty to suggest that Ferguson's ill-
fated stay at Rangers was condemned to failure by a toxic
mixture of appalling timing, managerial change, shabby treatment and creeping paranoia. Attempting to blame someone else
for his rare failures has, for some, come to be one of his defining
characteristics.

However poisonous Allison might have been, the fact
remained that Ferguson could hardly have picked a worse time

to join Rangers. They were at an all-time low because Celtic were at an all-time high. A few months before Ferguson arrived at Ibrox, Jock Stein's magnificent side had beaten the great Inter Milan team managed by Helenio Herrera in Lisbon to become the first British team to win the European Cup. Ferguson was in Hong Kong on a Scotland B tour on the night of the final and heard the result on the radio. He was proud for Scottish football, but the repercussions of that victory helped to seal his fate at Ibrox.

Celtic's unprecedented success heaped the pressure on the Rangers boss, Scot Symon, who had been manager since 1954 and had won six championships for the club. Ferguson idolized Symon, even though his methods were increasingly coming to appear outmoded compared with tracksuit managers like Stein. Ferguson admired Symon for his authority and work ethic and was struck by the silence that would fall over the dressing room when the manager walked in.

Rangers were top of the league when the club sacked Symon in November 1967. Ferguson had only been playing for the club for three months and suddenly the man who was his protector and his champion was gone. He was so distraught and disgusted that he tried to hand in a transfer request as soon as he heard the news. But he was talked out of it. His humour did not improve when he found out Symon's replacement was to be his assistant, Davie White.

There was a mutual antipathy between White and Ferguson. Ferguson thought White was weak and tactically naive. He distrusted the fact that he sought the company of the players. He thought that compromised the manager's authority. White thought Ferguson wasn't good enough. Even though Ferguson was the top scorer in his first season at Ibrox with 23 goals, White tried to get rid of him by selling him to Hibs.

It turned out that both men were right. Celtic led the title race for much of Ferguson's last season and then blew it when the going got tough. Jock Stein played a master stroke at the beginning of the run-in when he conceded the title to Rangers, a ruse which seemed to spook White and unsettle the players. Ferguson recognized Stein's move immediately as the work of a managerial genius and imitated it nearly twenty years later when he said Blackburn would have to 'do a Devon Loch' to lose the championship.

It didn't work for Ferguson but it worked for Stein. In the spring of 1968, Rangers began to fade. By the end of the season, the Old Firm giants were neck and neck. Rangers played their final game needing to beat Aberdeen at Ibrox to keep the pressure on Celtic, who would then have to beat Dunfermline away the following Wednesday if they were to pip Rangers to the title. Ferguson scored against Aberdeen but Rangers lost 3–2. It was their first home defeat of the season and they had handed the title to Celtic.

Their fans were furious. They hurled stones through the windows in the home dressing room and Ferguson and his teammates were holed up inside the stadium for two hours, hoping that the anger would subside so that they could go home. In the end, Ferguson plucked up the courage to poke his nose out of the front door and speak to his former St Johnstone colleague John Bell, who had been planning to meet him for a night out. He told Bell to bring his car to the entrance in ten minutes. He dashed out of there like Clyde Barrow after a heist but the fans hunted him down and kicked him on his way before Bell drove him off into the evening.

At least Ferguson had gone into that game with hope. During the close season, that hope was extinguished. First of all, Ferguson was humiliated on an end-of-season trip to Denmark when John Lawrence introduced his players to the British ambassador in Copenhagen and forgot Ferguson's name. Then, Ferguson's wife called to tell him that the Scottish papers were running stories claiming that his Rangers career was over and that Rangers were desperate to get rid of him. He felt humiliated a second time.

His first thought was to blame Allison. Ferguson had built him into a hate figure by now. After the defeat to Aberdeen, some of the criticism for the loss of the title was aimed at him but Ferguson had been far more concerned about the revival of rumours about his marriage. 'Much more serious was the evilly intentioned gossip about Cathy's religion that was swirling around Ibrox and the other gathering places of the supporters,' he said.

'I knew that the principal muck-spreader was Willie Allison, the bigoted public relations officer, who clearly felt that anybody married to a Catholic was not a fit and proper person to play for Rangers.

'Later, after our first son was born, Allison peddled the tale that Mark was christened in the Catholic church. To most normal people, where a child was baptised – in Mark's case, it happened to be the Church of Scotland parish church in Croftfoot – would have no relevance to the father's member-ship of a football team, but a diseased zealot like Allison was prepared to tell lies about the matter.'

After Ferguson had heard the rumours circulating about his Rangers future back in Scotland, he went out on a lunchtime bender in Copenhagen. He repaired to one of the many pictur-esque little bars inside the Tivoli Gardens with a journalist, Ken Gallacher, and a couple of Rangers players. Instead of drinking himself into a stupor, though, he drank himself into a whirling rage and staggered back to the King Frederick Hotel where Allison was eating in the dining room.

Ferguson harangued Allison until the other players dragged their teammate away. They were trying to bundle him into his room when Allison showed up, so Ferguson gave him another blast. Eventually, Greig put Ferguson in his pyjamas and shoved him into bed, but when he had left, Ferguson went downstairs in his nightclothes and resumed his attack on the hapless public relations man.

This time, Greig abandoned half-measures. He shoved

Ferguson in a cold bath and then stuck him under a freezing shower. He got room service to send up steak and chips and a pint of milk. In the best football traditions, Greig and the other Rangers players sobered Ferguson up and then took him out to get hammered all over again. The next morning, Ferguson was struggling to see straight at training. When it came to heading practice, Ferguson was heading thin air where he thought the ball should be. 'Mostly, he was missing by five feet,' his team-mate, Dave Smith, said.

That wasn't quite the nadir of Ferguson's relationship with Allison, though. A year later, when Ferguson had been consigned to a shadow life of playing in the Rangers third team, Allison, who he had nicknamed Colonel Blimp because of his florid countenance and pinstriped suits, stopped to talk to Ferguson while he was training with the apprentices. Allison told Ferguson he had cancer. Ferguson was unmoved. 'I know it is a terrible thing to say but I did not have a crumb of pity for him,' Ferguson said.

Ferguson's lack of compassion is the least surprising part of the story. He can be a ruthlessly vengeful man, as many of his former players and colleagues have discovered to their cost. The puzzling part of the incident is why Allison would have confided in Ferguson, particularly about something so personal and terrible, if he had devoted much of the past two years to trying to destroy and discredit him. It doesn't stack up. Some Rangers players felt Ferguson demonized Allison to help to excuse his failure at Ibrox.

Before the start of the 1968–69 season, Davie White told Ferguson he had been offered to Hibs as part of a deal to lure Hibs striker Colin Stein to Ibrox. Ferguson refused to be part of the plan. White tried again a couple of weeks later and at least prevailed upon Ferguson to travel to Edinburgh to talk to the Hibs manager, Bob Shankly, Bill's brother.

While he was at Bob Shankly's house, the phone rang and the Hibs boss picked up the receiver, listened for a couple of minutes without speaking and then put it down on the table and resumed the conversation with Ferguson. But Ferguson was distracted. He could hear someone still speaking at the other end of the line. 'Oh that's my brother, Bill,' Bob Shankly said. 'He rings me every Sunday and I can't get a word in edgeways so I just lift the phone now and again and say "aye".'

Ferguson still refused to be transferred to Hibs, so Rangers bought Colin Stein anyway and paid £100,000 for him. Ferguson's punishment was to spend much of his second season in the reserves. He played for the first team intermittently and scored in a Fairs Cup quarter-final against Atletico Bilbao. He got another break when Stein was injured before the Scottish Cup Final and White brought Ferguson back into the first team. But that final against Celtic turned into another sad chapter in Ferguson's cursed Rangers career.

He disagreed strongly with White's tactics, which he felt would isolate Rangers' centre backs against the quick Celtic striking pair of Bobby Lennox and Steve Chalmers. He was also uneasy about being asked to mark Celtic's towering captain, Billy McNeill, at corners. Two minutes into the game, his worst fears were realized. Ferguson lost McNeill at a corner and McNeill nodded the ball in for the opening goal. 'I always remember saying to myself: ' "How in the name of Hell did I get so free",' McNeill said.

The match turned into a rout. Celtic waltzed to a 4–0 victory. Ferguson was dropped for the remaining four games of the season and never played for the Rangers first team again. The next season, he found himself banished from training with the first-team squad. He led a shadow life, training with the apprentices and playing for the third team against sides like Glasgow Transport and Glasgow University. When Nottingham Forest bid for him towards the end of November 1969, Ferguson demanded £2,000, 10 per cent of the transfer, before he left.

Rangers were so desperate to get rid of him that they acceded to the request. Then Ferguson's old boss at Dunfermline, Willie

Cunningham, now in charge at Falkirk, rang and begged him not to finalize the move to Forest until he had had a chance to talk to him as well. Ferguson's wife wanted to stay in Scotland so he made his apologies to the Forest manager, Matt Gillies, one of the most progressive managers in England, and turned his back on what might have been a good career south of the border. He took the easy option and signed for Second Division Falkirk.

A week later, Davie White was sacked and Rangers appointed a manager, Willie Waddell, who was a confirmed admirer of Ferguson. 'You're an idiot,' Ferguson kept telling himself. 'Idiot, idiot, idiot.' He was only twenty-seven but his top-line career as a player was over. Falkirk won the Second Division championship in Ferguson's first season and he was full of the joy of being liberated from his torture at Rangers, but he had never won a winners' medal as a player and now he was never likely to. Instead, he had to be content with a Scottish Cup semi-final appearance.

He enjoyed his time at Brockville Park, a small ground packed with character and passionate supporters. The town motto fitted him, too. 'Better meddle wi' the de'il than the bairns of Falkirk,' it read. Ferguson thrived on the excellent team spirit Cunningham had helped to build and enjoyed chewing over football tactics with another future Scotland manager, Andy Roxburgh, his fellow striker.

He seems to have derived an equal amount of pleasure from 'the excellent bonus system' that the Falkirk directors introduced after the side was promoted. He waxed lyrical about it in his autobiography. 'It not only rewarded us healthily for wins and draws,' he said, 'but gave us an extra £40 for every week we were in the top ten of the First Division.' For a manager who accused Alan Shearer of turning his back on Manchester United for money reasons, Ferguson the player could never be accused of neglecting the financial implications of any element of his football career.

By the time he arrived at Falkirk, Ferguson had already begun to harbour lasting grudges against journalists and photographers. He refused, for instance, to pose for the Falkirk team photo at the start of the 1970–71 season because he spotted a photographer with whom he had had a disagreement at Rangers in the group waiting to snap the Falkirk side. In 1970 he was also elected the chairman of the Scottish Professional Footballers' Association, where he was a forceful advocate for his members' rights.

In March 1972 Hibs tried to sign Ferguson again, and this time he decided he wanted to go to Easter Road. Cunningham blocked the move and the two men had a furious row that would have turned into a fist fight if they had not been separated. By now, Ferguson's career was starting to peter out. He was out for several months with a serious knee injury and his most significant contribution to the season came when he led a threatened players' strike after Cunningham had withdrawn expense allowances for travel and lunches in response to a 6–0 defeat to St Johnstone. The threat worked and Cunningham's authority was undermined.

Ferguson was starting to look to a life beyond playing now. He earned his coaching badge and took over the running of a pub near the junction of Govan Road and Paisley Road West. It was called Burns Cottage. It was renamed Fergie's. It's still there today. In its latest incarnation, it's called The Angel Bar. Cunningham began to get him involved in coaching at Falkirk, too, although Ferguson let himself down when he was sent off for aiming a kick at Aberdeen defender Willie Young, hardly the action of a man ready for the responsibility of running a team. Still, when Cunningham stepped down at the end of the season he encouraged Ferguson to apply for his job. Falkirk ignored Cunningham's recommendation and appointed John Prentice.

Ferguson was restored to the ranks and then released from his Falkirk contract before the start of the 1973–74 season. There was the obligatory row about money before he left.

Ferguson claimed he had been diddled out of the last payment of his signing-on fee. He got his cash. Then he made the final move of his playing career and signed for Scottish football's last incurable optimist, Ally MacLeod, at Ayr United.

He juggled his time at Ayr with the day-to-day problems of running Fergie's. It was only a couple of miles west of Ibrox and close to the docks so it was not a place for shrinking violets. There were brawls, one man was attacked with a docker's hook that left him prone on the pavement outside with blood pouring from wounds in his neck and face, and one evening Ferguson even got a call to say a man had wandered in carrying a shotgun. Typically, Ferguson threw himself into the venture wholeheartedly. One Christmas, he even ended up cooking the bar meals in the kitchen because the chef was off sick.

Ayr gave his career a hint of an Indian summer. They had finished the previous season in sixth place in the top division and Ferguson scored seven times in his first eight games. In mid-October, after Ferguson had hit the winner at Motherwell, Ayr were second in the table and being acclaimed as shock contenders for the championship. It didn't last, either for club or player. Ferguson enjoyed sweet revenge over Prentice when he scored the winner against Falkirk, but by the spring his regular starting position at 3 p.m. was the bench. He scored his last senior goal in a 1–1 draw against St Johnstone in front of 1,900 spectators on 2 February 1974 at Muirton Park. That's gone, too, now. Like Brockville Park, there's a superstore on the land where footballers used to play. His last league appearance was against Falkirk at Brockville in April 1974.

Ferguson's last competitive game was a reserve team match at Ayr's Somerset Park ground against East Fife reserves. He scored a header but he used the match to revisit the memories of sixteen years of a football career that never quite fulfilled its promise and which had been disfigured by the bitter disappointment of his ordeal at Rangers. He even gleaned a wry amusement from being clattered again and again by his young marker,

Colin Methven, who went on to become a stalwart for Wigan Athletic. 'I had to smile as I looked at the enthusiasm of a young lad who reminded me of many of my own attitudes when I was starting out,' Ferguson said.

Playing football had taken him to within sight of the mountain top without ever letting him reach the summit. Now, as an aspiring manager, he was back at base camp and ready for the long climb that lay ahead.

7: Shankly and the New Breed

Brian Hall, the earnest little student who was the new kid on the block in the first-team dressing room, usually kept himself to himself. He made a point of being seen and not heard. But one morning he thought he had spotted a chance to impress the old guard that was too good to miss. He had read an article about the comedian Eric Sykes in the *Radio Times* the night before and now, as he sat in the first-team dressing room, he heard Roger Hunt, Ian St John and Ron Yeats, the three kings of the club, talking about him.

Hall, who had only just become part of the first-team squad and was a bright lad just out of university, didn't know that Hunt, St John and Yeats were friends with Sykes, so he piped up about how the comedian was deaf in one ear. Hunt, St John and Yeats pretended to be amazed. They looked at each other in mock astonishment. Encouraged, Hall rattled out everything he had read in the magazine. Hunt said he was flabbergasted. Hall kept going. Eventually, Emlyn Hughes, another new boy, dug Hall in the ribs and told him he was making a fool of himself. The next morning, at the team hotel, Sykes walked into the breakfast room.

'Sykesy,' St John shouted across the room, 'I believe you're deaf in one ear.'

'What?' Sykes shouted back.

Hall had to smile. 'The whole place burst out laughing,' he said.

This was Shankly's Liverpool in the late Sixties. Two generations rubbing shoulders with each other in uneasy fraternity. One not ready to be consigned to the past, the other itching to take hold of the future. One belonged to television's black and white era, which ended in 1968 when the BBC broadcast its first match live in colour. That was the FA Cup Final between West Brom and Everton, and the players who came after that were the children of a new generation. Trapped in black and white, watching the footage of Yeats, St John and Hunt now makes them seem as if they played in a different world.

The thing was, Shankly's first great Liverpool team was getting old. Getting old like the Beatles, who had beards on their faces and disharmony on their minds. John, Paul, George and Ringo were getting ready to split and Shankly knew that a reckoning was coming at his football club too. He was a loyal man, but by the end of the Sixties the team he had built around Hunt, St John and Yeats had not won anything since the league title in 1966. That team had got tired and stale like all great teams do. It had worn itself out, and although Shankly was a loyal man, he could be ruthless, too. He was getting ready to turn to the new breed.

He had been buying steadily since that second title win in 1965–66, squirrelling some of the brightest young talents from the lower leagues away in the reserves. That year, the year of England's World Cup triumph, Liverpool strolled to the championship. They had won the FA Cup the year before and reached the semi-finals of the European Cup and now they were at their peak. They crushed everyone who stood in their way. They put five goals past West Ham, five past Northampton Town and five past Blackburn Rovers. Most satisfying of all, they put five past Everton too. That was sweet. Shankly had been telling his players for days that he had been watching from the upstairs windows at his home as Harry Catterick ran the Everton players into the ground at Bellefield. He told them Everton would be exhausted. When Everton leaked four goals in the second half of their humbling at Anfield, he must have seemed like a prophet.

That was the last of the great seasons for Shankly's first side. They only used fourteen players throughout the entire campaign, and one of those, Bobby Graham, played just once. The sky was the limit. Three of the team – Ian Callaghan, Gerry Byrne and Roger Hunt – made it into Alf Ramsey's England World Cup squad. Callaghan played in the first group game before he was replaced by Alan Ball, but Hunt played every minute of every match including the final. When the new season resumed, Liverpool and Everton put on a special display before the 1966 Charity Shield at Goodison Park. Yeats walked round the ground holding the Championship trophy, Brian Labone carried the FA Cup that Everton had won against Sheffield Wednesday, and Hunt and Ray Wilson held the World Cup aloft. It was a formidable display of Merseyside football power and Liverpool, in particular, felt they were invincible.

'If you are very lucky,' St John said, 'you know days when you don't believe you can be beaten. When we beat Everton 5–0, we played so well that it seemed we could do anything. We were not so much a football club as an empire and I lived at the heart of it ... Shankly likened me to one of the best middleweights, quick and hard, and for an old fighting man, that was another reason to believe in a future without bounds. Our second title was virtually in our pockets by Christmas and even when we lost a game, it seemed like the merest slip along the way to unlimited glory. We were fighting cocks who had to resist the urge to strut on to the field, a resolution that was not always kept. We believed it would never end.'

St John didn't see what was coming. After he had achieved so much and grown so close to Shankly, perhaps it was unreasonable to expect that he should. Liverpool wrapped up the title by beating Chelsea at Anfield in late April. The Chelsea players formed an honour guard to welcome them on to the pitch just as Manchester United's players were to do for Chelsea at Old Trafford thirty-nine years later. Liverpool didn't just show great skill and togetherness in that 1965–66 season. They showed tenacity, too. The previous season had ended with the shattering blow of a controversial European Cup defeat to Inter Milan when it seemed they had been cheated out of a place in the final by several suspicious refereeing decisions. It would have been easy to let that poison the 1965–66 season, but Shankly avoided that fate. Instead, Liverpool took another tilt at European glory, this time in the European Cup Winners Cup. They beat Juventus, Standard Liège, Honved and Jock Stein's Celtic on the way to the final at Hampden Park where Borussia Dortmund were waiting for them.

Dortmund were a step too far. The pitch was sodden after a day of hard rain, the crowd just 41,000. Hunt, who wasn't fully fit, equalized the Dortmund opener early in the second half but then missed a late chance to win the game. It went to extra-time. Early in the second period the Liverpool keeper, Tommy Lawrence, rushed to the edge of his area and punched a high bouncing through ball clear because he felt that if he caught it his momentum would take him outside the box and he would be penalized for handball.

It was a good punch but it fell to Reinhard Libuda, who was standing near the right touchline about 40 yards out. Libuda, also known in his homeland as 'Stan', lashed the ball back towards goal. He could not have weighted it any better. It sailed over Lawrence and eluded the desperate last efforts of Yeats to clear it, bouncing off a combination of the post and the Liverpool captain's long legs before it nestled in the bottom of the net.

Defeat was a hard blow. Another long and emotionally draining European campaign had ended in failure. After that, others took up the mantle and there was a clear sense that Liverpool were being overtaken and shunted back into the shadows. In 1966–67, Liverpool went out of the European Cup in the second round. They had needed three games to get past Romanian no-hopers Petrolul Ploiesti in the first round. Then they drew Ajax. Shankly was optimistic. He didn't rate Ajax.

He even said that if he had had a choice of who to meet at that stage, he would have picked the Dutch champions.

Ajax responded by humiliating Liverpool. The teams played the first leg in Amsterdam in a thick fog so gloopy that Shankly later claimed he had run on to the pitch to give instructions to Willie Stevenson and that none of the officials had seen him. But nothing could obscure Liverpool's humiliation. They were thrashed 5–1 by a side that included a young Johan Cruyff, and could only draw 2–2 back at Anfield. It was a prelude to the great Ajax European Cup triumphs of the early Seventies but it seemed like an epitaph for Liverpool's European ambitions.

As Liverpool fell back, others began to step up. Shankly had been desperate to make legends of himself and his players by blazing a trail in Europe and establishing Liverpool as the country's greatest footballing export. Scaling the peak of the European Cup would have been his Everest, whatever he might have said later to Shelley Rohde about the FA Cup being the most important competition of all. He knew that even by the mid-Sixties the European Cup held more kudos than any other competition and now he was forced to sit and watch as other men and other teams seized the immortality he had hoped would belong to him and Liverpool.

As Liverpool sank into a state of atrophy, Stein's Celtic, the same Celtic that Liverpool had beaten in the Cup Winners' Cup the season before, beat Inter Milan in Lisbon in late May 1967 to become the first British team to lift the European Cup. And so it was the Lisbon Lions, not the Liverpool Lions, who passed into legend. It was Billy McNeill, not Ron Yeats, who stood on the ledge in the old open-air Estadio Nacional in the low hills outside the Portuguese capital and lifted the great trophy above his head. It was Celtic, not Liverpool, who took their place alongside Real Madrid and Inter in the pantheon of the game. It was Celtic's players who suddenly stood side by side with Puskas and Di Stefano and Gento and Fachetti as the lords of the European game.

A year later, Liverpool slipped out of the Fairs Cup in the third round, losing home and away to the Hungarians, Ferencvaros. Shankly still clung to the hope that Liverpool could be the first English team to win the European Cup, but a few months later, that was taken away from him too. This time it was Manchester United's turn to remind Shankly how far back he had fallen in the queue. On a great tide of emotion, Bobby Charlton, George Best and Brian Kidd scored the goals that beat Benfica at Wembley. The football world was enthralled by the romance of Matt Busby's return from the horror of the Munich Air Crash to claim the trophy he had always felt was his club's destiny. And in Best, United had a player of such charisma and genius that he overshadowed any of the talent Shankly had at his disposal.

Shankly grew restless. He knew what had to be done. He knew that the team he continued to acclaim in later years as the best side England had known since the Second World War had to be dismantled and reinvigorated. So he acted. He began to build a team in waiting. In February 1967 he paid Blackpool £65,000 for Emlyn Hughes, who was nineteen and was to become closer to Shankly than any of his players. Shankly had first seen Hughes more than a year earlier when he made his Blackpool debut at Blackburn. He offered the Blackpool directors £25,000 for him on the spot but they turned him down. Shankly continued to monitor his progress, though, and when he finally sealed his signature he could not conceal his glee.

'Emyln was one of the major signings of all time,' he wrote in his autobiography. 'As soon as we had sorted things out at Blackpool's ground and finalised the transfer, we went to Emlyn's digs for his belongings and then drove him to Liverpool. On the way, another car ran into the back of mine and smashed one of the rear lights. I got out and said to the driver, "What the bloody hell do you think you are doing?" Before he could answer, I told him, "Never mind, it's only a rear light, I've got what I want in the car."' A little further on, Shankly was stopped by a policeman. Shankly asked him if he knew who was in the car. 'I believe you're Mr Shankly,' the policeman said. 'Not me,' Shankly said, exasperated. 'That's the future England captain in the back seat.' Behind him, Hughes was writhing in embarrassment.

Four months later, he bought Ray Clemence from Scunthorpe United for £18,000. Concerned because he was left-footed, Shankly went to watch Clemence eight times before he satisfied himself he was the right man. His logic was typically eccentric. 'I don't like left-footed goalkeepers,' he said, 'especially if they are left-handed. I'm not suggesting they are not good enough but I have always felt they are short of balance. Ray was left-footed but right-handed and that was good.' Clemence was brought from Scunthorpe to Anfield in the Scunthorpe chairman's Rolls-Royce like a precious work of art ready to be delivered to a proud new owner.

'The first time I ever met the Great Man was at the reception doors at Anfield that Saturday morning,' Clemence said. 'For the first couple of hours, we never spoke about what I was going to earn or anything like that. It was all about Shanks convincing you that you were joining the best club in Britain at that time. He showed me the dressing rooms and what a great playing surface the Anfield pitch was. He showed me the Kop and said the greatest set of supporters would be behind me every week. He took me down to the training ground and showed me all the training facilities. He even took me into the toilet area and I wondered what was going on. He pressed the flush and said: "This will refill in 15 seconds, we have everything right here." He just impressed on you that he knew everything there was to know about that football club.

'He wanted it to be the best and he wanted you to be the best and he would do everything he could to make sure that happened. All those things were in my mind before he sat me down and asked me if I wanted to sign. Well, I'd made my mind up I wanted to sign before I had even come across from

Scunthorpe that morning. But if there had been any doubt in my mind, Shanks would have got rid of it. He was so enthusiastic and so believing in the fact that he had the best team and that his team would conquer all. They had had great success but he was looking around by then thinking he might have to change one or two.

'On the day I signed, he told me: "Carry on improving the way you are doing and you'll be in our first team within the next year. Tommy Lawrence is thirty coming up thirty-one and he's past his best. There's no problem." So I went home and told my mother and father what Shanks had said. When I reported for pre-season training a few weeks later, I soon found out that Tommy was twenty-seven and at his peak. I had to wait two and a half years to get into the team. But Shanks could get away with that kind of thing.'

The same year, Shankly bought Tony Hateley from Chelsea for £96,000. He went straight into the team but things didn't work out. Injuries thwarted his progress and Shankly didn't like injuries. He sold him on to Coventry at a slight loss after one season. Alun Evans didn't make it either. After Shankly had paid £100,000 to bring him from Wolves in September 1968, he was injured in a nightclub incident when a glass was shoved in his face, and it seemed to shatter his confidence. But the signings continued. Alec Lindsay arrived from Bury in 1969 and Larry Lloyd, a towering centre half very much in the mould of Ron Yeats, was bought from Bristol Rovers.

Then there was Steve Heighway, who was studying at Warwick University, and Hall, who was doing a degree at Liverpool University and working part-time as a bus conductor. Predictably enough, they were nicknamed 'the two Bambers' by the other players after the University Challenge host Bamber Gascoigne. 'The first time I had a conversation with Shanks – or rather when I listened to him – would be some time in July 1966,' Hall said. 'The only opportunity I had to train with the professionals was during the summer holidays. I had a job with a bus company called Ribble who ran from Preston to Liverpool. With my busman's uniform on, I could get a free ride there and a free ride back. So I had to turn up at training in my busman's uniform. I was nineteen but I looked about sixteen. You can imagine the stick I got from the senior pros when I walked in with this busman's uniform. I got shown into the apprentices' dressing room, which was the away dressing room underneath the paddock. I was told where my hook was. I put my bag down and the next minute the Great Man walked in. He looked me up and down and he said: "You're the student, aren't you son. Where are you from?" I told him I was from Preston and he then went into this terrific eulogy about Tom Finney. In the middle of all of this, and this is gospel, he stopped and looked at me and said: "Do you need a degree these days to be a bus conductor, son?"'

Shankly was building a shadow team of hungry young players ready to step in when the time came. It was to become his second great Liverpool side and it was built entirely from signings from the lower leagues and the products of Liverpool's youth team. Clemence, from Scunthorpe. Lawler, from the youth team. Smith, from the youth team. Lloyd, from Bristol Rovers. Lindsay, from Bury. Callaghan, from the youth team. Hall, who had risen through the ranks. Hughes, from Blackpool. Heighway, from non-league Skelmersdale. Up front there was Kevin Keegan, who followed Clemence from Scunthorpe in 1971, and John Toshack, bought from Cardiff City a year earlier.

His recruitment policy seems strange, almost dull, in an age when we are accustomed to managers with pretensions to winning the Premiership stocking their teams with players from outside the British Isles. That option was not really open to Shankly. Very few imports played in the English league, even though Denis Law, John Charles and Jimmy Greaves all played in Italy for a time during the early Sixties. Anyway, Shankly would have found it hard to cope with having players from abroad in his side. He had a xenophobic streak and he valued traditional British qualities like full-blooded commitment. Quite how a foreign player would have coped on Shankly's preferred diet for his Liverpool team of steak, steak and more steak, we will never know.

Nevertheless, Shankly's reliance on signing players from the lower leagues to rebuild his side in the late Sixties shines a sad light on the breakdown of the progressive hierarchical structure in English football in the twenty-first century. Shankly believed that there was enough quality in the Second, Third and Fourth Divisions to help him fashion a renewed assault on the biggest prizes in the game. And he was right. But the trust Shankly had in the potential of players from Scunthorpe and Bury no longer exists, largely because young players of potential are picked up by the big clubs earlier and cosseted in their extensive youth systems and academies. It is hard to think of modern players making the same kind of leap that Clemence, Lindsay or Keegan did. Jonathan Stead moving from Huddersfield Town to Blackburn Rovers is one of the few examples, and that was hardly a roaring success. Ferguson flirted with the idea of signing both Simon Davies and Matthew Etherington from Peterborough United but backed off. Spurs took the plunge instead. Neither lasted long at White Hart Lane.

Partly, it's just a product of the times. The ending of restrictions on the number of foreign players who could compete for a team in European competition opened up a vast new market of football raw material. It's cheaper to buy young talent from a European club than it is to try to pluck them from the Championship. The cost of English players has become inflated. The catch is that an eclectic mix of players often fails to engender the same kind of team spirit at a club as when the nucleus of a side provides an indigenous base. The influx of foreign players has even started to provoke a backlash at some clubs now. Some Premiership chairmen have begun to speak openly of the need to build the team around an English spine – a policy Jose Mourinho has adopted at Chelsea.

It could be argued, in fact, that Ferguson's problems at Old Trafford began in earnest when he tried to move away from the base of English players that had brought him so much success in the 1990s. High-profile signings like Juan Sebastián Verón, Fabien Barthez, Laurent Blanc, Kleberson and Eric Djemba-Djemba – so bad they named him twice, the United fans said – were conspicuous failures, but Ferguson's production line from the youth team had dried up, and he too felt the quality of talent in the lower leagues did not merit high spending.

Shankly managed in a different time, though, and when the moment came to give his hungry young recruits their chance, he did not hesitate. The catalyst for radical change was an FA Cup quarter-final defeat to humble Watford at Vicarage Road. The date was 21 February 1970, and it marked the changing of the guard, the day when one great team was flushed away and another emerged from the cupboard. The signs had been there for some time. Gordon Milne, who had been supplanted by Hughes, and Willie Stevenson had each been sold for £50,000, to Blackpool and Stoke respectively.

Ten days before the Watford game, Hunt's turn came as well. He had scored 13 goals in his 38 games that season, way below the prodigious marks he had set in his pomp. In the first half of an FA Cup fifth-round replay with Leicester, Shankly substituted him and replaced him with Bobby Graham. It was a dramatic move and a clear and strong signal of intent. Hunt was furious. Substitutions were new to the game and usually only used when a player was injured. Hunt felt humiliated, and as he stalked off the pitch he tore his shirt off and hurled it at the bench. He and Shankly had a furious row at half-time. He made a couple more appearances but was substituted again against Stoke a couple of weeks later. His time had passed.

No one felt more bitter about the way he was discarded than

St John. He has nursed the hurt and the pain of his fall from grace for more than thirty-five years and still the agony persists. He was considered to have been close enough to Shankly to be asked to be one of the pall-bearers at his funeral, but when St John's autobiography was serialized in *The Sunday Times* in 2005, a big banner headline ran across two broadsheet pages. 'Shankly: The Hero Who Let Me Down,' it said.

The words that ran underneath it, beautifully sculpted by St John's ghost writer, James Lawton, told of a man who found it impossible to forgive Shankly for ending his period in the magic circle. St John tried to rationalize his bitterness by saying that Shankly mishandled the occasion when he first dropped him, but sadly football is full of tales of footballers who cannot cope with the enormity of the moment when their top-line career comes to an end and forever seek to blame someone else. Keegan's personal hate figure was to be Bobby Robson, who dropped him from the England squad. St John's was Shankly.

In his autobiography, St John described the shock and the anger he felt when he discovered Shankly had dropped him for a match against Newcastle United at St James's Park in the autumn of 1969. St John was chatting with the Newcastle scoring legend Jackie Milburn in the club foyer, when Milburn was handed a team sheet and told St John he wasn't playing.

'Bill Shankly had dropped me without saying a word, without even meeting my eyes,' St John wrote.

'. . . As I hurried down the corridors of St James's Park, I thought of the great relationship I had had with Shankly, all the warmth and the intimacies and the endless laughter and the deep sense that beneath all the passing pressures of the game and sometimes the terrible tension and cruelties it produced, we had a deep understanding. If it wasn't father and son understanding, it was something very close indeed – or so I had thought.

'Despite all the triumphs we shared and the good memories, to this day I cannot shake the belief that at the end, Shankly let me down. I was terribly disappointed that he didn't handle it better. He should have taken me to one side, even in the hotel in Newcastle, on the eve of the match. He could have said any of a hundred things. He could have shown a little courtesy. When I got to the dressing room at St James's, my boots had been placed beneath the no. 12's peg. Shankly was nowhere to be seen and I presumed he was lying low. I ranted and raved and Paisley and Reuben Bennett were trying to calm me down.

'On the Monday morning, I went to Shankly's office. "Why didn't you tell me I wasn't playing?" I asked him. "After all these years, didn't you think I deserved something better than hearing it on the steps of another ground." He said I should have been in the dressing room when he made his team announcement. I said that wasn't the point. He wasn't sympathetic. The conversation slipped into a full-blown row.'

When Phil Thompson, who would force his way into the first team a couple of years later, made his debut for the reserves, he found himself playing alongside St John in midfield. Thompson was a young kid in awe of Shankly but he grew used to St John referring to Shankly simply as 'that bastard'. 'You do hate a manager when he starts to leave you out,' Thompson said. 'But I was quite taken aback when I heard St John and a couple of the other older players talking like that. This was Shankly. I was overpowered by listening to them. As they got older, they realized the reasons why they were left out. But at that particular time he was hated by the players for what he was doing. I couldn't understand the way they felt at the time. I was only a kid. I was thinking: "You can't be saying that, this is the fella who has brought greatness to Liverpool and given you star status." So it wasn't all roses.'

Shankly would not be deflected. After the Watford game, he quickly organized a behind-closed-doors friendly against Blackburn Rovers at Ewood Park. The players on the bus were the new breed. The ones who weren't were on the outside. Brian Hall was the exception. He realized the significance of the game and was distraught when he didn't get a seat on the coach, but he forced his way in later. 'The wind of change was blowing,' Hall said. 'I knew this was an opportunity and I wanted to get at it. A couple of weeks later, the weekend came along and for once, I stayed in on a Saturday night. We hadn't been married long and we'd bought a semi-detached bungalow in Rainford. We usually went for a beer down to the Wheatsheaf with our next-door neightbours. I had played for the reserves on the Saturday and for some reason we were playing Blackpool on the Monday. We usually had Sunday off. I got a phone call about 10 p.m. on the Saturday evening from Shanks and I am convinced he did it to see whether I was in. He rang to say I was in the squad on Monday so I had to go training on Sunday morning. If I had gone to the pub that night, my life would have been so different, I am convinced of it.'

Ray Clemence was on the bus. He had been in the reserves for two and a half years and had reached the point where he felt he might have to ask for a transfer. But Joe Fagan, the reserve team manager, had assured him his chance would come in that 1969–70 season and he was right. Unlike St John, Tommy Lawrence, the man Clemence usurped, betrayed no anger towards his successor. Ian Callaghan was on the bus, too. He and the other couple of established players who took their seats on the journey to Blackburn felt as though they were the survivors of a purge. They looked around them on that coach and saw the fresh, eager faces of the next generation. There was no St John, no Yeats and no Lawrence. They were the disappeared. The aftermath of Watford was Shankly's Night of the Long Knives.

'I would think about the players we had,' Shankly recalled, 'and I could see that some of them were going a bit. When you have had success, it can be a difficult job to motivate yourself. You have done it before, like walking up and down the same road all the time. I felt that was happening to some of the players. I had vouched for that team that won so much in the Sixties. There had been games during which I hadn't batted an eyelid. I knew we would win. It was just a question of how long it would take and how many we would score. Sometimes, Tommy Lawrence would play a whole game and never touch the ball. But now it was obvious that while some of the players still had an appetite for success, others hadn't and might do better elsewhere. After Watford, I knew I had to do my job and change my team. I had a duty to perform for myself, my family, Liverpool Football Club and the supporters. It had to be done and if I didn't do it, I was shirking my obligations.'

Perhaps if Alan Hansen had been a *Match of the Day* analyst in 1970 he would have looked at what Shankly was doing and told him that you don't win anything with kids. But Shankly had had enough of mediocrity. He felt he and the club had endured too many barren years. He had spent too long watching other teams garner the honours he had coveted for himself. He had done what had to be done. His team was dead and another was being born.

8: Ferguson — A Frightening Bastard from the Start

Firs Park, besieged by the march of twenty-first-century commercialism, is a metaphor for the career of Sir Alex Ferguson. Dominated by the concrete walls and neon signs of Falkirk's Central Retail Park, it has surrendered some of its character and integrity, but its solitary stand with its curved roof, tucked away in a corner in front of Curry's, is still a thing of beauty. Even though long grass grows out of the shingle on the wooden terraces, East Stirlingshire's home feels like an oasis of originality in a desert of Glanford Parks and Bescot Stadiums.

To see it now, cowering in the shadow of the superstores and the sheltered housing, is to realize how long was the journey that Ferguson travelled as a manager from the moment he arrived at Firs Park at the end of June 1974 to take up his first post. He threw his first managerial tantrums here, told his first set of directors to stick their job up their arse, kicked his first tray of half-time teacups into the air, played his first mind games, launched his first vendetta against one of his own players and switched on his first hairdrier.

The home of East Stirlingshire is as far removed from Old Trafford as it is possible to be, but at least it is still clinging to life. In 2003, Falkirk, the club where Ferguson found himself late in his playing career, surrendered its Brockville Park ground to the developers. A Morrison's stands there now, little more than half a mile away from Firs Park.

Ferguson was only thirty-two when he arrived at East Stirlingshire. In his autobiography, he wrote that the club had finished the previous season rock-bottom of the Scottish Second Division. 'The worst senior team in the country,' he said. Statistically that wasn't quite true. It was Ferguson's first piece of managerial dramatic licence. In the 19-club division, they had finished 16th. They weren't exactly flying high, but Albion Rovers, Forfar Athletic and Brechin City were all below his new charges.

The odds were still stacked heavily against Ferguson at East Stirlingshire, though. He only took the job after he had ruined his first interview for a managerial vacancy at Queen's Park a couple of months earlier. On that occasion, he had become intimidated by the fact that most of the panel of directors talking to him were men he had played alongside when he was starting out as a footballer with the club.

But even though he had enjoyed his last season of being a player, under Ally MacLeod, Ferguson had begun to prepare seriously for management in the summer of 1973 when he went to the National Sports Centre at Lilleshall in Shropshire to attend a course for managers and coaches. Ferguson was particularly impressed with the teachings of Jimmy Sirrell, then the manager of Notts County.

'The principles of management he laid down with such emphasis were often simple but their importance was so undeniable that I have always tried to adhere to them,' Ferguson wrote. ' "Don't have the contracts all running out at the same time" was one of his tenets. "Watch the ages of your team" was another. It was a reminder that common sense, when there is enough of it, amounts to wisdom.'

MacLeod had put Ferguson forward for the Queen's Park job and recommended him again when he was sounded out by one of the East Stirling directors, Bob Shaw. Ferguson agreed to meet the chairman, Willie Muirhead, out of courtesy but the two men liked each other instantly. The job was part-time, the pay was only £40 a week and Ferguson still had Fergie's to take care of, but when Muirhead pestered him, he agreed to take it. Alex Ferguson was a manager.

The club's situation was parlous when he arrived. The new season was only a few weeks away and the club had only eight players signed up. There was no goalkeeper, either. 'As I mentioned to the board,' Ferguson said, 'it always helps if you start a match with a goalie.' Ferguson was given £2,000 to spend, so he began to trawl through the ranks of the unemployed, the players who had been granted free transfers by their clubs, football's underclass.

He took Partick Thistle's overweight reserve team goalkeeper, Tom Gourlay, and their diminutive centre forward, Jimmy Mullen, paying them a total of £1,000 in signing-on fees. Then he splashed out and negotiated a £900 signing-on fee with Clyde centre forward Billy Hulston. By the start of the season he had assembled a squad of fifteen players.

He worked on their touch by starting every training session with an exercise known as boxes that teams still use today as a matter of course. Five or six players stood in a tight circle with one or two in the middle of the circle. The players on the outside passed the ball to each other with the intention of keeping it away from the man in the middle. When a player plays a loose pass and the ball is intercepted, he moves to the centre of the circle instead.

It didn't take long for Ferguson to earn the players' respect. Partly, it was because of his passion and his intensity. When he had signed Hulston, he had offered to give him £50 out of his own pocket to seal the deal. He even took his wallet out of his pocket and put the notes down on the table. The phone call Hulston wanted to make to the Stenhousemuir manager never happened.

But he also scared them. His first game in charge, the first competitive game of his managerial career, was a Scottish League Cup tie away to Forfar, a team known as the Loons. Some of those who have fallen foul of Ferguson's Vesuvian temper in the intervening years might say, tonge in cheek, they were fitting opponents.

East Stirling were 3–0 down at half-time, and the players trudged back to the Station Park dressing room expecting a festival of abuse. 'Already he terrified us,' winger Bobby Mc-Culley said. 'I'd never been afraid of anyone before but he was a frightening bastard from the start.' But there was also something inspiring about him from the start as well. Ferguson didn't give them the treatment at half-time. He was encouraging. He said they had played well. He has always been at his best in adversity and this was the first foreshadowing of the hundreds of times he has rallied teams to superhuman comebacks. East Stirling scored three unanswered goals in the second half. The game finished in a 3–3 draw.

The first real test of his authority came when centre forward Jim Meakin, Shaw's son-in-law, asked Ferguson for permission to miss an evening training session for a family break in Blackpool and mentioned that he was going with Shaw. 'I don't care if you are going with the Queen,' Ferguson said. 'You are training Monday, end of story.'

Late on Monday afternoon, Meakin rang up to say his car had broken down and that he would not be able to make it. Ferguson asked him for his number so he could ring him back. Meakin confessed. Ferguson suspended him. Indefinitely. Meakin missed three or four games before Muirhead begged Ferguson to reinstate him. His point made, Ferguson relented.

The directors quickly realized that Ferguson was not a man to be crossed. The new boss initiated the beginnings of a youth policy by authorizing a £40 payment for a coach to bring a junior team called Glasgow United to Firs Park to play a friendly against some local prospects. At the next board meeting, Ferguson was reprimanded for not seeking permission for the payment. Ferguson hurled £40 on to the table, told the old boys what they could do with their job and stormed off.

He was persuaded to rescind his resignation, and next it was the chairman himself who provoked his wrath. Midway through the second half of one of the early season games, East Stirling were trailing 2–0 when Muirhead suddenly appeared and sat down next to Ferguson in the dug-out.

'What are you going to do?' Muirhead asked.

'I'm going to throw you out of this fucking dug-out if you don't move now,' Ferguson said. The chairman moved.

Ferguson was quickly stamping his character and his antagonistic attitude on the club. He felt the same need to change the club's kit that Shankly felt in his first managerial post at Carlisle. He wanted to get rid of East Stirling's traditional black and white hoops and change the strip to white shirts, black shorts and red socks.

It was important to Ferguson. He said he couldn't wait to make the change. For both men, it was as if changing the kit was a sign of their ownership of the club, a bit like a woman changing her name when she married. Both men were control freaks. They wanted to dominate every aspect of their clubs. Shankly did it again when he was at Liverpool, switching the kit to its famous all-red.

By the time Ferguson arrived at Old Trafford, though, changing the kit on a whim was beyond the remit of a manager. There would have been fits of apoplexy in the boardroom, the commercial department, the superstore and the design houses of the sportswear manufacturers. Even at East Stirling, the board rebuffed him and made it plain they considered it an impudent request. For once, Ferguson let it lie.

Results were going well, though. Ferguson had transformed the struggling, demoralized side of the previous season into a club climbing towards the top of the table. By the end of September, they were in third place and Ferguson had even started to talk to the local newspaper, the *Falkirk Herald*, about the prospect of winning the league.

In just a few months, he had got the players believing in themselves. He accentuated the positives about his own team and devoted even more time to withering assessments of the opposition. Before a derby showdown against Falkirk, Ferguson went into overdrive. 'He spent an hour identifying all their weaknesses,' East Stirling captain Gordon Simpson said. 'So-and-so lacked pace, that guy's only got one foot, this player is weak in the tackle. We went out there believing we were by far the better team.'

Simpson was a moaner and a whinger who spent much of every match complaining to the referee. Ferguson made it plain he liked that. He also honed the players' competitive instincts with sharp, intense practice matches. The matches lasted until Ferguson's side won, even if it had gone dark. 'He was ferocious, elbowing and kicking,' McCulley said. 'We'd say to each other: "Just let him score and we can all go home".'

Ferguson's instructions to his side for the match against Falkirk covered every detail. He was especially desperate to win it because he had been discarded and treated shabbily at the end of his playing days with the club by their manager, John Prentice. Ferguson had been bundled out of Brockville in the summer of 1973 and had watched sadly as Prentice took the club down. He was keen to exact a measure of revenge.

Before the days of dossiers, Ferguson even told his strikers what to do if they found themselves through on goal with only the 'keeper to beat. He said that if they tried to dribble it around the goalkeeper, he would dispossess them. They had to pick their corner and shoot. He wanted them to be right psychologically too. And he was particularly keen to try to unsettle Falkirk.

So he obtained permission from the board for his players to stay in a local hotel the night before the game. Ferguson knew it was the same hotel where the Falkirk players stayed. The following morning, Ferguson orchestrated a scene where his team walked past the picture window of the dining room where he knew the Falkirk lads were having their breakfast. He told his players to laugh and joke and josh with each other as they wandered past. When the Falkirk team stared over, they saw a team whose morale appeared to be formidably high.

So many of the ruses that Ferguson pursued throughout his

managerial career manifested themselves in those early months at East Stirling. He told his players they would have their work cut out against Falkirk because they were the big team in the town and that everybody wanted them to win. He told them even the *Falkirk Herald* was biased against East Stirling. It was a theme he revisited again and again and again, especially at Aberdeen and in his later years at Old Trafford.

It all worked. Falkirk were beaten 2–0 at Firs Park in front of a bumper crowd of 4,650. East Stirling started to switch into a higher gear. They won 4–3 at Hamilton next and then trounced Alloa 4–0 at home. By then, the average crowd had risen to more than 1,200 compared with the 400 'the Shire' had been drawing at the start of the season.

But then Ferguson took a telephone call from his former boss at Falkirk, Willie Cunningham, who was now in charge at St Mirren. Cunningham had been a major influence on Ferguson in their time together at Brockville, and when Cunningham asked him to go down to St Mirren's Love Street ground to see him, Ferguson assumed it was just for a chat about old times.

It wasn't. Cunningham told Ferguson he had grown disillusioned with football and was giving up the game to run a sports shop. He wanted to put Ferguson forward to the board as his nomination for his successor. Ferguson hesitated. St Mirren were a couple of places below East Stirling in the Second Division and Ferguson had formed a close bond with his players at Firs Park.

He had a three-hour meeting with the St Mirren chairman, Harold Currie. Currie was impressed. He asked Ferguson if he really believed East Stirling could ever become a big club and told him to go away and think about his decision. Ferguson agonized. He rang the Celtic boss, Jock Stein, and told him about his dilemma.

Stein gave him a wonderful piece of advice. He told him to go and sit in the highest point of the main stand at St Mirren and the highest point of the stand at Firs Park and stare out over both grounds. Stein said that would make Ferguson's choice for him. The main stand at Firs Park was about 20 ft tall and held a couple of hundred people. The main stand at Love Street was a handsome two-tier building that held a few thousand. Ferguson made his apologies to everyone at East Stirling and left.

There were no recriminations, though. Just gratitude from the club. He had only been in charge for 117 days but he had revolutionized attitudes at Firs Park and made the club believe that that they could embrace respectability again, maybe even become a rising force in the Scottish game. Ferguson had taken the underdog and made it snarl.

'He was only a few months at the club,' Shaw said, 'but by God he did a lot for us. We knew it would only be a stepping stone for him but I'm proud we gave him his first chance. The man is a winner through and through.' Muirhead was just as grateful, although he was distraught when Ferguson left. 'It was a bloody tragedy for East Stirlingshire when he left,' Muirhead said. 'He was the best thing that ever happened to the club.'

There were pangs of regret from Ferguson, too. The management bug had hooked him and he had grown attached to his players. He had put everything into the running of the team and he felt that his players had reciprocated. Everything was going well and he had almost been seduced into thinking that anything was possible. Currie had appealed to his ambition, but even before Ferguson had taken over at Love Street, he felt nostalgic for what he was leaving behind.

His players were shocked when he told them. Many of them had felt that he represented a chance for them to escape from the football basement where they had played out their entire careers. 'You bastard,' wing-half Tom Donnelly said. Ferguson forgave him. He was feeling the pain of the departure, too. 'Tom was a good lad and showed his disappointment as honestly as he lived his life,' Ferguson said. Sadly, the players could not maintain the momentum they had built up under Ferguson after he left.

Ferguson recommended former Arsenal player Ian Ure as his successor, but Ure could not guide East Stirling to the top-six place they needed to be included in the First Division the following season under the reorganization of the Scottish leagues that created a Premier Division for the first time. Instead, they finished in ninth place, six points off promotion. The team that finished sixth was St Mirren. The Shire soon slipped back into their old ways. Firs Park became a den of mediocrity again, famous for giving Sir Alex Ferguson his first foothold in management and little more.

After a spell when crowds bottomed out at about 70, they are back up towards 300 again now. But the players are part-timers. There are a couple of students from Edinburgh University in the team, a policeman, an electrician and a couple of plumbers. At the start of 2006, East Stirling were rock-bottom of the Scottish Third Division, even lower than when Ferguson arrived.

He moved on. They slipped back. 'As I left East Stirlingshire for St Mirren,' he wrote in his autobiography, 'there was no trace of exhilaration but rather a dull sense of failure, of a task unfinished. I had no right to assume that the players awaiting me at Love Street would serve me as well as the diamonds I was leaving behind at the Shire.'

9: Shankly and a Vision of Hell

It was easy for Jimmy McInnes to slip out of his office at Anfield unnoticed on the day he took his own life in May 1965. The club was agog with excitement. The night before, Liverpool had won a tumultuous European Cup semi-final first-leg tie against Inter Milan in front of their own fans. Three days before that, they had won the FA Cup for the first time.

McInnes had been the club secretary for ten years. He had joined from Third Lanark as a player in 1938 and played in the same half-back line as Matt Busby. But he retired after the Second World War and rose up through the ranks of the club administration. A dour, round-faced man, he was only fifty-one on that spring day when he walked through the deserted stadium, still echoing with the exhortations of the previous evening, and made his way towards the Kop.

McInnes, who Ian St John remembered as a 'small and kindly man', had started drinking heavily and spending night after night sleeping on the couch in his Anfield office instead of going home. He headed for the Kemlyn Road entrance to the Kop and, once beneath the giant terrace, he sought out the darkness of one of the booths where a turnstile attendant would sit on match days to take admission money from the fans as they clicked their way in. McInnes rigged up a noose in the booth and hanged himself from it.

The world McInnes lived in had changed so fast that he couldn't cope any more. Success had come in a dizzy rush under Shankly and suddenly everything at Anfield had altered. Mc-

Innes was a one-man band, a relic from the era when Liverpool was a football backwater. Now it was a hub. And now he was being asked to organize European Cup trips to places like Reykjavik and Cologne, deal with the rush for FA Cup final tickets, sort contracts and field press inquiries. It was too much.

McInnes was a tragic symbol of how far the club had travelled in so short a space of time. He was a casualty of the club's rise and the bewildering cultural shift that had swept through the country. Society was changing. The austerity of the Fifties had given way to the liberation of the Sixties and Liverpool was in the vanguard of the revolution. The Beatles were at Number One that May with 'Ticket to Ride' and Shankly and his team were already on board.

Shankly was desperately upset about McInnes. He felt he was partly to blame. The Liverpool party that left a few days later for the second leg against Inter in Milan was subdued, but there was no time to grieve. Jimmy McInnes had committed suicide at a time when Shankly and his side stood on the brink of immortality as they tried to become the first British club to win the European Cup.

It is heartbreaking now to think how close Liverpool came to finding that grail in 1965, because winning it would have brought Shankly the peace that he could not find in the last years of his life. His epitaph would not just have been that he was the architect of all Liverpool's later European Cup triumphs.

He had travelled to Rome to see Liverpool win their first European Cup in 1977, but his pleasure that night was stained by regret that he was no longer in charge. He hadn't seen the job through to the pinnacle like Busby at Manchester United and Jock Stein at Celtic. And that meant that when people talked about the greatest managers of all, Shankly's name was sometimes overlooked.

He was aware of that when he was alive. Now, sometimes in death, too, there are occasions when he is frozen out of

accolades and awards ceremonies. As part of Uefa's celebration
of fifty years of the European Cup in 2005, in November the
organization made a presentation on the pitch at Anfield at half-
time of Liverpool's Champions League tie against Real Betis.
Phil Neal and Kenny Dalglish were both called on to the pitch
to receive commemorative shields, and the sons of Bob Paisley
were asked to collect an award on behalf of their late father. No
mention was made of Shankly. There was no reason why there
should have been.

But when Liverpool set off for their date with Inter at the
San Siro in May 1965, anything seemed possible. The side
Shankly had built was in its prime and brimming with confidence after its extra-time FA Cup Final victory over Leeds and
the 3–1 humbling of Inter at Anfield. They travelled to Italy
believing they were favourites to make it through to the final
where the Benfica of Eusebio would be waiting for them.

Instead, what awaited Liverpool in Milan was a reception so
hostile that it unsettled the players. They were still relative
novices in European terms and they were shocked at the intensity and excess of the emotion that met them when they touched
down in Italy. Liverpool had outplayed Inter so comprehensively
at Anfield that rumours had started to circulate in Milan that
Shankly's players must be on drugs. When they emerged from
customs at the airport, Italian fans were there in force waving
placards to that effect. It was the kind of welcoming party that
has become routine when visiting teams land in Istanbul now.
The Welcome to Hell banners have become a cliché, but Liverpool's players had never witnessed anything like it and felt
shaken as they made their way to the team hotel in Como, a
pretty lakeside town north of the city.

When they got there, they were confronted by a new problem. To Shankly's horror, he found that the peace of the hotel
where Liverpool were staying was regularly shattered by the
pealing of church bells nearby. Shankly and Bob Paisley went to
see the priest and tried to persuade him to let them silence the

bells for the duration of their stay. Shankly's determination to quieten God in the pursuit of football glory set a new standard for his obsession with the game, but he was unapologetic about it.

'It wasn't so bad until about eleven o'clock at night,' he wrote in his autobiography. 'The noise of the day had ceased then and there was nothing to hear but the bells. One, in particular, was like doomsday. Bob Paisley and I went to see the Monsignor about it. We tried to get him to stop the bells ringing for the night so the players could sleep.'

Shankly told the priest it wasn't fair. He told him he and his players had come to Como to prepare for the most important football match in the world that year. His rationale for that was that if Liverpool beat Inter, they would win the European Cup, too. The priest was sympathetic towards their plight but said he could do nothing to silence the bells. And still Shankly did not give up.

'I said: "Well, could you let Bob here go up and put a bandage on them and maybe kind of dull them a bit?"' Shankly wrote. 'Crepe bandages and cotton wool. Bob was killing himself laughing. That would have been one of the funniest things Bob had ever done, one of his greatest cures as a trainer, creeping up the aisle with cotton wool and bandages. But we just had to put up with the noise.'

The noise in Como was one thing. The noise at the San Siro was quite another. Like the welcome at the airport, the sheer hostility and vehemence of the Inter fans took Shankly and his players off guard in the same way that, thirty years later, the visceral desire of the Liverpool fans bewildered Jose Mourinho's fine Chelsea side when it came to Anfield for a European Cup semi-final second leg.

As the teams emerged at the San Siro, the Inter fans hurled smoke bombs on to the pitch that threw up a purple haze. 'One of them landed on the steps,' Shankly said, 'and Bob Paisley's clothes were covered in the stuff.' For Shankly, it seemed like a vision of hell. What followed was bedlam, a football match gone mad, a game played outside the accepted rules, a contest that seemed to be weighted in favour of Liverpool's illustrious opponents.

Part of the reason why the bitterness of what happened that night in Milan lingered so long with Shankly and cast such a shadow over his career was that he realized how close he had come to beating one of the great sides of world football. Victory that night in the San Siro would have confirmed Shankly's European graduation and made Liverpool a power in the world game more than a decade before Paisley took them to the summit.

When Liverpool walked out to try to defend their two-goal advantage that night, Inter were commonly regarded as the best club team in the world. Managed by the Argentine Helenio Herrera, they were the reigning European champions, having beaten Real Madrid in 1964. They were about to clinch the second of three successive Serie A titles and they were packed with brilliant players.

Herrera was the architect of the notorious catenaccio system, Italian for 'door-bolt'. He used four man-markers in his defence with a sweeper behind them. His Inter side set a trend in Italian football for trying to strangle teams and then attempting to hit them on the break. Their manager was Machiavellian and ruthless. 'He struck me as a remarkable little fellow,' Shankly said, 'a cut-throat man who wanted to win.' He and his team were a tough enough proposition without any help from a referee.

But help was what they got. After eight minutes, Inter were awarded an indirect free kick on the edge of the Liverpool area and Mario Corso curled the ball round the wall towards the near post. Tommy Lawrence flung himself to his left. He would have touched it if he could but he did not reach it so the goal should not have stood, but the referee, a Spaniard called Jose

Maria Ortiz de Mendibil, pointed back to the centre circle. Liverpool's players protested wildly but in vain.

A few minutes later, Inter were level on aggregate. Lawrence retrieved the ball in his area after an overhit pass had eluded Inter centre forward Joaquin Peiro. Lawrence started bouncing the ball as a prelude to kicking it upfield, but as he bounced it Peiro stole in from behind him and nicked the ball away. He took one touch and slid it into the empty net.

Other players have done the same over the years. Most famously George Best when he was playing for Northern Ireland against England. Best whipped the ball out of the hands of Gordon Banks and headed it into the net. But that goal was disallowed and Peiro's should have been wiped out, too. The rules stated that what he had done should have led automatically to a Liverpool free kick, but once again Ortiz de Mendibil ignored the rules and allowed the goal to stand.

Liverpool's players were beside themselves with anger and disbelief this time. Tommy Smith had to be restrained from confronting the referee. Ortiz de Mendibil was still surrounded by men in red but he would not change his mind. That finally broke Liverpool's spirit. 'At that moment, we knew we weren't going to get much out of the game,' Callaghan said.

Later in the game, with Liverpool's morale crushed, Inter scored a third. This time it was a thing of beauty in the midst of all the ugliness, a lovely build-up featuring Luis Suarez finished off by a sublime strike from Giacinto Fachetti. But as the 90,000 fans in the San Siro went wild, Liverpool went off knowing that they had been cheated. When Shankly saw Ortiz de Mendibil laughing and joking with Inter officials near their dressing room, it confirmed his suspicions.

'I was told before the game in Milan that whatever happened, we would not go through to the final,' Shankly said. 'I had the feeling that something was wrong politically and I believe there were some investigations later about that game.

The decisions on the pitch were queer. We can't really prove anything but we went close to winning the European Cup at a time when no British club had won it.

'I was delighted for Jock Stein when Celtic did it two years later and there are no sour grapes from me when I say that the Inter team they beat that year couldn't compete with the one we played. Nor was the Benfica side beaten by Manchester United at Wembley in 1968 nearly as good as the Benfica team Inter defeated after they played us in 1965.'

Afterwards, as the Liverpool team bus drove back to the airport, Shankly told his players they could be proud of themselves. He told them to look at the fervour and relief with which the Inter supporters were celebrating victory and pointed out that Inter were regarded as the world champions of club football. But Shankly nursed the resentment about the injustice that was visited upon Liverpool that night for the rest of his life. He referred to it again and again, and the pain of it only grew as first Celtic and then United superseded Liverpool in the scale of their European achievements.

Some thought that one of Shankly's tales, about seeing a brown paper bag being handed to Ortiz de Mendibil that night, was embroidered with the bitterness of a man who could not accept defeat and that Liverpool's manager was making ever more outlandish excuses for his side's reverse. But many years later the excellent journalism of the renowned football writer Brian Glanville and his colleague Keith Botsford suggested that Shankly's conspiracy theories had been entirely vindicated.

Glanville is an expert on Italian football and a fluent Italian speaker. Whatever Premiership ground he is gracing, his voice can still be heard drawling the half-time scores from Serie A across the press box. Glanville is both a lover of football and a cheerful iconoclast. He does not respect reputations. He challenges them. And he and Botsford discovered that Inter had made three offers to bribe referees in the second legs of European Cup semi-finals. Including the 1965 tie against Liverpool.

Glanville and Botsford called that period of Inter's history 'The Years of the Golden Fix'. They discovered that club president Angelo Moratti and club secretary Italo Allodi made the offers in 1964 and 1965, when they were successful against Borussia Dortmund and Liverpool respectively, and in 1966 when, because of the integrity of an Hungarian official called Gyorgy Vadas, they were knocked out by Real Madrid.

Glanville and Botsford tracked Vadas down and tried to persuade him to talk. But he was still too nervous to give up his secret, and it was only later that a Budapest journalist prised the truth out of him and related his story in a book, *Only the Ball Has a Skin*. It transpired that Vadas and his linesmen had been wined and dined by Moratti at his villa on the morning of the match against Madrid. Each had been given a gold watch and Vadas was offered the equivalent of about £50,000 to bend the match. Vadas's response was to referee the game impeccably. His reward was never to be assigned to a significant European fixture again.

And so a few Italian rich men and a weak Spanish referee cheated Shankly out of his destiny. He was never to come so close to winning the European Cup again. He was denied the chance to join the elite of British managers who have won the trophy that is seen as the pinnacle of achievement in European club football. Jock Stein, Matt Busby, Bob Paisley, Brian Clough, Tony Barton, Joe Fagan and Sir Alex Ferguson have all won it. Shankly was denied his shot at the prize.

Ronnie Moran played his last game for the club that night. He did not feel Shankly was unduly affected by it. 'We got cheated in Milan,' Moran said. 'Shanks was upset about it but he would be upset if we lost a five-a-side.' Others, though, felt the game cast a lingering shadow over Shankly's otherwise brilliant career. It was, after all, the one significant absentee in his list of great triumphs.

'The boss never got over what happened at San Siro,' Ian St John said. 'Not really. It fuelled his distrust of foreigners on a football field. He believed that it was natural for them to cheat, something quite separate from his own culture, which was hard to the point of ruthlessness but purged of cheap trickery. Heaven knows how he would have reacted to some of the behaviour on show in today's Premiership. The blatant dives indulged in by some of the most honoured players of today, stars such as Robert Pires and Ruud Van Nistelrooy, would have filled him with scorn.

'What happened in Milan was one of the heaviest blows he ever suffered. Had we got by Inter, we believed we had every chance of beating Benfica, the team of Eusebio, Torres and Simoes. They were a talented side but had weaknesses the boss believed we could exploit. For Shankly, it would have been the coup of his footballing life. He would have beaten Jock Stein, the man he worshipped, to the great peak of the European game by two years, Busby by three. When you thought of his impact at Anfield and the speed with which he had turned us into a side that could compete properly with any force in football, who could say it was a distinction he didn't deserve.'

That night in Milan should have been Shankly's night. That was his Terry Malloy moment. That was when he was cheated. That was his brush with the summit. And through no fault of his own, he couldn't take the final step. He didn't end up with a one-way ticket to Palookaville, but he didn't get the shot at the title, either. Shankly didn't take a dive but the referee took it for him.

When Ferguson got to the same point, Roy Keane was there to give the performance of his life in the Stadio delle Alpi to take United beyond Juventus in the 1999 European Cup semi-final. And in the final at the Nou Camp, Ferguson beckoned history towards him when he told his players they would be tortured for the rest of their lives if they came so close to winning the European Cup and let the chance slip away.

Shankly never got the chance to make that speech. He never even got to the final, never got to try and turn things around like Ferguson and, later, Rafael Benitez, in the Olympic Stadium in Istanbul in 2005 when Liverpool produced the greatest comeback of them all. That night in Milan robbed Shankly of that.

Victory in the European Cup Final puts the gloss on anybody's career. Player or manager. Without it, something is missing. Terry Venables never won it. Don Revie never won it. Nor Bobby Robson. Nor Kenny Dalglish. But if you aspire to greatness, it should be there.

When George Best died, because he had won the European Cup with United when he was just twenty-two, no one could say with conviction that he had underachieved as a player. However much of his talent he subsequently wasted, he would always have that magical night against Benfica at Wembley to point to, and the fact that he not only played in the final but he scored a sublime goal as well.

Shankly got two other shots at the European Cup. Ajax and Red Star Belgrade ended his dreams on those occasions. But it was the night of 12 May 1965 that stuck with him no matter how hard he tried to shake it. Time and again, his mind raced back to the images of that cursed night at the San Siro. Of the purple smoke. Of the hate etched on the faces of the Inter fans. Of Ortiz de Mendibil being pursued by disbelieving Liverpool players. And most of all, of Ortiz de Mendibil laughing his knowing laugh with the Inter officials after the match.

'Of all the people I have seen and met,' Shankly said of Ortiz de Mendibil a few years before his own death, 'that is the one man who haunts me to this day.'

10: Ferguson and a Case Dismissed

Alex Ferguson wanted a Jaguar. He had decided he deserved one. The manager of Motherwell had one, he told the board of directors at St Mirren, so he figured it was only fair that he should have one too. He had done a lot for St Mirren in the three and half years since he had arrived from his first managerial job at East Stirlingshire in the autumn of 1974. He had transformed its fortunes, bolstered its crowds and taken it into the newly-formed Scottish Premier Division. He imagined he was in the big time now and that his status demanded he drive a flash car. The board said no.

Ferguson was angry. He felt that the chairman, Willie Todd, and the directors were not giving him his due. His relationship with them was in meltdown. He had worked tirelessly to turn the club into something approaching a force in Scottish football again. St Mirren had been marooned in the middle of the old Second Division when he took over. Their gates were bottoming out at around 1,200 supporters at a time when the Love Street capacity was 53,000. Their average attendance was more than 11,000 when he left.

When he arrived, St Mirren was just a team on the edge of Glasgow that had fallen on hard times. Just like its home town, Paisley, which was full of industries in recession. 'When I was at St Mirren, it was a desolate place,' Ferguson said. 'Even the birds woke up coughing.'

Football fans from Paisley caught the bus into the city to watch either Rangers or Celtic on a Saturday afternoon. Ferguson had started to change that to the point where the St Mirren fans backed him with their money as well as their attendance. At the start of the 1976–77 season, Ferguson signed the experienced centre back Jackie Copland from Dundee United with the help of a £14,000 loan from the St Mirren Supporters' Association.

Ferguson used his raging enthusiasm, his proselytizing fervour and his coaching talent to transform St Mirren from a side of demoralized part-timers into a club that was able to make the giant leap to going full-time the year after he left. He took them into a new era. He modernized St Mirren single-handed. At the end of his first season, Ferguson had nursed the club into the top six and ensured that they took their place in the new First Division at the start of the 1975–76 season.

They finished that season fifth. The season after, with the help of Copland and young talents like Billy Stark and Frank McGarvey, who Ferguson had drafted into the side, they won the First Division championship. St Mirren only lost two games all season and won the title with a record total of 62 points. It was Ferguson's first trophy as a manager.

He deserved it. His appetite for improvement and self-improvement at Love Street was gargantuan. He didn't just run the team, he ran everything at St Mirren. He had the turnstile booths rebuilt so that fans who had bribed the gatemen couldn't vault over them into the ground. Perhaps he had already forgotten the days when he used to try to sneak into Ibrox without paying when he was a lad growing up in Govan. At Love Street, Ferguson was the archetypal poacher turned gamekeeper.

He tackled the development of the club with a missionary zeal. On the morning of a match day, he would tour local housing estates in a car with a loudspeaker like a politician on the hustings, urging people to start supporting their local team. He clamped down on the quaint system that had been allowed to exist at the stadium where the groundsman, Jimmy Ritchie, was given responsibility for programme sales and club catering.

Alex Ferguson, the proud socialist, took great pride in suddenly making programme sales profitable and telling Ritchie's wife she could no longer use the club kitchen to cook Sunday lunch for her family. 'You could say that I was a hands-on boss,' Ferguson said.

It was at Love Street that he established the model for the network of snitches he was to use at Aberdeen and Manchester United to monitor the off-the-field activities of the players. In those days his brother Martin and his pal John Donachie were his most reliable snouts. They did not appear to find it strange to phone Ferguson to inform on the St Mirren players if they saw them out drinking or generally doing anything that did not conform to their master's rules of professional conduct.

The consequences for the players were severe if they were spotted out on manoeuvres. When Martin Ferguson phoned one night with a particularly juicy tip about seeing some of them in the Waterloo Bar in Glasgow city centre and hearing them bragging about the size of the bonuses they were earning, his big brother waited until the aftermath of a victory over Partick Thistle before attacking them with a ferocity that even unsettled him.

'The quickness of my temper and the depth of my anger often worried me,' he said. 'After the match, I told the culprits to sit on one side of the dressing room so I could let rip at them. My anger intensified with each decibel until I lost control, lifted a bottle of Coca-Cola and smashed it against the wall above their heads. Not one of them moved as the Coke ran down the wall and the glass dropped on to their strips. I told them the whole team would be staying at Love Street all night, training, unless they signed an agreement never to enter the Waterloo pub again.'

Ferguson was also fond of telling his players that if they lost, they needn't bother returning to the dressing room unless they were prepared to soak up an almighty torrent of abuse. The players responded, but they responded to his innovative training sessions and his boundless enthusiasm and energy even more. Ferguson made bold decisions at St Mirren. He made an eighteen-year-old, Tony Fitzpatrick, his captain because he was so impressed with his work-rate, his attitude and his technique. He wanted to make a statement that he was breathing youth and life into a club that had been stagnant when he arrived.

Fitzpatrick, Stark, McGarvey and Copland were the bedrock of the side. Their arrival and Ferguson's demented level of commitment spread new levels of enthusiasm for St Mirren around Paisley. In January 1977 more than 19,000 supporters flocked to Love Street to see St Mirren humble Dundee United 4–1 in the Scottish Cup. According to Feruson:

'That was a period when my development as a manager was accelerating. Sheer hard work was a huge factor in bringing success but I am sure that sticking to my beliefs was equally important. I believed strongly that being able to pass the ball well was crucial and I don't think there was a training session that did not incorporate passing. But I was also trying to add imagination to my coaching, emphasising the need for players to have a picture in their minds, to visualise how they could have a creative impact on the shifting pattern of a game.'

Unfortunately for Ferguson, his learning curve also included trying to coexist with a chairman he distrusted and who distrusted him in return. Harold Currie, the man who had hired him, had been replaced by Todd, the Conservative Party leader on Paisley council. They were hardly ideological bedfellows. Todd also wanted to be hands-on and to have a media profile. He attracted attention by being provocative and insulting to bigger clubs like Rangers. Ferguson soon grew to dislike him intensely.

Things began to disintegrate quickly during St Mirren's first season in the Premier Division. St Mirren struggled near the bottom of the table for much of the campaign and only dragged themselves clear of relegation a couple of weeks from the end of the season when they beat fellow strugglers Ayr United at

Somerset Park. By then, Todd and Ferguson were no longer speaking to each other.

The relationship between the two men had grown fraught. Ferguson felt the antagonism from Todd and reacted badly. He demanded the Jaguar and was rebuffed. He had a blazing row with his office secretary, June Sullivan, after he asked her to pay one player his travelling expenses free of tax and she refused. Ferguson swore at her and was livid when she sided with Todd over the issue. According to reports in Michael Crick's excellent biography of Ferguson, *The Boss*, he tried to get her sacked, an industrial tribunal reported later, and when that failed he did not speak to her for six weeks.

By then, Ferguson had turned down an approach from Ally MacLeod, the Aberdeen manager, about the prospect of taking over from him at Pittodrie. He was starting to regret it. 'Later,' he wrote in his autobiography, 'I would understand that there are fundamental distinctions of scale that apply to football clubs. Just as East Stirlingshire cannot be a St Mirren, so St Mirren cannot be an Aberdeen and Aberdeen cannot be a Manchester United.'

It is an obvious theory, interesting only because it shone a light on the pragmatism, the financial advancement and the ambition that have always been Ferguson's guiding principles. Ferguson claims loyalty has been the bedrock of his life, but sometimes in his case it appears to have been a one-way arrangement. He expects absolute loyalty from those around him but is the personification of ruthlessness when a player, an assistant or a friend has outgrown their usefulness to him. It could be argued by some that it is a necessary quality for a manger.

Ferguson had a point about the size of clubs and their related ambitions, of course. It is one of football's timeless realities. Then again, did 'fundamental distinctions of scale' hinder Brian Clough when he was winning two European Cups with a small club like Nottingham Forest in 1979 and 1980? That's one more European Cup than Ferguson has won in twenty years at Old Trafford.

Ferguson admitted in his autobiography that he received another approach from Aberdeen at the end of the 1977–78 season after their then manager, Billy McNeill, moved to Celtic. Ferguson wanted to take it this time but he did not tell St Mirren immediately because he was worried they might sue him. Before he could break the news, the club sacked him. Ferguson was called into a boardroom meeting on the last day of May 1978. Todd had a piece of paper in front of him with thirteen accusations typed on it. Each was a separate allegation of a breach of contract. Ferguson began to laugh bitterly as Todd read out the crime sheet. 'I thought you only needed one reason to sack anybody,' Ferguson said, 'that he's not good enough at his job.'

But according to Michael Crick, Todd cited other reasons. These reasons came to light largely because Ferguson took the then unprecedented decision of taking St Mirren to an industrial tribunal, claiming unfair dismissal and seeking compensation. The case was heard in November and December 1978, when Ferguson had already taken over at Aberdeen. St Mirren contested his claims vigorously.

Crick wrote that Ferguson's contemporaneous account of his dealings with Aberdeen before his sacking by St Mirren differed sharply from his recollections in his 1999 autobiography. In the autobiography, Ferguson was candid about the fact that he received two approaches from Aberdeen, or Aberdeen representatives, while he was at Love Street. But he told the tribunal that the first time there had been any contact was on the night after his sacking. 'These two Ferguson accounts cannot be reconciled,' Crick wrote.

Crick examined the report of the industrial tribunal in detail. In it, St Mirren's accusations against Ferguson were laid bare.

Some of them were minor financial infractions: paying the players an unauthorized bonus for winning a relegation clash, offering a goalkeeper a £500 tax-free bonus, allowing Love Street to be used for a Scottish Junior Cup semi-final free of charge.

But according to Crick there were more serious charges. The club alleged that Ferguson had taken £25 from the club each week to cover expenses without the knowledge of the directors. When they told him to stop, he carried on anyway, St Mirren said. In the end, they had to block his access to the club's petty cash. Club officials were worried that Ferguson's payments to himself would leave them open to charges of tax evasion.

Ferguson countered by producing a letter that he claimed stated that he was entitled to unreceipted expenses of £25 a week, but the tribunal was suspicious of his explanation. At worst, the tribunal report said, Ferguson 'took sums of money belonging to St Mirren to which he ought to have known he had no right'.

Next, there was an accusation that Ferguson had regularly given advice to a friend who was a bookmaker about the outcome of St Mirren matches. Ferguson's association with the bookmaker, David McAllister, had emerged when Ferguson was driving the editor of the *Paisley Daily Express*, James Neil, to a lunch in Glasgow and stopped en route to hand over a couple of tickets to McAllister.

When Ferguson got back in the car, he told Neil that he had recently suggested to McAllister that St Mirren would beat Ayr United in their crucial relegation encounter. McAllister had won £3,900, and on the Monday after the game a crate of champagne from the bookie was delivered to Love Street.

The tribunal treated this revelation less seriously. For a start, if Ferguson had had something to hide he was hardly likely to chat about it to the editor of the local newspaper and flaunt his contact with the bookie in front of him. Nor was there any suggestion that Ferguson had ever advised McAllister to bet against St Mirren. Ferguson denied he had ever received champagne from McAllister and the tribunal report said the charge was inconsequential. 'Managers' punditry in greater depth than this about the prospect of their side the following day, can be read any Friday for the price of a newspaper,' the report said.

The tribunal was appalled by Ferguson's behaviour towards June Sullivan, though. During the period when Ferguson refused to speak to her, the tribunal report said, any contact between the two of them had to be conducted through a seventeen-year-old secretarial assistant. 'It shows him as one possessing neither by experience nor talent, any managerial ability at all,' the report said. 'When he was the author of a particularly absurd situation, it was more than ever his duty to resolve it. His reaction was a childish one and one likely to stultify and cripple the day-to-day office activities.'

Sadly, that kind of petulance, that willingness to pursue a vendetta, still plays a key part in Fergerson's behaviour today. He is still ridiculously sensitive to the mildest criticism. One of his favourite refrains, familiar to most younger newspaper and television reporters, is: 'You're finished ' In some ways, he has not changed much since he tried to bully June Sullivan.

Ferguson made a series of counter-allegations. One of them, the complaint that some of the St Mirren players were earning more than he was, has been a recurring theme throughout his years as a manager. He also mentioned the Jaguar car. And his lack of one. Again.

But the three-man panel decided in favour of St Mirren. 'They were entitled to think that the deterioration in relations was likely to be irreversible,' the tribunal report said. 'In his event, it was only a short, logical step for St Mirren to decide that they had no choice but to dismiss Ferguson and, in the Tribunal's view, this was a conclusion reasonably arrived at.'

Ferguson was devastated when the verdict was delivered, four days before Christmas 1978. He was having a difficult time in his first season at Aberdeen. His father was desperately ill. This just made things a lot worse. In time, he came to regret deeply the fact that he had bothered with the tribunal in the first place.

But he had felt slighted and humiliated. His career seemed to be falling into a pattern of setbacks and rejections. He had been damaged psychologically by his treatment at Rangers when he had been marginalized as a player by a manager who didn't rate him. He had been cut loose at his next club, Falkirk, too.

He felt echoes of those experiences in what was happening to him at St Mirren. At the time, he was also determined not to be beaten by someone like Todd, whom he considered to be part of the privileged establishment. Ferguson had a healthy contempt for football's ruling classes in general and club directors in particular in those days, an attitude that seems more and more distant now that he has seemed to morph into the Glazers' man.

At St Mirren, though, the insurrectionist soul of the man who had led a strike of apprentice toolmakers when he was a shop steward at American company Remington Rand, the man who had spearheaded a threatened players' strike at Falkirk and who had been chairman of the Scottish PFA, still burned bright. Back in the late Seventies, Ferguson was still willing to indulge in cussed defiance of authority.

His defeat in the tribunal taught him a lesson. It told him he needed to be a bit more cute in future, that sometimes confronting authority head-on was not necessarily the best way of achieving success. 'Even if you hate your chairman,' he said later, 'you have to find a way of getting on with it. My single-mindedness meant that I was always ready to argue my corner with Todd and in the power-struggle I had no chance.'

It was the only time in his managerial career that somebody got the better of him. Since then, he has bent with the wind. He has done what he has had to do to preserve his hold on power. Chairmen and chief executives have come and gone at Old Trafford and Ferguson has outlasted them all. He owes his longevity, in part, to the lessons he learned at Love Street.

11: Shankly's Greatest Day

The Liverpool players listened to *Desert Island Discs* on the coach that took them from their hotel to Wembley for the 1965 FA Cup Final against Leeds United. Radio 4 was not the station of preference for hard, uncomplicated men like Ron Yeats and Tommy Smith, but on this particular May Day they had no choice. The castaway that morning was Bill Shankly, and as the presenter began to play Shankly's chosen songs and the interview he had recorded a couple of days earlier, the more confident players hooted their derision at his selections. Shankly leant forward towards the bus driver and asked him to turn the volume up.

And so on the most important day of their footballing lives, Ian St John and Roger Hunt, Yeats, Smith and the rest, did not listen to 'King of the Road', 'You've Lost That Loving Feeling', 'Doo Wah Diddy Diddy' or any of the other chart hits of the last twelve months. Instead, the radio blared out Shankly's voice and the strains of 'A Red, Red Rose', 'Danny Boy', 'When the Saints Go Marching In' and 'Because'.

The songs he chose betrayed Shankly's ruling passions of desire and commitment and, of course, his attachment to the Scottish writer and poet Robbie Burns, a man Shankly idolized as an early socialist. But if Burns was thinking about a woman in 'A Red, Red Rose' when he wrote that he would love her 'till a' the seas gang dry', it is easy to imagine football as the object of Shankly's ardour.

The only time the players stopped smirking and sang along

with the music was when 'You'll Never Walk Alone' started playing. There was cheering, too, when the presenter asked Shankly what solitary luxury item he would take with him to his island to comfort him in his isolation and Shankly replied 'a football'. It was the obvious answer. Football had always been his salvation. From the time when it took him away from the pits to his last years when he played two-a-sides with Jock Dodds against the waiters from the Norbreck Castle Hotel on the Blackpool seafront. Without a football, he was lost.

Shankly had made painstaking preparations for the hours leading up to the Cup Final. The stakes were as high as they could be that day. The FA Cup was still king back then. It had not been devalued by the demands of the Champions League or the proliferation of domestic cup competitions. It was regarded as on a par with winning the league, by players and supporters alike. 'I've seen boys sitting in T-shirts soaking wet at FA Cup games and drinking Oxo,' Shankly said. 'They might not do that for the League but the Cup's a different story.' In terms of a single day's experience, an afternoon at Wembley in May was still prized above all other things for a British footballer.

Particularly for a club like Liverpool, which had never been accorded quite the same respect as teams like Arsenal and Manchester United, the Cup was the key to acceptance among the elite. Winning the league didn't do it. It was regarded as a victory for dogged perseverance, not quite the mark of class it is today. But the Cup, well the Cup was about glamour and sophistication. It was about basking in the limelight and treading the biggest stage.

Until then, and for a few years beyond, all the dominant images and stories of our national game were rooted in the drama of the Cup Final. Victory in a Cup Final could still define a player then, just as now it takes a title win or, even better, a European Cup Final success, to cap a player's career. Most famously of all, there was the Matthews Final in 1953 when Sir Stanley Matthews finally got his hands on a winner's medal.

Bert Trautmann broke his neck in the 1956 Final, Charlie George scored one of the most replayed goals in football history to win the 1971 Final and Jim Montgomerie produced his astonishing double save to deny Leeds in 1973.

There was even more riding on it for Shankly and Liverpool, though. Like Leeds, Liverpool had never won at Wembley – they lost to Arsenal in 1950 in their only previous Cup Final – and their repeated failure had even led to the growth of a legend that the copper statues of the Liver Birds would have to fly from their eyrie atop the Pier Head on the banks of the River Mersey before Liverpool could ever lift the trophy. The birds seemed to have been primed for take-off a couple of seasons earlier, but then Liverpool lost to Leicester City in the semi-finals. Their team was more mature, more settled and more confident now. It was their big chance.

Shankly was so determined that nothing should go wrong that he arranged for an empty coach to follow the Liverpool team bus all the way from their hotel in Weybridge to England's great cathedral of football just in case the bus broke down. As they began to draw nearer to the Twin Towers, the pavements started to fill up with Liverpool supporters dressed all in red and making their way towards the ground. Shankly, whose mantra was that the players must never do anything to betray the fans who supported their team so loyally, stood up and made a brief speech. 'See these fans, boys,' he said, 'they've travelled down to give you their support. They've spent money that some of them can't afford and they've worked all week, so don't let them down.'

From another voice, perhaps, that speech might have sounded insincere, but no cynicism crept into the attitude of Shankly's players towards their boss. They knew he was for real when he talked about his sense of duty to the supporters. It was part of his dictum of accountability. It was also deeply rooted in his socialist principles and his obsession with treating the working man with respect and dignity.

That kind of accountability, that feeling of communion with the supporters, has largely disappeared now. It has been replaced by a deep mutual mistrust that is merely suspended from time to time. The players are wary of the attentions of the supporters, partly because their rocketing wages have isolated them from the working-class communities in which they grew up. Their riches have marooned many modern players in a purgatory suspended somewhere between their origins and an aristocracy that despises what it regards as vulgar wealth. Witness the horror of the inhabitants of Cobham, Surrey, at the invasion of their village and its surrounds by legions of Chelsea millionaires.

Nor do the fans still feel the same unconditional admiration for their heroes as they did in Shankly's day. Their heroes have feet of clay now. Many supporters harbour deep and nagging suspicions about the lack of loyalty of many of the players to their Premiership sides. There is a presumption now that a player's allegiance to a club is almost wholly dependent on whether he could earn more money elsewhere. The seemingly nakedly mercenary behaviour of men like Rio Ferdinand, the Manchester United defender, has exaggerated that impression. The disillusion felt by some fans at the invasion of the game by extortionists masquerading as footballers has persuaded swathes of them to abandon the game and leave it to the neophytes Roy Keane memorably branded 'the prawn sandwich brigade'. Agents and players seem to have clubs over a barrel as their contracts draw to a close.

Back in 1965, though, the players and the manager still had a bond with the supporters. A year earlier, St John and Yeats had celebrated the clinching of the title by drinking the night away with supporters in a Liverpool pub called the Maid of Erin. And by the time the Liverpool coach pulled on to Wembley Way – the broad avenue that used to run from Wembley Park tube station all the way to the foot of the Twin Towers – Shankly was clutching a pair of Cup Final tickets in his hand.

When the bus pulled up, Shankly got off and gave them to two
Liverpool supporters. When they got over the shock, they
offered to pay him for the tickets. 'Pay me next season,' Shankly
said. But he didn't mean it.

In their dressing room, the Liverpool players were met by
Frankie Vaughan and Jimmy Tarbuck, two Liverpool entertain-
ers, one a singer, the other a comedian. They helped to stave off
the tension. Tarbuck told a few jokes. Frankie Vaughan took
requests. He sang a few bars of 'Gimme the Moonlight, Gimme
the Girl'. Shankly popped out into the tunnel to see if he could
hear any noise coming from the Leeds dressing room. He
couldn't. 'This is great boys,' he said. 'Revie has got those poor
buggers locked up next door.'

The Leeds boss, Don Revie, was to become Shankly's greatest rival. The 1965 FA Cup Final marked the beginning of a
decade of fierce competition between the two men. Shankly did
not dislike Revie exactly, but he did not feel the same respect
for Revie as he did, say, for Matt Busby, because he believed
Leeds were ready to attain their objectives by fair means or foul.

They already had a fine side, though. Jackie Charlton and
Norman Hunter were a formidable central defensive pairing,
Billy Bremner and Johnny Giles were tenacious and classy in
midfield, and their captain, Bobby Collins, was a fearsome and
cynical competitor, similar in some ways to Dennis Wise. They
had just missed out on that season's league title to Manchester
United on goal difference and they believed they were going into
the Final as favourites.

But the Liverpool side, Shankly's first great Liverpool team,
was at its peak, and on that damp, drizzly day in northwest
London it was about to reward all Shankly's tutelage with a
performance that set new boundaries for courage, for endurance
and for determination. It was an experienced, mature Liverpool
side whose confidence was still brimful after their title victory
and which had been freshened by the emergence of Tommy
Smith.

Smith was not yet considered the hard man of the side. That distinction went to Gerry Byrne, and he was about to earn it. Byrne, who played at left back and had ousted Ronnie Moran from the starting line-up, was the only man who was banned from making tackles in Melwood five-a-side matches for fear of the damage he might do to his own players. Even Smith got skittish when he sensed Byrne bearing down on him.

Smith formed a formidable partnership with Yeats at the back, in front of Tommy Lawrence, the goalkeeper that Manchester City manager Joe Mercer labelled 'the first sweeper-keeper', because of his speed off the line. Lawrence was not quite as commanding as Shankly would have liked, but he made up in calmness and agility what he lacked in stature.

Chris Lawler, who had been working part-time on the ground staff when Shankly arrived at Anfield in 1959, had come into the side at right back. He was solid and dependable. And he was the quietest man at the club, a quality that earned him the nickname Silent Knight and gave Shankly the material for one of his great one-liners. At the end of a typically competitive five-a-side training match, one of Shankly's team hit the underside of the bar with a shot and Shankly claimed it had bounced down and crossed the line. A fierce argument ensued, until Shankly turned to Lawler, who had been watching because he was injured.

'Did you think that was a goal, Chris?' Shankly implored.

'No, boss,' Lawler said.

'Jesus Christ,' Shankly shouted at him. 'This is the first time I've heard you speak to me and you tell me a bloody lie.'

In midfield, Gordon Milne should have been partnering Willie Stevenson in the centre, but Milne had been injured a fortnight earlier against the hard-tackling Chelsea side of Ron Harris when he chased a bad ball from St John and was caught off-balance by Chopper's sidekick, Eddie McCreadie. 'It was the last kind of match in which you wanted to deliver a hospital ball to one of your teammates,' St John said, 'and I couldn't shake off the guilt that I had done precisely that to Gordon.'

Milne was replaced by Geoff Strong, but Liverpool's real strengths were on the flanks. On the right, Ian Callaghan worked tirelessly up and down and provided a steady stream of straightforward and reliable crosses for the forwards. On the left, Peter Thompson, bought from Preston for £37,500 a year earlier, tormented opposing defences with his pace and his brilliant, mazy dribbles. He was a winger in the mould of Tom Finney and Stanley Matthews, a twister and a turner and elusive as hell. His only weakness was his inability to recognize the best time to release the ball, a trait shared by many wingers before and after him, and one that was to cost him a place in Alf Ramsey's World Cup-winning team.

Perhaps Liverpool's greatest advantage over Leeds was in attack, where St John and Hunt had formed a formidable partnership. Both were proven goalscorers, but as they had grown accustomed to playing alongside each other St John had adapted his game to act more as a provider for his teammate, who was a lethal finisher. Both men were forwards of the highest quality and idols of the Kop.

Together, these men, with Shankly at their head and the Leeds players striding beside them, made the long march from the mouth of the Wembley tunnel to the place in front of the Royal Box where they stood for the singing of the national anthem. The Queen was wearing red and the Liverpool fans, revelling in the novelty of a big day out at the fine old stadium, roared out their delight when the music began to play. 'God Save Our Gracious Team,' they sang and the stage was set.

Perhaps because of the relaxed build-up, perhaps because Shankly's incessant preaching about their superiority had seeped through, Liverpool's players were sure they were going to win as the referee's whistle signalled the kick-off. 'I actually spent more time worrying about what I was going to say to the Queen than about the match itself,' Yeats said. 'That may sound big-headed but it is the truth. Leeds had a hard reputation but we had done well against them in the league that season. We had also beaten some very good European sides so facing Leeds held no fear for us.'

But if Liverpool were confident, they were soon dealt what ought to have been a serious blow. Only three minutes of the final had gone when Bobby Collins overran the ball and launched himself at Byrne with a late lunge that was also a shoulder barge. Byrne was knocked off his feet and sat down hard on the turf. When Bob Paisley, doubling up as the trainer, ran on Byrne told him he thought he had just hurt his leg. But when he stood up and felt the searing pain in his shoulder and upper chest, both men realized he had fractured his collarbone.

Normal men would have come off, even in an era when neither team was allowed a substitute. But Byrne played on and Shankly resisted the urge to put him out of harm's way on the left flank because that would have made it obvious Byrne was a passenger. Somehow, even though the two pieces of his collarbone were grinding together, Byrne managed to disguise his pain and condition. He even set up Liverpool's first goal. 'He stuck it out,' Shankly said. 'He should have had all the medals to himself.'

The game had been dour and chanceless, not helped by a pitch made slick from the day's rain, and it slipped into extra-time. Three minutes into the first period, Byrne summoned the courage to overlap down the left and crossed for Hunt to nod the ball past Gary Sprake. Liverpool thought the Cup was theirs and they began to tighten up. Bremner punished them by bringing Leeds level with a sweetly struck half-volley that was still rising when it bulged the back of the Liverpool net.

But then, nine minutes from the final whistle, Callaghan raced away down the right and cut the ball back from the byline. St John was waiting, anticipating the flight and the direction of Callaghan's cross, and he powered his header across the line. 'If you haven't found God in your life,' St John wrote in his autobiography, 'you find him at times like that. You hear yourself praying "please, God, give me this." I never had such an attack of instant religion.'

In the moment of triumph, Shankly was exultant. He pushed both his fists up into the air in that familiar stiff-armed gesture of his that looked as if he was trying to make a 'V' out of his upper body. Before Ron Yeats had lifted the Cup and as Liverpool's delirious supporters chanted 'Ee-aye-addio, we've won the Cup', Shankly ignored the falling rain and in a gesture of solidarity with the fans, took off his coat and strode towards them. The pitch was pockmarked with puddles and the water and mud spattered his trousers. The chalk from the pitch markings turned his black shoes white. He didn't notice.

Shankly was transported by the emotion of the occasion, more than he ever had been, more than he ever would be again. He created his own piece of football history that day. He gave a city a great gift. Now, football had joined music, its twin opiate, in heaping honour and pride on Liverpool's working classes. Like the Beatles, Shankly and Liverpool were ambassadors for the city now. They were the face of success and the proof that passion and ability, discipline and nobility, thrived on the banks of the Mersey.

'I went to the supporters because they had got the Cup for the first time,' he said later. 'Grown men were crying and it was the greatest feeling any human being could have to see what we had done. There have been many proud moments in my career. Wonderful, fantastic moments. But that was the greatest day.'

The players celebrated with a banquet at the Dorchester Hotel on Park Lane. Shankly made a rousing speech but it was clear his thoughts were already turning to the first leg of the European Cup semi-final against Inter the following Wednesday. The waiters stopped topping up the champagne glasses early in the evening. The next morning, Shankly and his players were up early to catch the train from Euston back to Liverpool Lime Street.

In these days of conspicuous emotional outpouring spawned by the death of Princess Diana and confirmed by the reaction to the passing of the dissolute former genius George Best, we have grown accustomed to mass displays of grief and joy. Huge crowds met Manchester United when they came back from Barcelona with the European Cup in 1999. Crowds thronged Oxford Street and Regent Street for the Rugby World Cup winners in 2003. Hundreds of thousands lined the streets of west London when Chelsea won the league title for the first time in fifty years in 2005. Win a World Cup or a Test match series, and you are a shoo-in for a spot in a parade.

But Liverpool had never seen anything like the fervour that greeted Shankly and his team when they arrived back in their home city. That 1965 final had marked a sea-change in football mores and the awareness of provincial football culture in the country at large. When the Kop transplanted itself to Wembley, it imposed its passion on the arena like no group of fans had ever done before. Television beamed back pictures of joyful Liverpool supporters belting out 'You'll Never Walk Alone' and 'Ee Aye Addio We Won the Cup' and marvelled at the spontaneity of the chanting. The days of orchestrated singing, prompted by military brass bands, were gone for ever.

The popular joy that assailed Shankly and Liverpool as they clambered aboard buses at Lime Street surprised them too. There were 50,000 outside the station, crowded around the exit and massing in front of the beautiful neoclassical façade of St George's Hall opposite. Their coaches took them to the Town Hall on the other side of the City Centre where it was estimated that another 150,000 supporters crammed into Castle Street and Dale Street to see Shankly hold the cup aloft from the balcony.

'The reception in the city centre was unbelievable,' Shankly said. 'The emotion was tremendous. When we came out of the station, we couldn't see anything but buildings and faces. People were climbing up the walls of shops and banks and hoardings to get a better view. They were in dangerous places but their name was on the Cup at last and that was all that mattered. The FA Cup win was the most emotional day for Liverpool in their entire history. Winning the European Cup was also a great achievement but that was virtually new. The FA Cup had been in existence since football began and people had lived and died without seeing Liverpool win it.'

After the reception, Shankly took his players to Blackpool for a short break. Chris Lawler stayed behind to get married. Then he joined them. After Wembley on the Saturday, some thought that Inter the following Wednesday could only be an anticlimax. But it wasn't. If anything, it was even more intense, even more visceral, mainly because it was played out in the Anfield bear-pit in front of a baying Kop. They closed the gates an hour before kick-off that night because the ground was already full to its 54,000 capacity. The Liverpool fans summoned a spine-tingling atmosphere that unsettled even the well-travelled Inter players and dismayed the scheming Herrera (known by the Inter fans as The Black Magician because of the dark overcoat that seemed to be draped permanently over his shoulders).

It was stage-managed by Shankly down to the last detail. Late in the afternoon, he had hatched a plan to send the injured Gerry Byrne and Gordon Milne out on to the pitch to parade the FA Cup before the game. He talked it over with Paisley and they agreed it would have more psychological impact on Inter if they could unveil the trophy when Inter were already on the pitch.

So Inter sprinted out first, ran straight to the Kop end by mistake and were sent back to the Anfield Road end by a fusillade of boos. It was a good start. Then Ron Yeats led the Liverpool team out and there was a deafening roar. Then Byrne, the injured hero of the Final, and Milne, the man who had missed out, walked up the steps and out of the tunnel in their suits and started limping their way around the perimeter of the pitch with the gleaming trophy. The right sleeve of Byrne's jacket flapped loosely by his side, his arm in a sling. The din nearly took the roof off. 'Dear God,' Shankly said, 'what an eruption there was when our supporters caught sight of that Cup.'

It was a wonderfully dramatic piece of theatre, a scene that worked in so many different ways. St John, still haunted by guilt over Milne's injury, watched with tears in his eyes and felt his determination to excel redouble. The denizens of the Kop swayed and surged. Phil Thompson, who was sitting in the Kemlyn Road Stand with his mum, watched as steam rose from the masses behind the goal. They sang 'Go Back to Ital-ee' at the Inter players to the tune of 'Santa Lucia', a chant that was to be echoed in Istanbul thirty years later when AC Milan were the opponents.

That night at Anfield was the kind of night when you feel privileged to be a football fan, the kind of night when you can lose yourself in the anonymity of the crowd and the exhilaration of the occasion and when you can wonder at the strength of the will around you. The masses on the terraces swayed and surged and rolled. It was the kind of night that is all but extinct in the sanitized atmosphere of the Premiership where it is a bookable offence if you celebrate a goal the wrong way.

In that atmosphere, Liverpool began the game feeling as if they were superhuman. They played that way, too. They were ahead within 4 minutes. Once again, Callaghan was the pro-vider, racing on to a pass from Strong and pulling back a cross for Hunt to hook a volley past Inter goalkeeper Giuliano Sarti. Six minutes later, though, Inter were level. Yeats made an uncharacteristic mess of a clearance just inside Liverpool's half, Peiro raced away and squared the ball to Mazzola who fired it high into the net.

But this had the aura of a special evening, the Kop did not lose its voice and Liverpool were not to be denied. They regained the lead 10 minutes before half-time with a free kick of stunning invention and flawless execution. Placing the ball just outside the area, Callaghan lined up the kick but ran over it instead of shooting and dashed onwards towards goal. Stevenson played the ball to Hunt, who curled it over the wall into the path of Callaghan. Callaghan reached the ball a split second before Sarti and he dinked his shot past the goalkeeper and into the corner of the net.

Liverpool might have gone further ahead, but a shot from Lawler that beat Sarti was ruled out because a Liverpool player was deemed to have strayed offside. Still, 15 minutes from the end Sarti failed to cling on to Hunt's fierce drive and St John was on the loose ball in a flash, stabbing it into the empty net. 'You showed that magician and his boys how to play tonight,' Shankly told his players in the dressing room.

Herrera was unstinting in his praise for Inter's conquerors. 'We have been beaten before,' he told the press, 'but tonight we were defeated.' That night at Anfield was the first of the great European nights. The first of the nights when Liverpool and their fans felt heady with invincibility and the power of their passion.

Herrera was saving up his own box of tricks for the San Siro a week later that stopped Liverpool in their tracks, but that night at Anfield, and the Saturday before at Wembley, did not mark the close of an epic pursuit. It was, in fact, a beginning. That Cup Final and the match against Inter four days later formed the gateway through which Shankly and Liverpool surged. On the other side, fame and glory waited. And in Shankly's case, immortality.

12: Ferguson and his Father's Eyes

Alex Ferguson was under siege in the summer of 1978 when he turned his back on the Glasgow conurbation where he had lived his entire life and headed northeast to Aberdeen. His father, his great hero, the man who had forged his character and whom he respected more than any other, was dying. His wife was worried about uprooting their young family. And he was reeling from the first great setback of his managerial career after being sacked by St Mirren and then accused by the club of a variety of misdeeds that included giving tips to a bookmaker and bullying a female employee.

He did not arrive at Pittodrie like a bull ready to run amok, which was his usual style of giving first impressions. Instead, he felt humbled and rather vulnerable. He also felt grateful to the Aberdeen chairman, Dick Donald, and his vice-chairman, Chris Anderson, for taking him on when he was at such a low ebb. He had achieved much at St Mirren but his reputation had been tarnished by the accusations that had been levelled at him, and his future clouded by his insistence on taking St Mirren to an industrial tribunal. Which he lost.

Ferguson came to Aberdeen looking for a place that could be both a sanctuary from the troubles pursuing him from his former life and a base for a sustained revenge attack. Suddenly, Ferguson, the man born and bred in Govan on the Clyde, was preaching suspicion of all things Glaswegian and inculcating a hatred of the Old Firm clubs, Celtic and Rangers, in the minds of his new charges at Pittodrie.

English football fans have long been used to his habit of winding up the Manchester United players with all manner of conspiracy theories about the plots he imagined were raging against his team. Ferguson had dabbled with creating a siege mentality when he was manager at East Stirling and St Mirren, too, but a combination of his own troubles and Aberdeen's geographical isolation, three hours by road from Glasgow, gave him the ideal opportunity to take his rage against the supposed iniquities of the establishment to the limit.

'He built the model of the idea that "everyone hates us" at Aberdeen,' his centre forward, Mark McGhee, said. 'I don't know if he decided early on that that was going to be part of his strategy but he was relentless about it. He would talk about how the journalists and the TV guys hated coming up the road for three hours from Glasgow to watch us. He'd tell us that the reporters all wanted us to get beat. It got us really wound up. He leant very heavily on that.'

When Ferguson took over at Aberdeen, it had been thirteen years since anyone other than Celtic or Rangers had won the league title. It was Kilmarnock who broke the stranglehold briefly in 1965 but that was their first and last championship triumph. As Ferguson drove northeast to take up his appointment in June 1978, he wanted to be seen as the man from the Monopolies Commission, the manager who was going to take a wrecking ball to the duopoly exercised by the Old Firm.

The upheavals in his personal life obscured the fact that Aberdeen represented a clear opportunity for Ferguson to take a giant leap forward professionally. It was the next step on the ladder. The manager's job had become vacant when Billy McNeill, the legendary Celtic captain, was persuaded to return to Parkhead. But he bequeathed Ferguson a side that had finished second in the league to Rangers and which had reached the final of the Scottish Cup. Nor were Rangers quite the side they once were, and Celtic had just lost Kenny Dalglish to Liverpool.

The city of Aberdeen was thriving, too. Oil had been discovered beneath the North Sea in the early 1970s and Aberdeen was caught up in the rush for black gold. Texans flooded in, money flowed and *Newsweek* magazine even gave the Granite City a new moniker. Sin City, they called it, alleging that the creation of a new cash-rich generation of oil-rig workers had turned Aberdeen into a city with a thriving sex trade.

The oil money did not have any particular impact on the football club. Dick Donald ran a tight ship at Pittodrie and there was little chance of Ferguson embarking on a spending spree. But the oil brought a feel-good factor to the area and rid it of some of its small-town, hurdy-gurdy, Highland hicksville reputation. Oil helped to put Aberdeen on the map. Ferguson completed the job.

He inherited a fine bunch of players from McNeill. The captain, Willie Miller, defender Stuart Kennedy and prolific forward Joe Harper had all played for Scotland. There were fine young talents, too. Alex McLeish was there, Gordon Strachan, John McMaster, Drew Jarvie, Doug Rougvie and Steve Archibald. Goalkeeper Jim Leighton was coming through the ranks and in March 1979 Ferguson paid £70,000 to Newcastle for striker Mark McGhee.

His first season, though, was not easy. In fact, it was one of his darkest times in football. He was not a man given to questioning his own ability but he questioned it that year. His confidence was low, and in later years he admitted he made many mistakes in those first months at Pittodrie and that his personal circumstances did not allow him to give everything he wanted to the job.

His family was still living in the new town of East Kilbride, south of Glasgow, and given that most Scottish Premier League clubs were concentrated in and around the Glasgow conurbation or in Edinburgh, Ferguson made a habit of heading off to see his wife and sons after away matches rather than catching the coach back to Aberdeen.

It might seem insignificant but it is the kind of habit that can undermine a manager very quickly at a football club. It erodes respect for him because it suggests that he is not fully committed. In his first seasons at Newcastle, for instance, Graeme Souness left himself open to criticism by going back home to Cheshire after away games in northwest England rather than travelling back to the northeast with his team.

The same formula contributed to Ferguson's struggles in his early months at Aberdeen. There was some resentment about his methods and his attitude among senior players and strong characters like Miller and the long coach journeys back to Pittodrie without the manager gave them plenty of scope to chew over their shared discontent.

'One of the minor personal irritations I had to endure at first,' Miller said, 'was having St Mirren's Jackie Copland constantly held up as a model on which I should base my play. Every time we had a practice game, the manager would at some point remark: "Jackie Copland would have cleared that ball" or "Jackie Copland would have done it this way." Much as I respected Jackie as an excellent player, frankly, I thought my method of doing things was just as effective and I did not appreciate the constant comparison. It took some time for Alex Ferguson and me to build up the relationship of mutual respect and understanding which we finally achieved.'

There were other problems. At thirty-six, Ferguson was still a young manager. Some of his senior pros were only a few years younger than him. Most of them had played against him and he had never been the most generous or chivalrous of opponents. Some felt they had a score to settle. Strachan was struck by how quiet the new manager was, but that was never going to last long.

The friction between Ferguson and his players meant that his first months in charge were turbulent. He and Miller had several eyeball-to-eyeball confrontations, and although Ferguson never backed down, the atmosphere at the club was hardly conducive to building the kind of formidable team spirit that Ferguson has always taken such a pride in achieving.

Ferguson didn't usually need an excuse for being uptight and highly strung and allowing his hair-trigger temper free rein, but in this period of his life, he had one. His father had developed lung cancer and was failing fast. He travelled to Dens Park in Dundee to watch his son take charge of Aberdeen's League Cup semi-final against Hibs in December 1978. Ferguson remembers looking up at him in the stand and seeing him wave. He was wearing the Crombie coat Ferguson had given him as a present. It was the last game he attended.

Two weeks after that, Ferguson's industrial tribunal against St Mirren went south. They found against him. Ferguson connected the decision and the humiliation that was heaped upon the Aberdeen manager with a hastening of his father's decline, and that was almost more than he could bear.

His father was a noble man. A fine father and a strong figurehead for his family, he had tried to teach Ferguson the virtues of humility and perseverance and had passed on his own unwavering commitment to hard work. He had also borne his own health problems with great stoicism. He had developed bowel cancer in 1960 and had lived uncomplainingly with the indignity of a colostomy bag ever since.

'My father had been ill for a while,' Ferguson said. 'When he was 47 he had to start using a colostomy bag and that was a terrible thing for him because there was no bathroom in our house in Govan so he had to try and clean himself at the sink. The thing he found hardest was the terrible lack of dignity. He just wanted the privacy to be able to look after himself.'

His father gained that privacy when Ferguson's parents were relocated to new flats in the early Seventies when their tenement on the Govan Road was demolished. But he had also started smoking in his late thirties and was diagnosed with lung cancer before Ferguson moved to Aberdeen.

Ferguson's mother died of the same disease. He had only been at Old Trafford for three weeks when he learned that Elizabeth Ferguson had been struck down by lung cancer too. 'I found out over the phone,' he said. 'I had bought my mother a house near to the local Catholic church, because at that point, her life was the church, and I used to phone her every day to see how she was and have a chat with her but this time nobody answered.

'I remember that I was in London because we were playing Wimbledon that Saturday. I rang my brother's home and my sister-in-law, Sandra, answered and said: "You're wondering where your mother is aren't you? She was admitted to hospital last night." I flew back to Scotland and when I got to the hospital, the doctor sat me down, told me she had lung cancer and then said: 'She's got about four days to live.' He was right. She died four days later – and all I could suddenly think of was how final it was. The absolute finality of death.'

Before his father died, Ferguson visited him one last time in the Southern General Hospital on the eve of Aberdeen's away game at his old club, St Mirren. Ferguson was shocked by how quickly his condition had deteriorated in the fortnight since he had last seen him and there is something incredibly moving about his description of that final meeting between father and son.

'As I sat with him, all I could do was hold his hand and look into his eyes,' Ferguson wrote in his autobiography. 'They had gone a very pale blue, which was actually quite beautiful. "It's just one of those things, Alex," he said to me as I left.'

The next day, 24 February 1979, the match at Love Street turned into a war full of rage and emotion and seething controversy. Aberdeen led 2–0 at half-time but in a frenzied five-minute period midway through the second half, at exactly the time Ferguson's father was breathing his last in the hospital, the referee sent off Willie Miller and Ian Scanlon and St Mirren fought their way back into the game and salvaged a 2–2 draw. Ferguson flew into an uncontrollable rage.

After the game, the St Mirren electrician, an old friend of Ferguson called Fred Douglas, tried to approach Ferguson to tell him that his father had died. Ferguson wouldn't let him speak at first. He was hammering on the referee's door. 'He was blazing,' Douglas said. 'He said "I want to see this cunt".'

Eventually, after the referee had told him he would be reported to the Scottish Football Association because of his behaviour, Ferguson listened to the pleadings of Douglas and the rage stopped long enough for him to be guided away to a small room so that the news could be broken to him. He crumpled. Grief drowned his anger. 'I was completely broken up,' he said. 'Fred, Dick Donald and Chris Anderson all did their best to console me but, like most of us at such times, I was beyond consoling. When I asked my brother what time dad had died he said: "4.23." It was strange that dad had slipped away just when all the mayhem was breaking out at Love Street.'

It was almost as if Ferguson felt there was something supernatural about those minutes, as if the pain his father's death caused him had been foreshadowed by the fury that had descended on the pitch at the moment when his life ended. It was a desperately sad and difficult time for Ferguson, and his team's fortunes did little to lift his spirits. A month later, Aberdeen lost his first final as a manager when they were beaten by Rangers in the climax of the League Cup.

Aberdeen finished the season in fourth place in the league, well adrift of new champions Celtic. It was hardly the step forward the Aberdeen board had hoped for when they appointed Ferguson to replace Billy McNeill. Ferguson's second season did not start promisingly either. Aberdeen had lost five league games by November and in December they lost another League Cup Final, this time in a replay against Dundee United.

Ferguson found it impossible to sleep the night after that defeat. He rose before dawn and went to the training ground early to greet the players as they arrived. Most of them were expecting a dressing down, but Ferguson congratulated them on their efforts and promised them they would never lose another final while he was manager. It was a turning point in their season.

Gradually, his players were growing accustomed to his abrasive, confrontational style. Some of his antics in those early days at Pittodrie cemented his reputation as the dressing-room equivalent of the nutter on the bus. On one occasion, at a reserve team game at Forfar Athletic, Mark McGhee saw him boot a laundry basket across the dressing room with such force that a pair of underpants landed on a player's head. The lad concerned was so petrified that he sat motionless until Ferguson ordered him to remove them.

McGhee and Strachan still laugh about those incidents. They were two of the strongest characters in the team, men who were able to look beyond Ferguson's ranting and raving and wait for the fit to pass so that they could get some sense out of him. Some time in 2005, with Strachan manager of Celtic and McGhee at Brighton, they both went to a match at Kilmarnock to watch a player and found themselves reminiscing about another of Fergie's managerial moments.

Kilmarnock was in the Ayrshire countryside, southwest of Glasgow, and players whose families still lived in the city usually stayed down to visit them rather than catching the team coach back to Aberdeen that night. But on this occasion, Aberdeen only managed a draw and the performance left Ferguson in a typically foul humour.

'One of the lads, Walter McCall, had his wife and his kids in a car in the car park and they were all going to spend the weekend at his parents,' McGhee said. 'But Fergie was so angry he made us all go straight back to Aberdeen on the bus. So his wife had to follow the bus all the way back to Aberdeen. As much as it made a point, it was a little bit unnecessary.'

A couple of years later, at half-time of a European Cup Winners' Cup tie away at Romanian side Arges Pitesti, the rage of Ferguson reached its apogee in a violent tirade against Strachan. Ferguson felt Strachan had ignored his instructions in the first half when he refused to play right wing. When he had gone to the touchline to point it out in forthright terms, Strachan shouted back: 'Away and shut your face.'

He knew there was an explosion coming at half-time, but he still could not resist winding Ferguson up even further. Eventually, the volcano blew. 'The wee man was in one of his nippy sweetie moods,' Ferguson said, 'full of caustic comments. What he regarded as smart ripostes struck me as senseless meanderings and as I intensified my onslaught, I swung a hand in anger at a huge tea urn that was nearby.

'It was made of pewter or iron and striking it nearly broke my hand. The pain caused me to flip my lid and I hurled a tray of cups filled with tea towards Strachan, hitting the wall above him. The other players were also sitting on that side of the room and a fair amount of the tea dripped down on to them. Strachan obeyed instructions in the second half.'

The braver ones still chanced their luck. At Pittodrie, the snooker room doubled as a weights room where injured players often began their convalescence. Some of them preferred the green baize to the effort of pumping iron. Ferguson, of course, was alive to the possibility of them shirking their duties and used to carry out regular checks. But by now he had developed a nervous cough that acted as a warning signal for the guilty men.

The cough manifested itself most obviously before matches when Ferguson would retreat to the dressing-room toilets. The tension gripped so badly in those minutes before kick-off that the cough turned into a prolonged retching. But on normal days, it was nothing more than a regular clearing of his throat. 'In the weight room, they could hear him coming because they heard the cough,' McGhee said. 'The boys would drop their cues and start doing press-ups.'

By then, Ferguson had acquired the nickname 'Furious' at Pittodrie. For obvious reasons. Most players accepted his rages as part of the deal. Some of them made intermittent protests. The chair on the opposite side of his desk in his office was known as the Archibald chair because the striker sat in it so often to air his grievances.

Once, after Archibald had scored a hat-trick against Celtic, he kept the match ball as a souvenir. Ferguson, who was so obsessed with wise husbandry at the club that Mark McGhee said he counted how many toilet rolls the players used each week, objected and said Archibald should give it back. The next morning, Ferguson was sitting in his office with a couple of assistants when Archibald burst in. He booted the ball into the room so that it ricocheted violently off the four walls and smashed a light. 'There's your fucking ball,' Archibald said as he stormed off.

But only Harper decided to take Ferguson on consistently. Ferguson was already in constant conflict with Harper over what he viewed as the player's indisciplined lifestyle, and one night the two men bumped into each other at a house party thrown by a mutual friend. Harper was eating a plate of haggis and neeps. 'What the fuck are you doing?' Ferguson said. Then he grabbed the plate and swept its contents into the sink. 'So me being a shy, unassuming person,' Harper said, 'I went over and got a plate and put the double the amount on it and started to eat it and my wife was staring at me and saying "Joe don't" and I could see her praying.'

Harper was injured early in Ferguson's second season at Aberdeen and never regained his place. Ferguson did not tolerate open rebellion against his way of doing things and gradually his methods began to pay off. Most of the players in his side were strong enough men to recognize that behind his ranting and raving, Ferguson was a man with the means to further their careers.

'We've all told the stories about the laundry basket and the teacups,' McGhee said, 'but those things weren't the important things.' We all had enough about us to know what was required. We weren't playing well because he was threatening us with cups. We were playing well because at the end of throwing the cups, he would say something that helped you. So as much as the cups bit would get you listening and would get your attention, it was what he said that was the important thing.

'He would go on spying trips to places like Ujpest Doza and Arges Pitesti and when he came back, he knew the names of all their players off by heart. He would talk about them one by one and he had acquired such a level of knowledge about them that it felt as if he knew as much about them as if we had been playing Dundee or Celtic. He had it all sussed. That was something I always found very impressive about him

'The hairdrier stuff was his way of reacting to situations where he was probably right. I don't react like that to the same situations but the same situations arise for me as a manager and I have to do something about it. Because of his personality, his way of dealing with it was to rant and rave. But he was usually right. He had a very economic way of giving instructions. He was succinct. You knew exactly what it was he wanted you to do.

'He helped me a lot. A couple of years earlier, when I was at Newcastle, I made my debut against Leeds at Elland Road and I played against Gordon McQueen and I gave him a torrid time, I really did. We won 2–0 and it was the first time Newcastle had won there in twelve years. The next home game against Middlesbrough, I scored and we drew 1–1. But the next game, I was totally anonymous. That was down to my style. Either the things I could do naturally came off or if they didn't, I was anonymous. I was trying to do the same things, beating people.

What it meant was that when I wasn't playing well, I wasn't contributing much to the team.

'The one thing that Fergie gave me – and this was the turning point in my career – was a structure where he said 'the starting point is this: you have to try and win the first header, you have to try and dominate the centre half and win that battle first, you have to keep the ball for us and then after that come all the bits and pieces'.

'So instead of being in the bathroom before the game saying to myself 'hope I play well, hope I play well', I was thinking 'got to keep the ball, got to keep the ball'. It sounds obvious but it was different. It gave me a foundation. After that, he kept the pressure on you. If you didn't do it, he was on your case.

'He would not give you credit for the things he knew you could do. Once, when we played Morton, we were winning 4–0 at half-time and I hadn't scored but I had made the four goals. I had made them all by running with the ball and beating three or four men and I expected to come in at half-time and get praise. But he slaughtered me. He called me a greedy bastard, asked me who I thought I was and told me I should be passing the ball. It was the things you weren't good at that he would keep urging you to improve. He wanted to see improvement in a player.'

The improvements started to come, although for much of the winter of the 1979–80 season they were hidden by a veneer of frost and snow. It was such a severe winter that Aberdeen played only once between 17 November and 5 January. In the same period Rangers played six times and Celtic four, so even though Aberdeen trailed both teams throughout January and February, Ferguson's side had plenty of games in hand.

They lost 1–0 at Morton on 5 January. A bad mistake by the Aberdeen left back Dougie Considine cost Aberdeen the game. Although McGhee was usually sanguine about Ferguson's outbursts, he felt that the manager went too far when he singled

Considine out in the dressing room after the game. 'He used to take advantage of the ones he knew he could bully,' McGhee said. 'He picked on the more vulnerable ones. Dougie Considine only played a few games for us. He was from up near Aberdeen somewhere, Ballater or Banchory or somewhere like that. He was a real Highland country boy. Totally harmless. A really nice big guy.

'He wasn't a great footballer but he was all right. He played against Morton and he made this horrendous error and Morton beat us 1–0. Fergie came in afterwards and set on him. 'You will never play for Aberdeen again,' he told him. And he never did. I always thought that was totally out of order. It was unnecessary. It was almost as if he was prepared to sacrifice that lad for the rest of us. To make the point that if you are going to make mistakes like that, you are going to be out. I thought that was wrong. A few years later, the lad was running a dry cleaner's in Pitlochry.'

Ferguson might argue that the sacrifice of Considine worked, just as the sacrifice of Leighton worked after the 1990 FA Cup Final. After the defeat to Morton, Aberdeen suffered only one more loss throughout the rest of the season, a home reverse against Kilmarnock. Relentlessly, they began to rein Celtic in and Celtic began to feel Ferguson's hot, eager, hungry breath as they ran.

The chase intensified in April. Aberdeen beat Celtic 2–1 at Parkhead at the start of the month with a second-half winner from McGhee. In the middle of the month, Celtic were hammered 5–1 by Dundee at Dens Park. At the end of the month, Aberdeen beat them at Parkhead again. This time it was 3–1. Goals from Strachan, McGhee and Archibald did the damage.

Ferguson's great achievement was to keep the eyes of his players away from the prize as they grew tantalizingly close to their goal. Aberdeen had not won the league title since 1955, but Ferguson kept them free of nerves in the run-in. It was almost like he played a con-trick on them right up until the day when they clinched the title with a game to spare with a 5–0 thrashing of Hibs at Easter Road. McGhee recalled:

'There was no real feeling of anticipation about how we were on the brink of winning the league. It was game to game. It was "win this game", then "win this game". It was almost only in the last game that we realized where we were. The news of the result came through that Celtic had drawn and we were winning 5–0 and Easter Road which meant we had won the league. There was an overwhelming feeling of disbelief on the pitch as if nobody had realized.

'I don't remember going into those last few games under pressure. One of the great things about Fergie was that he distracted us. It was almost cavalier, game to game. He didn't go on about the opposition. He didn't build them up. He didn't talk about them in the press or look forward to winning the league. He kept it specific to what was happening that day.'

Ferguson danced a jig on the pitch that day at Easter Road. He went to the end of the ground where the Aberdeen fans were singing and celebrating and gave them a clenched-fist salute. Everybody hugged each other. Ferguson went up to the announcer's box when the stadium had emptied of Hibs fans and thanked the Aberdeen faithful for their support. He told them they were welcome back at his house to continue the party.

His brother Martin hopped on the team coach back to Aberdeen and he and Ferguson sat up most of the night drinking and watching the video of the Hibs game. In the early hours, there was a knock at the door. Two intrepid fans had decided to take Ferguson up on his offer. True to his word, he invited them in and they all sat drinking until dawn in the house of the manager of the new champions of Scotland.

For Ferguson, that day at Easter Road was a beginning, not an ending. It was the start of him being recognized as a winner rather than a loser. He had never won a major honour of any kind before.

13: Shankly and Napoleon Bonaparte's Big Idea

In the summer of 1964, flushed with the success of winning his first league title a couple of months earlier and ready to ride the wild frontier in Europe, Bill Shankly took his Liverpool side to America on a pre-season tour. The club had been making regular journeys across the Atlantic since the Second World War. They were pioneers of the US market when Peter Kenyon, football's most eager modern chaser of the American dollar, was still in nappies. In New York, Shankly and his players appeared on the *Ed Sullivan Show*, only deemed of interest to an unknowing American audience as Beatles spin-offs rather than footballers playing to a strange code.

In Chicago, Shankly sought out the haunts of Eliot Ness, his hero from *The Untouchables*, his favourite television show back in England. He asked to see the site of the St Valentine's Day Massacre and made a pilgrimage to Soldier Field, where Gene Tunney fought Jack Dempsey in 1927 and hung on to win because of the famous Long Count.

While he was on the tour, Shankly wore a row of wristwatches up his left arm to keep himself abreast of the times in London, New York and Chicago. But he lived on English time. In America, he rose from his bed at midnight and handed out team sheets at 3 a.m. He made his team train on the exact spot where the ring had been erected in Soldier Field. He treated it as if it was holy ground. 'We played five-a-side games where they had pitched the ring,' Ian St John said, 'and Shankly's eyes glowed as we did our work. He believed that somehow the spirit of those great fighters might be transferred to his team.'

One thing upset him so much, though, that it marred his trip. He mentioned Tom Finney's name at a press conference in New York and some of the pressmen there looked puzzled and asked him who Finney was. Shankly was mystified. And he was outraged. 'Christ,' he shouted, 'that's it. If you don't know who Tommy Finney is, you'll never have a fucking team in this country.' He strode out into the hotel lobby. 'Can you believe it,' he said. 'Never heard of Tommy Finney. There's no hope for them.'

Shankly was not a worldly man. He was a Little Englander, an isolationist who was suspicious of foreigners. In fact, he was a xenophobe. Ferguson was making a point about the Italians' cunning on the football field when he said before a game against Inter Milan in 1999 that when an Italian told him it was pasta on the plate, he checked under the sauce to make sure. But Shankly's views, like many of his generation, were partly conditioned by living through the Second World War. They were a product of growing up in a tight-knit community and rarely travelling abroad until relatively late in life.

And yet in the early 1960s Shankly was leading Liverpool into a new era of rapidly expanding horizons. Initially sceptical about European football, he became a zealous proselytizer for it and his old prejudices did not affect his admiration for the great players of Real Madrid and Inter. Liverpool came from a port city after all, and now they were about to explore distant shores and embark on great adventures overseas. The joy of promotion from the Second Division, secured in the summer of 1962, soon seemed like an embarrassing reminder of a time when the club had fallen on hard times. In the next three years, Shankly and Liverpool embraced a brave new world.

Fast-paced progress seemed to pervade every facet of life on Merseyside in the early Sixties. Liverpool was a humming, buzzing hub of change. The Beatles became a worldwide phenomenon and Harold Wilson, a Huddersfield-born MP for Huyton, the birthplace of Steven Gerrard, was elected the first grammar school-educated British prime minister. For the first time in thirteen years, the Conservative Party was ejected from government as the people turned their back on Tory grandees like Harold Macmillan and Sir Alec Douglas-Home. The composition of the ruling classes was altering in politics, in music and in football and Liverpool was in the vanguard of it all.

The early to mid-Sixties were a thrilling period in English football, a time when the First Division was bursting with great individual talents and strong-minded managers setting out on rivalries that would last for a decade. Matt Busby had rebuilt Manchester United after the Munich Air Crash and George Best began to emerge as one of the most talented players the country had ever seen. In 1961, Spurs under Bill Nicholson became the first team since Aston Villa in 1897 to win the Double, Leeds were being moulded by Don Revie, Everton were thriving under Harry Catterick and Chelsea bore the brash, hard, entertaining stamp of a young Tommy Docherty.

Then there was Liverpool. And Liverpool could match them all. In Shankly they had the most charismatic manager of the lot. In Peter Thompson they had a winger who was second only to Best in bewitching trickery, and in St John and Roger Hunt they had two goalscorers who were a match for any in the division. It was a golden age, an era when teams were massing for glory and engaging in titanic season-long struggles where only the strongest stayed standing.

Shankly had dragged Liverpool into that mix. He had changed things so fast at Anfield in his first three years in charge that Liverpool were ready to vie with the elite by the start of the 1962–63 season. He revolutionized the club's ambitions and upgraded its hopes and dreams. A few weeks after Liverpool had won the Second Division title, he went to a meeting of the club's shareholders. They were grateful for what he had achieved and so they presented him with cigarette boxes for all the players. 'Next time we come back here for presents,' Shankly told them, 'we will have won the Big League.' They looked at him as if they thought he was mad. But Shankly knew where his team was heading. 'My idea was to build Liverpool into a bastion of invincibility,' he said. 'Napoleon had that idea and he conquered the bloody world.'

To almost everyone else, the idea of Liverpool conquering the world seemed like an impossible dream. Most people dismissed it as Shankly bombast. Liverpool weren't even the best team in Liverpool in the early Sixties. In Liverpool's first season back in the top flight, Catterick's Everton won the title by 6 points from Spurs. Shankly disliked Catterick intensely. And he never stopped raging against the assumption that existed at the time that Everton were the city's natural aristocrats and Liverpool were destined to follow them like good forelock-tuggers.

Shankly was especially angry when he read an article by one of the club directors in the Liverpool programme soon after he arrived that suggested Everton would always have the upper hand. John Moores, the owner of the Littlewoods empire, was a leading shareholder in Liverpool but was chairman of Everton and ploughed most of his resources into Goodison Park. Liverpool was more of an investment. He wanted the club to do well. But not too well. He certainly did not envisage Liverpool as a real rival to Everton.

Everton had more seats, 21,000 to Liverpool's 11,000. They also had more money to spend on players, a better ground and a wealthier chairman. The odds were stacked in their favour. But soon after Shankly arrived, Moores installed one of his brightest Littlewoods executives, Eric Sawyer, as his representative on the Liverpool board. Sawyer changed the culture at Anfield and gave Shankly money to spend on top players. 'Putting Eric on the board at Liverpool,' Moores told Peter Robinson many years later, 'was the worst mistake I ever made in business. I should have made him a director at Everton.'

Sawyer was not quite Shankly's Roman Abramovich but he

did have a massive influence on his career. Before Sawyer arrived, Liverpool's directors had placed a ceiling of £12,000 on any bids Shankly might want to make for players. The average price of a leading player capable of excelling in the First Division was more than double that. Without Sawyer, Liverpool might just have been another stride in the journey for Shankly, another club where his talents would have been emasculated by an absence of financial backing.

It is difficult to believe now that we know how much he went on to achieve that anything could ever have stopped Shankly becoming one of the greatest and most revered characters in the history of the English game. But if Shankly had not made a breakthrough at Anfield, it is difficult to know whether he would ever have got a shot at a club that would give him the platform for success. Without Sawyer and the money he released, Shankly might have played out his time as a frustrated bit-part player.

No matter how talented he is, every manager needs financial backing if he is to win the big prizes. It doesn't matter how good the racing driver is if his car isn't quick enough. The claims that Chelsea bought the title in 2005 might be true, but they only did what Manchester United and Arsenal and Blackburn did in the decade before them: they entrusted a manager they believed in with the funds to go out and build a Championship-winning side. Jose Mourinho delivered for Abramovich. Shankly delivered for Sawyer.

Sawyer allowed Shankly to spend almost £70,000 on Ian St John and Ron Yeats in the summer of 1961. The dividend was immediate promotion. But Shankly did not rest. Two years later, he was badgering Sawyer for another £40,000 to spend on the flying Preston winger Peter Thompson, who was just twenty years old. The relationship between Sawyer and Shankly was based on mutual respect, but Sawyer was not afraid to warn Shankly of the consequences of failure. 'I'll back you on this, Bill,' he said, 'but if it doesn't work out, I'll sack you.'

There never really seemed much chance of things not working out for Shankly once he had taken Liverpool into the top flight, though. Now that he had the full financial backing of a club, the might of Shankly's force of character accelerated Liverpool's growth. The club united around him: supporters, players, even the board. It was as if everything flowed from his dynamism, his energy and his determination.

He made great communion with the masses who stood on Spion Kop, the most famous of all the behind-the-goal areas of terracing that dominated football grounds before the Taylor Report ordered that they be gelded by transforming them into rows of plastic seats. The Kop was named after a bloody battle in the Boer War in 1900 when British soldiers were cut down as they tried to force their way up a hill called Spion Kop. 'Spion Kop' is Afrikaans for 'Lookout Hill', and it seemed like a fitting tribute to name the great incline where the supporters gathered in its honour.

Supporters still stand on the Kop at Liverpool now, despite the pleadings and admonitions of the club. The seats are there but they don't use them. Except to rest their programme on, perhaps. It's as if the tradition of standing at football matches is buried way too deep in the psyche of many football supporters for them to submit to the comfort of sitting down. There are no surges any more. Nobody gets crushed against crowd barriers for a few seconds like they used to in the days before Hillsborough, when it seemed like an innocent delight, just part of the visceral experience of watching a game. But still they stand to watch as though they are clinging on to part of football's history.

And the Kop at Liverpool is still capable of producing a febrility of atmosphere no other English ground can match. To see the supporters standing there, their scarves held aloft in a great wall of red, in the spring of 2005 when Chelsea came to contest the second leg of a European Cup semi-final felt like travelling back thirty years or more in football culture. The noise was louder than anything at an English ground since the abolition of the terraces. John Terry, the Chelsea captain that night, admitted he was taken aback by the volume of the supporters' imprecations. A child of the all-seater era, he had never heard anything like it before.

It still wasn't close to the way it was when Shankly took Liverpool up to the First Division in 1962 and began the assault on the summit of English football. Things were changing fast in football culture then and Liverpool fans were among the first to realize the power of their own voices and the joy of collective wit in chanting. As Liverpool grew into a force in football, the Kop was there to provide the backing, a seething, swaying, sweating, gesticulating giant male-voice choir belting out the Beatles and the sounds of Merseybeat.

In the winter of 1963, as Shankly gathered his players for a tilt at the league title, Liverpool band Gerry and the Pacemakers released their version of 'You'll Never Walk Alone', a song written by Rogers and Hammerstein for the 1945 Broadway musical *Carousel*. It went to Number 1 in the charts and stayed there for five weeks. But even when it fell from the top spot, Liverpool fans continued to sing it with gusto. Other songs came and went but somehow 'You'll Never Walk Alone' endured and became a Liverpool anthem and the club's signature tune.

It's exclusive to them. The supporters of other English clubs recognize that and don't even try to appropriate it for themselves. It's part of the Liverpool legend now. Part of the call to arms, of the special heritage that sets the club apart from most of the rest. There are a couple of rivals, Newcastle United fans are associated with 'The Blaydon Races' and West Ham fans have been singing 'I'm Forever Blowing Bubbles' since the late 1920s, when an advertising campaign for soap hit the billboards. It featured a child blowing soap bubbles and the little boy was supposed to be a dead ringer for one of the West Ham players. The song has the same kind of pathos that 'You'll Never Walk Alone' possesses.

Shankly never tired of listening to the Liverpool anthem. It meant plenty to a man who had had his own share of struggling and wondering whether he would ever get to the end of the storm. The lyrics always moved him.

Shankly romanticized the people who roared out the song, too. To him, the denizens of the Kop were like soldiers in his Liverpool army. They reciprocated his faith in them. Their banners identified them as Shanks's Red Army. 'If you're a member of the Kop,' he said: 'you feel as if you are a member of a big society where you have got thousands of friends all round about you and they are united and loyal. I'm Scottish and the people of Scotland have got humour and spirit and I think it's the same in Liverpool. They are spirited, they have got life in them, they've got humour and I am the same as them.

'I identified myself with the people because the game belongs to the people and if you don't have the people on your side, then you've got nothing. I was a working-class boy. I was part of them. I wouldn't let anybody say anything against the Kop. They are my kind of people. They are arrogant, they are cocky and they are proud and that's what I wanted my team to be.'

Shankly could not summon quite the same enthusiasm for the club's directors. When Peter Robinson arrived at the club in 1965 after the suicide of Jimmy McInnes, Shankly loitered in the boardroom until the new secretary had finished his first meeting with the directors. Then, he ushered Robinson downstairs into his office and warned him that he must not trust them. Even when regular success came, Shankly had an uneasy relationship with the Liverpool board.

His socialist principles and his impoverished working-class upbringing explain that distrust. As a manager, Shankly never tired of trying somehow to improve the lot of the working men who followed the club, even if it was largely in the form of palliatives. 'My aim was to bring the people close to the club and the team and for them to be accepted as part of it,' Shankly said. Almost every player who worked under Shankly recalls witnessing him paying for train tickets for Liverpool fans at Euston when they were trying to get back north after the club had played in London. He was also insistent that any complimentary tickets he had went to genuine fans and he dispensed them like alms.

'My late grandfather was a Liverpool fan all his life,' Liverpool supporter Colin Watt said, recounting one story of Shankly largesse. 'Upon his retirement from the docks in the late 1960s, he received his season ticket. He was shocked to find that the club had moved him from his regular seat to one where he wasn't near the people he'd sat with for years and where he'd get wet when it rained. My uncle took him to Anfield to try and get his old seat back. He explained he had just retired after working down the docks as man and boy. The people in the ticket office were completely unsympathetic, telling him that his seat was no longer available.

'On leaving the office, he noticed Shanks walking in. "Bill, Bill," shouted my grandfather, and the Great Man came over. My grandfather explained the situation about his retirement, his time down the docks (working every night during the blitz) and a lifetime as a Liverpool fan. Shanks told him not to worry, to hang on and he'd sort it out. Five minutes later Shanks reappeared with the season ticket for my grandfather's seat, and said: "If you have any bother ever again, ask for me."'

Stories like that are legion. Conversely, Shankly was uncomfortable around privilege and old money. He felt a basic antipathy towards it and he railed against it. He lived in a modest, semi-detached house in the anonymity of suburbia. He was different to Ferguson like that. Ferguson has seemed easily seduced by the thrill of mixing with people who have more money than him. Shankly did not have that trait. He led a thrifty, almost frugal, lifestyle. He didn't drink. He didn't smoke. But his job compelled him to report to the board every week and discuss the progress of the club. He didn't have to

consult them on team selection – a relatively new development
for most managers at the time – but he did have to enter into
sometimes lengthy dialogue about the club's results and performances and his plans for the future. 'Bill absolutely hated
those meetings,' Peter Robinson said.

Shankly hated the recurring short-sightedness of the board,
too. He took any momentary reluctance to back a signing he
had proposed as a grievous slight. 'I used to fight and argue and
fight and argue and fight and argue until I thought "is it
worthwhile, all this fighting and arguing,"' Shankly said. 'Many
times during my career with Liverpool, I felt like saying "that
will do, I will get my jacket on and go." It is bad enough fighting
against the opposition to win points but the internal fights to
make people realise what we were working for took me close to
leaving many times.'

With Liverpool back in the First Division, though, Shankly
did not have to fight quite so hard. With Sawyer's help, he had
wrung support from the board and won promotion. Gradually,
things began to run much more smoothly, and the problems
that Shankly had to deal with as Liverpool continued to climb
towards the summit stemmed from issues arising from success
rather than failure. Players like Moran, who had been guaran-
teed a place when the club wallowed in mediocrity, found their
places under pressure. He, and others, resented the increasing
Scottish influence, personified by St John and Yeats.

Moran was a devotee of Shankly's teachings and a regular
in both the promotion side and the championship-winning team
of 1963–64 that stuck to the old 2-3-5 formation. He had made
his debut in 1952 but he was thirty when Liverpool won the
title, and the higher Liverpool climbed, the more vulnerable he
became. In the season after Liverpool became champions, Chris
Lawler came in on the right, Byrne moved to the left and Moran
was pushed out. The evolution of a side is bound to claim
casualties or else there would never be progress, and Moran
began to feel the tension of a man whose claims to a starting

place are being overtaken by others. A few years down the line, St John felt it, too.

'We played down at West Ham one season in the mid-Sixties,' Moran said, 'and when we got down to the ground, I found I'd been left out. I went outside to the main reception because I wanted to give a friend of mine a couple of complimentaries. There was a guy from the *Liverpool Echo* there. He wondered why I was getting changed so late and I told him I wasn't playing. Shanks played a young Scottish lad instead. I told the fellow from the *Echo* that I would have gone and got the train home from Euston if I'd had any money with me. He said: "Oh, don't do that." I went back in and sat on the touchline. I went to see Shanks in the Monday in his office but whenever you did that, you came out feeling ten foot tall because he'd gone on for so long about what a great player you were.'

St John and Yeats were both aware of the hostility towards them from the contingent of Liverpool-born players when they arrived from north of the border. St John called it an 'Anfield mafia' and it consisted of Jimmy Melia, Ronnie Moran and Johnny Morrissey. On a pre-season trip to Czechoslovakia, St John overheard Moran referring to him and Yeats as 'the Scottish bastards'. Late in 1962, the problems came to a head when Melia kicked out at St John during a practice match on the flat sands of Southport beach. Shankly had to separate them and St John spent the coach journey back to Melwood hurling threats at Melia. When they arrived at the training ground, St John told Melia to follow him to the gym where they could settle their differences with their fists. Melia refused and St John felt in that moment that the domination of the Anfield mafia was broken.

The first season back in Division One was hard work. Liverpool did not start well. They lost their opening game at home to Blackpool and scraped a draw against Everton at Goodison with a late equalizer from Hunt. Morrissey, who had been sold to Everton against Shankly's wishes, scored for Catterick's side. Consecutive defeats to Leicester, West Brom and Burnley at the end of October shoved Liverpool down towards the relegation zone and it began to seem as if they might be destined for an immediate return to the shadows of the Second Division.

Shankly acted fast. He promoted goalkeeper Tommy Lawrence from the reserves for the West Brom game, ousting Jim Furnell, and paid £20,000 to buy the creative midfielder Willie Stevenson from Glasgow Rangers. Stevenson was a neat, clever passer of the ball, a man whose pretensions to sophistication were not confined to the pitch. 'He never quite said it,' St John said of Stevenson, 'but as he lit up a fine cigar and sipped a good brandy, the implication was that the rest of us were pretty much peasants.'

The changes worked. In fact, they were a dramatic success. After the defeat to Burnley, Liverpool won nine consecutive games, a sequence that lifted them out of trouble and banished the spectre of relegation. They finished the season in eighth place and reached the semi-finals of the FA Cup against Leicester. They lost 1–0, beaten not so much by the winning goal from winger Mike Stringfellow but by an inspired performance from Leicester goalkeeper Gordon Banks.

Shankly felt he was close to having a side that could challenge for the title, and in the summer of 1963 he bought Peter Thompson to replace Alan A'Court on the left wing. A'Court was a fine player who had been capped by England but he only played once more for Liverpool. Thompson was the last piece in the jigsaw, and even though Liverpool lost four of their first nine games in the 1963–64 season, two goals from Ian Callaghan crashed them through the psychological barrier of beating champions Everton at the end of September. After the turn of the year, they climbed fast up the table.

With Thompson and Callaghan on either side, St John dropped deeper to bolster central midfield with Stevenson and

Gordon Milne. St John scored 21 goals that season. 'He could have been the best midfield player of all time if he had been used there regularly,' Shankly said. There was no question of moving Hunt back, though. He scored 31 of Liverpool's 92 goals that triumphant season. Wolves, Stoke, Sheffield United and Ipswich all had 6 goals stuck past them at Anfield. Alf Arrowsmith played enough games in attack to score 15 goals as well.

Liverpool won the title with three games to spare and finished 4 points ahead of second-place Manchester United. Shankly was nonchalant when he talked about how he had motivated his team for the title run-in: 'At Easter, I said "Right boys, we've jogged along nicely, let's go out and get it going. Never mind anything that happens, off we go." We won seven games on the trot, running through teams and tearing them to pieces, and we rounded things off by drubbing Arsenal 5–0 at Anfield.'

There was a carnival celebration at Anfield after that merry dispatch of Arsenal on a sunny April afternoon. But there is a curious lack of emotion in the recollections of that triumph in the accounts of the protagonists. In his autobiography, Shankly mentions it almost in passing. And in his own autobiography, St John spends more time talking about his post-Championship celebration in the Maid of Erin pub. It was a momentous day, the first time Liverpool had won the title since 1947, but it had been done before and therefore the triumph of doing it again could never match the fervour that flooded over the club when it won the FA Cup for the first time a year later.

In April 1964, winning the league felt like a huge achievement, but it was so quickly superseded by the melodrama of the FA Cup victory and the European Cup semi-final with Internazionale of Milan that by the mid-1970s it had been relegated to a happy footnote in the hierarchy of great memories. It was as if it was a foundation stone for the glorious architecture that was to spring up around it. On a more prosaic level, the title was eventually won so comfortably that season that the clinching of the Championship was shorn of much of its suspense and excitement.

It was a time of new challenges when the football world was changing and expanding. European competition was the new horizon and there was an exotic thrill about exploring new lands. Winning the league in 1964 bought Liverpool the passport to embark on their first adventure overseas, but as the years wore on the title victory was increasingly seen as a means to an end. It was swamped by the mission to end Liverpool's FA Cup curse and the romance of the club's attempts to conquer the best that the Continent had to offer.

The pre-season tour to America in the summer of 1964 ruined any chance Liverpool had of retaining the title. It exhausted the players and turned Shankly's side into a cup team for the season ahead, a team that could turn it on when the occasion demanded it but which was incapable of winning consistently. The low point of the league campaign was a 4–0 defeat to Everton at Goodison which sent Shankly scurrying home to scour the oven in his wife's kitchen, his traditional method of working out the anger and disappointment that overcame him after results like that. Shankly won the title three times at Liverpool but never once did his team retain the Championship, an achievement that in the modern era has come to be seen as a mark of real class and which Arsène Wenger, to Ferguson's great delight, has never managed at Arsenal.

But in 1964–65 Liverpool supporters forgot about their labours in the league as they were transported into a land of fantasy by the club's exploits in the cups. Liverpool's first European Cup match was away to Reykjavik in Iceland on 17 August 1964, a match they won 5–0. They won the return leg 6–1. The second leg at Anfield was so one-sided the Kop cheered the Icelanders' every touch and booed when Liverpool had the ball.

The second-round tie, though, was a different story. Liverpool were paired against Anderlecht, the champions of Belgium and one of the best sides in Europe. Shankly went to watch them play against Standard Liège one Sunday afternoon and returned full of foreboding. 'I thought we had a terrible match on our hands,' he said. Belgium had just taught England a footballing lesson in a 2–2 draw at Wembley and Shankly feared Anderlecht might be too much for a team as inexperienced as Liverpool were in European competition. 'Belgium murdered England,' Shankly said. 'When I came out of Wembley, I said to Joe Mercer: "Christ Almighty, how do you beat these?" When I got back to Anfield, of course, I said I didn't rate them.'

As he wrestled with his worries, Shankly hit on one idea he thought might even the odds a little. Liverpool had played in a kit of red shirts, white shorts and white socks, but Shankly decided his side would look bigger if they switched to an all-red kit. It would be impossible to make that change at such short notice now, of course. The shirt manufacturers would have a collective coronary and the kit sponsors would rip up their contracts. But things were simpler then. Shankly's only precaution was to get Ron Yeats to model the new kit first.

He dressed him up in it and got him to walk out on to the pitch at a deserted Anfield while Shankly sized him up. 'Jesus Christ,' Shankly said as Yeats walked up the steps into the light, 'you look enormous.' After the game, Shankly went home to his wife, full of enthusiasm for his innovation. 'You know something,' he said to her, 'tonight I went out on to Anfield and for the first time there was a glow like a fire was burning.'

Perhaps it was the kit, but something spooked Anderlecht. Liverpool overran them at Anfield and beat them 3–0. Tommy Smith, who was nineteen, was given his first chance to impress on the big stage, and together with Milne they choked the influence of Anderlecht's most influential player, Paul Van Himst. St John put Liverpool ahead inside ten minutes and Hunt scored a second before half-time. Yeats, resplendent in the kit he had modelled, put the tie out of reach with a third in the second half. Shankly had rubbished Anderlecht to his players before the match, but when they walked back into the dressing room after the final whistle, he was playing a different tune. 'You've just beaten one of the best sides in Europe.'

If the semi-final against Inter Milan later that season was packed with more drama and more atmosphere, the win over Anderlecht was the first of the big European nights at Anfield. 'It felt like a coming of age,' Chris Lawler said. Liverpool won the second leg in Brussels, too. Hunt got the winner in the last minute to clinch a 1–0 victory. Liverpool were in the third round and the European establishment began to wonder whether a new power was emerging in the game.

Liverpool played Cologne in the quarter-finals and fought out two goalless draws. In between, the first attempt to stage the second leg at Anfield was postponed because of a snowstorm just before kick-off. The only action Shankly watched that night was a snowball fight on the pitch between supporters from the Kop and the Anfield Road end. There were no penalties to settle a stalemate, so the teams played a third match in Rotterdam to decide the outcome. That ended in a draw, too, so the referee tossed a coin to decide who would advance to the European Cup semi-finals. The first time he hurled it into the air, it landed on its edge in the mud and the referee had to repeat the process. The second time, Yeats called correctly. Liverpool were through.

Cologne were inconsolable. 'Their number three was crying like a baby,' Shankly said, 'so I gave him a hanky.'

If a manager said that now, he would be derided as cruel. If Ferguson said it, it would be isolated as an example of Manchester United's insufferable arrogance. But Shankly got away with it. He got away with all the jibes about Everton and the mockery of his opponents. He got away with the insistence that Liverpool had no equal, wherever they finished in the league. The fact that he lived and worked in a different era to Ferguson, when the media did not seize on every saying and every taunt, explains part of that, but it is not the whole story. The crux was that there was a vulnerability about Shankly that Ferguson has never possessed. Jose Mourinho does not have it, either, and he too has been heavily criticized for his arrogance and his lack of grace. With Shankly, there was vulnerability, there was relentless enthusiasm and there was humour. It was a winning combination.

Liverpool were to be cheated against Inter in the semi-finals, but they would not be denied in the FA Cup. There was only one scare. Shankly missed the fourth-round tie at home to Stockport County to go and watch Cologne in Germany. He left Paisley in charge, presuming the Fourth Division side would pose little problem. When he got back to Euston station after returning to London by boat and rail, he asked the porters if there had been any cup upsets. He was told Peterborough had beaten Arsenal. Then he caught sight of a newspaper and saw the result from Anfield.

Liverpool and Stockport had drawn 1–1. Shankly brandished the paper at the porter in admonishment. 'What do you call that if it's not a shock?' he said. Liverpool won the replay at Edgeley Park and then beat Leicester and Chelsea to book their place in the final. A wider world beckoned and the old days when Bill Shankly had arrived at Anfield to find a ground without running water and a decrepit club mired in apathy seemed like another country.

14: Ferguson and the Glory of Gothenburg

In the autumn of 1980 when Alex Ferguson was still basking in the glory of prising apart the Old Firm's domination of Scottish football by leading Aberdeen to the title the season before, he and his assistant, Archie Knox, flew south to Liverpool to do some homework on the team they had been drawn to meet in the second round of the European Cup.

They turned up at Anfield to watch Bob Paisley's all-conquering side play Middlesbrough and were treated with great courtesy. A few minutes before the game, they were shown to their seats in the directors' box. Ferguson was delighted, although a little overawed, to find himself sitting next to Bill Shankly. It was the first time the two men had met and Ferguson was flattered when Shankly, who was in the last year of his life, heaped praise upon him for the job he was doing at Aberdeen. The pleasantries over, Shankly went straight to the kernel.

'So you're down here to have a look at our great team?' Shankly said.

Ferguson and Knox nodded.

'Aye,' said Shankly, 'they all try that.'

Ferguson tried. And failed. Liverpool were in their pomp then. They were a majestic team, packed with talents like Graeme Souness, Kenny Dalglish, Ray Clemence, Ray Kennedy, Alan Hansen and Terry McDermott. Aberdeen were beaten 1–0 at Pittodrie by a goal from McDermott and then humbled 4–0 in the return at Anfield. This time, it was an own goal from Miller and further strikes from Neal, Dalglish and Hansen that did the damage. Seven months later, Liverpool won the European Cup for the third time when they beat Real Madrid in the final.

'All we could do was try to ensure that we learned from painful exposure to proven masters of the techniques and discipline required in European competition,' Ferguson said. 'Above all, our players had to appreciate that there is no forgiveness in such games for teams who surrender possession cheaply.'

Despite that setback, Aberdeen's title triumph in 1979–80, Ferguson's second season at Pittodrie, had brought him a measure of respect he had not enjoyed before. It legitimized him. It turned him from a man perceived as a bully, someone who was all about sound and fury signifying nothing, into a figure of substance. But he was not satisfied with one title win. In fact, his success seemed to intensify his hunger.

He knew the hard part would be moving the club forward rather than falling back. Predators started to circle. Steve Archibald was sold to Spurs for £800,000. Ferguson himself was approached by Wolves and Sheffield United. He travelled down to Molineux to listen to what the board had to say but he was less than impressed. He knew there was much more to come at Pittodrie.

After the high of the previous season, the 1980–81 campaign was an anticlimax. Aberdeen finished a distant second to Celtic in the league and were brushed aside by Dalglish and co in the European Cup. The next season, the European experience improved when Aberdeen began their Uefa Cup campaign by beating the holders, Bobby Robson's Ipswich Town, in the first round. They squeezed past Arges Pitesti next, although not without Ferguson throwing the most spectacular tantrum of his managerial career at half-time of the second leg, but in the third round they were beaten by SV Hamburg. At home, they missed out on the title to Celtic again.

But they made an important psychological breakthrough in the Scottish Cup. The club had developed a habit of losing finals, but in May 1982 Aberdeen crushed Ferguson's old club, Rangers, 4–1 in the Final. They had beaten Celtic in the fourth round, too, and the victory was ample compensation for missing out on the league. When Dundee United took the league title the following season, it seemed the age of the New Firm had dawned on Scottish football.

The 1982–83 season was Ferguson's best north of the border because it brought him not just domestic glory in the Scottish Cup again but international recognition, too. When Aberdeen beat Bayern Munich in a classic Cup Winners' Cup quarter-final and then overcame Real Madrid in the Final, suddenly the magnitude of what Ferguson had achieved at Pittodrie was impossible to ignore. Their victory over Madrid in Gothenburg was one of those nights where English football supporters did that thing that infuriates Scots everywhere and adopted Aberdeen as a British team.

Until then, Aberdeen's success was vulnerable to being dismissed as relatively meaningless in the wider context of the European game. Ferguson's detractors could argue that Aberdeen were merely the best side in a desperately weak Scottish league and that they had taken advantage of a brief period when Celtic and Rangers were both in transition.

Those arguments were flawed anyway, but once Aberdeen won a European trophy, nobody could deny that Ferguson had created something extraordinary in the isolated Scottish city. In an era when English clubs were used to monopolizing British success in European competition, Aberdeen usurped their position for a season with a series of performances remembered as one of the classic club campaigns of recent decades.

There was a romance about what Aberdeen did because it was inevitable that they would be perceived as the underdog. They had only just emerged from the shadow of the Old Firm and those who had not seen them play assumed that they had reached their glass ceiling when they won the league title for the first time. Their Cup Winners' Cup run ruined that theory. They eased their way past Sion, Dinamo Tirana and Lech Poznan before running into the mighty Bayern in the last eight. Bayern had won the European Cup three times in succession in the mid-Seventies, and even if they had declined since then, they had still reached the Final again in 1982 only to lose to Aston Villa. Before they met Aberdeen, they gave Spurs a football lesson in an early round of the Cup Winners' Cup. They were still a formidable side with an intimidating pedigree and players of the calibre of Paul Breitner, Karl-Heinz Rummenigge and Klaus Augenthaler.

Aberdeen earned a goalless draw at Munich's Olympiastadion with a fiercely disciplined performance, but the weight of expectation when the teams played the second leg a fortnight later almost crushed them. Augenthaler put the German side ahead after 10 minutes with a thunderous free kick, Neale Simpson equalized, but then early in the second half it seemed the tie was over when Hans Pflugler volleyed Bayern back into the lead.

Aberdeen needed to score twice to have a chance of reaching the last four, so Ferguson was bold. He took off right back Stuart Kennedy, who had been struggling against Pflugler, and switched Doug Rougvie into his position, bringing on John McMaster to restore composure to midfield. Aberdeen improved, but with 13 minutes remaining they still trailed.

Ferguson gambled again. He took off midfielder Neil Simpson and threw on an extra attacker, John Hewitt. Straight away, Aberdeen won a free kick on the right side of the Bayern area. Gordon Strachan and McMaster pretended to bump into each other as they attempted to take the free kick and then staged a mock argument. Bayern lost concentration, Strachan whipped in a curling ball and McLeish headed an equalizer.

Thirty seconds later, Aberdeen were ahead. McMaster played a ball into the box, Eric Black headed it goalwards and when the goalkeeper parried it, Hewitt prodded it over the line. Ferguson's two substitutions had worked out spectacularly well.

They made him look like a genius. Aberdeen hung on for 12 nerve-racking minutes. Then they were in the semi-finals.

They beat Waterschei comfortably to progress to the Final, but lost Kennedy to a bad injury that finished his career. Ferguson admired Kennedy. 'He had real pride and belief in himself,' he said, 'and was quite simply one of the strongest and finest characters I have come across in football.' In a rare show of compassion and sentimentality that he has never repeated, Ferguson named Kennedy among the substitutes for the Final, even though he could hardly walk, let alone play.

In the run-up to the Final, which was to take place in Gothenburg, Sweden, Ferguson astonished the players with his demeanour. They expected him to be unbearably tense and irritable but he seemed more relaxed and good-humoured than he had ever been. He played jokes. He sent a spoof itinerary to the players' wives informing them that they would be staying in chalets and that they would have to take sleeping bags and other basic camping equipment with them to Sweden. It suckered them. For a couple of days, the wives were outraged. But they laughed when the scam was revealed. The players were mightily relieved.

Ferguson invited the great former Celtic manager Jock Stein to travel with the official club party to Gothenburg and leant on him for a few tips on how to handle the big occasion. Stein told him to present the Real Madrid manager, Alfredo di Stefano, one of the greatest footballers there has ever been, with a bottle of finest Scotch whisky the day before the game to make him think Ferguson and Aberdeen were just grateful to have made it to the Final.

Ferguson got the preparations for the match just right, too. For a start, he managed to banish his cough. He chose a hotel in a hamlet in the wooded countryside outside Gothenburg as a base so that the players were protected from the excitement that was building in the city as Aberdeen fans began to arrive in their thousands. He did everything he could to keep the minds of the players divorced from the scale of the occasion. Scottish clubs had only ever tasted success in European competition twice. Stein's Celtic had won the European Cup in 1967 and Rangers won the Cup Winners' Cup in 1972. That was it. There was an enormous amount of pressure on Aberdeen, but Ferguson did not let his players feel it.

On the eve of the game, there was a quiz at the team hotel and a game of Scrabble that ended in a fierce debate over spellings. Earlier in the day, Ferguson and Archie Knox had played the fool, challenging each other to a three-mile race to a nearby castle and back. 'The players thought we were off our heads,' Ferguson said, 'but it was all done just to keep everybody active.'

'By that time,' Aberdeen striker Mark McGhee said, 'we had played in a lot of European games so we had plenty of experience of that kind of thing. It wasn't new to us. It didn't seem much different from any other game. Fergie never really spoke about Real Madrid in the build-up. He totally played that down. We never gave Real Madrid a second thought. It was only when we got back to Aberdeen and we saw how people at home were feeling about it that we began to think "maybe this is bigger than we realised". That was a core part of the success: Fergie managed to keep it under control about who we were playing.'

Despite the presence of Di Stefano at the helm, Madrid were not the team of old. Nor were they a side even of the flawed beauty of Zidane, Ronaldo, Raul and Beckham. They had good players like Uli Stielike, Johnny Metgod, Santillana and Vicente del Bosque, later a successful manager at the club, but it was not one of the great Madrid teams. Their fans didn't think so either. Only two or three thousand made the journey to the Ullevi Stadium, compared with 15,000 who had travelled by sea and by air from Aberdeen.

It rained incessantly during the game. Aberdeen took an early lead when Eric Black scored from close range after Strachan had pulled a corner back to the edge of the box for Alex

McLeish to head goalwards. But Madrid were level before half-time when a backpass from McLeish slowed up on the sodden surface and Santillana stole in to take the ball round Leighton, who brought him down. Juanito converted the penalty.

Aberdeen were the stronger, better side but the game lapsed into extra-time and Ferguson began to suspect that Real were happy to take their chances in the lottery of a penalty shoot-out. He had already brought on John Hewitt for the injured Eric Black, but Hewitt was playing so badly that Ferguson considered substituting the substitute. He was glad he didn't.

Eight minutes from the end of extra time, Peter Weir played a cleverly weighted ball down the left wing to McGhee. McGhee ran at his marker and beat him on the outside. He looked up and crossed towards Hewitt in the centre. The Madrid goalkeeper, Agustin, came a couple of steps off his line and seemed to be about to intercept it. But he flung himself at it and missed. Even before Agustin had hit the floor, Hewitt had headed the ball into the empty net.

When Real got a free kick on the edge of the area in the dying minutes, Weir prayed. 'Please God, don't let them score,' he yelled into the night air. When the final whistle went, there was an explosion of joy from the Aberdeen supporters. As the team coach pulled away from the stadium after the players had celebrated for an age on the pitch, Leighton stared at Aberdeen supporters cavorting in a fountain. 'They probably reasoned they could not get any wetter,' he said.

A couple of days later, Ferguson and McGhee went down to the quayside to greet a couple of thousand fans who were arriving back from Gothenburg on a ship called the *St Clair*. The two men took the cup with them and shook the hand of every supporter as they disembarked.

There was a parade in Aberdeen. More than 200,000 people came to greet the team as they rode an open-top bus down Union Street. It was a momentous occasion. Even though Martin O'Neill's Celtic made it to the Uefa Cup Final in 2003, they lost in Seville to Jose Mourinho's FC Porto. Aberdeen remain the last Scottish club to have won a European trophy.

That triumph was the high-water mark of Ferguson's eight-year reign at Aberdeen. It was bound to be. Short of winning the European Cup, there was no way to exceed the thrill of conquering a new frontier. There were other great achievements in the mid-1980s. In many ways, the team went from strength to strength.

The three years after Gothenburg were Ferguson's most successful domestically. In 1984 Aberdeen won the domestic double of league and cup and added the European Super Cup by beating SV Hamburg. In 1985 they retained the title, a feat that gave Ferguson an immense amount of satisfaction. And in the spring of 1986 they won the Scottish Cup again, the fourth time they had clinched the trophy under Ferguson.

But after the victory in Gothenburg, more and more tensions began to creep into the Aberdeen squad. It was inevitable that leading players would start to receive offers from elsewhere that it would be hard for them to turn down. The same was true of Ferguson. In fact, only a week after the victory over Real Madrid he was offered the manager's job at Rangers.

Rangers was the club he had supported as a boy. The tenement building where his family had lived near the banks of the Clyde was only a few hundred yards from Ibrox. He had watched the team and he had gone on to fulfil his childhood dream by playing for them, too. Only the dream turned sour and he was widely regarded as a failure at Rangers. He left under a cloud. He had plenty of unfinished business if he felt like taking up the challenge.

Many of his friends urged him to take the job. It seemed like a natural fit, the job he had been destined to do. They felt it would give him closure on his unhappy playing days there, and in particular the way in which he was hustled out of the club. Most people assumed that Ferguson would jump at the chance to go back home.

But he turned it down. Part of his reasoning was that he did not want to play any part in ousting the existing manager, John Greig. Ferguson counted Greig as a friend and had also admired him when Greig was Rangers captain. But sensitivity to Greig's position was not the whole story. Ferguson's record suggests that if he had wanted the Rangers job, he would have found a way to justify taking it to himself. He did not, for instance, appear to harbour too many concerns about taking Ron Atkinson's job at Old Trafford.

Ferguson was also concerned that he might run into problems at Ibrox with the club's policy of refusing to sign Catholics. He felt he had not been treated fairly when he was a player at Rangers and he blamed his ordeal in part on entrenched attitudes towards his wife's Catholic background.

There were some bigots at Rangers who still frowned on so-called mixed marriages, and Ferguson did not want to expose Cathy to another battle based on religion. He also realized that if he did not have the stomach to challenge the club's policy on refusing to sign Catholics, his chances of buying the players he wanted would be cut in half. He had plenty of Catholic friends, too, and he worried that they might take offence if he aligned himself with Rangers' Protestant-only transfer policy. It was left to Graeme Souness to smash that policy by signing Mo Johnston in 1989.

Most of all, Ferguson was concerned that he would not have the same level of control over the job at Ibrox that he enjoyed at Aberdeen. Everything worked smoothly at Pittodrie as far as he was concerned. Nothing happened without him knowing about it well in advance. He had an excellent relationship with Dick Donald and he had a fine side in place. By the time he made his decision to turn Rangers down, he had made up his mind that Ibrox was too big a gamble.

His problems at Pittodrie were limited to trying to stop complacency creeping into his side and keeping his medal-laden team together. Ferguson was willing to achieve that by any means necessary. Usually, it involved bullying. Often, he tried to head off a player's move by threatening them with missing an important match.

Ten days after victory in Gothenburg, the relaxed Alex Ferguson the players had seen in the build-up to the Cup Winners' Cup Final had already been replaced by a man who seemed to them to have sunk to a new low of petulance and gracelessness. Aberdeen beat Rangers in the Scottish Cup Final at Hampden Park but Ferguson was disgusted with their performance.

At the end of 90 minutes, with the game goalless, Ferguson had prepared Leighton for extra time by giving him a withering stare and telling him he was Rangers' best player. Eric Black got the winner in extra-time but Ferguson was livid. Even as Willie Miller was lifting Aberdeen's second trophy of the season, Ferguson was denouncing his team live on television. He said they were the luckiest team in the world and he called them 'disgraceful'. 'I'm not going to accept that from any Aberdeen team,' he said. When Dick Donald brought a crate of champagne into the dressing room afterwards, Ferguson told them not to uncork it

He said Miller and McLeish had won the game on their own and that nobody else deserved any credit. 'I'll be looking for nine new players next season,' he said. The idea of cutting the players a bit of slack because many of them were running on empty after their heroics that season didn't occur to him. The coach journey back to St Andrews, where they were staying the night, took place in silence.

'We were stunned,' Leighton said. 'It seemed incredible that we were being lambasted by our boss at a time when we should have been savouring another victory. We went back to St Andrews that night but some of the players were so disgusted with the manager's reaction that they stayed away from what was supposed to be a celebratory party.

'There was a dreadful feeling of anticlimax within our ranks.

I've never since known anything quite like it. Ferguson knew he'd gone well over the top when he saw the newspaper head-lines the next day and apologized to us. The damage was done, however, and we did not feel like forgiving him.'

Aberdeen won the league the following season but the campaign was disfigured by running battles between Ferguson and a trio of players who intended to leave Pittodrie. Strachan let Ferguson know early that he would not sign a new contract but he contrived to make an awful mess of his departure by signing a variety of agreements with Cologne, Verona and Manchester United.

Ferguson had known nothing about the pre-contract Stra-chan had signed with Cologne and was scathing about his conduct. 'Though I always felt there was a cunning streak in Strachan,' he said, 'I had never imagined that he could pull such a stroke on me, not after everything I had done for him.' In the end, Ferguson and United untangled the paperwork and he went to Old Trafford.

Doug Rougvie, another player who had given long service to the club, left amid even more acrimony. Rougvie had received an offer from Chelsea that would double the wages he was on at Aberdeen and he asked Ferguson if there was any chance of Aberdeen matching it. Ferguson said Rougvie flew to London and signed for Chelsea before he had a chance to put his question to the directors.

Rougvie's recollection is reported to be different. 'When we met, he told me to fuck off,' Rougvie said. 'He kicked me out of his office and, on the following week, wouldn't let me inside the Pittodrie door. He slaughtered me in the press but I didn't respond. I must admit, I was hurt, though. My heart was at Pittodrie and I didn't want to leave. I have every respect for Mr Ferguson as a football manager but not for the way he managed people.'

The transfer that sheds the brightest light of all on Fergu-son's modus operandi, however, was McGhee's move to SV Hamburg, also at the end of the 1983–84 season. McGhee had made up his mind that he wanted to begin a new challenge the following season, but when Aberdeen made it to the Final of the Scottish Cup that year, Ferguson called all the players together.

'Three weeks before the Final,' McGhee said, 'he had us all in and he said: "Right, anybody who is not signing a new contract and staying, come in tomorrow and tell me and they're not playing in the Final. Except Gordon Strachan, because a year ago, I agreed with him that he could leave the club. But any of the rest of you, come in and see me and you're not playing."

'I went straight in the next day and I said: "I'm not staying." So he says: "Well, you're not playing." I said, "Fine." Three days later, he called me in. He said he had been thinking about it and he knew I wouldn't let him down and so I would be playing. I said, "Fine." Then, he gave me a long lecture about how the condition was that I mustn't get distracted by talking to agents or anything like that. He wanted me to save all that until after the season had finished. I said: "Fine." '

Despite the way Ferguson has treated him, McGhee will still not talk about what happened next, but other sources at Aberdeen have confirmed the story. A few weeks later, his doorbell rang and McGhee was alarmed to find the agent who was organizing his move to Hamburg standing on his doorstep. McGhee was concerned that Ferguson would find out about the visit and he was curious how the agent had found his house in the first place. It turned out that Ferguson had given him a lift.

It is to Ferguson's immense credit, though, that even though his side had been stripped of its three leading attacking talents, Aberdeen won the title again the next season with a record points tally. Ferguson had brought in Billy Stark, Frank McDougall, Stewart McKimmie and Tommy McQueen to replace Strachan, McGhee and Rougvie, and all had fitted in seamlessly.

The next season, Ferguson's last full season at Aberdeen, the club finally won the League Cup and added another Scottish Cup to their manager's trophy tally. But there was an unmistakable sense of progress slowing down. Ferguson had been appalled and disgusted when Strachan came to him the previous year and told him he was bored. But in his autobiography, Ferguson admitted that much the same state of mind had begun to afflict him in his last months at Pittodrie.

'My thoughts were dwelling increasingly on a change of some kind,' he said. 'I was finding that the afternoons at Pittodrie were becoming a bit of a drag. The club was run so well that the challenge for me had diminished and I can honestly say that I was feeling the need for the painful stimulation of again having to build a successful team.'

Ferguson had also grown distracted by his duties with Scotland. He had taken temporary charge of his country after Jock Stein collapsed and died at Ninian Park in September 1985. The caretaker job meant a long trip to Melbourne midway through the 1985–86 season for part of a two-legged play-off against Australia which Scotland won.

But Aberdeen suffered in his absence. Ferguson was particularly unhappy with the contribution of his latest assistant, Willie Garner, while he was away. He had come to believe that Garner was too laid back and too friendly with the players to be of real use to him. So Ferguson sacked him and brought back Archie Knox.

Ferguson said later: 'I'm glad that Willie has not harboured any grudge towards me.'

Garner said later: 'I'd just bought a new house, I had a young family and all of a sudden I had no job. I really detested the guy at the time.'

A couple of months later, Fergie flew south.

15: Shankly and the Building of the Boot Room

In the spring of 1960, a few months after he had become manager of Liverpool, Bill Shankly paid his first visit to Toxteth. It was the toughest, most deprived area of the inner city then, just as it is now, a home for migrant labour flooding in from Ireland and North Wales to seek jobs on the docks and for local workers from families whose fathers and sons had been stevedores for generations. Thirty years later, its terraces and tenements would yield up one of Liverpool's greatest strikers, Robbie Fowler, and now, right at the beginning of his fifteen year reign, Shankly made straight for the warren of streets perched on the bluffs above the Mersey to clinch his first significant signing.

There was something symbolic about his short journey from Anfield to the city's working-class heartland. A great blossoming was about to take place in Liverpool. Men and women who were to become cultural icons were still hidden in anonymity but were beginning to push their way to the surface. A girl called Cilla White, who was playing small halls in Tuebrook, was about to change into Cilla Black. A band that was was experimenting with names like Johnny and the Moondogs and the Quarry Men and that played one early gig on the back of a truck in Toxteth would soon turn into the Beatles. Ritchie Starkey, who lived in Admiral Grove, round the corner from the beautiful façade of the Empress Pub and close to the route Shankly took that afternoon, had just transformed himself into Ringo Starr.

Shankly drove to Toxteth in a Ford Corsair. It was flashy for the day. He might have been a thrifty, modest man in some ways but he was not averse to displays of grandeur. He was always immaculately dressed. In time, he would have all his suits made by Liverpool tailor Denis Newton, who boasted Jimmy Tarbuck and Frankie Vaughan as customers and whose clothes were thought to be the height of sophistication. Sometimes Shankly, who owned a modest Austin A40 when he first arrived in Liverpool, would borrow a more expensive car if he wanted to impress a young footballer he wanted to sign. He liked to leap out from behind the wheel of what he called 'a big car'.

When he signed Ian St John from Motherwell in the summer of the following year, he tried the same ruse. 'He swept into Fir Park like a one-man boarding party in a Rolls-Royce he had borrowed from a Liverpool director,' St John said. 'He was a sharp dresser – he told me his father was a tailor and he got his ties, which invariably had the colour red as a significant element, from Germany – and was filled with a quite amazing urgency.'

It is funny to think of that now in an era when reserve-team players can afford the cars of kings. Kieran Richardson, a bit-part player at Manchester United, was planning to buy a Bentley Continental until Roy Keane suggested in forthright terms that he might be getting a little bit ahead of himself. The basic point remains: it would be impossible for a manager to impress a modern player with a smart car, but back at the start of the Sixties, Shankly's Ford Corsair was still capable of acting as a recruitment tool.

As Shankly drew up to the kerb of Caryl Gardens, a tenement building in Caryl Street, a crowd of kids gathered round, and from a downstairs window Shankly's target smiled at the commotion. Ian Callaghan, who was to go on to win every club honour in the game and play for Liverpool more times than any other footballer, was a kid himself then. Just turned seventeen, he was serving an apprenticeship as a central heating engineer with a city centre firm called Bernard and Partners, and since Shankly's arrival at Anfield he had found himself promoted to the reserves.

Callaghan and his parents lived on the ground floor of Caryl Gardens. They didn't have to share a landing like the residents five floors up, but then neither did they have a view of the dirty river gliding silently past below or of the merchant ships queuing to unload their cargo at the Brunswick Dock, a couple of hundred yards away. The docks were thriving then, and so was Toxteth. Go there now and it looks as if it's dying. It looks like an urban wasteland despite the halting attempts that were made to regenerate it after the riots there in the 1980s.

Caryl Gardens was demolished long ago, and many of the houses that have taken its place have their windows boarded up with plywood. Shadows of people hover in the doorways of derelict pubs like the Wellington, mobile phones pressed to their ears. Parts of Toxteth are home to Liverpool's underclass now, and the dock buildings have been converted into smart new business parks full of people in open-plan offices staring at computer screens.

When Shankly drove there, past the looming hulk of the Anglican cathedral, Toxteth was raw, rough and tough, but vibrant. An overhead railway took the dockers from their homes to their jobs on the docks that crowded the riverside at all points from Garston in the south to Seaforth in the north. Callaghan and his mates used the overhead railway, which was torn down in the early Sixties, to travel down to the Pier Head and catch the ferry over to New Brighton for an afternoon out.

Callaghan's father had served in the Navy, and even though he had come out of the service he started working on the massive cruise ship the *Empress of Australia*, which Callaghan would watch surging out to sea from the mouth of the Mersey, taking his father away for weeks on end. The family was not poor but Callaghan's parents had been sceptical about a football career, especially as their son was learning a trade with a reputable firm. They needed persuading that he should sign professional forms. Shankly persuaded them.

'He came down in the big car,' Callaghan said. 'He called it "the big car". I remember seeing it outside the flats and all the kids gathering round. He came in and saw my mum and dad. I went out of the room but I knew immediately he had gone that they had been impressed by him. Everyone was impressed by him. He told them he'd look after me. He told them he'd feed me up with steaks. And he said he thought I could make it. My mum and dad forgot about the apprenticeship. They said I could sign and that was it.

'Shanks was always absolutely brilliant with me. Always, right from then until the day he retired. I don't know whether he was influenced by coming to see my mum and dad and the background I came from. We didn't have a lot of money and I think he could see that. I think that did influence him. I was an honest player, too. I never gave him any trouble. I was never late, all that kind of carry on. I don't think I ever asked for a rise. I think he appreciated that. There was a paternal attitude about the way he treated me. Sometimes, he would come up to me in training and tell me to go through the motions just for that session because he didn't want me tiring myself out. He seemed to look after me. He really did.'

Shankly paved the way for a signing who was to become a rock of the side for a generation that day. How significant that the first man he recruited to his new regime should go on to play 857 games for Liverpool. Right at the inception of his reign, Shankly identified a man who was to win a Second Division championship, five League Championships, two FA Cups, two Uefa Cups and a European Cup with the club.

Callaghan played a handful of first-team games that first season. Once again, Liverpool ended the campaign stranded in third place in Division Two, denied their place in the big time for another year. Shankly began to make radical changes. He was horrified by some of what he found when he took over.

Anfield, he said, was a slum. It was a dour, dilapidated stadium. Even the floodlights cast only a dim, funereal glare over the playing surface. Liverpool was sinking when Shankly arrived. The toilets didn't even flush and Shankly insisted the club spend £3,000 installing a network to channel water over from Oakfield Road, which ran adjacent to the ground.

Shankly was also shocked by what he found at Melwood. It was unrecognizable then from the state-of-the-art complex with its row of bowling green pitches that the players use today. Gérard Houllier was to oversee the building of the new Melwood with its gym, its pool, its hi-tech treatment rooms and its media centre at the turn of the century, but in 1960 the training ground was an expanse of pitches and a creaking, cold, draughty wooden pavilion. There was no heating, the baths were downstairs and the sanitation was basic.

Shankly was outraged to find that one pitch was given over to cricket for several months of the year. He stopped that immediately and turned the area into a couple of five-a-side pitches. The standard of the pitches was poor, too. There were bumps and bare patches everywhere and the grass was mowed irregularly. There was just one sprinkler tap to water them in summer. So Shankly insisted the Anfield groundsman, Bert Riley, should divide his time between the stadium and the training ground to improve the surface at Melwood.

'When I went to Melwood to take my first training session, it was in a terrible state,' Shankly wrote in his autobiography. 'There was an old wooden pavilion and an air-raid shelter and there were trees, hills and hollows and grass long enough for Jimmy Melia to hide in standing up. It was a sorry wilderness. One pitch looked as if a couple of bombs had been dropped on it. "The Germans were over here were they?", I asked.

'As time wore on, the place was levelled and cultivated and a suitable pavilion was built with proper changing facilities and a sauna bath. But that first day was a sight, I can tell you. The front pitch was bare, except for the middle. I was told this was a cricket pitch. "I'll cricket you," I said, and it was made into our five-a-side pitch.'

Changes were made quickly but Shankly established a routine that was to last throughout his time in charge where the players got changed into their training kit at Anfield and travelled by coach to Melwood. After training, the players would get back on the coach and get showered and changed at Anfield. Shankly was worried about them catching a chill if they showered while they were still sweating and came straight out into the winter air, but there were other reasons for maintaining the routine, too. He knew that there would be plenty of banter on the coach and he thought it was good for team morale. He liked to see the players talking and laughing and ribbing each other about what had just happened in training rather than all going their separate ways as soon as they left Melwood. He felt the two bus journeys were good for team spirit as well as for the health of his men.

He made one change in the pre-season format at the start of the 1960–61 campaign. In previous years, the players had run the few miles from Anfield to Melwood to try to start building up their fitness for the season ahead. They jogged down past Stanley Park and then down some side streets off Priory Road. They didn't attract much attention. Footballers were not celebrities then. No one honked their car horns or tried to run alongside them asking for autographs. They ran in three groups: fast, medium and slow. When they got to Melwood, usually within five minutes of each other, they worked there for an hour and a half and then ran back to Anfield. 'Bill said we weren't going to keep doing that,' Ronnie Moran said. 'He said we didn't run on roads during a match. We ran on grass.'

By then, Shankly had overhauled the training regimen at Anfield completely. He was part of a new breed of manager who coached players rather than exercised them. With men like Matt Busby and Joe Mercer, Shankly was in the vanguard of a generation of managers who seized control of their teams from club directors who had been used to selecting the players and dominating the decision-making process. Shankly demanded control of the playing staff and he got it. His coaching methods are often regarded now as rather basic, with their heavy emphasis on five-a-side games as opposed to complex tactical work, but he was obsessed with good technique and good habits like pass and move.

His secret was in the almost childlike enthusiasm he had for the game. He approached football like a breathless little boy who would have played all day if he could. Somehow, he had managed to keep the magic of first encounters with the game fresh in his mind. He had not become cynical or gnarled or drained of passion. He was like the Tom Hanks character in *Big*: on the outside there was an adult in a tracksuit or a shirt and a smart tie, but on the inside was a child whose love of football knew no bounds.

'He was the first one I ever met who really got into talking the game, training for it, living it and in effect bringing it back to those days when we were kids,' St John said. 'After the clockwork running at Motherwell, training under Shankly was an escape, a joy. As soon as you came out on the training field, he was there with bags of balls. After a brief warm-up, the balls would be rolled in your direction as if they were an astonishing treat. Then you would be crossing and heading and playing two-a-side games. You would be doing all the things you had done in a Scottish street or tenement backyard.'

In a way, Shankly's career was about achieving something that lies deep inside all of us but which is usually beyond our means. It was about perpetuating his childhood. That's why he still played in lads and dads matches on rough hillsides when he was manager of Huddersfield. That was part of his genius: awakening in grown men the intensity of the love they had felt for the game when they still dreamed of a life playing professional football.

Ferguson loves the game too, of course. It consumes him

too. But it's different to Shankly. For Shankly, his love of football was something he couldn't control. Ferguson has always been in control. Ferguson has used football and shaped it to his own ends. He has never lost his hunger for achievement, but that is another thing altogether to the boyish enthusiasm that shaped Shankly. An inner rage has driven Ferguson on, but even though Shankly could be a fierce and ruthless man, he never burned with that kind of anger.

One of Shankly's innovations became a landmark at Melwood well into the 1990s. Soon after he arrived, Shankly oversaw the erection of a maze of eight-feet-high wooden walls – known as boards – beside one of the pitches. The players took a ball into the complex of boards and smashed passes against each one. When the ball rebounded to them, they had to control it and move on to the next board. Shankly demanded that they repeat the exercise for two minutes. It was so intense, new players could not cope with it.

The boards feature prominently on old television footage of Melwood. On one occasion in the 1970s, every single player was away on international duty except Jimmy Case, and the BBC ran a feature on him training alone. Sure enough, there he was at Melwood banging the ball against the boards.

The boards were great for technique, control and stamina. By the Nineties, they had become faded. Times had moved on. 'They were practically rotting away by the time I arrived,' Stan Collymore said. 'But no one wanted to take them down. They were monuments to a time when Liverpool ruled Europe. Perhaps they should have turned them into a heritage site and organized coach tours so people could stare at them. Because that was all they were good for.'

But they were good for a lot more than that. The ceaseless practice in front of the boards honed control and passing accuracy, and those were Shankly's twin grails. 'If you can't pass the ball and you can't control it when it is passed to you,' he said, 'you can't play.' He stressed and stressed the importance of keeping possession, of playing the simple, easy ball and the value of being able to control a ball whether it came to a player chest- knee- or foot-high.

For Liverpool players blinking in the bright light of Shankly's new ways, the boards were a symbol of a new dawn. Players who had been used to long hours of fitness training and endless laps of the Melwood perimeter were suddenly liberated by Shankly's accent on working with the ball. The players were not just running and doing exercises any more. They were being coached and they responded. They could run all day if they had the ball at their feet.

Too many teams in the 1950s were controlled by drones who emphasized fitness and neglected ball skills. It seemed particularly profligate in an era when wonderful ball players like Tom Finney and Stanley Matthews were in their prime. Shankly's predecessor, Phil Taylor, had not encouraged ball practice and men like Moran, who was club captain, felt they had suddenly been given a new lease of life.

'I had only worked with him for a few weeks and I was already wishing he had come five years earlier,' Moran said. 'It was simple ball work and that was what he wanted to get over to players. Play it simple. Play the early ball. Play it to the nearest red shirt. Sometimes people used to take that too literally and they'd pass it to the nearest red shirt even if he had three men on him. If anyone did that, Shanks would go over and hit him on the head. I loved training under him. If he had come five years earlier, we wouldn't have been in Division Two all that time.'

And of course, the biggest change was Shankly himself. Shankly the Irrepressible. Shankly the Disciplined. Shankly the Eccentric. Shankly the Innovator. Shankly the Motivator. Shankly the Orator. Shankly the Witty. Shankly the Force of Nature. Shankly was, quite simply, an immensely likable and charismatic man and his presence began to transform Liverpool from a dour, down-at-heel club to a place that was suddenly brimming with enthusiasm and vitality. Shankly could do that. He could drag people along with him on the journey. Not because he bullied them. But because they worshipped him.

'He was a strict, strict man,' Callaghan said. 'But one of the things about the boss was that he had the utmost respect from all the players. You could be messing about in the corridor outside his office and he would come out of his door and straight away you would shut up and walk away and greet him with an "alright boss" as you were going. It was his enthusiasm for football and for life that made such a big impression on everyone when he first joined. He was full of beans. He was very rarely down.'

Amid the flurry of changes, Shankly chose continuity in only one aspect of the running of the team. He eschewed the new manager's usual habit of clearing out all the previous boss's backroom staff and kept them all on. Even for a clever man like Shankly, it was probably the wisest move he ever made. Bob Paisley, Reuben Bennett and Joe Fagan all kept their jobs. It was the first step in the creation of the legend of the Boot Room.

The Boot Room was a boot room. Just what it said on the tin. An outer room separated it from the corridor running under the main stand at Anfield. There was a work bench in that outer room and a cobbler's last and some brushes and a few big tins of polish. That was where the apprentices cleaned the boots, wedging them on the last, knocking the mud off them and then polishing them up and making them soft and supple again.

And then there was the inner sanctum. The place where the boots belonging to the first-team players were kept. There were a few bits of kit kicking around. The place had the air of a store room but it doubled as a meeting place for the football men who were in Shankly's brigade. Shankly himself did not spend as much time in there as he did working in his office. The Boot Room was more of a hideaway for Paisley, Bennett and Fagan, a place where they could get away from everyone, including

Shankly, and chew the fat. They went in there, closed the door, shared a tot of whisky or a beer and talked about the game.

It was several years into Shankly's time that it metamorphosed from an untidy storage room into a space that was said to be the hub of a great empire. Visiting managers used to go in there to seek out Paisley once he had become manager. The idea of this great dynasty being run from a room flecked with clumps of mud and strewn with spare kit fitted the image of a club that stressed the team ethic more than any other. A Liverpool side was always supposed to be a team of equals, a team of eleven good men.

It helped that the Boot Room boys were relentlessly down-to-earth. Paisley was a stoic who greeted success and failure evenly, a lugubrious northeasterner from Hetton-le-Hole who played more than 250 games for Liverpool at wing-half in the period after the Second World War. He was the bad cop to Shankly's beneficent dictator. When there were dressing-room bollockings to be handed out, Shankly delegated the job to his number two.

His role was often underestimated. Indeed, despite the fact that he won three European Cups in his time in charge, Paisley has often been dismissed as a mere beneficiary of the foundations laid by Shankly. In that respect, Paisley, a quiet self-effacing man, was a victim of Shankly's powerful personality. No one could quite believe that he had the wherewithal to be more successful than such a charismatic figure as his former boss.

But it takes a certain kind of strength to adhere to a profitable formula. It takes a man without ego to continue with the methods and principles laid down by another. Shankly might have found that tough, but Paisley just saw it as common sense. And in their time together, if Shankly painted with broad brush strokes, Paisley was more clever tactically. He took over from Shankly in 1974 and became the most successful manager in the history of the English game, but success did not change him. Phil Thompson remembers him packing a league championship trophy away in a cardboard box soon after it had been won. Paisley looked up at him as he was taping the box up. 'You get fuck all for that next season,' he said.

Of all Shankly's original Boot Room boys, least has been written about Reuben Bennett. He did not join the production line of managers like Paisley, Joe Fagan, Ronnie Moran (as caretaker) and, later, Roy Evans, which may explain why he has been overlooked. But Bennett, a tough, gritty Scotsman who had been the favourite to take over at Anfield before Shankly was appointed, was regarded by many as Shankly's right-hand man.

He was a colourful character, a fount of tall stories and anecdotes. He had lived out his life in football's lower echelons either side of the border. He kept goal for Hull City, Dundee and Queen of the South and then worked for Shankly's brother, Bob, at Dundee. He managed Motherwell, Third Lanark and Ayr United and was appointed head coach at Liverpool in December 1958 when the club was in the doldrums.

Under Shankly, he was also the the drill-master, the one who administered Shankly's famous endurance tests before the start of each season. Every manager likes to have someone on their staff who provides a bridge to the players, someone who can lighten the mood when the need arises without compromising the authority of the management team. Kevin Keegan and Graeme Souness both used Terry McDermott for that at Newcastle. Glenn Hoddle had John Gorman, Martin O'Neill had John Robertson. The nearest Shankly got to the role was Bennett.

'We would be getting on the coach at Anfield and it would be pouring with rain or freezing cold,' Wigan Athletic manager and former Liverpool squad player Paul Jewell said about his time at the club in the early Eighties. 'You might get on swearing about how cold it was. And Reuben would say, "Freezing, son? It's like the Bahamas."'

His apparent imperviousness to pain or any form of discomfort was one of his traits and something else that endeared him to Shankly, who made a habit of ignoring injured players. The son of an Aberdeen fisherman, he had served in the army through the Second World War and was proud of his physical fitness. He made a point of always being at the head of the pack when the players were running laps of Melwood.

He told one story of how, when he was playing for Dundee, he was ordered back to the dressing rooms because of a particularly grisly injury but was so determined to play on that he left the stadium, re-entered through a turnstile at the opposite end and hobbled back on to the pitch before anyone could stop him.

'Reuben was as hard as nails,' said Brian Hall. 'He didn't experience pain. No such thing as pain. That fitted in with Shanks's philosophy on things like injuries. He was like a sergeant-major. He would do the warm-up in the morning and bark and yell at us. He took the A-team when I was there in the late Sixties and he would shout at all the kids and it was real aggressive stuff.

'On the surface, he appeared to be a bit of a tyrant but he was close to Shanks. I sometimes think he must have exerted a lot of influence on him. And he had that wonderful knack of being able to take the warm-up exercises, shouting in that sergeant-major way in his Scottish brogue and yet being the one who could go out for a drink with you. He was the one who would sit down with the lads and have a beer. He went on these tours that were just a break for the lads. He somehow managed to bridge the gap and he got to know us and we got to know him.

'We could have a laugh and a joke and there was all that camaraderie thing that was part of the dressing-room spirit. Then the following day, he would go out and scream his head off at you and no one ever took any offence. I would have liked to have been a fly on the wall to see what kind of conversations he had with Shanks about the players. "He drinks too much, definitely", "He's not so bad", that kind of thing. I don't know.

'Reuben had some wonderful stories. So exaggerated they were untrue. Stuff like he kicked the ball out of the stadium in Dundee one day and it ran all the way to Edinburgh. Daft stuff like that. But you could talk to him and you could have conversations with him. I could have a conversation with him on a different level than I could ever have with Shanks. He was a lovely character, Reuben.'

The last of the men working happily in the shadow of Shankly, the last of the original Boot Room trio, was Joe Fagan. Fagan was eventually to take over from Paisley in 1983, the only Liverpool-born manager the club has had for more than half a century. Fagan's playing career was spent mostly at Manchester City and, like Shankly's, it was interrupted by the Second World War. He left Maine Road to become player-manager of Lancashire non-league club Nelson, combining that with a job inspecting gas meters in local factories.

The great Everton manager Harry Catterick recommended Fagan to the Liverpool board and he joined the club as an assistant trainer in 1958, a few months before Bennett. A kindly, avuncular man, he rose through the Boot Room ranks like Paisley. Sadly, the lingering memory of his time in charge was of his crumpled, broken face as he tried to take in the scale of the Heysel Disaster in Brussels in 1985 when 39 fans were killed in rioting and Liverpool lost a European Cup Final rendered meaningless by the tragedy to the Italian side, Juventus.

It was cruel that it should happen to him because he was a gentle, quiet man loved by everybody. It fell to him to try to cushion the blow when Shankly's ruthless pursuit of progress and excellence consigned some players who had grown used to the limelight to the dustbin instead. Fagan did that with St John when his time passed in the late Sixties. He told him that it happened to all the great players and that he needed to look at the bigger picture and help out the kids in the reserves until he found himself another club and continued with his career.

He liked a cigarette so the players called him Smokin' Joe. Some of them also called him the most important cog in the Liverpool machine. 'He was probably the most respected man in football and the guy given the least praise,' former Liverpool boss Roy Evans said. 'Others have been honoured for their contributions to football but Joe was the top man. I don't mean any disrespect to Bill Shankly or Bob Paisley when I say this, but Joe was the best.'

In a way, it seemed as if these men had been chosen for Shankly, rather than by him. It was as if they were disciples who had been gathered together so they could follow. They were not ambitious men who plotted against him. They were not motivated by personal ambition. They did not scheme. Perhaps the closest there has been to any of them in the modern game is a man like Ray Harford, the late coach so greatly valued and missed by Kenny Dalglish and Alan Shearer among others.

Their character and their temperament complemented Shankly's perfectly. They were happy to operate in his shadow, team players who recognized his greatness. They were there when Shankly arrived and, rather than discard them, he chose to lead them. He laid down a code of loyalty for them and, from Shankly's first day at Liverpool until his last, they adhered to it faithfully.

'I want one thing,' Shankly told them. 'I want loyalty. I don't want anybody to carry stories about anybody else. If anyone tells me a story about someone else, the man with the story will get the sack. I don't care if he has been here for 50 years. I want everyone to be loyal to each other. Everything we do will be for Liverpool Football Club.'

When he had satisfied himself about the quality of his staff, Shankly began to rebuild. The pace of change was so swift, the exodus so big, that Moran and his teammates stood around chatting after training, wondering aloud which of them would be next out of the door. The feeling of insecurity hardly improved when Liverpool were trounced 4–0 by Cardiff City at Anfield in their first match under their new boss. The date was 19 December 1959.

Liverpool had slipped out of the promotion race by then. They had lost nine matches by the turn of the year and were marooned in tenth place. Huddersfield, the team he was leaving, were sixth. Shankly's predecessor at Liverpool, Phil Taylor, had been one of the old guard even though he was only forty-two when he quit on the grounds of ill-health. Taylor was more of an administrator than a coach and had been happy to allow the directors to pick the team. He wasn't a training-ground man like Shankly.

Liverpool had been relegated from the First Division in 1954 and Taylor had taken over two years later. He presided over the autumn of the career of the great Billy Liddell, a winger who, despite all Liverpool's more recent glories, is still regarded as one of the club's greatest players. Liddell's influence was being slowed by injuries by the mid-1950s and Liverpool were in stasis.

Early in 1959, Taylor's Liverpool crashed out of the FA Cup in the third round, beaten 2–1 at non-league Worcester City. It was the greatest upset in the club's history and it convinced Liverpool chairman Tom Williams that change was needed at the top. Reuben Bennett and Joe Fagan arrived to overhaul training and run the reserves but Williams had interviewed Shankly once before in 1951 and was determined to get his man this time.

Shankly had baulked at the idea of taking over at Anfield eight years earlier because he was unwilling to accept a system where the manager had to bow to the directors when it came to team selection. This time, he received assurances that he would be in charge and he did not hesitate to accept. His wife, Nessie, was upset because she had settled well in Huddersfield but Shankly was adamant. His starting salary was £2,500 a year, £500 more than he had been paid at Huddersfield.

He made some early personnel changes. Gerry Byrne, the

man who was to perform so heroically for Shankly in the 1965 FA Cup Final, had fallen out of favour with Taylor and had been placed on the transfer list. Shankly took him off it. Plenty of others were moved on. By the end of the 1960–61 season, Shankly was hacking away at the dead wood and twenty-four of the players he had inherited from Taylor were transferred away from Anfield.

A few survived. Roger Hunt, who was to become one of Alf Ramsey's World Cup-winning side, was twenty-one when Shankly arrived and was turning heads with his goalscoring feats. Jimmy Melia, later to lead Brighton and Hove Albion to the 1983 FA Cup Final, was a prolific inside forward who had scored 21 goals the season before Shankly's arrival and went on to win a league championship medal under the new boss. The club stalwart Ronnie Moran quickly became a devotee of Shankly's methods and his voice on the pitch. And on 16 April 1960 young Ian Callaghan made his first-team debut at home to Bristol Rovers.

Shankly had lifted Liverpool to third place by the end of the season. They were still comfortably adrift of the promoted sides, Cardiff and Aston Villa, but they had only lost three games since the beginning of January. Shankly had failed in attempts to sign his protégé Denis Law from Huddersfield and Jack Charlton from Leeds United, which led to the first signs of tension between him and the Liverpool board. But then he persuaded them to pay a club record £13,000 for Kevin Lewis from Sheffield United to try to fill the gap left by Liddell.

Liverpool finished third again the following season, this time well adrift of Ipswich Town and Lewis's old club at Bramall Lane. Shankly was again rebuffed in his attempts to sign Charlton from Leeds and even considered resigning until his friend Matt Busby, the Manchester United manager, talked him out of it. Shankly looked up to Busby, who was finally beginning to recover from the terrible injuries he sustained in the Munich Air Disaster, and valued his advice.

But he was losing patience. He felt promises had been broken. The directors were trying to interfere in team selection and the money he needed to bring in leading players did not seem to be materializing. Crowds were down to 20,000 and his credentials were being questioned by supporters and by the board. Shankly had left Huddersfield because he thought Liverpool was a club with ambition and potential, but he was beginning to think he was mistaken.

But then, in the summer of 1961, everything changed. When he was almost at his lowest ebb, Shankly made the two signings that were to propel him and his team into the big league. He snatched Ian St John away from Motherwell and Ron Yeats from Dundee United and suddenly it was as if he had found the key to the door. Their arrival turned Shankly from a manager striving to prove himself into a real player. He changed from a little man on the outside to a big man with power. His personality and his methods had created the conditions for Liverpool's inexorable rise, but the arrival of St John and Yeats gave Shankly the raw materials he had been craving.

Shankly gave much of the credit for the transformation to an accountant called Eric Sawyer. Sawyer was the representative on the Liverpool board of Littlewoods Pools magnate John Moores, who at that time was chairman of Everton. But Moores still had a significant stake in Liverpool and was concerned that the club was still struggling to break out of Division Two. So he gave Sawyer, a finance executive at Littlewoods, the power to grant more funds to Shankly. It felt as if the floodgates had opened.

Shankly mentioned at a board meeting that Motherwell had put St John up for sale. The price would be close to £40,000 and he knew Liverpool had never paid anything remotely close to that for a player before. 'One of our directors said: "We can't afford to sign him,"' Shankly said. 'But Mr Sawyer said: "We can't afford not to sign him." That man, Mr Sawyer, was really and truly the beginning of Liverpool Football Club. Here was somebody who was willing to spend money. He said to me: "If you can get the players, I'll get the money." '

When he knew the money was available, Shankly shot up to Glasgow with his chairman and a director called Sid Reakes, who owned the Rolls-Royce. They watched St John play for Motherwell against Hamilton Academicals and were so keen to conclude the deal that they started negotiations with the Motherwell directors at the interval and didn't bother with the second half. The fee they agreed was £37,500.

Shankly convinced St John about the move in a blitzkrieg of persuasion. St John was being courted by Newcastle, too, and had been offered £1,000 signing-on fee. Shankly brushed that aside and made it clear Liverpool would match it. Then he told St John and his wife Betsy that he was whisking them straight back to Lancashire. 'Betsy, like me, was a little overwhelmed,' St John said. 'She said: "Mr Shankly, you know we have a baby . . ." He brushed aside the problem. "Take the baby to your mother's," he ordered, "we have important business here." '

Encouraged by the signing of St John, Shankly moved for Yeats, who had been put on the transfer list by Dundee United because he had asked for a £2 rise. They met at the Station Hotel in Edinburgh. Yeats didn't know who Bill Shankly was. He didn't even know for sure where Liverpool was geographically. He just knew that an English club was interested in signing him.

Shankly marched out of a crowd of directors in the hotel foyer when he saw Yeats coming and gazed up at him admiringly. He guessed he was seven feet tall. Yeats said he was only 6 ft 3. Then Yeats asked Shankly where Liverpool was. 'What do you mean, "Where's Liverpool?" ' Shankly snapped back at him. 'We're in the First Division in England.' Even though Shankly had misunderstood his question, Yeats was puzzled. He said he thought Liverpool were in the Second Division. 'With you in the team, we'll be in the First Division next year,' Shankly said.

And so Yeats signed, too. This time, the fee was £30,000, but Shankly knew he had just made a priceless acquisition. He took him back to Anfield and showed him off. 'I've signed a colossus,' he famously told reporters at the unveiling. 'Come in and walk round him.' It was such a good line that *The Sun*'s respected Manchester United reporter Peter Fitton appropriated it when Alex Ferguson signed Jaap Stam, another daunting figure of a man, from PSV Eindhoven thirty-seven years later.

Shankly promptly made Yeats club captain. He boasted that his giant could win the Second Division on his own. 'With him in defence,' Shankly said, 'we could play Arthur Askey in goal.' Shankly was always saying things like that. 'His whole life seemed to be a gesture of ambition and aggression,' St John said. Even if the regime he ran at Anfield was spartan in many ways, even if he abhorred the star system and insisted that the team ethic was more important than anything, Shankly could still behave like a braggart. His obsession with boosting the confidence of his own side by praising them to the skies often involved denigrating the opposition, too. But his wit was so sharp that he often got away with comments that would have made others appear utterly conceited.

He tried to sign Frank McLintock that summer, too. He marched up to him on the dance floor of the Dorchester Hotel in London where McLintock was drowning his sorrows after Leicester City's defeat to Spurs in that season's FA Cup Final. 'How would you like to play for a good team, son?' Shankly asked him. McLintock was amused and impressed by Shankly's impertinence, especially as he was being tapped up in full view of the Leicester directors. He gave a non-committal answer and when Shankly made a bid for him later in the summer, Leicester turned it down.

It didn't matter. The first season after he signed St John and Yeats was a landmark for Shankly. He had spent his whole managerial career telling his teams they were the best and watching them come up short. He'd been trying to convince players they were world-beaters even though they were playing in the basement of the Third Division North, scratching a living out of the game and struggling not to fall off the edge of the earth. Now, at last, he had a side that could live up to his prophecies and fulfil all his hopes and dreams.

Liverpool won ten of their first eleven games in 1961–62. Roger Hunt was on fire. He scored seven goals in the first three games. And the crowds started to flood back in. The public's apathy of the previous season disappeared. More than 50,000 supporters watched the first home game of the season against Sunderland. More than 42,000 saw them thrash Leeds 5–0 three days later. Their first defeat came against Middlesbrough at Ayresome Park but they rebounded from that and went on another winning run.

Hunt and St John thrived in each other's company. St John's clever runs and neat flicks made space and opportunities for Hunt and Hunt took them. He scored 41 league goals that season. Liverpool were 8 points clear of the rest by January and home free by 21 April when they clinched the promotion their supporters had craved so long by beating Southampton with two goals from Lewis. The Southampton players formed an honour guard to clap them off at the end and the Kop bayed for the players to come back on to the pitch to receive their adoration.

Half-naked, St John and Yeats were both hauled into the crowd and had to be rescued by police. Shankly made a victory speech. So did Tom Williams. They were heady, heady times. Elvis Presley was in his pomp, the Beatles were only a year away from their first Number 1, Gerry and the Pacemakers were about to release 'You'll Never Walk Alone', the River Mersey was still thronged with merchant traffic from all over the world, and Liverpool Football Club was back in the big time. That April day at Anfield felt like the start of something good.

'I was so fortunate that I got in at the beginning,' Callaghan said. 'The Sixties were brilliant in Liverpool. The football club took off. And there were the Beatles and Gerry and the Pacemakers. Liverpool was buzzing. Then you had a character like Bill Shankly. And God, he was a character. It was just a marvellous place to be, especially because I was a Liverpool kid. I felt like I was at the centre of the universe. All this was happening and I was part of it. People say to me now: "I bet you wish you were playing now with all the money." Well, no, actually, because what I got was unbelievable. I got more than money. Because I will never meet someone like Shanks again. I won't.'

16: Ferguson and the Death of his Hero

There have been traumas in Alex Ferguson's football life. He suffered his share of rejection and isolation as a player. He was familiar with being herded into acting the role of scapegoat. As a manager, he had difficult days, too. He had to tell Roy Keane he was no longer needed or wanted at Old Trafford. He had to tell Jim Leighton he was going to drop him for the 1990 FA Cup Final replay against Crystal Palace. They all hurt him. They all caused him awkwardness or pain. But nothing affected him like the death of Jock Stein.

Stein was one of the greatest managers Scotland has ever produced. His greatest achievement was leading Celtic to victory in the 1967 European Cup Final against Inter Milan. Celtic became the first British team to win the trophy. The side was made up of ten players born within 12 miles of Parkhead. The eleventh, Bobby Lennox, was raised 30 miles away in Ayrshire. That added to the magnitude of Stein's accomplishment.

Ferguson hero-worshipped him. The merest word or the slightest rebuke from the manager everyone called the Big Man made a huge impression on him. Stein upbraided him once in the mid-Eighties for ignoring a group of striking miners trying to raise funds and Ferguson was mortified that he had not noticed them. Stein, who had worked down the pit until he was twenty-seven, was real. It is hard to imagine him cosying up to New Labour and its acolytes in the way Ferguson has done.

After he had been discarded by Celtic, Stein was appointed Scotland manager, and in 1984 he asked Ferguson to be his assistant. Ferguson accepted with relish. He combined the job with his duties at Aberdeen and resolved to use it to learn everything he could from the man that he considered the master of the art of football management.

Ferguson enjoyed working with a good Scotland side that contained Kenny Dalglish, Graeme Souness, Alan Hansen and his own Aberdeen players, Willie Miller, Alex McLeish and Leighton. But the qualifying campaign for the 1986 World Cup in Mexico did not go smoothly and Scotland went into the last game, against Wales at Ninian Park on 10 September 1985, needing at least a draw to be sure of a place in a play-off against Australia.

The build-up had been marred by the late withdrawal of Hansen. Hansen had already disappointed Ferguson by refusing to talk about the best way to nullify the threat of Ian Rush, the Wales striker. Hansen and Rush were teammates in Bob Paisley's all-conquering Liverpool side and Ferguson was appalled that Hansen was putting club before country with his reluctance to provide any information about the player who might undo Scotland's hopes of reaching Mexico.

Stein, who was sixty-two, was nervous on the day of the game. Ferguson said Stein had been irritated by a couple of newspaper articles and by comments attributed to the Wales manager, Mike England. When he went to Stein's hotel room on the afternoon of the game, he noticed a medicine bottle and two bottles of tablets on Stein's dressing table. He said he appeared to be suffering from a heavy cold.

When the match began, Scotland were outplayed in the first half and fell behind to a goal from Mark Hughes. During the interval Ferguson was confronted with the first of the incidents that continue to haunt him even now. Stein called him away from the players into the bathroom area where Leighton, who had looked dreadfully uncertain during the opening 45 minutes, was sitting miserably, staring at his feet.

Stein told Ferguson that Leighton had lost a contact lens and did not have a replacement. He assumed that Ferguson, who had been Leighton's manager at Aberdeen for seven years, knew that he wore lenses. He was surprised that Ferguson had not mentioned it to him. 'He turned ashen-faced before storming away without saying a word,' Leighton said. 'Sadly, it turned out to be the last time I saw him alive.'

Ferguson's initial reaction was similar. 'I swear I had absolutely no idea that Jim used contact lenses,' he said in his autobiography. 'I was so dumbfounded and there was such a swirl of anger and embarrassment going through me that at first I didn't say a word. There I was, Leighton's club manager, somebody with a reputation for maintaining strict control over my players and for making it my business to know everything worth knowing about them. Jock was entitled to suspect that I had been holding back about the lenses. I think the secrecy represented terrible selfishness on Leighton's part . . . in football, where it should be all for one and one for all, that kind of behaviour is out of order.'

The incident unnerved Ferguson. Things got worse. Soon after the second half began, he noticed that Stein, who was sitting next to him in the dug-out, had turned grey and was beginning to sweat. There was another misunderstanding when Stein indicated he wanted to take Gordon Strachan off and replace him with Davie Cooper. At first, Ferguson thought he had said he wanted to take Steve Nicol off. Stein had to correct him. Again, the memory of something that would have been forgotten on any other night sits uneasily with Ferguson now.

As the second half wore on, Stein stressed to Ferguson that they must make sure they kept their dignity if Scotland lost. He repeated it to Ferguson several times. The same thought raced through Ferguson's mind in the second half of the 1999 European Cup Final. But just like in Barcelona, the match turned. Scotland equalized with a Davie Cooper penalty 10 minutes from time and Scotland went through to the play-off.

Stein didn't say a word when Cooper equalized. A couple of

minutes before the end, the referee blew for a free kick and Stein rose from the bench as if he was going to go to shake the hand of Mike England. After a couple of steps, he stumbled and began to fall. There is a picture of Ferguson, his face a mask of shock and horror, staring across at Stein in the instant the Scotland manager began to crumple. He was carried away by the Scottish doctor and a policeman. There were batteries of photographers gathered around the bench, ready to catch the reaction of the victorious manager. Suddenly, this was a terribly different kind of picture they were capturing.

When the final whistle went, Ferguson kept the players on the pitch for a short while. When he led them back to the dressing room, the initial reports suggested that Stein had suffered a minor heart attack and was recovering. Ferguson prepared to address the media and sling back a few of the barbs that had been aimed at Stein. Then Ferguson saw Graeme Souness standing at the door of the medical room. He was in tears.

Ferguson had to break the news to Stein's family. Then he had to tell the players. As they climbed on to the team coach outside Ninian Park, the fans surrounding the bus watched them in solemn silence. A few isolated voices shouted out: 'God bless you, Jock.' Ferguson kept his emotions in check until he broke down the next day but he was deeply moved. 'It was as if the king had died,' he said. 'In football terms, the king had died.'

The death of Stein hit Ferguson hard. He had begun to look upon the Big Man as a kind of father-figure. He was a wiser, older man that Ferguson revered. The distress he felt at Stein's death made him vow that he would retire from the game at sixty so that he would not suffer the same fate, so that he could spend more time with his family and escape the crushing stress that Stein had had to endure for so long.

When he got to sixty, of course, Ferguson abandoned that resolve. It was partly that time had dimmed the pain of Stein's death, and partly that, by then, Ferguson had realized it was too late to make up for lost time with his children. He realized that they regarded him as a friend more than a father and that they actually wanted him to carry on being a manager. He also realized that if the stress of football had helped to bring Stein's life to a premature end, the anguish of being exiled from football had done the same for Shankly.

Scotland won the two-legged play-off against Australia comfortably and Ferguson agreed to take charge of the side for the Mexico World Cup. His most controversial selection decision involved Hansen. The Liverpool defender pulled out of a warm-up game against England, citing a sore knee. That made Ferguson's mind up. When the squad was announced, Ferguson rang Hansen to tell him he would not be going.

Hansen took it well, but Ferguson was worried about the effect his omission might have on Hansen's close friend, Kenny Dalglish. Dalglish urged Ferguson to reconsider and include Hansen in the party. Ferguson refused to relent. Soon before the squad was due to fly out for the finals, Dalglish called to tell Ferguson he was not fit to travel because he needed a knee operation.

Dalglish has responded to suggestions that he refused to go to Mexico because he was in a fit of pique about Hansen with indignant anger. He said the idea was libellous nonsense and that he would not have been on the plane even if Hansen had been picked. But despite the fact that they are both Govan boys, the relationship between Ferguson and Dalglish has never really been anything warmer than tepid. Dalglish once murmured to a reporter who was interviewing Ferguson about a contentious refereeing decision that he would get more sense out of his baby daughter than his fellow manager.

Scotland missed the presence of Dalglish in Mexico. Mo Johnston was also left out, mainly for disciplinary reasons. Other than that, the preparation for Mexico went smoothly. Ferguson took the squad to Santa Fe in New Mexico for a few days of altitude training before the tournament and his players noticed how relaxed and comparatively permissive he was about the idea of granting them the occasional night out.

But Ferguson's duties with Aberdeen meant he had been unable to carry out the wider duties that a national team manager would normally perform, like scouting the choice of team hotel in Mexico City. 'The hotel was a disaster,' Gordon Strachan said. The rooms were small, there were no telephones and it was heavily guarded.

Scotland lost their opening game to Denmark 1–0. They lost again to West Germany, although Gordon Strachan put them ahead with a fine opening goal and at least gave their fans one happy image to remember when he pretended to try to vault the perimeter advertising hoardings but then settled for resting his right leg on the top of the boards, admitting that his lack of height had defeated him. The West Germans spoiled his celebrations by replying with two goals.

Franz Beckenbauer's side went all the way to the Final that summer, and even though Scotland had lost both their opening games, they knew they would still qualify for the next round if they won their last group game against Uruguay. Ferguson knew that his opponents, who only needed a draw, would play tough, cynical football, but he decided to leave out Souness because he was worried about his fitness in the sapping heat.

Ferguson later admitted he might have got that decision wrong. He also berated himself for leaving out players with Aberdeen connections like Steve Archibald and Jim Bett. Ferguson was too embarrassed to include them because he felt it might look as if he was biased towards men who had played under him at Pittodrie. With hindsight, he felt his awkwardness about that compromised his selections for the crucial third game against the South Americans.

He chose Graeme Sharp instead of Archibald and was desperately disappointed by his lack of aggression during the game. Ferguson felt Sharp was too easily intimidated by the Uruguayan tactics, although when one of those tactics was rumoured to include a Uruguayan defender ramming a finger up Sharp's backside, the startled countenance he wore for much of that ill-starred game is easier to understand. Leighton said that at corners, Uruguayan players spat in his face and tugged at the hair underneath his arms.

Uruguay played the vast majority of the game with ten men after Jose Batista was sent off after 40 seconds for a dreadful tackle on Strachan, but Scotland could not break them down. Again, Ferguson partly blamed himself. He had been distracted before his team talk by a blazing row with Archibald over the decision to leave him out and had not gathered his thoughts properly. The result, he said, was an address that was 'emptily Churchillian'.

The Uruguayans hung on for an equally empty goalless draw. Ferguson was appalled by the levels of their gamesmanship and their hounding of the French referee. At the end, Ferguson refused to shake hands with the Uruguay coach, Omar Borras, and accused him of 'historic hypocrisy' when Borras claimed Uruguay had played 'a fair game'.

A few months later, Ferguson left Aberdeen to take over at Old Trafford. He has never been tempted by international management again, although England have tried to lure him into The Impossible Job. North of the border, there are those who resent him for never having committed himself to managing his country full-time.

But once Ferguson arrived at Manchester United, the demands of international football became something he grew to abhor. The Scotland job was something he inherited because of a tragedy. He is a patriotic man, a man who even had "Scotland the Brave" as his mobile phone ring tone for some time. But his lust for glory was only properly fulfilled once he left Scotland behind him and headed south.

17: Shankly, Huddersfield and the Gateway to Immortality

There is a picture of Bill Shankly in middle age playing football in a field. It is clear from the still that the land is on a slope. The chimneys of Heights Farm are visible in the distance, close to where the modern M62 glides and dives across the Pennines today. There are twelve people in the frame, some of them lads, some of them dads, all of them looking at a football coming towards them in the air. A few have jumped to try and meet it but Shankly is above them all, so high it seems he must have rocket boosters in his boots.

Shankly, of course, is the oldest man there and the most formally dressed. He's wearing his everyday clothes: long trousers, a shirt with a stiff collar and a waistcoat with all its buttons done up. He couldn't wear his kit because he always told his wife he was just going out for a walk every Sunday afternoon when he left his house in the Huddersfield suburb of Lindley and strolled up to the field for a kickabout with the kids and their fathers.

His cover was blown occasionally. Once, when he was doing his regular Sunday chore of cleaning the gas cooker, a ten-year-old boy knocked at his front door and asked him if he was ready to play. Shankly told him to go and make sure the goalposts were set up and that he would be out to join the rest of them presently. When the boy had gone, Shankly turned to the Huddersfield Town assistant secretary, Eddie Brennan, who had been chatting to him while he cleaned. 'He's a dirty wee bugger, that lad,' Shankly said.

Shankly was forty-two when he arrived at Huddersfield in December 1955. He had been rescued from eight years of toil at dead-end jobs in the Third Division North by his old friend Andy Beattie, the Huddersfield manager and a man who had played alongside Shankly at Preston North End and for Scotland. Beattie was struggling to cope at Leeds Road. Huddersfield were bottom of the First Division and he wanted Shankly to help him share the burden and bring through players from the reserves.

It was Shankly's big chance. After spells in charge at Carlisle, Grimsby and Workington, this was his shot at the big time. His previous jobs had ended when he became exasperated by the failure of each club's directors to share his passion for improvement and back his sense of mission with transfer funds to buy new players. But they had all been clubs scrabbling at the margins. Huddersfield, a side with a glorious past, were much closer to the heart of things.

The problem was that Shankly wasn't cut out to be an assistant. He didn't want to be anybody's number two. He had too much energy for that. Too much drive and ambition. Too many ideas. So there was tension between him and Beattie almost from the start, tension that was exacerbated by the resentful presence of Eddie Boot, Beattie's former number two who had been supplanted by Shankly.

Shankly made it plain immediately that he cared far more about his reserve team than Beattie's first team. The reserves were to be his vehicle, his platform for success. Rather than subjugate them to the needs of the first team, Shankly set them up as a rival force within the club. When a player was left out of the first team and consigned to the stiffs, Shankly put an arm round his shoulder. 'I see you've been promoted, son,' he said.

As the first team continued to thrash about in the relegation zone, the reserves flourished in the Central League. Shankly had some bright prospects in his care. Denis Law was only fifteen, a raw kid fresh out of Aberdeen, when Shankly arrived, and even though he didn't look the part with his skinny frame, iron-rimmed glasses and a squint that made him terribly self-conscious, it was obvious he was going to be a master goalscorer.

Shankly began to pick Law and two other youngsters, Kevin McHale and Ray Wilson, later to become one of Alf Ramsey's England World Cup-winning side, in the reserves. Law was already attracting attention from elsewhere. After he ran Manchester United's young giants ragged in a youth team match, Matt Busby offered Beattie £10,000 for him on the spot. Beattie turned it down.

Law was a handful. Shankly was impressed by his sheer nastiness and will to win. One night, he got a call from Law's chain-smoking landlady to say there had been a fight. Shankly drove down to the digs. Law had punched another young lad in an argument after the boy had insulted him twice. Shankly sided with Law. He told the other boy to watch what he was saying next time.

Law also pestered Shankly and the rest of the staff constantly. He always wanted to play. When training was over, he badgered them to play five-a-side on the asphalt car park at Leeds Road. He played football all the hours of the day and even Shankly, the ultimate competitor, had to admit defeat. 'Denis worked all the usual stuff,' Shankly said. 'He was in and out and we couldn't get near him.'

Beattie's plan had been based on the idea that the fortunes of the first team would gradually recover and that once Huddersfield were safe from relegation, Shankly would join him in the running of the side. Shankly wanted more involvement immediately but bowed to Beattie's wishes.

The improvement in the first team never came, and on the last day of the season Huddersfield were relegated from the First Division on goal difference when their fellow strugglers Aston Villa beat Preston. Shankly's friend and hero, Tom Finney, missed a penalty for Preston that could have saved Huddersfield. The way things worked out, he did Shankly a huge favour.

Because things got worse when Huddersfield went down. They didn't take the Second Division by storm at the start of the following season. By early November, they were languishing in mid-table while Shankly's reserves had gone fourteen games unbeaten. When the first team lost 4–1 at home to Sheffield United, Beattie resigned. He recommended that Shankly should be appointed as his successor. Shankly was called to Leeds Road, told what had happened and offered the job.

He accepted but he also felt guilty. For the first time in his life, he thought he had left himself open to accusations of disloyalty. He was right. Boot, among others, felt he had manoeuvred his way into the job. Shankly drove round to see Beattie and was so nervous that he drove round the block a few times before he plucked up the courage to stop the car and knock on Beattie's door. Beattie had been watching the performance from a window.

It was a strange meeting. Shankly has always had a reputation for being a forthright and honest man, but at Liverpool he shied away from confrontation with his players and now he could not meet Beattie's eye or even talk about what had just happened. Ambition had swamped him when he was offered the job and now he realized he had not behaved honourably.

'I was surprised that Andy had packed in and was waiting for him to say something,' Shankly said. 'We sat in the house together and talked about this and that but the manager's job was never mentioned. I was waiting for Andy to say "Oh, you've done it, you've got the job, good luck", or something like that. Then I would have said "I'm sorry about this Andy, I should have come to see you before I accepted it".

'It was a kind of mutual embarrassment. How I got that job is one of my biggest regrets. In some way, I felt as if I might have let Andy down. I was embarrassed by the way it was done. I'm not suggesting that it was done dirtily . . . but it would still have been better if it had been done when Andy was there with me to hear it.

'Andy was the one fellow you would never let down, because he would never have done that to you. It was sad. Andy and I remained close friends and he did a lot of scouting for me at Liverpool but we have never discussed that Saturday night at Huddersfield when he left and I took his job.'

Shankly was not a grasping man. He certainly wasn't a dishonest man. But he had been through enough periods of hardship in his life to be ruthless enough to take his chances when they came. His period as understudy to Beattie at Huddersfield was not his finest hour. But at least it exposed the steel beneath the anecdotes and the quips.

Others recognized that in him, too. Every day, he picked Brennan up outside the George Hotel in the town centre and drove him down to Leeds Road in his baby Austin. Shankly usually talked about what he'd seen on the television the previous evening. He was particularly fond of gangster movies and cowboy films. 'He was always going on about James Cagney, George Raft, Humphrey Bogart and the rest,' Brennan said. 'He loved them. Little tough guys, just like himself.'

Shankly was finally in charge of a club outside the Third Division North. It wasn't quite the top of the greasy pole but it was one step closer. His first game as manager was a 5–0 win at Barnsley, Huddersfield's best postwar away result. When the side started slipping again, though, Shankly gave youth its chance and handed Law and McHale their debuts against Notts County at Meadow Lane on Christmas Eve 1956. On Boxing Day, in the return against County, Law scored his first goal.

Shankly knew he had a fight on his hands to keep Law at the club. When he turned seventeen in February 1957 he was free to negotiate with any club he wanted to. And there were plenty of admirers. So Shankly turned the screws to get Law to stay. He invited his father down from Aberdeen, plied him with whisky, took him to the chairman's factory and gave him a length of the finest cloth, and laid it on thick about how well the club and Shankly, in particular, had looked after his son.

There was a great commotion about where Law was going to end up. A gaggle of reporters and photographers had even surrounded Shankly at Huddersfield station when he had arrived to meet Law's father off the train from Scotland. One of the reporters followed Shankly into the Gents toilets and started asking who Law was going to sign for. 'I pushed him into the urinal,' Shankly said. 'His bottom was wet, I can tell you.'

Law was tempted by other offers but Shankly's grafting paid off. 'Shankly was a very persuasive man,' Law said, 'and by the time he had pleaded Huddersfield's case, I think both my dad and myself would have felt really bad if I had not signed. Shankly made a big difference to me because he was always so positive and enthusiastic about his team and his players.

'There has never been anyone quite like Shankly. He was one of the most passionate men I have ever known and expected his players to give everything every time they changed into their kit. He was a great manager and I enjoyed being one of his players. His team talks were something else. He would tear apart the opposition both as a team and individually. Had they heard him and taken him at his word, I think many of them would have retired from the game.

'Shankly talked up everything and everyone with whom he was involved. His own players were the best in the universe and his team could fly to the moon and back without transport.'

Huddersfield finished the season in mid-table, and in the summer Shankly had a clear-out. He got rid of centre forward Dave Hickson, a disciplinary ticking time bomb, to Everton and moved on a number of other senior players. But the 1957–58 season was much the same, made memorable on the pitch only for one of the craziest games in English football history when Huddersfield blew a 5–1 lead against Charlton at The Valley with twenty minutes to go and lost 7–6.

Off the pitch, of course, everyone remembered that season for the Munich Air Disaster of 6 February 1958, which killed so many Manchester United players. Shankly heard the news when a journalist phoned him as he sat in his office at Leeds Road. The early reports said Matt Busby had died as well. Shankly was devastated. He had played with Busby for Scotland and admired him as a man and a manager. The way he had conquered English football with a team full of young players, his Babes, was an inspiration to Shankly as he gave Law, McHale and Wilson their chance in the Huddersfield first team.

Shankly dashed home to watch the television pictures of the wrecked plane and the injured being taken to hospital. He saw footage of the United chairman, Harold Hardman, saying Busby was dead. Later, the picture became clearer and the reports said he was clinging to life. Shankly was still shaken. Tom Curry, his first trainer when he was a teenager at Carlisle United and now Busby's assistant at Old Trafford, had been killed when the United plane crashed on take-off in a snowstorm in Munich.

'Whenever Preston played United after the war,' Shankly said, 'I used to take Tommy a couple of dozen eggs. They were scarce in those days but I knew one or two people in Preston who could get them for me and I took them to Tommy because he had been so good to me when I was a boy.'

The next season, Huddersfield started badly and Shankly could feel the familiar old frustrations starting to return. At every club he had managed, he felt he had been damned by the board's reluctance to back him when it came to transfers. At Huddersfield, they wanted him to build a side from the products of the youth system. That was why they had given him the job in the first place. But Shankly knew he needed to support the younger players with a few signings of quality and experience.

They thrashed Liverpool 5–0 at Leeds Road even though Huddersfield had been reduced to ten men after five minutes. 'I remember the Liverpool directors leaving the ground in single file,' Shankly said, 'with their shoulders slumped, like a funeral procession.' That result probably did Shankly's future job prospects the power of good. But Law was injury-prone and the results were inconsistent, particularly when he was not in the team. Huddersfield dropped perilously close to the relegation places before they recovered and finished fourteenth.

Exasperated, Shankly drove through the night with Eddie Boot before the start of the following season to watch two players he rated highly playing in a representative match at Falkirk, north of Glasgow. Ian St John was playing for a Scotland side, Ron Yeats was playing against him for a Scottish Second Division Select team. 'What a battle they had,' Shankly said.

He took the memories back with him to Leeds Road and raised the players' names at a board meeting. He said it would cost £25,000 to get either of them. The directors dismissed his request out of hand. Shankly bit his lip. The reality was that Huddersfield were one of the poorest teams in the top two divisions. They were one of the last clubs in the country who still did not have floodlights. It would take the sale of Denis Law to Manchester City in March 1960 to bring them enough money to pay for some.

But Shankly left before Law. In mid-October 1959, Huddersfield lost at home to Cardiff City. Shankly was despondent. As he walked away from the ground in the early evening, two men approached him. One was Tom Williams, the Liverpool chairman. The other was Harry Latham, a Liverpool director. Shankly prepared himself to rebuff another offer for Law or Wilson.

'How would you like to manage the best club in the country?' Williams asked.

'Why,' said Shankly, as sharp as ever, 'is Matt Busby packing it in?'

18: Ferguson and the Great Purge of Old Trafford

Manchester City were bottom of the First Division. They had only been back in the top flight for a couple of months and already looked like certainties to go straight back down. Their manager, Mel Machin, was about to get the sack and his side was packed with local kids who seemed out of their depth. Manchester United and their fans thought the Manchester derby at Maine Road on 23 September 1989 would be one of the easiest internecine battles of recent times. Alex Ferguson didn't glimpse the ambush until it was too late.

That day in September was his blackest moment in charge at Old Trafford. United were beaten 5–1. They were humiliated. Their new £2.2 million record signing Gary Pallister, the defender who was Ferguson's last throw of the dice, had a dreadful game. He was culpable for three of the five goals. City seemed to score every time they attacked. They were 5–1 up after 62 minutes. Six, seven, eight, any amount of goals seemed possible at that point.

City's fifth goal was a peach. Ian Bishop hit a long ball out to David White on the right and his first-time cross floated perfectly into the path of Andy Hinchcliffe who was hurtling into the box like an express train. Hinchcliffe leaned into it as he ran and met it full on the forehead. It sped past Jim Leighton like a bullet and bulged the back of the net. Behind that goal, the United fans sitting on the wooden benches in the Platt Lane Stand looked at each other in disbelief as the rest of Maine Road went wild. Some of them got up to go.

City's victory was even sweeter because they had achieved it with a backbone of local players. White, Hinchcliffe, Paul Lake, Steve Redmond, Ian Brightwell and substitute Darren Beckford were all local lads. The result was portrayed as a victory for passion and commitment over the detached indifference of United's newly-arrived expensive imports like Pallister, Paul Ince and Mike Phelan. Ferguson had bought all three of them in the past few weeks and now his new recruits were being written off as duds.

Ferguson took the result hard. If there was any consolation for the United players as they sat in the away dressing room after the game listening to the City celebrations, it was that the manager was too stunned to tear them to pieces for their performance. 'He was shell-shocked,' Pallister said. 'There was no hairdrier or volatile temper that day. He just wanted to get home and gather his thoughts because people thought there might be quite serious repercussions.'

The defeat jolted Ferguson more than any other in his United career. It shook him right to his core. It made him feel ashamed. He tried to be defiant but it didn't wash. It was his fourth season in charge and United were beginning to look as if they were going backwards. Everything that he had worked for was on the line. After all he had achieved at Aberdeen, it appeared as though he had blown his shot at the big time.

If the United board lost patience with him, it would be a long way back. There's only one way for a manager to go from Old Trafford and it's not up. A long and painful rehabilitation would have stretched out in front of him if he had not managed to hang on. He would probably have had to go back to Scotland with his tail between his legs, or rebuild at a lesser First Division club like Aston Villa or Sheffield Wednesday.

Several days after the City game, when he spoke to his friend, Hugh McIlvanney, he was still raw. 'Believe me,' he told McIlvanney, 'what I have felt in the last week, you wouldn't think should happen in football. Every time somebody looks at

me, I feel I have betrayed that man. After such a result, you feel
as if you have to sneak round corners, feel as if you are some
kind of criminal. But that's only because you care, care about
the people who support you.'

Ferguson fretted about some of the speculation in the newspapers. Howard Kendall was being linked with the United job.
Others were, too. The fans wanted him out. They'd had enough.
They were giving up on him. They had stuck with him for three
years and watched as he had cleared out former favourites like
Norman Whiteside and Paul McGrath and now, after being
humbled by their local rivals, they had run out of patience.

Ferguson is rightly celebrated for the wonderful football his
United teams have played over the last two decades, but there
was a joylessness about his early years at United that had worn
the supporters down. Attendances were starting to plummet.
They regularly dipped below 40,000 in that 1989–90 season. It
was as if Ferguson had brought his Scottish austerity south with
him and clamped it around Old Trafford.

Under his predecessor, Ron Atkinson, United had been
flawed but hugely entertaining. They had won two FA Cup
Finals in 1983 and 1985, beating Brighton and Hove Albion
after a replay and then Championship winners Everton after
United had been reduced to ten men by the sending off of Kevin
Moran. They were a cup team in the great traditions of the club.
They had their Captain Marvel in Bryan Robson, and Whiteside,
who had been given his United debut when he was sixteen,
looked like a player who could go on to become one of the
legends of the game.

At the start of the 1985–86 season, United reeled off a run
of ten straight wins and looked as if they were finally going to
end their Championship drought. Atkinson had signed Peter
Barnes from Coventry City, and even though his best years were
behind him, in that early part of the season he seemed young
again and his dazzling runs and dribbling on the left wing helped
United tear teams to pieces.

Then it fell apart, like it always seemed to for United in the league. Liverpool won the title. United finished fourth. Behind West Ham. Their collapse effectively signalled the end for Atkinson, and when they began the next season badly, United moved to take Ferguson away from Aberdeen.

In his autobiography, Ferguson was singularly uncharitable about Atkinson's reign at United. He managed to disparage him and Gordon Strachan, who had played for him at Aberdeen, in the same couple of sentences by relating how Strachan used to call him regularly to tell him how chaotic, decadent and amateurish Atkinson's regime at Old Trafford had become. 'The training, Gordon suggested, was a shambles, with nothing done until Ron had a session on his sunbed as a preliminary to joining in a small-sided practice game.'

In *The Boss*, Michael Crick posits a theory that Ferguson had been lined up to take over at United for several months. Ferguson claimed for many years that there had been no contact between him and United until after Atkinson had been sacked. There is even an elaborate and flowery story in the official Manchester United history that involved a detailed recollection of Ferguson driving to Pittodrie on a sunny morning and arriving to be told by Aberdeen chairman Dick Donald that United chairman Martin Edwards had just made the first contact.

In fact, United chairman Martin Edwards contacted Ferguson at Pittodrie on 5 November 1989, the day after United had been beaten 4–1 by Southampton at The Dell. They were next to bottom of the First Division. A United director, Mike Edelson, got past the Aberdeen switchboard by faking a Scottish accent and pretending to be Gordon Strachan's accountant. When Ferguson picked up the receiver, he found himself speaking to Edwards.

They met later that night at a motorway service station at Hamilton in Lanarkshire. It was a routine tapping up, the kind that has always existed and always will exist. It was football realpolitik, although the presence of Bobby Charlton and the United solicitor Maurice Watkins would disappoint football purists. How men like Ferguson manage to protest against the transgressions of others and keep a straight face beggars belief.

The rendezvous was amateur theatrics meets *Tinker, Tailor, Soldier, Spy*. Edwards arrived at the services and jumped into Ferguson's car. Bobby Charlton, Mike Edelson and Maurice Watkins got into a car with Martin Ferguson. They all drove to Cathy Ferguson's sister's house in Bishopbriggs, in the northeastern suburbs of Glasgow, and struck a deal. Atkinson was sacked the next day. Aberdeen were paid compensation. A few hours later, United announced that Alex Ferguson was the new manager, the nineteenth boss in the club's fabled history.

Ferguson went at the job like a surgeon gouging diseased flesh from a sick man. He regarded what had been happening at United with undisguised disdain. He treated the club as though it was rotten and rancid. He was especially appalled that Atkinson had thrown a farewell party and invited the players forty-eight hours before United's game against Oxford United and the night before Ferguson was due to take his first training session. And he was disgusted with United's level of fitness as they slumped to a 2–0 defeat at the Manor Ground.

Strachan's briefings to Ferguson had emphasized that there was a drinking culture at United, headed by Robson, Whiteside and the lavishly gifted Ireland central defender Paul McGrath. Ferguson swept into Old Trafford bristling with hair-shirted indignation at the slack attitude of his new charges. 'When I arrived at United,' he said, 'I was astonished to find that there was a club rule forbidding players to drink alcohol "less than two days before a game". I replaced that feeble prohibition instantly with a rule that made it an offence for any player to drink while he was in training.'

United's players were in a state of shock. One day they were being managed by someone who indulged them, the next by a man who seemed to regard the idea of them enjoying themselves off the pitch somewhere in the same bracket as Original Sin. The contrast could hardly have been more stark. Bye-bye Mr Bojangles. Hello John Knox.

McGrath certainly felt that the problems existing between him and Ferguson right from the start stemmed from cultural and religious differences that were too fundamental ever to be bridged. It didn't help that Ferguson substituted McGrath at half-time of that first game at Oxford United. Nor did it help that McGrath and Whiteside continued to flout Ferguson's new rules. McGrath wrote in his autobiography: 'Fergie comes from a staunch Protestant background in working-class Glasgow, I was brought up in working-class Dublin and proud of it. Idealistically, our two worlds were far removed. Ferguson supported Rangers as a schoolboy. My contemporaries were sided well and truly with Glasgow Celtic. Politically, socially and historically, we came from opposite sides of the fence.

'Ferguson, by virtue of his background and upbringing, would never be able to understand the spirit of a Celtic Irish soul that drove me on in the thirst for life and my hunger for a good time. He could never work out where I was going. I could never understand where he was coming from. To the Irish, having a good time is life itself. It's an escape from the realities of life, a release valve from the pressure of living. To some Scottish Protestants, it appears having a good time in an hour of need is akin to turning your face away from responsibilities and flying in the face of reality.'

That is not fair to Ferguson, who was far more intelligent and flexible than McGrath ever realized. Ferguson was also ahead of his time in recognizing the damage alcohol could do to a player's body, the way it could sap his stamina on the pitch and affect his recovery time, particularly after injury. Ferguson didn't rage against the evils of drink for religious reasons. He did it because he thought it would affect his team's chances of ending their nineteen-year wait for a league championship.

But he did have double standards about who to punish and who to ignore when the players went out on a bender. Most of the team disregarded his new rules about drinking to the extent that his diktat turned into exactly the same kind of 'feeble prohibition' he felt Atkinson had presided over. Ferguson felt he could trust some players to cope with heavy drinking sessions, but when other players did the same it infuriated him.

The new United manager forced himself to ignore Robson's excesses, for example, because the United captain had a remarkable ability to shrug off a drinking session with what Ferguson described as the 'masochistic zeal' with which he threw himself into training. However much he had drunk the night before – and he usually drank more than anyone else – Robson was always at the front of the running pack the next day, always the most committed man on the training pitch.

The idea that Ferguson somehow stamped out the drinking culture at Old Trafford is a myth. He stamped out Whiteside and McGrath, but the culture remained largely unchanged. For much of the first decade of Ferguson's time in charge at the club, in fact, it was as rampant as ever.

'When we used to go out on one of Bryan Robson's sessions,' Lee Sharpe wrote in his book, *My Idea of Fun*, 'the round, starting at the Bull's Head in Hale, used to be: twelve Budweisers, six Beck's, a couple of shorts, a bottle of champagne for Eric Cantona, and two Cokes for Gary and Phil Neville.'

Sharpe wrote extensively about the drinking culture that still existed at the club in the early Nineties. The fact that he was so contemptuous of Gary Neville's abstinence suggests that Neville was still very much out on a limb at that time. It was obvious it took formidable mental strength and sureness of character for Neville to resist the entreaties of the drinking club.

It also suggests that the club might not have been quite the haven from excess that it was portrayed as when Paul Gascoigne was on the verge of joining in the summer of 1988. Ferguson thought he had sealed Gazza's signature and Gascoigne told him to go away and enjoy his holiday in Malta, secure in the knowledge that he had made up his mind to come to Old Trafford. Then he signed for Spurs.

It has often been said that Gascoigne's career and his life might have taken an altogether happier and more stable course if he had come under the guidance of Ferguson rather than Terry Venables. That underestimates Venables but it also exaggerates the influence that Ferguson held over his players, most of whom carried on their social lives in much the same way as they had under Atkinson.

Sharpe made it plain that drinking bouts with Roy Keane in the mid-Nineties, for instance, were a matter of routine. Time and time again, he said, he had to rescue Keane from drunken rows with either fellow footballers they had met at a nightclub or with members of the public to whom Keane had taken exception. Keane drank far more than Sharpe but, just as with Robson, Ferguson adopted a pragmatic attitude to his problem. According to Sharpe:

'Ferguson's attitude was that he wished Roy didn't drink like that but he was able to understand it, I think, more than the way I went out to have fun. Robbo could drink anyone under the table, but he was an awesome football man. I wasn't a big drinker like Keaney . . . but with Keaney it was a genuine, old-fashioned, working-class drink problem, and that he could relate to.

'I don't think it ever made him question Roy's attitude if he was up a back street in an Irish pub all day because he could understand that. If I was out dancing, though, being a bit flamboyant, the manager was convinced my head wasn't on the football. His attitude to the drinking culture was actually rather more subtle than wanting to ban it outright.'

Ferguson felt McGrath and Whiteside couldn't rebound from drinking sessions in the same way as Robson could, and later Keane. McGrath and Whiteside were regulars at a variety of Cheshire nightspots. Yesterdays in Alderley Edge, the Pinewood in Handforth, the Valley Lodge near Manchester Airport, Mulligans nearby, and a range of pubs in Hale and Altrincham. But by the time Ferguson arrived, a combination of their hedonistic lifestyles and long-standing injury problems were starting to catch up with them and they were spending more and more time on the treatment table.

'He was right about the drinking binges myself and Norman would go on,' McGrath said. 'We'd be in this pub or that pub and all the time somebody would ring Fergie at the club and give him a progress report. I can just imagine him now sitting at his desk with a map of the Greater Manchester area plotting our drinking route, putting down pins wherever we had been spotted. I'm glad he was keeping a note of where we were. Usually, by the end of the night we wouldn't have a clue if we were in Hale or Altrincham – and we'd care even less.'

Ferguson was particularly distressed by Whiteside's decline. Whiteside was still only twenty-one when Ferguson arrived at Old Trafford. He had already played in two World Cup finals tournaments for Northern Ireland. He set a whole raft of records for being the youngest in everything. When he played in the 1982 World Cup, he was the youngest player ever to appear in the finals, beating Pele's record set in 1958. In 1983 he became the youngest player to score at Wembley when he got the opener in United's Milk Cup defeat to Liverpool. In 1985 he scored the winner past Neville Southall in the FA Cup Final against league champions Everton.

Whiteside was a phenomenon, a kid who started off as a forward and matured into a midfielder of sublime vision. He had a sweet left foot, he was good in the air and hard in the tackle. He lacked pace but he was a player who captured the imagination of the supporters at Old Trafford, who always felt he was underrated in comparison with good, but less gifted, players like Frank Stapleton. For a while in the early Eighties, he seemed to have the world at his feet, but gradually, tortured by knee problems, he sank into a premature decline, burned out before his time.

Whiteside told Ferguson he blamed his injury problems on a course of physiotherapy that had gone wrong when he was fifteen. 'As a player, he was close to the genius category,' Ferguson said. 'It was natural to wonder if the pain of thinking about what might have been had something to do with the contempt for his career that was implied by his consumption of booze.

'The worst binges usually occurred when McGrath and Whiteside took to the bars as a double act. As swallowers, they could have been backed at even money against W. C. Fields and Rab C. Nesbitt.'

The decline of Whiteside and McGrath and the endless confrontations that their off-the-field antics created dominated Ferguson's early years at Old Trafford. There was an air of sadness about what was happening, a feeling that something was ending rather than beginning. It wasn't just Ferguson who felt the two men were squandering their careers. The supporters could sense the poignancy of the situation too.

Whiteside seemed to accept his fate with passive resignation and melancholic dignity. McGrath was more bitter. He was a wonderful defender, confident on the ball, good in the air and expert at reading play. He was a forerunner of Rio Ferdinand. But he had struggled with depression as a teenager and his drinking had deep-rooted origins. Crowds made him nervous, which didn't make him a natural for coping with 60,000 screaming punters inside Old Trafford. He was shy in the spotlight. He drank to take the edges off and give himself a bit of confidence.

Later in his life, after his career was over, he was treated for alcoholism at Tony Adams' Sporting Chance clinic in Liphook, Hampshire. He did not complete his rehabilitation. Ferguson felt McGrath ignored all his pleas to reform when he was a player, and as United continued to perform inconsistently in the league, their differences grew and grew.

McGrath's career at Old Trafford effectively came to an end in January 1989 when he appeared with Whiteside on *Kick Off*, Granada's Friday night preview show, on the eve of an FA Cup third-round tie with QPR. The two men had been drinking. They were giggly in front of the camera. McGrath had assumed he was not playing the next day because his knees were troubling him so he did not care how it looked.

The next day, Lee Sharpe pulled out of the team with flu and Ferguson told McGrath he was playing. McGrath said he wasn't in the right frame of mind or physical condition to play. 'The two of us exchanged words at a pace of knots, eventually almost coming to blows when I said I would play and that any comeback was on Ferguson's head,' McGrath said. 'After the mother and father of all rows, he finally accepted that I wasn't going to play.'

The following week, according to McGrath's autobiography, Ferguson and Martin Edwards tried to persuade McGrath that he should quit the game. They offered him a £100,000 pay-off and a testimonial in Dublin. McGrath was stunned. Then he began to grow angry. 'Without any warning, they started to discuss money and insurance and pay-offs,' he said. 'This was my career they were ending, as coldly and as ruthlessly as breaking a turkey's neck at Christmas. They thought they were offering me a great deal, that I would touch my forelock to the Lord of the Manor and say "thank you, sir," like a good little boy.'

McGrath decided to stay on even though he was shunned and made to train for the reserves. 'Eventually,' he said, 'I made an appointment to see Fergie and threw the bombshell back in his face. I would not quit. He was visibly devastated. He told me in no uncertain terms that I had made a mistake of the highest order . . . I asked for a transfer. That was turned down. They were prepared to let me quit but not to let me move to another club. Bitchy, to say the least.'

United stuttered towards another dismal finish in the league. Ferguson's finest moment that season was a gesture that no one knew about. He and Martin Edwards were early visitors to Anfield in the aftermath of the Hillsborough Disaster in April 1989. They brought a substantial cheque with them as United's contribution to the disaster appeal, an act of generosity and caring which is still remembered with gratitude at Anfield today.

As Arsenal and Liverpool played out their thrilling finish to that darkened campaign, United trailed in eleventh place. In the summer, Ferguson added Webb and Phelan to his squad. Pallister and Ince were coming soon, too. Getting rid of McGrath and Whiteside represented a huge gamble for Ferguson. He knew their departures would be unpopular with the supporters and leave him even more vulnerable if the following season started badly.

But Ferguson pressed ahead. McGrath was at a barbecue in Bryan Robson's back garden when Robson handed him the phone. It was Ferguson. There had been a bid from Aston Villa. Ferguson had accepted it. 'There was no "hello,"' McGrath said, 'only "I've given Graham Taylor permission to talk to you. This is his number, the deal is done between the clubs. Goodbye."'

McGrath went to Villa for £400,000. Two days later, Whiteside was transferred to Everton for £600,000. McGrath kicked and screamed to the end. He sold his story to the *News of the World* and slaughtered Ferguson. When he wrote his autobiography, one of the chapters was called 'Alex Ferguson, Ouch, Ouch, Ouch'. Its first few lines went like this: 'Alex Ferguson. A name that brings a lump to my throat every time I come across it. Alex Ferguson. Two words that stick in that throat every time I have to mention him. A man, a manager, a nightmare as far as I am concerned.'

Whiteside's exit was altogether quieter. It was tinged with sadness and regret. Whiteside didn't bear any grudges towards Ferguson. He was offered £50,000 to tell his side of the story of his United exit and pile some more pressure on Ferguson but he refused. He refused to cooperate with Crick's book and he refused to contribute to this one, too. 'No, I won't be doing that thanks,' he said.

In his own affectionate and wistful memoir of his time at Old Trafford, *My Memories of Man Utd*, Whiteside had only good things to say about Ferguson. 'I am not going to say that Fergie and I always saw eye to eye,' he wrote: 'but what I will say is that he was always fair with me and I think that despite the problems, I never hid the truth from him.

'Before I got the chance to speak to the Everton manager, Colin Harvey, Fergie told me what sort of figure I should ask for salary-wise. Thankfully, I listened to his advice and upon joining the Goodison Park side I was suddenly earning more than I had been at United. This was thanks to someone who I was apparently not getting on with.

'Perhaps he saw something of himself in me, a lad from a working-class background who went into every game with the intention of winning and someone who would go for every ball with the intention of winning it. At the end of the day, Alex Ferguson did what he thought was best for both United and for me.'

The end for Whiteside was desperately sad. He only played one full season at Everton. United's fans booed him the only time he played there in an Everton shirt. 'I was bewildered and disappointed,' he said. In September 1990, after he was tackled from behind by one of the Everton juniors in a practice match at Bellefield and injured again, a surgeon told him he would spend the rest of his life in a wheelchair if he carried on playing. He was twenty-six years old when he was forced to retire.

Even in retirement, the fates were unkind to him. United granted him a testimonial at the end of the 1991–92 season and for a while it seemed as if the game would provide them with an opportunity to celebrate winning their first league title for twenty-five years and parade the Championship trophy. But

United blew it, Leeds won and Whiteside's testimonial was a drab afterthought. Only 7,434 supporters turned up to watch the match between United and Everton. It was the last game at the stadium before the Stretford End was demolished.

Whiteside still turns up at Old Trafford to do some match-day corporate hospitality. 'Occasionally, I bump into Sir Alex and we'll stop for a chat,' he wrote, 'something that many might find surprising as there are people out there who believe that we just don't see eye to eye or haven't done so in the past. I remember walking down one of the corridors after the championship win of 2001 and I saw him celebrating with his family and friends. Next thing I knew, he has dragged me in, stuck a bottle of champagne into my hand and told me to get it down my neck.'

Whiteside must have seemed like a ghost from a troubled past on that day of triumph at Old Trafford. Selling him and McGrath back in the summer of 1989 didn't solve Ferguson's problems. Not immediately anyway. United won their first game of the season 4–1 against champions Arsenal, and when the eccentric Michael Knighton offered to buy the club, his promise of an infusion of cash unlocked transfer funds for Ferguson to buy Webb, Phelan, Pallister and Ince. But then United ran into City.

The 5–1 defeat at Maine Road and its aftermath shattered United's confidence. 'That game was as low as it ever got,' Pallister said. 'When I came out of training at the Cliff the following Monday, there were four or five big burly fans waiting for all of us outside the gym and they were caning each of us as we came out. I was the record signing so I was getting plenty of stick but it wasn't just me. We all got panned. It was intimidating.'

The result sent United into a tailspin. They were jeered after a 3–0 home defeat to Spurs in the League Cup in October. That game yielded an iconic banner, the symbol of Fergie's dark times at Old Trafford. '3 Years of Excuses and It's Still Crap,' the banner said. 'Ta-Ra Fergie.' Ferguson started going to Glasgow for the rest of the weekend after Saturday matches just so he couldn't bump into United fans.

In December 1989, United lost at home to Crystal Palace and Spurs again and were trounced by Aston Villa at Villa Park. They rounded the holiday programme off with a goalless draw against QPR. 'I wouldn't walk round the corner to watch them play,' George Best said. He didn't want to watch them play until Ferguson had been sacked, he said. It's doubtful whether that was one of the 'million memories, all of them good' that Ferguson referred to when Best died in 2005.

Most observers felt Ferguson would be sacked if United lost to Brian Clough's Nottingham Forest in an FA Cup third-round tie at the City Ground on 7 January 1990. Martin Edwards says now that that was not the case. But it's easy to say it now. If United had lost that tie, their season would have been over five months early. And it would have been an awfully long five months for Ferguson.

'Before the game at Forest,' Pallister said, 'we were told in the dressing room that Jimmy Hill had said on the television that we looked like a beaten side even in the warm-up. That fired some of the lads up a bit. We realized that the manager was under a lot of pressure and we knew we were the under-dogs. We were expected to lose that game because Forest were playing some nice football at that time.'

United won 1–0. Mark Robins, otherwise a bit-part player in the history of Manchester United, got the goal. Mark Hughes played a brilliant ball into the box from the left. He hit it with the outside of his right foot so that it curled round the back of the Forest defence and Robins ran in and nodded it past the Forest goalkeeper. That morning, Ferguson had placed a bet on United to win the FA Cup. He got odds of 16–1.

United scraped past Hereford United in the fourth round and Newcastle in the fifth. They beat Sheffield United at Bramall Lane in the quarter-finals and then drew 3–3 with first-division

Oldham Athletic in the semi-final at Maine Road. United won the replay 2–1. Mark Robins extended his fifteen minutes of fame by scoring the winner.

United played Crystal Palace in the Final at Wembley. Palace nearly stole it. It was the match when Ian Wright burst on to the national stage, scoring twice after he had been brought off the bench in the second half. But even though Hughes earned United another 3–3 draw with an equalizer late in extra time, after the match Ferguson was weighed down by the realization that he was about to have to take one of the most difficult decisions of his managerial career.

His goalkeeper, Jim Leighton, who had served him so well at Aberdeen and been with him for all his triumphs north of the border, had lost his confidence. Ferguson had agonized about dropping him for the semi-final against Oldham but had been talked out of it by his assistant, Archie Knox. But Leighton was at fault for two of the goals in the Final against Palace, and this time Ferguson decided he could not risk him letting the team down again in the replay. He dropped him.

It was a brave and ruthless decision. But it was also correct. Leighton had become a liability. He had been worrying so much about his loss of form in the past couple of months that he had developed a stomach ulcer. He was getting migraines. Leighton will never admit it to himself and most of his friends will never tell him straight, but it was obvious he was in no fit state to play.

Ferguson wasn't just thinking about himself when he replaced Leighton with Les Sealey, on loan from Luton Town, for the replay. He knew that his job would be on the line again if United lost to Palace and let the promise of his first trophy slip away. But he was thinking about the rest of the team and the supporters. Leighton had nearly cost United the first match against Palace and his mistakes were not isolated incidents. They were part of a pattern. They told of a goalkeeper who needed to be taken out of the line of fire.

In his own way, Ferguson has paid heavily for the decision too. He was condemned as heartless and vindictive for what he did. He was blamed for ruining Leighton's career and blighting his life. A decade later, Leighton was indignant when Ferguson claimed he had behaved selfishly by refusing to accept that he bore part of the responsibility for being dropped. He also poured scorn on Ferguson's claim that he had tried to mend their relationship by calling to encourage Leighton while he was playing for Scotland at the 1990 World Cup. 'The only call I remember getting from him in Italy,' Leighton said, 'was about tickets for each of our three group ties. His own allocation had not turned up and he was looking for some assistance.'

Before the replay against Palace, Leighton and his wife Linda reacted with considerable melodrama to a footballing decision and Leighton is still deeply bitter about the trauma he says Ferguson inflicted upon him when he broke the news that he was dropped on the eve of the game. Leighton was one of the only players from either Palace or United who refused to play in Geoff Thomas's testimonial match.

'I've no clear recollection of what else was said because I was numbed by his decision,' Leighton said. 'I could not see straight and was rendered speechless. I was also dreading the thought that my first task would be to call Linda to tell her my bad news. I knew it would devastate her and, when I plucked up enough courage to lift the phone, had my fears confirmed. Both of us were in tears during that conversation . . . Getting through the next day proved to be one of the toughest tasks of my life. I was in a trance, hardly aware of all that was happening around me.'

But Ferguson's decision was vindicated. Sealey kept a clean sheet. United won 1–0. Neil Webb picked out the young United left back Lee Martin with a searching long ball over the Palace defence and Martin took it on his chest and crashed it into the roof of the net. After three and a half years in the job, Ferguson was a winner at last.

When the squad congregated at Wembley station for the journey back north, Ferguson was the picture of relief and happiness. He made a point of kissing each of the players' wives and girlfriends as they waited on the platform. When he got to Linda Leighton, she turned her back on him.

19: Shankly and the New Creed at Workington

Bill Shankly became manager of Workington AFC on 6 January 1954, four days after he had resigned his post at Grimsby Town. Workington were struggling at the foot of the Third Division North. A year later, Shankly had saved them from having to apply for re-election and was busy trying to fashion a promotion challenge when he typed an extraordinary letter on the club's headed notepaper.

The official print at the top of the page told the reader that the club colours were 'red shirts, white knickers'. The Chairman was E. D. Smith, the manager was W. Shankly. The club's phone number at its ramshackle Borough Park ground in the lowlands at the foot of the hill where the town was built was Workington 871. Shankly had typed the date underneath. It was January 17th, 1955. He was forty-one years old.

The letter was addressed to Reg Drury, a prominent reporter at the *News of the World* and one of the most respected figures in Fleet Street. Drury, who had the best contacts book in the business, made a point of getting on well with managers – until shortly before Drury's death in a car accident in 2003, the former Blackburn Rovers and Internazionale boss Roy Hodgson made a point of attending the Football Writers' Annual Dinner with him – and had struck up an acquaintance with Shankly.

Shankly liked journalists and, particularly at such a precarious stage of his managerial career, he was aware of how important it was to have influential friends among the Fourth Estate. He sent the letter to Drury on the pretext of thanking him for a favour – a special delivery of a copy of the *News of the World* to read on a train journey taking him from London back to the north – but its content went way beyond that.

It was stark in its candour and intensity and it reveals more about Shankly's obsession with football and his asceticism in the pursuit of success than anything else that is known about him. The letter to Reg Drury shows us the man who took his wife out twice in fifteen years during his time in charge at Liverpool. It shows us the man who was prepared to devote his life to football at the expense of everything else. It went like this:

Dear Reg

Thanks for paper, actually I lost my copy on the way home last Sunday.

Note your remarks on Page 5 and am in complete agreement with you, this being good losers, is being exagerated [*sic*]. We were good losers at Luton, but although outwardly I took the defeat well, inwardly I was boiling, I have no time for losing Reg, and I'm possessed with a killer instinct, which in my playing days paid dividends, without using shady tactics, I made sure that my immediate opponent drew a blank. I used to think that it would be better to die than lose. To enable me to reach the top, and keep their [*sic*], I went to all extremes, no woman, no smoking, early to bed, good food, this went on for years but it was worth while. If all players in the game did the same, the game would improve and would reach such a high standard that it would be a honour to be defeated.

You will be thinking I'm blowing a trumpet instead of giving my opinion of your article but it's perfectly honest. Hope you are well Reg. All good wishes. Yours sincerely. Bill.

At this remove, some of what Shankly said and did in the course of a career heavy with anecdotes can seem like self-parody, but the letter he wrote to Drury underlines how reverentially serious he was about the game. A puritanical streak ran through Shankly, forged by his loosely Presbyterian upbringing in Ayrshire, and his God was football.

Even at Workington, even before that when he was working at other outposts like Grimsby and Carlisle, he didn't want relief from football. He wanted total immersion. Towards the end of Ferguson's career, he threw himself into horse-racing and seemed to gain more enjoyment from it than football for a while. Ferguson seemed to be looking for a way out, trying to prepare himself for a life after football. But Shankly wasn't interested in that kind of diversion.

Shankly's obsession was undiluted. In that sense, he was closer in philosophy to someone like Arsène Wenger. Football turned men like Shankly and Wenger into hermits. In the autumn of 2005, Wenger told a group of journalists that he was going to go to a restaurant with his wife to celebrate his fifty-sixth birthday but that there were strings attached. It had to be a place near his north London home and he had to be back by 10.30 pm so he could watch *Match of the Day*. Wenger also revealed once that despite managing Arsenal since 1996, he didn't know central London at all. He never had any occasion to go to the West End. His day-to-day life was spent either at the training ground near the M25 or at home watching Spanish, French, English and German football.

Sometimes, Shankly's obsessional determination spawned unintentional slapstick. When he arrived at Workington, he was horrified to learn he had to share the Borough Park pitch with the local rugby league side, Workington Town. Rugby league was king in Workington – they had won the Championship in 1951 – and every Thursday night the Town players trained on the already muddy pitch and trod it into a morass. If it froze, its contours were moulded into a series of ankle-twisting bone-hard ridges.

But that wasn't the only thing that enraged Shankly. He was

furious that Town's coach, Gus Risman, another fearsomely strong personality, insisted on having the sidelines several feet narrower than Shankly wanted. The unfortunate groundsman, Billy Watson, who was to spend thirty-nine years trying to keep the quagmire of Borough Park at bay, soon found himself at the heart of a bitter row between two stubborn men.

'Shankly wanted me to make the pitch as wide as possible to encourage his style of football,' Watson said. 'But Risman thought otherwise because when the pitch was extended, his players were ending up on the cinders of the running track when they got tackled. I spent a few weeks rubbing out the rugby league lines with a stiff brush, painting the football lines on when Shankly's team played, rubbing them out, painting the league lines on again for Risman, and so on. But there soon came a point when the pitch could take no more.

'One day, Shankly came to me and said: "What time does Risman start?" He went to see him and said his piece. Technically, the rugby league side were the guests at the stadium so Gus just said: "You're the boss, Bill." And that was it. The lines stayed out wide, right near the cinder track.'

It took a driven man to do what Shankly was doing, to haul his young family from the eastern extremities of the country to one of its westernmost points, swapping the maritime grime and fish stink of Grimsby for a port in decline and a town dependent on a coal-mining industry that started dying in Workington thirty years before Margaret Thatcher and the brutal realities of capitalism killed off the pits in the rest of Britain. It was cold in Grimsby but it was colder and even more exposed in Workington, where the squalls and the gales howled in off the Irish Sea. 'There was always this film of dirt everywhere in Workington,' Nessie Shankly said. 'I think it must have come from a chemical plant or something. Every time I put the washing out, it was always dirty when I brought it back in.'

These were football outposts that Shankly was haunting now. Geographically, economically and meritocratically, places like Workington, Grimsby and Carlisle were at the margins of the game. Borough Park didn't even have electricity when Shankly became manager. It still ran on gas. The football club shared the stadium with the rugby league club. It was riven by boardroom disputes. And Workington had no money, even though they were occasionally drawing crowds that seem out-landishly good by today's lower-league standards. In Shankly's time at Borough Park, the club attracted 10,193 supporters for an FA Cup first-round tie against Hyde United and more than 14,000 for a league match against top-of-the-table Port Vale. But unemployment was high in the town and for much of the time attendances were sparse.

Shankly's consolation was that he was close to home again. Mary Queen of Scots had taken refuge briefly in Workington as she fled south to England in 1568. Galloway was on the other side of the Solway Firth and Ayrshire beyond that. The friends he and his wife had made in Carlisle were not far away, either. The tranquillity of Bassenthwaite Lake was close, too, but Shankly did not own a car when he was in charge at Borough Park, and anyway searching out a bit of peace in the Lakes wasn't really his style.

He threw himself into the job. He had to. Workington had finished the previous season next to bottom of the table and a few weeks before Shankly took charge they were at the foot of the division with 12 points from 21 games. Workington was one of those clubs that seemed to be engaged in an eternal fight for survival. Shankly's period at the helm was like a fleeting glimpse of light in a long tunnel of darkness.

Men like Shankly and, some years after him, Keith Burkin-shaw, were just passing through. Borough Park, squatting beneath an incline across the road from a new Tesco, is a dirge on the ephemerality of football management at clubs that live on the edge of the precipice. What Shankly achieved at Liverpool is still celebrated more than thirty years after he retired and will continue to be remembered as long as the club exists. He made

Liverpool the special club it is. At Workington, he stuck a few plasters on the wounds and tended to the club as assiduously as he could and then he moved on.

Borough Park is as dilapidated now as it was in the mid-Fifties. It's a wasteland of bricked-up windows and shattered glass. A heavy roller rusts in the weeds. At the Town End, behind one of the goals, there's a stand with an apology for a roof made out of corrugated iron that looks as if it could have been decaying ever since Shankly's two-year sojourn. The sweep of the terraces has been interrupted with rows of dirty white plastic seats opposite what used to be the main stand, but you can still see the cupola of Trinity Methodist Church up on the hill in the town. There are four seats in the press box, two rows of two, and four puny floodlights mounted on the type of towers sentries might use in a prison camp.

The club, more commonly known now as Workington Reds, played in the Conference North in 2005–06, sharing their place in football's pyramid with Kettering Town when Paul Gascoigne was their manager for a fleeting and unhappy spell in 2005. They slipped out of the league in 1977. They won four games all that season and finished rock-bottom for the second year in succession. Their average crowd had fallen below 1,000. They were replaced in the old Fourth Division by Wimbledon.

A giant billboard outside Borough Park flakes old posters. Barbed wire sits atop cracked slabs of concrete fence. On the stone wall outside what looks like the main entrance, names daubed in white paint many decades ago mark out the spaces where the chairman, the president and the directors parked their cars. Furthest away from the entrance are the spots reserved for the players. Behind one of the stands, a straight line of bare ground runs off into the distance where the railway sleepers used to lie in more prosperous times.

An air of foreboding and gloom hangs over the place. You know things must have got pretty grim when a three-volume history of the club has been given the title *So Sad, So Very Sad*.

And why some of the last surviving footage of the club's Football League past, its final home game against Newport County in May 1977, is called *Rejected FC*. This is not a club that has enjoyed its fair share of the glory years.

But while he was there, Shankly did everything he could to engender a pride in the place. Every morning, he met Watson at the bus station. Shankly dressed in a smart suit and tie and carried his leather briefcase. On the walk to the ground, they would pick up a bottle of milk from a doorstep in William Street as part of an arrangement with the woman who lived there. Occasionally, a motorist shot them a suspicious glance. Shankly glared back so fiercely that none of the drivers held his gaze for long.

He spent a lot of time with Watson, especially in the afternoons when training was over and the players had gone home. The groundsman remembers the sound of Shankly's steel-tipped heels echoing around the cold, empty corridors of Borough Park. And the two men, who in their very different ways dedicated their lives to football, sat in the boiler house for hours on end, talking about the game.

'I'd put the kettle on,' Watson said, 'and we would put the world of football to rights. He would pull up a lemonade crate to sit on and I would say to myself in anticipation: "What will he reminisce about today?" Would it be Tom Finney or maybe West Brom's Ronnie Simpson with his emerald-green overcoat? That was how it went. It was enthralling. I never married and I think it's because I was married to football. Shankly did marry but he was totally immersed in the game.'

On match days, Shankly led the team into Borough Park on foot an hour or so before kick-off. 'He would march past, eyes straight ahead, and say: "Close the gates, Billy, we're all inside,"' Watson said. 'It was the way he said it in that Scotch twang. It was very much: "Lock the gate, we're all in here, it's time for the big fight."'

It was a big fight, too, but Shankly drew his first game in

charge and Workington only lost twice throughout January and February. More than 13,000 watched Shankly's managerial bow against Carlisle and a thousand more than that watched the victory over Port Vale soon after. When they beat Barnsley a fortnight later, they moved out of the bottom four.

The Workington captain was Jack Vitty, a man who looked like a cross between Norman Hunter and Tommy Smith. Predictably, he had a reputation as a player who did not take prisoners. Shankly's first signing was a squat, stockily built centre forward called Ernie Whittle, an ex-miner who had had a decent career at Lincoln City. Whittle scored six times before the end of the season and Workington went into the last two games needing one point to ensure safety.

They got it by beating Halifax 3–1. Whittle scored twice. Workington finished 20th in the 24-team division with 40 points, 4 points more than Halifax, who had to apply for re-election. Under Shankly they had won 22 points from their 20 games under Shankly, compared with 18 points from the 26 games before he arrived. It was quite a rescue act and the club's directors were pleased. Four of them even decided to cut their ties with the rugby league club so they could concentrate on reviving the fortunes of the football team.

In the summer break, even Shankly found himself being dragged into a few community activities. He judged a beauty competition, appeared at some of the club's fund-raising dances and organized Sunday morning training for the A-team so he could form an idea of the quality of some of the young players he might be able to draw upon the following season. He decorated the club house he and his family had been allocated in Harrington Road, about a mile from the ground. It was a neat new semi-detached place with a trimmed hedge.

Shankly made a clutch of new signings, and early in the 1954–55 season Workington rose to the heady heights of ninth place, the highest they had ever been. He had got the players on his usual routine of playing five-a-sides in training. Not Young v Old or English v Scottish this time, but Bachelors v Married Men.

Towards the end of 1954, Workington enjoyed what was probably their greatest triumph under Shankly when they knocked Leyton Orient out of the FA Cup in the second round at Brisbane Road. The team had travelled by coach to Carlisle station where they caught the midday Flying Scotsman to London. On the train, Shankly had discovered that the great Hungarian team of the 1950s, the team that had humbled England 6–3 at Wembley the year before, inflicting the first home defeat on football's mother country, was camped in first class, travelling back to the capital from Glasgow where they had just beaten Scotland 4–2.

They were all there. Gyula Grosics, the goalkeeper, Jozsef Bozsik, Nandor Hidegkuti, Sandor Kocsis and the Galloping Major himself, Ferenc Puskas. Shankly took the Workington side up the train to meet these footballing gods. He asked Puskas for his autograph. 'Some of their magic rubbed off on us,' Shankly told reporters after the win over Orient, and the Hungarian FA sent Shankly a postcard to Borough Park. 'Congratulations on your historic win,' it said.

By December, Workington were up to fifth place and the board was considering a plan codenamed Prepare for Promotion, which entailed raising the £10,000 that would be necessary to bring Borough Park in line with the standards required of the Second Division. In the New Year, though, the team slumped. They finished the season in eighth place and in the summer the board accepted a proposal to cut players' wages by £1 a week to bring them into line with the rest of the Third Division. Shankly was told there was no money for transfers. The previous season, Workington had spent more than £18,000 on new signings and now the club was flat broke.

Shankly did his best to promote a youth policy. He even put adverts in the *Workington Times and Star* to encourage youngsters to attend training sessions. He packed the reserves with local lads under twenty. And Workington started his last season in charge well. Shankly even made a rather optimistic bid to sign Blackpool and England striker Stan Mortensen, who was now in the autumn of his career. Mortensen chose Hull instead, Workington lost a top half of the table clash with Accrington Stanley 5–1 and Shankly decided it was time to move on.

In November 1955 he was approached by Beattie and offered the job of assistant manager at Huddersfield. He accepted. He had had enough of the grind at Workington. There had been a few highs but plenty of lows. After that FA Cup victory over Leyton Orient, inspired by the brief encounter with the Hungarians on the train, for instance, Workington had been trounced 5–0 by Luton in the third round.

That was the defeat Shankly referred to in his letter to Reg Drury. Results like that crushed him. Worse than dying, that's what he said. There were always going to be plenty of days like that at Workington. Huddersfield held out the promise that it might feel a bit more like living.

20: Ferguson Breaks the Dam

There was a card school at the back of the team coach on away trips. Alex Ferguson didn't just turn a blind eye to it, he was part of it. He'd always liked a bet. When United trained at The Cliff, in Salford, he used the youth team's flying winger, Keith Gillespie, as a runner to place his wagers. When Gillespie moved to Newcastle, he developed a tidy little gambling habit that once cost him £47,000 in a single day. And when it was revealed in the spring of 2006 that Wayne Rooney had amassed gambling debts of £700,000, payable to Michael Owen's business partner, Ferguson dismissed the story as 'nonsense'.

Bryan Robson, Gary Pallister, Steve Bruce, Denis Irwin and the physio, Jim McGregor, were the card sharps on the bus in the early Nineties when United finally became the high rollers of English football again. Ferguson was the unexploded bomb in the corner. The manager always started the coach journey sitting at the front of the bus with the rest of the staff. But after a while, he sauntered down the aisle, making a few cracks along the way, and took his place at the gaming table. He loved cards. Just like Shankly did. And he hated losing a hand. The lads on the bus played a game of trumps called Hearts. The players sat there, laughing and joking with their boss, knowing this was the closest they would ever get to having any kind of real social interaction with him.

Ferguson never went out drinking with them. He frowned on that level of fraternization. He wanted to maintain a distance between him and his players. A game of cards was as far as it ever went. Even in those games, the Ferguson they knew best, the incendiary manager who was such a tightly-wound taskmaster, was never far away. 'If the game didn't go his way,' Pallister said, 'he would have a tantrum and chuck the cards. I have seen him throw a deck of fifty-two cards right across the bus because he had lost. Nobody laughed but it could be quite comical.'

Somehow, this scene gets to the nub of Ferguson. That was the way he was when he was still the hungriest man in British football, when he was ravenous for respect and for glory. He was a manager who walked the line. He could be a benevolent, caring father-figure one moment, a guy who could have a laugh and a joke and play the players' buddy. And the next minute he could be a brute, an ugly dictator who brooked no dissent and regarded any kind of levity or leeway as the enemy. He could be a nice guy and then he could try and destroy you, really destroy you. Get to the heart of you in front of your teammates and systematically humiliate you.

When Ferguson speaks of loyalty as his guiding principle, it is hard to know quite how to reconcile that with the regular bullying and goading of players that has always been part of his management style. It reached its apogee in his first eight years at United when he was spring-loaded with job fear and vaulting ambition. He could be avuncular when it suited him but more often he would let out his dread of being thwarted and his despair at defeat in a series of vicious spluttering tirades that earned him his nickname, The Hairdrier.

Once, famously, he drove round to Lee Sharpe's house in April 1992 when he found out that Sharpe and Ryan Giggs had defied him by going on a night out to Blackpool after he had told them both to stay at home. The Championship was slipping away from United again that season and Ferguson was at snapping point.

Ferguson was at an English Schools Football Association black-tie dinner in Morecambe when someone told him they had seen Giggs and Sharpe in Sharpe's Range Rover in Blackpool. Ferguson marched straight out without finishing his meal, drove back to Manchester and went to confront Sharpe at his house. He found Giggs there as well as a couple of youth team players. And a few girls. They were getting ready for another night on the town but Ferguson stopped that.

He ordered the girls and the apprentices out of the house, clipping the lads on the back of the head as they left. Then he started on Sharpe and Giggs. Even though Sharpe maintains the Easter Monday jaunt to Blackpool had been Giggs's idea, Ferguson saved the worst of his venom for Sharpe.

'He subjected us to the father, no, the grandfather, of all hairdriers,' Sharpe said. 'It was industrial strength; he could have dried the hair of a battalion of the Chinese army. His face was an awesome colour; you wouldn't know a face could turn that crimson. He leaned into us so he was an inch from our faces and tore shreds off us.

' "You're losing your pace," he started in on me, his face so close to mine I could feel the heat. "You're going down the pan, but the worst thing is that you're not just taking yourself down, you're dragging all the young lads with a bit of talent down with you." '

It got personal with Ferguson quickly. Abuse like that left Sharpe with ambivalent feelings towards a manager he had once worshipped. He blamed Ferguson for ruining his romance with his childhood sweetheart, Debbie, by ordering him out of the house they shared and back into spartan club digs. Separated from her, Sharpe became a womanizer. Ferguson didn't like that either. The result was that Sharpe was left with a reluctance to commit to a relationship. Ferguson's strictures and the spirit he built at Old Trafford and Pittodrie have enhanced many lives but they have harmed their fair share, too.

'If you were a young lad like me, loving it, but beset in private by doubts,' Sharpe said, 'his method wasn't what you needed. There was, though, something in his fury, his relentless, obsessive desire to win, to be better, never to be satisfied, to rant when standards fell, which did push everybody on. I just feel you can have that but be positive and treat people like grown-ups, too.'

Ferguson treated some players like adults. He rarely turned on Bryan Robson. And Eric Cantona was totally immune. The rest of the team were vulnerable. Ferguson twice came close to exchanging blows with his players in the early Nineties. One time was with Paul Ince at half-time of a 4–0 Champions League humiliation by Barcelona in the Nou Camp in November 1994. Ferguson called Ince 'a fucking bottler' over and over again, shouting it in his face until eventually Ince snapped and the two men had to be separated by Brian Kidd.

The other occasion was in early January 1994 when United blew a three-goal lead against Liverpool at Anfield and drew 3–3. Ferguson screamed abuse at Peter Schmeichel for the quality of his goal kicks and Schmeichel gave as good as he got. He questioned Ferguson's management and attacked his character. Ferguson threatened to throw a cup of tea in Schmeichel's face.

The row was so bad Ferguson told Schmeichel he was going to sack him. Schmeichel, it should be remembered, was recognized as the world's best goalkeeper at the time. Ferguson only reconsidered when he overheard Schmeichel apologizing to the rest of the team for the way he had behaved.

Schmeichel was one of Ferguson's favourite targets. His number one, though, was Pallister. Like Schmeichel, Pallister was a strong character. He was very difficult to upset or to unsettle but he had a difficult time when he first arrived at Old Trafford, burdened by the size of his record transfer fee and identified by Ferguson as one of the prime causes of United's struggles in the league in the 1989–90 season. Pallister recalled:

'I am loath to say I was scared of him, but I was intimidated by him. I have seen so many players have stand-up barneys with him where it has got to the point where you think there is going to be a punch thrown. The good thing about him was that you could have a stand-up row with him, but by the time Monday came around it was all forgotten about. I have had other managers who would ignore you for a week if they'd had a disagreement with you, but Fergie wasn't like that.

'He took me to one side once after I had had a row with him at half-time over something he had said. He told me that he had ten minutes to get his points across at half-time and that maybe he might sometimes put it too bluntly. But he said that he could not afford for players to be arguing with him in those ten minutes because there wasn't time.

'I was one of his favourites when it came to him dishing out stick. He felt I needed a kick up the arse. Sharpey got plenty, too. The only player that I never saw him have a pop at was Eric. I suppose you are dealing with a different temperament altogether there. But I have seen him stand toe to toe with Peter Schmeichel. I have seen him do that with Roy as well. You think of someone the size of Schmeichel and Fergie still never took a backward step. He wasn't afraid of anything. He would front up to anyone. He was never going to shout and scream and then cower behind his coach.

'He can cut you to pieces with words and belittle you. He said things to me. He said to me once "You will never make a centre half as long as you have got a hole in your arse". When you are confronted with something like that, you can either wither and die or you can prove to him and your teammates that he is wrong. In a way, it was a challenge. He gives you pelters and if you mope around the place, you are not going to have the character to win a league title, you are not going to be able to stand it in the muck and bullets at Plough Lane. You needed to have character to stand up against him.

'He would tear you off a strip. He was clever at making you feel a bit small. Nobody likes to be belittled in front of their mates and there were times when I thought he was out of order. In that first season I was there, 1989–90, I was copping a lot of flak and he was on my case a lot and there were times when I thought he was unfair and that I was being picked on. But now I can go back and he will invite me in for a chat. I still enjoy being in his company. It is part of the way of life at a football club. It is part of the relationship between a manager and his players. You are always going to have differences and you are always going to have strong personalities.'

The United team that emerged from the dark days of the late Eighties into the bright, shining light of the early Nineties was built on strong personalities. Ferguson's policy of buying a strong character, not just a good football player, was the bedrock of his success when his fortunes turned and the honours started to mount up. He found it hard to maintain the same policy after the European Cup win in 1999 and somehow felt unable to challenge men like Laurent Blanc, Fabien Barthez and Juan Sebastián Verón to raise their game when their performances fell below the level United required.

The recruitment of men like that diluted the team spirit at United and was one of the main reasons behind the slow decline that has gripped the club since its last Championship win in 2002–03. A decade earlier, though, Ferguson could count on men with steel in their souls to bring the club the Championship that had eluded United for so long.

Bryan Robson was the king of these men, a player regarded as a hero by his teammates and by his manager, too. Robson gave everything for the United cause and was a man of immense and unwavering physical courage. He was the leader of the dressing room and he and Ferguson had a close and trusting relationship. If the players had a grievance, it would be channelled back to the manager through Robson. If the manager wanted to get a point across to the players, he used Robson as his mouthpiece.

Led by Robson, United came desperately, heartbreakingly close to the title in 1991–92. They seemed to hold the advantage over Howard Wilkinson's Leeds side all season. With five games left to play, United were 2 points ahead with a game in hand.

Then United lost 2–1 to Nottingham Forest on Easter Monday and 1–0 to West Ham at Upton Park, a couple of days after Giggs and Sharpe had taken their illicit trip to Blackpool. Ferguson was starting to crack under the pressure. He called West Ham's performance 'obscene' and 'almost criminal' because they had raised their game so far above their norm.

Liverpool killed United off with a 2–0 win at Anfield, but by then Leeds had all but won the title anyway, beating Yorkshire rivals Sheffield United 3–2 at Bramall Lane earlier in the day. 'That was one of the worst days of my career,' Ryan Giggs said. 'It was terrible. Leeds had won in the morning, so we knew we had to beat Liverpool on their home patch to keep our faltering challenge alive. We lost 2–0, which confirmed Leeds as champions. Anfield was in raptures and took a lot of pleasure from our failure. After the game, as I was making my way to the team coach, a couple of Liverpool fans asked me for my autograph. I obliged, only for them to tear it up in front of me. The manager always reminds me of that incident to motivate me when we play Liverpool.'

Ferguson blamed his side's collapse on fixture congestion. United had had to play four games in seven days. Leeds fans hailed the influence of Cantona, who had been signed in the winter and had helped to ease the title away from United. It did not improve Ferguson's state of mind to be reminded over and over again that Leeds' most influential player that season was Gordon Strachan, the man he had discarded several years earlier.

His bitterness about Strachan spilled over in his autobiography. He had fallen out with him once when the two men were at Aberdeen and Strachan had become entangled in the messy transfer saga that finally saw him leave for Old Trafford. When the time came for Ferguson to bid him farewell at United in 1989, he did so with little affection.

Their relationship had been poisoned terminally by Strachan's manoeuvrings when he attempted to leave the club in the summer of 1988. Ferguson felt he had been duplicitous. 'I decided that this man could not be trusted an inch,' Ferguson said. 'Our lives had been enmeshed for most of a decade but I knew in that moment that I wouldn't want to expose my back to him in a hurry.'

Ferguson felt then that his team did not mirror his own personality. He did not feel confident in its fighting qualities. By the time he stole Cantona away from Leeds, though, that had changed. Ferguson did not inherit his first great United team. He built it brick by brick. Just like Shankly did in the years after he arrived at Anfield in 1959. Nor did Ferguson build it on sand. Instead, he hewed it out of rock.

In goal, Schmeichel had been bought from the Danish side Brondby in 1991 for £550,000, probably the best buy of Ferguson's career. Paul Parker was at right back; the durable, obdurate Steve Bruce, bought from Norwich City for £850,000 in December 1987, was Pallister's partner in the centre of defence; and Denis Irwin, metronomic, expressionless and unflappable, was a fixture at left back after his arrival from Oldham Athletic in 1990.

Andrei Kanchelskis was signed from Shakhtar Donetsk in the spring of 1991 and tore opposing defences apart with his pace on the right wing. Ince dominated midfield, first with Robson, then with the young gun, Roy Keane. On the left, Giggs, who had made his debut in March 1991 at the age of seventeen, was the closest thing United had seen to a genius since the departure of George Best.

Giggs was a bewitching winger. His friend and rival Sharpe had raw pace and great dynamism but he did not have the subtlety or the skill that Giggs had, and soon began to be supplanted by him. Partly because of his youth, partly because of his talent, Ferguson protected Giggs steadfastly from the demands of the media and refused to allow him to conduct interviews.

Ferguson spoke of the first time he saw him play with great

lyricism. In fact, he imparted a kind of mysticism to the experience of witnessing the beauty of a flowering talent. 'A gold miner who has searched every part of the river or mountain and then suddenly finds himself staring at a nugget could not feel more exhilaration than I did watching Giggs that day,' Ferguson wrote in his autobiography. 'I shall always remember my first sight of him floating over the pitch at the Cliff so effortlessly that you would have sworn his feet weren't touching the ground.'

The reclusiveness that Ferguson imposed on Giggs added an air of mystery to him. When that was combined with his good looks and status as the heir of Best in a United side that was suddenly beginning to click, Giggs became the leading icon in English football at a time when the game was riding the post-1990 World Cup boom inspired by the national team's dramatic run to the semi-finals and the impact of the tears shed by Paul Gascoigne. He was football's favourite pin-up until David Beckham came along. Giggs, far more mischievous than his dull public persona suggests, handed over the mantle gladly.

Giggs and his contemporary at Liverpool, Steve McManaman, were hailed as a new breed of winger, lightning-fast but elusive, too. They did not rely on a long ball over the top of an opposing defence. They were happier picking the ball up from deep and weaving in and out of back-pedalling defenders. Neither was a touchline hugger. McManaman did not even see himself as a winger, more as an all-round midfield player.

Giggs scored outstanding individual goals, too. There is a Canadian boxer, Arturo 'Thunder' Gatti, who is also known by fight fans as The Human Highlight Reel because his fights are almost always spectacular. Giggs was the football version of Gatti. He could always be relied on to provide something special. One goal against Queens Park Rangers at Loftus Road in January 1993 set the standard. Giggs hurdled tackles and beat four players with his pace and trickery, running from close to the halfway line before clipping a left-foot shot past the goalkeeper and into the far corner of the net.

Giggs seemed like a throwback to an earlier generation. His appearance and style recalled the best of United's past. His emergence and the way he thrived was the clearest indication of all that United really were on the road back to the same kind of greatness they had enjoyed under Matt Busby. In many ways, in fact, Giggs is Ferguson's finest achievement in football. His career is a monument to the way Ferguson chaperoned him through his youth. Giggs' longevity, his loyalty to United and his personal stability are a reproach to the critics of the Ferguson way.

Shankly had not applied the same fervour to controlling his players, partly because he didn't need to. The demands on them were not as great when Shankly was in his prime. The pace of the game was slower then. They did not need to be as fit. And the media did not report on their private lives. Shankly was not above telephoning the homes of players like Brian Hall to check with his parents on his whereabouts a couple of days before a game, but his own protégé, Kevin Keegan, did not drink anyway and did not need a controlling presence like the one Ferguson attempted to foist on Giggs.

Giggs was blessed with sublime talent and Ferguson has helped him to eke every last drop of worth out of it. Even though Giggs is coming to the end of his career now, it is still possible that he will beat Sir Bobby Charlton's all-time appearance record for United. He is often damned with faint praise when he is compared with Best, but actually, he is the living, playing embodiment of what Best might have become had he not had such a strong self-destructive streak. Compare the two careers and Giggs wins hands down.

Giggs supplied plenty of the ammunition. Mark Hughes fired a lot of the bullets. Hughes had been brought back from Barcelona in the summer of 1988 to spearhead United's attack. He was probably the most combative striker the Premiership has ever seen, a man who could give it out and take it, too. League clashes with Arsenal were particularly feisty then, just as they were to be a decade later. In October 1990 there was a 21-man brawl at Old Trafford when the two teams met that scandalized the public. Arsenal were docked two points, United lost one.

Hughes gave United their consolation for finishing sixth in the league that season. He scored two goals against Barcelona in the Cup Winners' Cup Final in Rotterdam. The first was a tap-in. The second was one of the greatest goals a United player has ever scored, especially in such a big game. Hughes burst in behind the Barcelona defence 15 minutes from time, but when the Barca goalkeeper, Carlos Busquets, rushed out to meet him, Hughes pushed the ball so far wide, it seemed the chance had gone.

Lee Sharpe was waiting in the middle, expecting that Hughes might try to square the ball to him. But Hughes looked up once and as the ball rolled towards the touchline he swivelled and drove it towards the goal. It never went above knee height but its trajectory was sweet and true. Busquets could not even get close to regaining his ground and the ball nearly burst the net. Ronald Koeman got one back for Barcelona but it was not enough.

Ferguson, who had also won the competition with Aberdeen in 1983, became only the second man, after Johan Cruyff, to win the European Cup Winners Cup with two different sides. But the tournament was the weakest of the three European competitions and it was abolished soon afterwards. It was little more than a palliative for the ongoing illness of underachievement in the league.

For that to change, it took the arrival of one last man. One superhero to gather Schmeichel, Bruce, Pallister, Ince, Robson, Kanchelskis, Giggs, Hughes and the rest for the final push. That man, of course, was Eric Cantona, the player who United fans still revere alongside Roy Keane as the greatest of all their modern-day icons. Perhaps he is regarded even more highly than Keane because it was Cantona, more than even the Irishman, who turned United from losers into winners.

Cantona had a chequered past. He had played for Olympique de Marseille, Bordeaux, Montpellier and Nîmes. It was while he was at Nîmes that he became so infuriated by a referee's decision that he picked the ball up and threw it at him. The French Football Federation banned him for a month, but at his hearing Cantona went up to each board member and yelled "Idiot" in his face. The suspension was raised to two months and Cantona decided he was going to quit the game.

But then he came to England. He had a trial with Sheffield Wednesday, where Trevor Francis was manager, but it didn't work out. Then he went to Leeds, who were vying with United for the title, and in February 1992 Howard Wilkinson gave him a contract. Cantona made six starts and nine substitute appearances and quickly became a cult hero with the Leeds supporters. Leeds held their nerve, United lost theirs. Cantona had an English championship medal to go with the one he had won at Marseille the year before.

There were no suggestions that Cantona was unhappy at Leeds. Quite the opposite. But when the Leeds managing director Bill Fotherby called United chairman Martin Edwards in November 1992 to inquire about buying Denis Irwin, Ferguson, who had been encouraged in his admiration of the Frenchman by Gérard Houllier, then the manager of Paris St-Germain, told Edwards to ask about Cantona. To Ferguson's surprise, Fotherby did not dismiss the prospect of Cantona moving on.

It later became clear that Cantona had already asked for a transfer after Wilkinson had dropped him for a league game. Cantona and Wilkinson were not getting on. It is difficult to imagine two stranger bedfellows than them. And United needed goals. Dion Dublin was injured, Hughes was struggling for form and Mark Robins had been sold. By the end of October 1992, United had already lost four league games and drawn five more.

Ferguson had built a formidable side by now. It is not even possible to say that it was a side lacking fantasy. With Giggs, Kanchelskis and Sharpe all vying for places in the side, no one could claim that Ferguson's team lacked players who could produce touches of magic and flair. But when United captured Cantona for a paltry £1.2 million and drafted him into the side, the difference was pronounced and immediate.

Part of the reason for the transformation was the belief and the confidence that Cantona brought to the players around him. There was a mystery and a haughtiness about him that made his teammates feel as though someone special was in their midst. It made them feel as if they had something that no other team had.

Cantona had an immediate impact on his teammates away from matches, too. He surprised Ferguson by asking if he could practise aspects of his game after normal training had finished. Soon, other players were joining him for extra work. He had raised the hunger at the club. He made his debut against Manchester City at Old Trafford on 6 December 1992 and Ferguson noticed how he always played the easy pass if it was available. 'Like all truly exceptional creative players,' Ferguson said, 'Cantona did something extravagant only when it was necessary.'

Cantona has become such a hero for United fans, a man whose name is still sung during every match at Old Trafford, because he was the start of it. He was the man who made it happen for Ferguson, the final piece in the jigsaw. Without him, maybe there would have been more near-misses. More heartbreak. Maybe the obsession with winning the league would have got more and more intense and then dwindled away in disappointment. Maybe there would have been no Sir Alex Ferguson. No knighthood, no friendships with the great and the good, no celebrity, no racehorses. Just a bitter Scotsman sent back north of the border to live out the rest of his life in anticlimax.

With Cantona in the team, United began to turn up the heat.

Norwich City had been leading the title race, but they began to falter in the New Year and it soon came down to a fight between United and Ron Atkinson's Aston Villa, the team of Mark Bosnich, Earl Barrett, Dean Saunders, Dalian Atkinson, Kevin Richardson, Ray Houghton and Shaun Teale. And, of course, Ferguson's bête noire, Paul McGrath.

The date when Manchester United finally cast off the burden of expectation that had been weighing them down for twenty-six years was 10 April 1993. United were trailing Villa by a point going into a game against Sheffield Wednesday at Old Trafford, and memories of how they had thrown it all away the previous season were beginning to crowd in on them again.

The fans' hopes shrivelled in the second half when Ince fouled Chris Waddle in the box and John Sheridan, a dead-eye from the spot, tucked away the penalty. Ferguson had spent much of the second half complaining to the linesman, John Hilditch, that Wednesday were wasting time and he felt his constant moaning paid off when Hilditch had to replace referee Michael Peck when he succumbed to an injury. As the clock ticked down, Hilditch estimated there were 7 minutes of added time to play.

Steve Bruce grabbed an equalizer at the end of normal time and then United laid siege to the Wednesday goal. Eventually, as news came through that Villa had only managed to draw at Coventry, United surged forward again. Giggs took a free kick from the left that was cleared to the right touchline. It was retrieved by Pallister of all people and when his cross back into the box took a deflection, Bruce ran on to it and guided another header into the net.

Old Trafford went wild. But nobody went quite as wild as Brian Kidd, who had taken over from Archie Knox as Ferguson's assistant. Kidd was so excited he did not know what to do with himself. Both he and Ferguson ran down from their perch in the stand and Kidd fell to his knees on the pitch and looked up to the heavens. For a second, it looked as if Ferguson was going to do the same. Then he caught himself, made do with a clenched-fist salute, and walked back up the steps.

'That was the result that really made us feel as though it was going to be our year,' Pallister said. 'We got out of jail a wee bit. But Fergie still looked ridiculous when he ran on to the pitch. I think he thought about doing what Kiddo had done and then thought better of it. The lads gave him a bit of stick about that. Looking at Kiddo, you would have thought he'd just scored the winner in the World Cup Final. That was how desperate everybody was. The club was a laughing stock because it had gone so long without winning the Premiership.'

Suddenly, it seemed as if United's long pursuit of the English league championship was not cursed after all. Suddenly, it seemed that this really might be the year. United won their next three league games against Coventry, Chelsea and Crystal Palace. Villa faltered against Blackburn. United's fate was in their own hands. If Villa beat Oldham at Villa Park on Sunday 2 May, United would have to beat Blackburn at Old Trafford a week later to win the title.

Ferguson could not bear to watch the Villa–Oldham game. He chose to play golf with his eldest son, Mark, at Mottram Hall, near Prestbury in Cheshire. It was a new course then, created partly to capitalize on the money that footballers and their princely wages had brought to the archipelago of villages south of Manchester. Ferguson was on the 17th fairway when a stranger jumped out of a car on the drive that connects the hotel to the road and told him that Oldham had beaten Villa. United had won the league.

Ferguson hugged his son and then walked up the 18th fairway, thinking of Arnold Palmer's march through the massed ranks of his fans to the 18th at Troon when he won The Open in 1962. 'That's how I felt,' Ferguson said. 'Like a real champion.' He was the first manager to win the Championship in both Scotland and England.

He quickly got used to feeling like a champion. United won

the title again the next season. And this time there were no nerves, no occasions like Sheffield Wednesday. United were superb that 1993–94 season. Freed from the pressure of breaking their league title jinx, they played with great expression and power as they eased their way to Ferguson's second title and United's first league and cup Double.

Many still believe that that side, bolstered by the signing of Keane from Nottingham Forest in the summer of 1993, was the best team in Ferguson's long reign at Old Trafford. Nobody could match them for skill and grace. Keane, Ince and Robson, in his last season, fought for two central midfield places. And nobody could match them for physical strength or intimidatory savagery. They were beautiful and they were ugly all at the same time.

Cantona was the worst offender that season. He was sent off for a horrific tackle on Norwich's Jeremy Goss in February 1994 and again for taking a fiendish relish in stamping all over Swindon's John Moncur. Ferguson lost his temper with Cantona for the first time over that. Cantona was sent off again the week after, this time for a clash with Arsenal's Tony Adams. Hughes and Schmeichel were also shown red cards that season and Keane and Ince were hardly shrinking violets.

But those transgressions could not dull the majesty of United's performances. One goal, against Wimbledon at Selhurst Park in an FA Cup fifth-round tie, typified their mastery. United strung together a move of twenty-seven passes untouched by an opponent's foot, until Irwin added the coup de grâce. Ferguson was particularly enthralled by Cantona's performance in November 1993 against Manchester City at Maine Road when United came back from 2–0 down at half-time. Keane scored one, Cantona two. Ferguson called the Frenchman's exhibition 'a display that should have been recorded as a coaching film'.

United never looked like being caught that season. They sealed the Championship with a 2–1 victory over Ipswich Town at Portman Road on 1 May. The same weekend, Ferguson became a grandfather when Tania, the wife of his son Jason, gave birth to a baby boy they named Jake. Two weeks later, United beat Chelsea 4–0 at Wembley to win the FA Cup. Cantona scored twice, both penalties. Mark Hughes got one, substitute Brian McClair finished things off.

Ferguson could not even find a place for Robson, one of the club's greatest servants, on the bench. He picked Ince and Keane in the centre of midfield and chose Sharpe and McClair as substitutes. He rationalized his decision by saying that Robson was leaving for Middlesbrough after the final while McClair would remain part of the family. Later, he admitted maybe he should have allowed sentiment to hold sway.

But Ferguson has never been in football for the popularity. And popularity has duly eluded him. Shankly could be ruthless and hard, too, but he avoided the pettiness that Ferguson sank into, and when he boasted on behalf of his club it was so overt and good-humoured that no one took offence. The public loved Shankly for his enthusiasm in the same way they have come to dislike Ferguson for his sourness, even though Ferguson often seems to reserve his worst moments for the public view.

In private, away from the glare, he is capable of acts of great generosity. When the former Crystal Palace player Geoff Thomas organized a replay of the 1990 FA Cup Final between his former teammates and the players who had represented United, Ferguson astonished everyone connected with the match by going out of his way to be helpful and supportive. He agreed to manage the United team even though the match, which was in aid of a leukaemia charity, came at a crucial stage of United's doomed attempt to catch Chelsea in the spring of 2006. When he believes in a cause, particularly if it involves helping a member of the football community, Ferguson can be a man of great beneficence.

But he has never shirked the idea of making enemies, sometimes for life. If the way to win meant trampling on the feelings of a player who had been a loyal servant, then he felt it was his duty to do it. He was football's Malcolm X, doing it by any means necessary. 'He was a right sod at times,' Pallister said, 'but he gave us the chance to play for Manchester United and we will for ever be in his debt for that. You don't forget about that.'

21: Shankly at the Outposts

Fifteen minutes before every game, Bill Shankly climbed up into the stand at Brunton Park and addressed the crowd through the Tannoy from the announcer's box. He had been impressed by the newsreel footage of the great demagogues of World War Two, and as he stood there in the rickety old stand that he once described as a pigeon loft, he sounded like a general commanding his troops before the battle.

He knew he had been born to manage. He had been planning for it for a long time. He had had a fine playing career and Carlisle United was hardly a glamorous stage for him to launch his new career as a boss. But Shankly relished it. It felt natural to him. He had been bossing players around his whole life. He had always been old and responsible before his time. He was a fitness freak and he was a control freak. He was a healthy eater, a non-drinker and a clean liver sixty years before Arsène Wenger made abstinence fashionable in English football.

And if Carlisle could not be pushed any further to the extremities of the game geographically, there was something about the club that Shankly loved, something about him and Carlisle that seemed meant to be. It had started life as Carlisle Red Rose at the turn of the century, an echo of Shankly's favourite Robert Burns poem. And his mother's brother, Billy Blyth, was a director on the board.

There was even an element of nostalgia about the place for Shankly. He had begun his playing career at Brunton Park, too, and used his solitary season there as a launch pad for a move to

Preston North End, two FA Cup Finals and international caps with Scotland. Now, the club was about to do the same for his managerial career.

Shankly poured everything he had into his first managerial role when he arrived at Brunton Park in April 1949. He had fallen out with Preston, the club he had played for since 1933, a few months earlier when their directors started leaving him out of the side even though he was club captain and then refused him a benefit match because he told them about the offer to manage Carlisle.

Shankly, who was thirty-five, was interviewed for the Carlisle job at the end of February 1949 and played his last match for Preston in March. But Preston refused to release him to Carlisle until the start of April. His first game as the manager of a football club was on 4 April 1949, when he took charge of Carlisle in the Cumberland Cup Final against Workington at Brunton Park. Carlisle won 2–1 and Shankly had won a trophy in his first match. One game, one trophy. A sign of things to come.

Carlisle was not a big club. The chairman, Johnny Corrieri, owned a fish and chip shop in the city. One prospective signing invited to view Brunton Park by Shankly described it as a 'rabbit hutch'. Nor was Carlisle an ambitious club. It had a big catchment area geographically but it was sparsely populated. In league terms, the club was becalmed in mid-table in the Third Division North, but even though they were safe from relegation and had no chance of promotion, Shankly threw himself into his task with gusto. His future depended upon him making a success of managing Carlisle because he wasn't qualified to do anything else except work down a mine. The usual occupation of the ex-footballer, running a pub, wasn't open to him. He was teetotal.

So he gave it everything. He took training, played in the practice matches, did the scouting, cleaned the boots and brushed out the dressing rooms. He also burned the training kit.

He said it stank. He felt that if the players wore filthy shirts and shorts when they were training, it would affect them psychologically.

One day, when the team coach was driving through Doncaster bound for an away match with Lincoln City on the other side of the country, Shankly spotted a new set of playing kit in a sports shop. He stopped the coach and paid for it with his own money. Carlisle played in it at Sincil Bank. It was the first sign of the policy Shankly adopted with his players throughout his managerial career: if you talked to them as if they were special and treated them as if they were special, sooner or later they would begin to play as if they were special.

By then, Shankly had qualified as a masseur. He had taken a course while he was at Preston so he gave the Carlisle players rub-downs as well, just to add to his duties. It was partly because he liked having a captive audience. If he wanted to admonish a player for some late-night carousing or some other form of indiscipline that had been brought to his notice, he would save his words for when he had the player lying on the massage table in front of him.

He sharpened up training. The players had been bored by long running sessions. Shankly got them playing five-a-sides. The emphasis was on ball work straight away. He was already sure of what he was doing. There was no sense of Shankly feeling his way into the job. He had been preparing himself for this for years. His transformation from player to manager was seamless.

'If a man can't go out and train a team in every aspect,' Shankly said, 'coach players and tell them how to play, and know about injuries and how long they might take to mend, he's not a manager at all. He might as well go home and change his title because that is the whole essence of the game. The rest is a waste of time. All the talk and the stuff you get from books is rubbish. Only the actual things that happen matter.'

Shankly took charge of seven games in his first season. Of

those he won one and drew four. But he was making plans for the following year. He converted Geoff Twentyman, later his chief scout at Liverpool, into a centre half and signed a clever right-winger called Billy Hogan from Manchester City. Carlisle had finished 15th in the season Shankly arrived. In 1949–50, he had dragged them up to ninth place, 8 points behind champions Doncaster.

The improvement in the club's fortunes created a stir in the border town and crowds of almost 15,000 were common. Then Carlisle were drawn to face the mighty Arsenal at Highbury in the FA Cup third round in January 1951. Arsenal had won the league title two seasons before and were still the most glamorous side in the country. There was a great clamour for tickets in Carlisle.

Nobody gave Shankly's side a chance, particularly as one of their regulars, Jack Lindsay, was out with a broken jaw and Twentyman was not fully fit. But Shankly believed they could win. The team stayed at the swanky Mount Royal Hotel, just off the Edgware Road, near Marble Arch, and as they prepared to take the pitch, Shankly told them that they were a credit to the city of Carlisle.

'That day, we had a confidence instilled into us by Shankly that I don't think has ever been equalled,' forward Jimmy Jackson said. 'The Shankly brand of enthusiasm made you feel there was no team in the country that you were not able to match.' And Carlisle did match them. They fought out a goalless draw with Arsenal that was every bit as big a shock as Exeter City's stalemate with Manchester United at Old Trafford in 2005. The Cup was more prestigious in those days. Arsenal played their first team, not their reserves.

When the final whistle went, Shankly walked on to the pitch with his arms raised above his head in that gesture of triumph that was to become so familiar. It was the first time anything he had achieved as a manager had been the subject of national attention. Even though Carlisle lost the replay 4–1 in front of

22,000 at Brunton Park, the result at Highbury put Shankly on the map and alerted potential suitors to the strides he was making.

Shankly applied for the vacant manager's job at Liverpool that year, and even though he had little chance he effectively ruled himself out by insisting that he would only take the job on the condition that he, and not the directors, would pick the team. The directors chose not to take him up on his offer. Eight years later, though, he didn't have to apply for the Liverpool job when it became vacant again. That time, they approached him.

Shankly was growing restless at Carlisle by the spring of 1951. He was frustrated by the board's refusal to release significant funds to strengthen the team. When Second Division Grimsby Town asked him if he would consider joining the club in a coaching role in March, he was tempted but decided that it would be a backward step after spending a year in management.

But when Carlisle finished third in the table at the end of the season to underline again what a dramatic improvement Shankly had effected, Grimsby approached him once more. They had been relegated from the Second Division and their manager, Charlie Spencer, who had been taken seriously ill earlier in the season, had told the club that he was not fit to return. Grimsby turned to Shankly to restore their fortunes and Shankly, seeing potential in a club that had been big enough to be in the First Division three years earlier, accepted their offer.

Things didn't start well. Grimsby lost their first home game of the season to Lincoln, but the defeat was the good part. His goalkeeper broke a finger and his centre forward broke a leg. Shankly had already arrived at Blundell Park to find his resources depleted after the directors sold some of the club's best players without telling him. His wife was homesick, his eldest daughter was complaining about the ubiquitous smell of fish. After the first couple of games, Shankly felt overwhelmed.

But he rallied quickly. He persuaded his assistant manager,

George Tweedy, to come out of retirement at the age of the
thirty-nine and pull on his goalkeeping gloves again. Shankly
made a couple of bargain signings and results began to improve.
In fact, they strung together a sequence of eleven straight wins
in the early months of 1952 that is still a club record and which
pushed them into contention for the solitary promotion spot to
the Second Division.

They thrashed promotion rivals Stockport 4–0 at Blundell
Park in April but they could not quite close the gap on Lincoln,
who clinched the title by dint of that early victory against
Grimsby's nine men. Grimsby missed out by 3 points and
finished second, but it did not stop Shankly paying his side an
extravagant compliment. 'That Grimsby team was, pound for
pound and class for class, the best football team I have seen in
England since the war,' he said. He didn't write that in 1956
either. He wrote it in 1976 in his autobiography.

Grimsby did not quite live up to their star billing the
following season. They started well, winning their first five
games, but blew it at Easter when they lost four in a row and
ended up in fifth place. The following season, Shankly started to
grow disillusioned. His wife was still homesick and now his
youngest daughter, Jeannette, was old enough to complain
about the smell of fish, too.

They found it hard to adapt to living on the east coast when
they had been used to Preston and Carlisle and quick trips home
to Scotland. So when Workington, rock-bottom of the Third
Division North, as low as you can go, asked Shankly in December 1953 if he would be interested in saving them, he did not
dismiss the idea. He asked for Christmas to think about it. It
was a huge gamble, the type that could have finished his career.

He had spent four seasons in the Third Division North
without achieving a single promotion. He was hardly Dave
Bassett when it came to getting lower-league clubs promoted.
And now he had left a team that was at least in the upper
reaches of the division for one rooted to the bottom.

The first night he went to have a look at Workington's bleak ground, Borough Park, he walked through the main door and felt around in the darkness for the light switch. He tried in vain. Eventually somebody told him. Borough Park didn't have electricity yet. It still ran on gas. Shankly hadn't exactly traded up.

22: Ferguson at the Peak of his Powers

They say that his best team was the Double-winning side of 1994 that mixed strength, guile and obduracy. His most successful season was 1998–99 when Manchester United won the Treble and brought him the great glory of the European Cup. But it was the years in between that illuminated the greatness of Alex Ferguson. Those were the days of his managerial life.

Forget the wrangling over his contract that rumbled on and on, with Ferguson's constant complaints that he was underpaid. Back then, Ferguson was right about the United board's lack of appreciation of what he had done for them. It is hard to comprehend now that the United hierarchy could have been so parsimonious with its praise and its riches during those years that it drove Ferguson to the brink of resignation.

Between 1994 and 1998, Ferguson did his job masterfully. He lost the title to Kenny Dalglish's Blackburn Rovers in 1994–95 and Arsène Wenger's emerging Arsenal team in 1997–98, but those reverses did not dull the significance of what he achieved in those years. Fate and circumstance cast a number of obstacles in his way that others would have considered insurmountable but Ferguson vaulted them all. He dealt with the loss of Paul Ince, Andrei Kanchelskis and Mark Hughes seamlessly. He blooded the army of new talent from the team that won the FA Youth Cup in 1992 at just the right time.

He nursed Eric Cantona through his eight-month suspension and kept him in the game. No one else could have done that. He harnessed the incendiary brilliance of men like Roy Keane and Peter Schmeichel. His psychological teasing destroyed Kevin Keegan when it seemed Newcastle United were bound to win the title in 1995–96. United won the Double that year. They won the Premiership again the year after that. Ferguson was at the peak of his powers.

He brought United out of one great era and led them straight into another. He managed the transition seamlessly. Not many managers have been able to do that. Most live and die with one great side, but Ferguson built two. The second one was infused with the romance of youth. Fergie's Fledglings were an echo of the Busby Babes, a proud and sentimental nod to the club's great heritage. And they played a brand of breathtaking attacking football that was a tribute to the principles of their manager.

Think of the players Ferguson brought through in those years. Think of David Beckham and Gary Neville, two men who are nearing the England appearance records set by Bobby Moore, Sir Bobby Charlton and Billy Wright, two men who won everything there was to win with United, two men who have been the epitome of professionalism and dedication throughout their careers.

Think of the majesty of Ryan Giggs, that goal against Arsenal in the 1999 FA Cup semi-final, all the service he has given to the club, the fact that he will come as close as anyone to breaking Charlton's appearance record for United. Think of the talent of Paul Scholes and the dedication of Phil Neville and the fact that Pele thought Nicky Butt was the outstanding player of the 2002 World Cup. Think of all these things and Ferguson's contribution to the heritage of United and the fabric of English football shines like gold.

The man that bestrode the two eras with him was Cantona. And if Ferguson deserves praise for the way he nurtured the club's bloom of young players, he is also owed a debt of gratitude for how he harnessed one of the most bewitching and unpredictable talents ever to have graced the English game.

Others had tried and failed, but Ferguson went out of his way to understand Cantona and accommodate his temperament.

He treated him differently. He didn't try to hide that. He allowed Cantona leeway that the others didn't get. He would overlook it if Cantona was occasionally late for training. He did not make the Frenchman adhere to the same dress code as the rest. He cursed at Lee Sharpe if he arrived at a function in a garish tie but he said nothing if Cantona showed up in a pair of trainers. At first, some of the other players resented it. Then they realized, too, that Cantona was a special case.

The greatest test of Ferguson's relationship with him came in the long aftermath of Cantona's notorious kung-fu kick attack on a Crystal Palace supporter at Selhurst Park on Burns Night, 25 January 1995. Cantona had been sent off for kicking out at the Palace defender Richard Shaw in the second half of a Premiership tie United were hoping would draw them closer to Blackburn at the top of the table, and as he walked down the touchline towards the tunnel at the far end of the ground he was subjected to a tirade of abuse from Palace fans.

One of them, Matthew Simmons, ran down one of the aisles and yelled insults at Cantona. Simmons himself later claimed he had spoken to Cantona with the formality of an English gentleman. 'Off you go,' he claimed to have said, 'it's an early bath for you.' The reality, of course, was vastly different, and Cantona lost control. He launched himself at Simmons with a high kick that caught the supporter in the chest and then aimed a few punches at him before he was dragged away and hustled back to the tunnel.

Ferguson was not fully aware of what had happened. He had still not seen the incident when he got back to his home in Wilmslow in the early hours of the morning. His son Jason was waiting for him and told him how terrible Cantona's attack looked. Ferguson waved him away and went to bed. But he couldn't sleep. He got up and put the video in the machine and he was horrified by what he saw. The next night, he met with

United chairman Martin Edwards, Professor Sir Roland Smith, the chairman of the plc board, and Maurice Watkins at a hotel in the Cheshire village of Alderley Edge. They decided to try to pre-empt any FA punishment by suspending Cantona for four months, which would rule him out until the end of the season.

But the FA doubled the ban. Cantona was tried at Croydon Crown Court and sentenced to two weeks in jail. On appeal, that was reduced to 120 hours of community service. 'It was supposed to consist of controlled coaching sessions for school-children which he probably would have enjoyed,' Ferguson said. 'But with the mixture of ages and sexes presented to him, proper coaching was impossible. The sessions were apparently just an excuse for a lot of people to meet him. I began to change my mind about his chances of surviving in the English game.'

Cantona's court case unleashed an unprecedented media feeding frenzy, even if it was one that would be matched three years later when Beckham returned home in disgrace from the 1998 World Cup in France. The madness got worse when Cantona read out a one-line statement after his court case. 'When the seagulls follow the trawler,' he said, 'it is because they think sardines will be thrown into the sea.' The statement was greeted as incontrovertible proof that Cantona had gone stark raving mad. Actually, it was just an elegantly simple jibe about the way he felt the vultures had been circling him.

Without Cantona, United were unable to catch Blackburn. They still exerted tremendous pressure on them, and Ferguson got under Dalglish's skin by conceding the championship early and saying that the only way United could win was if Blackburn 'did a Devon Loch'. That was a ploy he had learned from Jock Stein back in Ferguson's playing days at Rangers, when Celtic had come from behind to snatch the title. This time, United would have done the same if they could have beaten West Ham on the final day of the season, but Ferguson's new £7 million signing from Newcastle, Andy Cole, missed a hatful of chances, West Ham defended as if they were at the Alamo and United were held to a draw. Blackburn lost to Liverpool at Anfield but it didn't matter. They were champions. In the dressing room afterwards, Ferguson told shattered young players like Gary Neville to remember the feeling and make sure they never let it happen again.

By then, Ferguson had grown more confident that he could persuade Cantona to stay in the English game and at Old Trafford. He was still involved in training every day, and at the start of the next season Ferguson arranged some behind-closed-doors training matches at The Cliff against local lower-league clubs like Oldham, Rochdale and Bury that he believed did not breach the terms of the FA ban. After the first game, the news leaked into the press and the FA insisted Cantona was not eligible to play in any form of arranged match.

Their attitude dismayed Cantona. He felt as if he was being victimized and that the FA wanted to drive him out. He fled back to France and at first Ferguson was resigned to losing him. But his wife Cathy said she was surprised he was giving up so easily. Ferguson decided to make one last effort to persuade Cantona to return. He organized what was supposed to be a clandestine trip to Paris to meet Cantona but had to give a gaggle of supporters the slip when he arrived at Charles de Gaulle airport.

He checked in at the George V Hotel near the Champs-Elysées and then the trip turned into a scene out of *The Bourne Identity*. A porter smuggled him out of the hotel down some back stairs and through the kitchens to an exit where Cantona's lawyer was waiting on his Harley Davidson motorbike. Only a lawyer working for Cantona could wear black leather and ride a Harley. Ferguson was handed a helmet and rode pillion through the back streets until he arrived at one of Cantona's favourite restaurants which the owner had closed so that Ferguson and Cantona could have some privacy.

The two men spent the night chatting, mostly about great matches of the Fifties and Sixties. But Ferguson also assured

Cantona that United would redouble their efforts to make his life easier until the suspension lapsed. He told him that he had begun to make arrangements to find him a house so that he could escape the claustrophobic environment of the hotel where he was living. 'I believe he wanted me to put an arm around him,' Ferguson said, 'and convince him that everything would be all right, and in a sense, that was what I was doing . . . Those hours spent in Eric's company in that largely deserted restaurant added up to one of the more worthwhile acts I have performed in this stupid job of mine.'

It worked. Cantona was reassured and duly returned to the United side on 1 October 1995 against Liverpool at Old Trafford. Of course, he scored. His penalty gave United a 2–2 draw and his happy slalom down a white pole behind the goal became one of the images of the season. His return came just at the right time for the team and for Fergsuon, who had been heavily criticized for his part in the previous summer's sales of Ince, Kanchelskis and Hughes.

There was only one Guvnor at Old Trafford in those years. And it wasn't Ince. Ince might have been one of the main men at the club when United won the 1994 Double, but Ferguson had started to harbour serious misgivings about his positional play. He had also grown bored with Ince's insistence that the other players should call him the Guvnor. Ince claimed that the nickname was just a joke, but Ferguson felt there was more than an undertone of seriousness about it. He considered it a childish conceit.

Ferguson's main problem with Ince, though, was professional, not personal. The Guvnor stuff was a sideshow. What frustrated Ferguson more was the player's refusal to conform to the defensive midfield role that Ferguson wanted him to adopt. Ince saw himself as an attacking midfielder and felt that what Ferguson was asking him to do amounted to a snub to his talent.

So Ferguson decided to sell him. His resolve hardened when

Ince was dispossessed in the 1995 FA Cup Final against Everton at the end of the kind of forward surge that Ferguson had urged him not to make. United were exposed by a swift counter-attack, and after Graham Stuart's shot bounced down off the bar Paul Rideout headed the winner.

But the United board were not convinced. In fact, they were deeply concerned about Ferguson's intention to sell their central midfielder, even though Ferguson knew that Butt and Scholes were waiting in the wings. Martin Edwards even rang Ferguson when he was on holiday in America to urge him to try to persuade Ince to stay. Ferguson didn't quite do that. He phoned Ince and told him he was surprised he was thinking of moving to Inter Milan because he didn't have the game to cope with playing in Italy. Funnily enough, the move went ahead.

If Ferguson had been more than complicit in Ince's transfer, he was disappointed when he learned that Hughes had moved to Chelsea. Hughes had been unsettled by the arrival of Cole and had become embroiled in a dispute about his pension arrangements, but it was still a shock to Ferguson when he was told Hughes had moved on.

The third prong of that summer's treble was Kanchelskis's move to Everton. It was the most protracted and troubled move of all three. Kanchelskis, a powerful, fast and direct right-winger, had agreed a new three-year contract at United in the summer of 1994. Unbeknown to Ferguson, the contract included a stipulation that if he was sold, Kanchelskis would receive one third of the transfer fee. According to Ferguson in his autobiography, early in the 1994–95 season one of the player's Russian advisers, Grigory Essaoulenko, took Ferguson aside after United had arrived back from a midweek night game at Nottingham Forest. He gave him a parcel and said it was a gift for him and his wife.

Ferguson said he assumed the parcel contained a samovar or another kind of Russian ornament. When he got home, he unwrapped it. He lifted the money out of the package and laid

£40,000 in cash on the table. The next day, Ferguson took the money to Old Trafford and Maurice Watkins told him to put it in the club safe and document what he had done with the club solicitors.

It seems likely now that the money was intended less as a gift for past deeds and more as an attempt to smooth the passage of upheavals that lay ahead. By early in 1995, Kanchelskis appeared to be deeply unhappy at United and criticized Ferguson heavily in a newspaper article. Ferguson described the piece as 'sewage' and it soon became obvious that the winger was determined to leave and that Everton was his preferred destination.

When United baulked at the terms of the transfer to Goodison, Essaoulenko came back into Ferguson's life. The two men attended a meeting in the chairman's office at Old Trafford to try to thrash out the differences over the Kanchelskis move and Ferguson handed back the £40,000 from the club safe. Essaoulenko protested at first but Martin Edwards insisted Ferguson could not accept the gift.

Then things turned nasty. Essaoulenko demanded that Kanchelskis be allowed to leave the club, and when Edwards restated United's position that they were not happy with the money they were being offered for the player, Essaoulenko lost his temper and began screaming at Edwards. He threatened Edwards and told him to sell Kanchelskis immediately. As far as Ferguson was concerned there was no doubting the seriousness of the threat made. In August 2005, Kanchelskis was sold to Everton for £5m.

United fans were in shock. They did not understand why Ferguson had sold three of the club's best players in a bout of summer madness and failed to recruit any replacements. The *Manchester Evening News* ran a poll on whether Ferguson should be sacked. The majority said yes. Manchester City fans voted in force. Ferguson never forgave the *Evening News* for that and his relationship with them has never been the same.

The clamour grew when United lost their opening game of the 1995–96 season 3–1 away at Aston Villa on 19 August. Ferguson had laced the side with six graduates from the 1992 youth team. The line up, with three centre backs starting the match, went like this: Mark Bosnich – Paul Parker, Gary Pallister, Gary Neville – Phil Neville, Nicky Butt, Roy Keane, Lee Sharpe, Denis Irwin – Brian McClair, Paul Scholes. The substitutes, who came on at half-time, were David Beckham and John O'Kane.

Beckham scored United's goal, but on *Match of the Day* that night Alan Hansen was scathing about United's performance and their prospects. 'You'll never win anything with kids,' he said. He has been eating those words for more than a decade.

The kids did not let anyone down. They were magnificent. Soon the criticism of Ferguson abated and gave way to a rush of excitement about the fearless energy and ravenous hunger the lads brought to the team. Newcastle, under Keegan, had got off to a flying start and were playing dream football that made them the darlings of the media and everyone's second-favourite team. But Cantona came back in the autumn and United kept in touch.

At the start of March they were still 12 points behind Newcastle, but Keegan's team was starting to tie up and Ferguson could sense it. Keegan had brought the Colombian striker Faustino Asprilla to help Newcastle seal the title, but he upset the balance of the side and United began to close in. As Newcastle wobbled, United were ruthless and clinical. They won seven of their matches in the run-in 1–0 and Cantona scored the winner in five of them.

When United travelled to St James's Park on 3 March, few gave them a chance of overhauling Keegan's cavaliers. Peter Schmeichel made a series of outstanding saves in the first half and then, after the interval, United took over. When Phil Neville made his way to the byline and crossed to the back post,

Cantona was waiting to volley the ball down into the ground and into the net. United won 1–0. The chase was on.

Six weeks later, Keegan and his side were on the verge of cracking up. United were catching them and Ferguson was doing all he could to crank up the pressure. On 17 April, after United had beaten Leeds at Old Trafford, Ferguson pointed out that if Leeds had played with that kind of commitment all season they would not be in the poor league position they found themselves in. Ferguson also said he hoped Leeds would show the same kind of determination when they played Newcastle at Elland Road twelve days later.

Twelve days later, Newcastle won at Leeds, and after the game Kevin Keegan donned his earphones, stared straight into the Sky cameras and delivered the quivering diatribe of a doomed man that will for ever be the epitaph of Newcastle's season. 'I think you have to send a tape of the game to Alex Ferguson,' Keegan said, his voice breaking. 'Isn't that Leeds performance what he wants? You just don't say that about Leeds.

'I would love it if we could beat them. He's gone down a lot in my estimation. Football in this country is honest. You sometimes wonder about abroad but not in this country. I would love it if we beat them. Love it.'

Ferguson was unrepentant. 'I was stopped dead in my tracks by Kevin's outburst,' he said. 'God, I felt for him. Looking at replays later, I was better able to digest what he said and at first it made me feel a bit guilty. Then I thought to myself that I had done nothing wrong. I had said something that related to the honesty of the game, which I had a right to do.'

Nevertheless, what Ferguson had accomplished, intentionally or not, was the public psychological dismemberment of his greatest rival that season. Ferguson is a hard, driven man. He may be quick to anger and easy to ruffle but he would never break the way Keegan broke. Keegan was vulnerable, he was emotionally fragile. He always has been. And Ferguson knew it.

Three days after they won at Leeds, Newcastle were held to a draw by lowly Nottingham Forest and United sealed the title with a 3–0 triumph over Middlesbrough at The Riverside. It was Ferguson's third title triumph and one of his sweetest.

A week later, United became the first English team to do the Double twice when they beat Liverpool in the FA Cup Final. After the White Horse Final of 1923, this was the White Suit Final, although David James would probably maintain it was cream. Liverpool added to their Spice Boy reputation of the time by strolling on to the pitch for their pre-match walkabout wearing white Armani suits. It was a symbol of their reputation for style over substance. Stan Collymore, the gifted Liverpool centre forward, admitted to 'feeling a bit of a knob in that suit'. The United forward, Andy Cole, came up to him and said: 'What the fuck are you boys wearing?'

Even Ferguson admitted that Liverpool's choice of attire handed United an immediate advantage. 'All our players would acknowledge that they were given a boost before a ball was kicked when our opponents turned up looking like a squad of bakers in cream-coloured suits,' Ferguson said. 'The sight gave our lads a great lift.'

It was not a good final but United won it 1–0. Inevitably, it was Cantona who scored the winner. James came for a Beckham corner late in the game but could only punch it weakly to the edge of the area where the Frenchman was lurking. Cantona adjusted his body shape to the bounce of the ball and gave himself space and time to drive the ball back past James and the defenders on the line.

Ferguson didn't quite know it then, but Cantona was approaching the end of his reign at Old Trafford. The next season, as the kids lambasted by Hansen matured into men, United won the league at a canter, finishing 7 points ahead of Newcastle. But still Ferguson was haunted by his failure to lift the European Cup. Even though they progressed further than they had before under Ferguson by reaching the semi-finals,

United squandered chance after chance in both legs against Borussia Dortmund and lost 1–0 each time.

Cantona was particularly subdued in both matches. Ferguson described him as 'low-key and marginal'. The day after United's exit, Cantona asked for a meeting with Ferguson and told him he wanted to retire. Ferguson asked him to think about his decision for some time but gradually, as he studied the dullness in Cantona's eyes and a broadening of his physique, he began to understand that the Frenchman was making the right decision.

Three days after the 1996–97 season ended, Cantona met Ferguson again at the Mottram Hall Hotel where Ferguson had learned United had won the title for the first time. Cantona confirmed he was going to quit. He said he felt he had become a pawn of United's merchandising department and he was disappointed in the club's lack of ambition in the signing of elite players.

Ferguson kept the news secret for several days in accordance with Cantona's wishes. However, his behaviour at that time sheds more light on his character. Rumours began to circulate at some newspapers that Cantona had quit. Two of the reporters closest to Ferguson, Bob Cass, of the *Mail on Sunday*, and Peter Fitton, then of the *Sun*, were asked to check the story out with the United manager.

Cass and Fitton were not the type of journalist Ferguson despised. Cass and his great friend, the late Joe Melling, were both regular dining partners of Ferguson's. Cass and Fitton are also brilliant reporters and men of principle who felt great loyalty to the United manager and always treated him fairly. Both men asked Ferguson whether Cantona had told him he was going to retire. Ferguson continued to abide by Cantona's wishes, even though he must have known it would make them both look stupid back at their papers.

They still do not talk about the way Ferguson treated them at that time, out of a continuing loyalty to him. It is a shame

Ferguson does not hold the same values. At the end of the press conference that announced Cantona's departure officially, Ferguson turned to Fitton as he filed out. 'Off to get your P45 now, Peter?'

Ferguson was at it again the next season, playing silly games and concealing the truth when Roy Keane snapped his cruciate ligaments when he kicked out at Alf Inge Haaland in a league game at Elland Road. Keane's injury did not inhibit United at first, but after the turn of the year Arsenal gradually reined them in at the top of the table much as they had done to Newcastle two years earlier. A late Marc Overmars goal gave Arsenal a 1–0 victory at Old Trafford on 14 March and successive draws against Liverpool and Newcastle allowed Arsenal to steal in.

The way Arsenal claimed the Double that season marked the joining of the great battle between Ferguson and the Arsenal boss, Arsène Wenger. Ferguson has enjoyed many significant rivalries in his two decades at Old Trafford but it is the contest with Wenger that has defined him. Wenger built a side at Highbury that competed with United in the beauty and the vibrancy of their attacking play, but Ferguson found it more difficult to cope with facing an enemy far more urbane and assured than him.

Ferguson is a bright man but he was no match for Wenger when it came to verbal jousts. When Wenger responded to a bout of Ferguson bragging about United by saying that 'everyone thinks they have the most beautiful wife at home', Ferguson thought Wenger was aiming insults at Lady Ferguson. Ferguson was also scathing about Wenger's reluctance to share a glass of red wine with him in his office after a match. The two men share an obsession for football and very little else.

Even though Wenger caused him such discomfort, Ferguson has come out on top in their struggle. He won the European Cup while Arsenal were struggling even to reach the knock-out stages. In Wenger's ten years in charge at Highbury, Arsenal have won the Championship three times to United's five. Against that, Ferguson has spent more money and Wenger has been hobbled by the expense of Arsenal's move to a new stadium.

One advantage Wenger certainly held over Ferguson is that he always felt wanted by the club's hierarchy. At the end of the 1997–98 season, when he had achieved so much and was on the brink of winning so much more, Ferguson felt so disillusioned with the manoeuvrings behind the scenes at Old Trafford that he offered to quit.

He had been unsettled initially by a concern that he was being undermined by his assistant, Brian Kidd. Before he had left for a summer holiday in the south of France with his wife, children and grandchildren, Ferguson had told Martin Edwards that he was keen to sign Dwight Yorke from Aston Villa. When he called Edwards from his rented villa in Cap Ferrat to find out how talks with Yorke were progressing, Edwards told him that Kidd thought United should sign West Ham's John Hartson instead.

Ferguson was livid. Edwards also told him that Kidd had been offered the manager's job at Everton and wanted to take it. Ferguson called Kidd and confronted him about what he had been saying about Yorke. The two men reached an uneasy accommodation and Ferguson even promised to intercede on Kidd's behalf and press for an improved contract for him at Old Trafford to lessen the pull of Everton.

When Ferguson next spoke to Edwards, the chairman told him he wanted to see him in London and that he should break his holiday. Ferguson flew to Heathrow and was driven to the headquarters of the Hong Kong and Shanghai Bank, where the United plc board chairman, Professor Sir Roland Smith, held a directorship. Ferguson thought the discussion was going to be about Yorke and Kidd. It turned out it was about him.

Edwards told Ferguson that he had taken his eye off the ball. He said that Ferguson was not concentrating on the job as he once had done, an observation that was aimed at his new-found love of horse-racing. Next, they questioned his continuing desire to sign Yorke. Ferguson responded with a list of great players he had signed. He could rightly point to a long line of great players he had brought to the club, headed by Keane, Schmeichel and Cantona. The meeting ended in a frosty truce that left Ferguson feeling more undervalued than ever.

He got back to France just in time to see David Beckham being sent off for England against Argentina. Beckham had scored one of the Premiership's greatest-ever goals at the start of the 1997–98 season, chipping the Wimbledon goalkeeper Neil Sullivan from inside his own half at Selhurst Park. Back then, he was one of Ferguson's favourite sons. 'He may look as if butter wouldn't melt in his mouth,' Ferguson said, 'but underneath the boyish appearance and all the trappings of trendiness, there is a steely determination that has to be admired.'

Ferguson called Beckham as the hounds of hell pursued him and an effigy of him was hung from a gibbet in south London. Ferguson was there for him. He told him that he would make sure Old Trafford became his sanctuary and his support. Beckham has never forgotten that kindness. The way Ferguson handled him was just another example of the sure touch in man-management he possessed then and another reminder that, once, he too was regarded as a father-figure for his players.

23: Shankly, Tom Finney and the War

People poked gentle fun at Bill Shankly in his later days as Liverpool manager because of his enduringly obsessive competitiveness on the practice pitch. Sometimes, their affectionately mocking remembrances of the simple joy in the game that he took into his sixties obscures the fact that Shankly was not an impostor belatedly living out a fantasy of sharing the same field or five-a-side court as a group of international-class players.

Because at his peak, Shankly was a real player, too. He played with the greats and against them. In April 1939, five months before the outbreak of the Second World War, he played for Scotland against England in front of 150,000 fans at Hampden Park and tried in vain to stop Stanley Matthews laying on the winner for the England centre forward, Tommy Lawton. But Matthews lobbed the ball over him and Shankly was close enough to Lawton to hear him growling: 'Get in, you fucker' in his Bolton brogue as he smashed the ball over the line. It was a wet day and Shankly caught the sound of the rain swishing off the net as Lawton's shot bulged it. He was so distraught about losing that he wished in that moment the ground would open up and bury him.

He spent much of his club career seeing greatness at close range, too. Apart from his first season at Carlisle United and brief spells with other clubs during the war years, Shankly's playing days were devoted to Preston North End, and he felt privileged to spend many of them tucked in at right half behind the flying right-winger Tom Finney, the greatest player Shankly ever saw.

Shankly had joined Preston in the summer of 1933, and he began to notice Finney a few years later when he saw the kid playing for Preston Schoolboys and practising for hours by kicking a ball against the walls of one of the stands at Deepdale. Shankly recognized that Finney was a special talent straight away, and he made a point of watching youth team matches and encouraging him constantly.

In the midst of the unseemly deification of George Best that followed his death in November 2005, Finney was largely forgotten in the rush to acclaim the former Manchester United winger incontrovertibly as the greatest player and the most noble human being Britain, or indeed the world, had ever seen. Perhaps Finney's reputation has suffered because he was a quiet, modest man, not a high-profile hell-raiser, but some voices that went largely unheard at the time of Best's passing protested gently that Finney had a claim at least to be his equal.

'If all the brains in the game sat in committee to design the perfect player, they would come up with a reincarnation of Tom Finney,' one newspaper tribute read when he retired. Finney played for England at right wing, left wing and centre forward. He was a genuinely two-footed player who could score goals from 30 yards out with his left boot or his right. He had speed and balance. He was a great dribbler and a sublime passer. He wasn't tall but he had a spring like Les Ferdinand's and could head the ball with surprising power.

Hugh McIlvanney heard Shankly round on a journalistic colleague who had suggested to Shankly that Finney might not have been robust enough to survive in the modern game. 'Tommy Finney was grisly strong,' Shankly said. 'Tommy could run for a week. I'd have played him in his overcoat. There would have been four men marking him while we were kicking in. When I told people in Scotland that England were coming up with a winger who was even better than Stanley Matthews, they laughed at me. But they weren't bloody laughing when big Geordie Young was running all over Hampden Park looking for Tommy Finney.'

Finney won 76 caps for England, even though the early years of his career were wiped out by the war. He scored 30 goals from the wing playing for England and held the scoring record for his country until it was beaten by Bobby Charlton. He did not win any honours for his club because when football resumed in 1945, Preston were unhealthily reliant on his talents. 'Tom Finney should claim income tax relief . . . for his ten dependents,' was a popular jibe against the Preston team of the time.

Shankly loved playing with Finney. When Finney turned professional in 1940, Shankly played a few wartime games with him before Deepdale was commandeered by the army and Preston was wound up for the duration of the war. Finney was still only twenty-three when the war ended and Shankly acted as his minder on the pitch until he moved into management in 1949.

Shankly's admiration for Finney was reciprocated. Shankly spoke so often about what a great player Finney was that others made fun of him for it. But even now that Finney is a sprightly, white-haired man in his eighties, with streets called after him and a stand at Deepdale named in his honour, the icon who is now the Preston North End president is almost as effusive about Shankly.

'I was with the juniors at Preston before the war,' Finney said at Deepdale in 2006. 'But I played in wartime football and Bill was behind me. I always had a great admiration for him and a great respect. All the other players did, too. He was an outstanding player as far as I was concerned. It was fantastic playing in front of him because he gave you so much encouragement. Everybody improved as a player as a result of being around him. He played when I came into the side in 1940–41 and we won the Northern League and played the top of the Southern League at Wembley.

'It was classed as a wartime Cup Final. I was playing against Eddie Hapgood, who was then the captain of Arsenal and England. Bill used to say before the game: "You just go out there. You will probably play against quite a number of players who will be on to you about what they're going to do to you and with you being a youngster they'll try and frighten you out of the game. Just let me know and I will deal with them, you just go on and play your own game."

'He used to come down and watch a lot of the junior games. He would come in and have a chat with us and encourage us. It was a great achievement for us to have someone like him taking an interest in our matches. He was someone I really looked up to. He was so wrapped up in the game, so enthused with it, one couldn't really help but feel that he would be lost without it.

'When I was fifteen or sixteen, to think a first-team player was prepared to come and watch the game and talk to you about how you had played was wonderful. Sometimes, he would invite you down for tea on a Sunday so we could all talk about the game that had been played the previous day. He lived in Deepdale Road, just across from the ground. It's called Sir Tom Finney Way now. I went on two or three occasions and he talked nothing but football.'

Shankly remained Finney's champion until the end of his days. He picked him in his side when he was asked to name his Greatest XI of all time. The only stipulation was that he could not name Liverpool players. It went like this, in the 2-3-5 formation that was prevalent in Shankly's playing days: Gordon Banks – George Young, Ray Wilson – Billy Bremner, John Charles, Dave Mackay – Stanley Matthews, Raich Carter, Tom Finney, Peter Doherty or Denis Law, George Best.

If Finney's career was shortened by the war, Shankly's was cut to shreds by it. He celebrated his twenty-sixth birthday the day before war was declared on 3 September 1939. Ever the consummate professional, he had gone into Deepdale for a pine bath and massage the day after Preston's game at Grimsby

Town. 'Some people were trying to sweat the beer out of themselves while I was getting ready for the next game,' Shankly said.

The next game never came. While he was still at the ground, he heard the Prime Minister, Neville Chamberlain, announce on the radio that England was at war with Germany. Later that afternoon, long lines of wagons and trucks from the barracks at Preston Castle rolled past his house on Deepdale Road, taking troops to the trains to begin the process of transporting them to the front.

Shankly was in his prime, about to enter what should have been the most fruitful years of his career. Preston had been improving gradually since he arrived in the summer of 1933 as Lancashire suffered in the grip of the Great Depression that had swept the USA and Britain. Suddenly, £6 a week seemed like the height of luxury as unemployment rose to affect 20 per cent of the workforce in England.

Cotton towns like Preston were particularly badly hit, and Shankly began to realize how privileged he was, particularly when, midway through the season, he broke into the first team at right half and played for the remainder of the campaign. At the end of that season, Preston pipped Bolton Wanderers to promotion to the First Division. Shankly's wages went up to £8 a week.

Shankly was able to live comfortably on his wages because he was single. He could send a significant percentage of his salary back home to help his parents. But there was poverty and hardship all around him. Families who needed help were subjected to the humiliation of the household means test. To be working-class and live through these times in England was to have a character forged in adversity.

Like so many people of his generation, Shankly's behaviour in his later life was shaped by living through great periods of hardship. In his childhood in the 1920s, he and his brothers stole food so their family of ten could survive the long winters in their mining community. In the 1930s, he grew used to seeing deprivation and human misery all around him as the Depression bit. And in the 1940s, he lived through all the hardships the war brought and the grim times of postwar austerity. It is little wonder that by the time he became Liverpool manager he distrusted extravagance and authority and lived for fifteen years in a modest semi-detached home in suburbia.

When Preston were promoted to the First Division, Shankly had gone from being a raw prospect at a basement club like Carlisle a year earlier to an established player preparing to face the great teams and the great players of the 1930s. He was only twenty but he would be up against the star names of the era, men like Dixie Dean, Hughie Gallagher, Cliff Bastin, Alex James, Raich Carter and Peter Doherty. It did not faze him. He went back to his home village of Glenbuck, an Ayrshire mining community, and ran relentlessly in the hills to ensure he was fitter than ever when he returned to Preston in July.

Preston held their own in the First Division. They finished eleventh in that first season. Arsenal won the title again even though their visionary manager, Herbert Chapman, died of pneumonia midway through the campaign. 'Arsenal were the kings in the 1930s,' Shankly wrote in his autobiography. 'They had everything: the marble halls of Highbury and aluminium massage baths. Their players walked about the dressing rooms wearing white hooded robes like Muhammad Ali does today. Arsenal thought big.'

Preston were seventh the following season and back down to fourteenth in 1936–37, although Shankly's reputation was on a steady upward curve. Doherty, a Northern Ireland international, even spoke admiringly about the day when he made his Manchester City debut against Preston and Shankly 'blotted me out completely'.

'Shankly has always been a wily tactician,' Doherty said, 'but that day he excelled himself. He dogged my footsteps all afternoon, muttering: "Great wee team, North End, great wee team" and subduing me so effectively that I must have been a great disappointment to all the thousands of City fans who had come along to see the club's expensive capture.'

Preston reached the Cup Final in 1937, too. They had seven Scots in the first team by now, including Andy Beattie, the man who was to give Shankly his big break in management by plucking him from Workington to become his assistant at Huddersfield Town. Team spirit was excellent, and under manager Tom Muirhead and trainer Billy Scott, Preston played a neat, clever brand of football that Shankly used as his template throughout his own managerial career.

They took the lead against Sunderland at Wembley, but Sunderland had been league champions the previous season and they came back strongly. They equalized early in the second half and then took the lead through Carter 17 minutes from time. They went further ahead in the 85th minute and Preston travelled back to the northwest empty-handed and distraught at falling at the last hurdle.

The next season was Shankly's finest as a player and Preston came desperately close to winning the title. Preston, Wolves and Arsenal were all level on points at the top of the table with three games to go and Arsenal still to visit Deepdale. The next Saturday, more than 42,000 fans crammed into the ground to see the showdown, but Shankly's teammate Jimmy Milne broke a cheekbone before half-time and Preston had to play the rest of the match with ten men. Bastin, who held Arsenal's goalscoring record until Ian Wright broke it in 1997, scored twice in Arsenal's 3–1 victory. The Gunners went on to win the title with Preston 3 points back in third.

The result had been different, though, when Arsenal and Preston met in the FA Cup fifth round at Highbury. Arsenal had a team packed with stars like Bastin, Ted Drake, who had scored seven goals in a single match against Aston Villa a couple of seasons earlier, Eddie Hapgood and the fearsome Wilf Copping, the Tommy Smith of his day. Preston won 1–0 in front of

72,000 fans and Shankly could not control his elation in the dressing room afterwards.

When Sir Frederick Wall, who had just retired as secretary of the FA after thirty-nine years in the post, but was still regarded as one of football's most powerful men and had formed an association with Arsenal, walked in to congratulate the Preston players afterwards, Shankly roared with laughter because the old man was wearing a long, astrakhan coat. 'Oh Christ,' Shankly said, 'it's Methuselah.'

Shankly was starting to get a reputation as a bit of a sharp wit around Deepdale by now. He once dressed up as John L. Sullivan, the former world heavyweight champion, and larked around the changing rooms in boxing gloves and a robe. And he learned from the humour of others, soaking up their way of making people laugh just as he absorbed the training methods he encountered as a player.

Shankly was impressed, for instance, by the urbanity of the Preston chairman, James Taylor. Taylor added to the atmosphere of hilarity in the Preston dressing room that day at Highbury when he began to mock the idea that a small-town team like Preston should be able to beat the mighty Arsenal. 'It's not right that a little village team can come down here and beat Arsenal,' Taylor said to Sir Frederick.

Shankly liked that. 'That was real sarcasm, salt into the wound,' he said. 'Taylor could have been prime minister. His brain was so alert and he was so witty.' Shankly, of course, went on to become a master of sarcasm himself. Once, when he was asked during the 1965–66 season if he was troubled by a recent defeat, he looked grave. 'Oh yes,' he said, 'here we are struggling at the top of the league.'

Preston felt after that victory at Highbury that they were destined to win the Cup at last. They beat Brentford comfortably in the quarter-final and Aston Villa in the semis. The people of Preston clamoured for Wembley tickets. There were 50,000 applications for the paltry 10,000 allocation that clubs received in those days. The match, though, was hardly a classic. Shankly complained about the length of the grass. It was short and dry, he said. The ball raced along the surface, making it difficult to control passes and catch long balls. Both teams were paralysed by tension, too. The match went to extra-time.

There was only a minute left when Shankly played a pass into the path of George Mutch, the Preston centre forward. Mutch hurtled towards the Huddersfield area but was sent crashing to the ground by a mistimed tackle from Alf Young. The referee blew for a penalty even though still photographs showed the tackle seemed to have taken place just outside the area. Then, as now, controversy raged over a referee's decision. Then, of course, they did not have the technological means to give the referees help if they had wanted to.

In the tension of the situation, Shankly appears to have had a rare failure of nerve. Mutch was clearly dazed by his heavy fall. In fact, he was briefly knocked unconscious. But no one stepped forward to take the penalty off him. He told reporters afterwards that he was so disoriented that he wondered why his teammates were handing him the ball. He didn't even realize a penalty had been awarded, and when he ran up to take the kick he couldn't see the goal. But Shankly, a regular penalty taker, who scored eight times from the spot during his Preston career, did not volunteer this time.

He was lucky. Mutch hammered the ball so hard that it took paint off the underside of the bar as it crashed off it and into the back of the net. Mutch was still reeling. He fell over again after he had taken the penalty. Shankly, who had been following up in case of a rebound, was first to him. 'I picked him up and lifted him above my head,' Shankly said. 'He knew it was in.' It seems astonishing now that Mutch should have been allowed to take the penalty and just as surprising that somebody like Shankly did not take the responsibility away from him.

After Mutch had scored, there was just time for the restart and for Andy Beattie to hoof a clearance into the Wembley crowd and then the final whistle blew. It was the happiest moment of Shankly's playing career. 'Of all the things that can happen in the game, when the whistle blows at Wembley and you've played in a final and you've won, that's the greatest thrill of your life as a player. No doubt about that. I thanked God for that. The feeling is unbelievable.'

Shankly collected his winner's medal from King George VI, and when he got back down to the pitch he saw Young in tears. 'A big, strong man crying,' Shankly said. 'Alf was not crying because he was soft. He was crying with emotion because he felt he had been responsible for losing the Cup.' Other reports suggest Shankly was rather less sympathetic. 'Aye and that's nae the first one you've given away,' Shankly is supposed to have said to his inconsolable opponent.

More than 80,000 people thronged the streets of Preston to welcome the players home the Monday after the Final. Shankly stood alongside the captain, Tom Smith, on the first of the four coaches that carried the team through the town to Market Square. A band played the team theme song, 'Keep Right on to the End of the Road', and Shankly drank it all in. A few weeks earlier, he had made his international debut for Scotland at Wembley and Scotland had beaten England 1–0. His career was scaling the peaks he had dreamed of. And then, just over a year later, Adolf Hitler invaded Poland.

Shankly didn't join up straight away like some other footballers. At some clubs, in fact, entire teams of men joined up together. At the start of the First World War, the Hearts team had marched to the recruiting station together. Seven of them were killed at the Battle of the Somme. Now, at the start of the Second World War, the Bolton Wanderers team did the same. Their captain, Harry Goslin, led the players to the recruitment station and they enlisted en masse in the 53rd Field Artillery Regiment of the Bolton Artillery. The West Ham team did the same thing in London. Goslin rose to the rank of lieutenant and was killed in Italy.

Maybe Shankly felt he had too much to lose to do that. Maybe his career was too precious to him. Maybe he disagreed with the idea of the war. Maybe he just loved football too much. And, like many others, he probably assumed the war would be over in a few months and normal life would resume. He probably even thought the 1939–40 season would be reinstated in some sort of abridged form. So one of the Preston directors found him a job in a reserved occupation in the town and Shankly began work as a riveter at English Electric, who were making Hampden bombers.

Shankly hated it and left after a few months. He joined the RAF. He had no ambition to rise through the ranks. He did not yearn to fight. He did not crave the buzz of the front line like some or feel that it was his duty to be sent somewhere where he could risk his life. 'My aim in the services was to do my bit,' he said. 'Whatever I could.' All he wanted to do was keep himself fit. He didn't shirk his duties, of course. If he was assigned to cleaning the latrines, he wanted to make sure he did it better than anyone else, but nor was he the kind of gung-ho airman who thrust himself forward and attempted to excel.

It seems incongruous, somehow. Shankly was a restless man. His football reputation was of someone who wanted to be at the centre of everything and hated the idea of hanging back. But he was utterly unadventurous as an airman. He was content to remain in the background and harboured no regrets about never having been posted abroad. Bob Paisley, in contrast, fought in North Africa with Field Marshal Montgomery's Desert Rats as part of a tank crew. He first saw Rome, for instance, through the turret of his fighting vehicle when the Allies liberated the Italian capital.

Shankly was posted to different camps all around Britain – Padstow, St Athan, near Cardiff, Manchester, Arbroath, Great Yarmouth, Henlow, in Bedfordshire, and finally to Bishopbriggs in Glasgow, so he could be close to his dying father – but he never once flew a sortie or climbed into a cockpit. He never got off the ground. The closest he came to seeing action was when an enemy aircraft bombed the hangars at the Manchester camp, but Shankly was not injured.

He seemed faintly embarrassed about his lack of advancement in the service. 'The highest rank I reached was acting corporal,' he said. 'Not very high but I hadn't any ambition to reach any great rank. Even so, I was possibly a better example to the men than some of the sergeants were. I gave more advice than the sergeants did and without the bull. I felt some of the boys were put upon. Some deserved it for being lazy and dirty but some seemed to be victimised for the sake of it.'

But Shankly's war was not about battlefields, bodies, dodging bullets, waking up in field hospitals or suffering from shell shock. Shankly's war was a sanitized thing. It was six years of a man desperately trying to pretend everything was normal and clinging on to the remnants of the career that had been taken away from him when he was at his peak. It was six years of denial and keeping his head down.

He used football as his escape. Just as he had always done. Football was his escape from the mines once and now it was his sanctuary from war. It was his pretend world. Shankly's life during the war was an elaborate conceit and football was the mechanism he used to protect him from the stark reality of what was occurring on the other side of the English Channel.

Hitler's name is not mentioned once in Shankly's autobiography. Instead, his war annals are packed with a list of his sporting achievements and the details of the various eating establishments across the country where, by a variety of means, he managed to procure the meals of steak, egg and chips that allowed him to stay in the same shape he had been in before the outbreak of war. It's not quite *King Rat*, but nor is it *In Which We Serve*.

His station team in Manchester won the Manchester and District Services League. He boxed for the camp there, too, at middleweight. The boxing team won the Duke of Portland Cup, whatever that was. He played for East Fife when he was at Arbroath, he refereed the final of a camp football competition at Henlow and played for Arsenal eleven times but was offended when they left him out of their wartime Cup Final side to play Charlton in May 1943.

He played for Scotland against England at Wembley again and was proud because a newspaperman made him man of the match. He was irate when he picked up a knee injury playing for Preston against Halifax and travelled from Halifax to Manchester on a bus over the moors with his leg badly swollen. He was treated at Crumpsall Hospital and later had to have a cartilage removed.

Perhaps his finest hour during the war came in May 1941 when he played with Finney in the Preston team that beat Arsenal in the second year of wartime Cup Finals. The two teams drew at Wembley and Preston won the replay at Ewood Park on 31 May. A year earlier, West Ham and Blackburn had contested the first War Cup Final on 8 June. In Jack Rollin's book, *Soccer at War*, a navy sailor remembered hearing the commentary of the final on the radio as he helped drag the bodies of English soldiers out of the sea in the wake of the evacuation from Dunkirk a few days earlier.

Shankly never seemed to wrestle with issues like that. Some of those who did not fight in the war, for whatever reason, rightly or wrongly, were haunted by guilt because so many had died and they had stayed at home. But guilt didn't cross Shankly's mind. It never appeared on his radar. To him, the war was a bloody inconvenience, a nuisance that wouldn't go away, a cataclysmic event that had interrupted football.

Shankly ignored it as best he could. He claimed, for instance, to have played in three FA Cup Finals: 1937, 1938 and 1941. It didn't seem to occur to him that maybe 1941 shouldn't carry quite the same weight because some men who might otherwise have been eligible to play professional football that year were preparing to die in the Battle of Britain.

In 1944, at the end of June, Shankly married Agnes Fisher, a member of the WRAF who was stationed with him in Glasgow. He wooed her by taking plates of toasted cheese over to her section. A year later, their first daughter, Barbara, was born and in January 1946, several months after the end of the war, Shankly was demobbed. The next day, he played for Preston in an FA Cup match against Everton.

It was almost as if the war had never happened. Shankly was bursting for football's return, and when Preston and Everton played the second leg of their tie at Goodison Park a few days later, it was Shankly who stepped up to take the decisive extra-time penalty at the Gwladys Street End. He was almost overcome by the joy of the moment. Every detail was pin-sharp. 'I had the wind and the rain at my back and there was a bit of a slope at that end of the pitch,' he said. 'I hit the ball with the side of my foot and it was maybe three feet inside the post. It skidded in like a bullet. Wet day, heavy ball – everything was perfect.'

For a while, everything was perfect at Preston, too. Shankly slipped easily back into the old routine and moved his wife and daughter down to Preston with him. The Labour government pegged football admission prices to make them affordable and crowds flocked to grounds in record numbers. Finney was a huge draw, the equal of Stanley Matthews, and he and Shankly, who was now club captain, formed a fine partnership on the right.

But things soon began to sour. Even though Shankly had kept himself fit, he was nearly thirty-three by the time the first proper postwar season began in the summer of 1946. Preston finished seventh that season and seventh the season afterwards. By then, rumours had begun to circulate that he was planning to retire. Shankly issued furious denials, but by the start of the 1948–49 season he found himself banished to the fringes of the team.

He was recalled for a victory over Huddersfield Town in

October but then dropped again when Preston were thrashed 6–1 by Manchester United in the next game. The club wanted him to stay on to help the reserves, but in January 1949 a managerial vacancy occurred at his old club, Carlisle United, when the player-manager, Ivor Broadis, transferred himself to Sunderland for £18,000.

Shankly's uncle, Bob Blyth, was still on the Carlisle board and told Shankly to apply for the job. He had an interview on 28 February and Carlisle offered him £14 a week to be their next manager. Tom Finney wanted him to stay. Preston tried to persuade him not to go. They threatened to withhold his benefit match, which would have been worth around £750, about a year's wages.

They said he would be given a benefit match if he stayed, but Shankly said they should give him one anyway after all the years of service he had given them. They refused. He played his 297th and final game for Preston against Sunderland at Deepdale on 19 March 1949. Preston were in deep relegation trouble by then. They went down at the end of that season. Shankly's best years had coincided with theirs. At least the Preston fans recognized his loyalty. They instituted a testimonial fund for him that raised nearly £170.

'At one time, I thought Preston North End was the greatest place in the world,' Shankly said. 'It would have broken my heart to have left. But in the end, I went without shedding a tear, bitter because I never got what I was promised. I felt the people who were running Preston at the time had cheated me out of my benefit match and that was the biggest let-down of my life in football.'

His playing career was over at the age of thirty-five. For some football men, the dawning of that day heralds a slow decline that lasts for the rest of their life. Shankly's life followed a very different pattern.

24: Ferguson and the Wonder of Barcelona

Alex Ferguson had a collection of favourite team talks. Some of his players knew them almost by heart. There was the one about the American billionaire Armand Hammer, who continued to rise at six o'clock every morning to go to his office even when he was in his eighties. And there was the parable about a man who kept banging into the glass doors at a branch of Marks & Spencer. He used that to upbraid players who were having difficulty learning from their mistakes.

Sometimes, he sat his players down in the dressing room before a big game and challenged them about what they wanted out of life and football. He told them that some people were content to take their holidays in Blackpool every year, buy kiss-me-quick hats, eat ice-creams and stroll on the promenade. And then there were some people who wanted to fly to the moon. Shankly liked Blackpool. 'Me,' Ferguson said, 'I want to fly to the moon.'

But at half-time in the Nou Camp in May 1999, with his team trailing 1–0 to Bayern Munich in the European Cup Final and his life's dream slipping away, Ferguson didn't go for any of the old favourites. Instead he remembered something that Steve Archibald, who had played for him at Aberdeen, had said the night before when they met at the side of the pitch in Barcelona's giant bowl of a stadium.

Ferguson had worn a red replica shirt with a white round collar as a nod to United's history when he took United's final training session before the final. When the players strolled off,

Archibald had told him that he was still tortured by what had happened to him in the moments after the end of the 1986 European Cup Final when his Barcelona team lost to Steaua Bucharest on penalties in Seville. When Archibald was called to the podium to collect his loser's medal, he had to pass within a few feet of the great jug-eared trophy, knowing that he could not touch it. Ferguson asked his players to imagine the same fate and then sent them back out up the steps and into the great cauldron of the stadium.

Ferguson had tried to make the build-up to the match as relaxed as possible. The squad had flown to Barcelona on Sunday, the day after their FA Cup Final victory over Newcastle United, and then driven 45 minutes south to the seaside resort of Sitges, the town where Bobby Robson lived when he was in charge at the Nou Camp. They set up camp in a hotel on the edge of the resort, and even though Ferguson was initially dismayed to find the foyer thick with United fans, he did his best to recreate the low-key, isolated build-up he had organized for Aberdeen's European Cup Winners' Cup Final against Real Madrid in Gothenburg sixteen years earlier.

His most difficult task was team selection and, specifically, where to play David Beckham and Ryan Giggs. Roy Keane and Paul Scholes, Ferguson's first-choice central midfielders, were both suspended for the final and Ferguson knew their absence had the potential to create a power vacuum at the heart of the side. His dilemma was whether to play Beckham or Giggs alongside the dependable Nicky Butt. He plumped for Beckham, brought Jesper Blomqvist in at left wing and moved Giggs to the right flank.

It didn't work. Mario Basler put Bayern ahead in the sixth minute with a straightforward free kick that he curled round the defensive wall and which left Peter Schmeichel strangely flat-footed. Bayern were generally the better side. Ferguson has tried to rewrite history in the years that have elapsed since, but Bayern outplayed United. They looked more authoritative and more confident. Lothar Matthäus, the great German captain, was playing within himself, and the Bayern markers, Sammy Kuffour and Thomas Linke, did not give United's prolific forward pairing of Andy Cole and Dwight Yorke a hint of an opportunity.

Ferguson's half-time team talk didn't have an immediate effect. United were still second-best. In fact, they were on the verge of being overrun. Midway through the second half, Bayern midfielder Mehmet Scholl left Schmeichel stranded with a deft chip that looked as if it was going to float gently into the net and kill United off. It hit the crossbar and bounced to safety but it seemed as if it could only be a stay of execution. In the stands, George Best got up from his seat and left. Up in the press box, most of the contingent of English journalists were busy filing the first takes of reports to the effect that Ferguson's gamble had failed. Much of that copy survived in the next day's first editions. Ferguson loved that.

Even Ferguson had begun to tell himself that, above all, he must remain dignified in defeat. He knew that the disappointment would be crushing and that it would leave him with his last great ambition unfulfilled, eating away at him even more voraciously. It would rob him of the chance of being bracketed with Jock Stein and Sir Matt Busby, his managerial heroes, who had both won the trophy with Celtic and United respectively. But he steeled himself nonetheless and told himself to be gracious when he shook the hand of the Bayern coach, Ottmar Hitzfeld, after the final whistle blew.

He made a couple of substitutions. A last gamble. He brought on Teddy Sheringham for Blomqvist and Ole Gunnar Solskjaer, who had turned down a move to Spurs earlier in the season, for Cole. The Germans were starting to celebrate. Not just their fans. On the touchline, Matthäus, who had been substituted late in the game, seemed to be mocking the United players. High fives were exchanged. Backs were slapped. Then, just after the fourth official had held up his board indicating that there were three minutes of added time left, United won a corner on the Bayern right.

Schmeichel came up for it. Beckham took it. He curled it right into the danger area. There was a mêlée. Schmeichel flung himself at it but it went to Yorke who headed it back towards goal. The ball fell to the Bayern defender Thorsten Fink, who had come on for Matthäus ten minutes earlier. Fink had time to control it and clear, but he panicked and slashed at it. The ball spiralled in the air, and when it came down Giggs volleyed it towards goal. It was a weak shot because it had fallen to his right foot, but as it bobbled through the players Sheringham pounced on it and swept it into the corner of the net. Sheringham looked towards the linesman to make sure he was not offside and then the madness and the glory took hold.

Ferguson had a feeling that his whole life was going to be condensed into the next 90 seconds. He was reaching out for everything he had worked towards for so long. Seconds ago, it had almost gone. Now it was within touching distance again. On the touchline, Steve McClaren tried to be the sane voice in the wonderful chaos. He had always told himself that when everyone around him was losing their heads, it was his job to stay calm and try and think rationally. In the mayhem, he asked Ferguson how they were going to change the team formation now that they were back in the game. 'Stay as we are,' said Ferguson.

McClaren wondered what he meant. As we are? McClaren didn't know how they were at that moment. There was no discernible formation at all. Then United won another corner on the Bayern right. Beckham ran over to take it. A kind of lust for glory had gripped all the United players, a feeling that suddenly the European Cup was theirs for the taking.

It was like the rope-a-dope. United were Muhammad Ali and Bayern were George Foreman. United had been battered and beaten all match long, and now Bayern were exhausted and United were coming out swinging. Beckham looked around him.

'It was all happening so quickly that when I went over to take the corner,' he said, 'I could see United supporters still jumping around shouting into their mobile phones and celebrating Teddy's goal. I think the Bayern players were still trying to get to grips with what had happened, too.'

Beckham curled in another perfect corner. The legs of the Germans had no spring left in them, but Sheringham leapt. He glanced the ball on just as he had glanced on a thousand corners in hundreds of games less important than this one. The ball flew across the face of the goal. Solskjaer reacted fastest. He stuck out his right leg and guided the ball towards the goal. It flew past the left hand of Oliver Kahn, who was helpless. It rose and rose. It went under the crossbar and into the roof of the net. Some of the Bayern players fell to the floor as if they had been clubbed. Some of them burst into tears. From the restart, they forced the ball into United's half one more time. Then the whistle blew. It was over.

As the United players flung their hands in the air in joyful amazement, the flashbulbs from thousands of cameras lit up the Nou Camp as if it was noonday in the Spanish sun and froze the players in triumph for a split second. After Schmeichel had lifted the trophy, the United players cavorted on the pitch for an hour. They formed a guard of honour for Keane and Scholes, who looked awkward in their club suits. Ferguson posed with them all for a team picture. David May, a non-playing substitute, felt the need to dominate every picture. He will, at least, be a great quiz question for future generations.

While the players were still celebrating, Ferguson made his way to the post-match press conference. He was applauded when he came in. He was almost lost for words, still dazed by being the beneficiary of the most dramatic denouement there has ever been to a European Cup Final. He invoked the memory of Sir Matt Busby. It would have been the great man's ninetieth birthday that day. And then, Ferguson paused to try to sum up what had just happened. 'Football,' he said. 'Bloody hell.'

After the celebrations had finally petered out, the players changed and then spoke to the massed ranks of the media for the best part of an hour. Then they climbed back on board their coach and travelled to the Hotel Arts on the seafront. Their party lasted until dawn. Many of the United players spent the time trying to come to terms with the enormity of what had just happened.

Gary Neville and Ben Thornley, his former teammate from the great United youth team of 1992, wandered out of the party as dawn was breaking and walked through the half-light and the deserted streets to the marina at Port Olimpic, talking about everything that had happened to them in the last seven years. When they got back to the hotel, the party was still going strong.

It is a measure of the increasing control exerted by Ferguson over every aspect of the club that he tried to insist through his obedient press officer Ken Ramsden that his next day's press conference should be attended only by the beat reporters who covered the club week in and week out. It was pointed out to Ramsden that Manchester United had pretensions to being the biggest club in the world and had just won the European Cup for the first time in thirty-one years, so trying to limit the press conference to five or six people was not only farcical and ridiculous but totally impractical.

Ramsden was insistent. Even in his moment of triumph, Ferguson was still obsessing about his petty feuds and resentments with journalists he did not like. In the end, of course, the reporters who had turned up at the hotel brushed aside Ramsden's feeble protestations and joined Ferguson in a kind of conservatory at the back of the hotel where he was holding court. He was happiness and charm itself. He did not say a word about the ban he had tried to impose. On the morning after the best night of his professional life, even he lacked the stomach for a shouting match.

He felt fulfilled at last. He talked that morning about

wanting to create a dynasty at Old Trafford, about wanting to emulate teams like Real Madrid and Juventus and AC Milan by winning the trophy with something approaching regularity. He foresaw great days ahead. He thought that now United had won the European Cup once under him, they could go on to win it many times. After the season his team had just had, it was hard to blame him.

The 1998–99 season, which will always be known as the Treble season, was probably the most remarkable performance by a team in the history of English football. Arguments rage about whether other English sides were more accomplished, and of course there are plenty of backers for the great Liverpool teams of the Seventies and Eighties, the United team that won the club's first Double in 1994 and the Arsenal team that went unbeaten for an entire league season in 2003–04.

But nobody won the three most important trophies like United did that season. Liverpool won a Treble of their own a few years later but it wasn't *the* Treble. It was the Worthington Cup, the FA Cup and the Uefa Cup. Pretty good. Special, in fact. But not really close to what United had achieved in 1998–99. Liverpool's Treble was remarkable but it was seen as preparation for a tilt at the big trophies.

Other English teams may well come close to emulating what United achieved, but even if they do, none will ever achieve it with quite the style, the panache, the determination, the refusal to quit or the unremitting melodrama that accompanied United's waltz towards history. To watch them that season was to wonder at them. To see Ferguson marshalling them was to gaze upon a magnificent manager at the peak of his powers.

It has been largely forgotten now because of the breathtaking excitement of the comeback at the Nou Camp, but the season was largely defined by the rivalry between United and Arsène Wenger's first great Arsenal side. The famous Arsenal back four was still intact then and enjoying its last hurrah: Marc Overmars was running like a human rocket down the left, Emmanuel Petit and Patrick Vieira were controlling the heart of the side, and Dennis Bergkamp and Nicolas Anelka combined subtlety and blistering pace in attack.

They went head to head that season. They could not escape each other. The season will be for ever associated with United now, but it could so easily have been Arsenal's. Just one extra goal to go for them or one extra goal against United and the title would have been theirs. Just one successful penalty kick in an FA Cup semi-final and the Cup would have gone to north London too.

The struggle between United and Arsenal in the league was titanic. It went right down to the wire. At the beginning of May, with four games still to go, United thought they had ceded the advantage to Arsenal when they blew a two-goal lead against Liverpool at Anfield. To Ferguson's disgust, Denis Irwin was sent off for time-wasting, a decision which meant he missed the Cup Final.

Then Paul Ince, still smarting from being discarded by United four years earlier and newly stung by being derided by Ferguson as a 'big-time Charlie', got the Liverpool equalizer two minutes from time. Ince's celebrations suggested that revenge was very, very sweet – 'Gloatingly excessive,' Ferguson called them.

On the United bench, Steve McClaren thought Liverpool had won it when Jamie Carragher rose to meet a cross in injury time. McClaren thought it was going in. When he thinks back to the season now, the way that that header seemed to curl away from the goal at the last instant is one of several moments in that season that he felt had an almost supernatural quality. The draw meant United were 3 points behind Arsenal with a game in hand.

But United wrested back the initiative when they won their game in hand with a goal from Dwight Yorke against Middlesbrough at the Riverside. Ferguson had paid £12.6 million for

Yorke at the start of the season in the face of considerable opposition from the United chairman, Martin Edwards, and his own assistant, Brian Kidd, who preferred West Ham's John Hartson.

Ferguson never forgave Kidd. He thought his assistant had gone behind his back and tried to undermine him with Edwards. He was scathing about Kidd in his autobiography, published in 1999. Kidd was a popular man and Ferguson's attack was ill-judged. But he got Yorke in the end, just before the transfer deadline in August 1998.

After United won at Middlesbrough, Arsenal faced an awkward trip to Elland Road the following Tuesday night. The atmosphere in the ground was febrile and the Leeds players tore into their opponents. A young Alan Smith, full of snarling iconoclasm and glorious disrespect, rattled Tony Adams with his robust tackling and some colourful comments about the Arsenal captain's liaison with the model Caprice. Adams, unusually, lost his cool. Leeds were brilliant. A few minutes from the end, Jimmy Floyd Hasselbaink grabbed the winner with a bullet header.

The following evening, United went to Blackburn Rovers. Kidd had taken charge at Ewood Park by then and had been unable to drag Blackburn out of the relegation zone. No one knew then the depth of the vindictiveness Ferguson felt towards his former assistant, but when United ground out a goalless draw that sent Blackburn down, he exchanged the briefest handshake with the man who had worked with him for seven years and then disappeared down the Ewood Park tunnel. After the game, when reporters asked Ferguson if had felt any sympathy for Kidd, he said he hadn't realized that Blackburn were now relegated. It was hard to believe.

So United were a point clear of Arsenal going into the final weekend of the season. Arsenal were at home to Aston Villa. United were at home to Spurs. It was in United's hands. Arsenal fans were convinced that United had the perfect opponents. How could Spurs live with themselves if they got a draw at Old Trafford and handed the title to Arsenal?

Anticipation mixed with tension at Old Trafford on the final day. Russell Watson, a tenor from Salford, strode out onto the pitch before the Tottenham game and belted out a rousing rendition of Nessun Dorma to crank up the atmosphere. Not that it needed it. The supporters in the stadium knew what was at stake. Among other things, they knew that this would be Peter Schmeichel's last home game for the club. But with the FA Cup Final and the European Cup Final both lying ahead in the next ten days, they wanted this to be a beginning, not an ending.

Spurs went ahead after 24 minutes when Les Ferdinand looped a high lob over Schmeichel. The tension increased. United struggled. Then, three minutes before half-time, the ball was worked to Beckham in space on the right side of the area. Beckham looked up and hit a high swerving shot across Ian Walker and into the top corner of the Spurs net. Relief flooded around the stadium.

Ferguson brought Andy Cole on for Teddy Sheringham at half-time. The two strikers didn't like each other. They didn't even speak to each other. Cole has mellowed considerably now and is one of the most intelligent commentators on the game, but back then he could be defensive and difficult. Around that time, a journalist was invited to his house to do an interview. Cole asked him if he wanted anything to drink. The journalist said that a cup of tea would be nice. Cole glared at him. 'Andy Cole don't make tea,' he said.

But Cole was still an assassin in front of goal. He had improved immeasurably from the time he was a pure goalscorer at Newcastle under Kevin Keegan. His touch was better. His movement was better. His contribution to the team was better. Ferguson's substitution that day was inspired. Two minutes after the interval, Gary Neville floated a lovely ball over Justin

Edinburgh and into the path of Cole. Cole controlled it sweetly and then lifted it over Walker and into the net.

It didn't matter what Arsenal did after that. It didn't matter that they beat Villa 1–0. Because United hung on. Paul Scholes missed a couple of chances and Ferguson brought on Phil Neville and Nicky Butt to keep things tight. When the game was won and the celebrations were in full flow, Russell Watson came back out on to the pitch and sang an aria made famous by Freddie Mercury and Montserrat Caballe. It was called 'Barcelona'.

Before United could get to Catalonia, though, they confronted Newcastle in the FA Cup Final at Wembley in the second leg of their Treble attempt. The Cup was the least important of the three trophies they were hunting but in the Treble season, the competition still entwined United in two of the most dramatic games in their history.

The first came at Old Trafford on 24 January when Yorke and Ole Gunnar Solskjaer scored twice in the last two minutes to take United to a 2–1 victory over Liverpool. It was the first of the remarkable last-gasp comebacks that defined their season and gained them a reputation as the team that refused to die.

If that game was dramatic, their semi-final replay against Arsenal at Villa Park on 14 April surpassed it with ease. That match, pitting two wonderful sides against each other at their peak, has a claim to be one of the greatest FA Cup ties of all time. If the Cup Final against Newcastle was a walkover, a straightforward 2–0 win that gave United their third Double but which was still, essentially, an anticlimax, the replay triumph over Arsenal was crammed with the best that football has to offer.

Ferguson rested Cole and Yorke and gave Teddy Sheringham his seventh start of the season. The Arsenal fans taunted him with their favourite chant. 'Oh Teddy, Teddy,' it went, 'you went to Man United and you won fuck all.' Teddy, of course, was about to put that right. After 17 minutes, United took the lead when Beckham drilled a low shot past David Seaman from the edge of the area.

It took Arsenal until midway through the second half to strike back. Dennis Bergkamp got the equalizer, courtesy of a thick deflection off Jaap Stam. Five minutes later, Keane was sent off for a second bookable offence after he chopped down Overmars near the touchline. The referee was David Elleray, who was rarely sympathetic to United. Keane knew there would be no mercy from him. United's Treble chance was hanging by a thread. In injury time, it seemed the thread was about to be severed.

Ray Parlour won a penalty. Bergkamp took it. If he scored, not even United could have come back. He stroked his penalty low to Schmeichel's left but the United keeper guessed right and parried it before it was kicked to safety. Bergkamp never took a penalty again. His miss cost Arsenal a second successive Double and pushed United on towards glory.

At the start of the second period of extra-time, Vieira played a loose ball from left to right across the pitch just inside the United half and it was intercepted by Giggs. Giggs was the fittest player at United. At pre-season training, he was always the player who won the first cross-country race after the holidays. He had sat on the bench for the first hour of the game, too. If that loose ball could have gone to anyone, United would have wanted it to go to him. Giggs got it and set off for goal.

He eluded Vieira's lunge and hurtled into the area, avoiding Overmars too. Lee Dixon came for him next and Giggs side-stepped him. That move took him a little wide but instead of squaring the ball, Giggs shot with his left foot and the ball took off like a guided missile. It arrowed over Seaman's head and into the roof of the net.

There was a postscript too. The kind of postscript that underlined what a magical rivalry it was that season between United and Arsenal. After the game, both sides were exhausted and Arsenal's players were shattered by their loss. But when United eventually made it back to their dressing room, they found Lee Dixon and Tony Adams waiting by the door for them. Dixon and Adams shook the hand of every United player as he walked past. United players like Gary Neville never forgot that gesture of good sportsmanship.

But the drama of that season was relentless. There were no troughs, ahead, only peaks. A week after the semi-final replay, still on a high, United travelled to Turin for the second leg of their European Cup semi-final against Juventus at the Stadio Delle Alpi. Even though they were in the midst of such an enchanted spell, even though it was beginning to seem as if they would never lose, no one gave them much of a chance against Juventus.

United had not had a smooth ride to the semi-finals. They had been forced to begin their campaign on 12 August at home to the Polish side LKS Lodz before the Premiership season had kicked off. Because they had finished second to Arsenal in the league the previous year, United had to play in the second qualifying round of the European Cup. They won 2–0 on aggregate but their reward was to be drawn in a group that comprised Barcelona, Bayern Munich and Brondby.

Brondby were easy enough. United beat them heavily twice. But they also took part in two breathless 3–3 draws against Barcelona and a 2–2 stalemate with Bayern at the Olympiastadion in Munich. It meant they went into the last group game against Bayern at Old Trafford on 9 December 1998 still needing to win to be sure of progressing to the quarter-finals. Instead, they drew again. But they were lucky. They finished as runners-up to Bayern but went through to the last eight as one of the two best second-placed sides.

In the quarter-finals, in March, they eased past an Inter Milan side who rushed Ronaldo back from injury for the second leg. United had a two-goal advantage from the initial encounter at Old Trafford but there was still widespread anxiety about the havoc the Brazilian might wreak. In fact, he was anonymous and United ground out a goalless draw at the San Siro.

But Ferguson's hopes of emulating Sir Matt Busby and winning the trophy for United for the first time in thirty-one years seemed doomed when Juventus outplayed their opponents in the first leg of the semi-final at Old Trafford at the beginning of April. Juventus were a formidable side. They had been runners-up in the European Cup the previous two seasons and winners the year before that. Their team was dominated by the balletic Zinédine Zidane and the combative Edgar Davids. Zidane was elusive as a ghost. Davids snarled like a pit bull. When Juventus drew 1–1 in the first leg against United, the return in Turin was presented as a formality.

Formality appeared to have turned into embarrassment when Juventus went two goals up in the first ten minutes. Filippo Inzaghi opened the scoring when he sneaked in at the back post to meet a cross from Zidane after five minutes. Inzaghi scored again five minutes later. His shot hit Jaap Stam and spiralled into the air over the stranded Schmeichel and into the net.

But then Roy Keane took over. Keane will always be remembered for his performance that night. He was the game's tragic hero. It was at once his finest hour and his most exquisite agony. The pain stayed with him for the rest of his career at United. He got United to that final but suspension meant he could only watch from the stands. When United won it, it stripped them of the hunger to do it again and Keane never played on the stage he craved most of all. He raged against that injustice for the last seven years of his career at Old Trafford.

'Anybody looking to throw the towel in,' Keane wrote in his autobiography about the moment when Inzaghi scored his second, 'now had the perfect opportunity. Anybody seeking to prove that they were worthy of playing for Manchester United also had the chance to fucking prove it. It is at moments like this that football – any sport for that matter – becomes a mind game. How strong were we mentally? How strong were Juventus?'

Keane soon provided the answers. He dragged United back into the game in the 24th minute when he met a Beckham corner at the near post and glanced it into the net. Eight minutes later, Keane mistimed a tackle on Zidane. It was easy to do. The referee booked him. He knew that would put him out of the final. Most men would have crumbled. Like Paul Gascoigne had in similar circumstances in the same stadium eight years earlier. But Keane did not cry.

Instead, he was filled with a furious passion. He drove United on. He couldn't go to Barcelona but he was determined that the team should get there. He was everywhere. He stifled everything Juventus tried to create. They were unsettled by the force of his play. Even Davids seemed taken aback by his power.

'I didn't think I could have a higher opinion of any footballer than I already had of the Irishman,' Ferguson wrote of Keane that night, 'but he rose even higher in my estimation in the Stadio Delle Alpi . . . I felt it was an honour to be associated with such a player.' Ten minutes before half-time, United were level on the night and ahead on away goals. Cole and Yorke came good again. Cole chipped into the box, Yorke rammed a diving header past Peruzzi. Juventus were stunned. United put the semi-final beyond Juventus 6 minutes from the end with a goal from Cole.

It was another heady night. Another night that season when it really seemed as though there was magic in the air. But straight away, there was sympathy and admiration for Keane. Most of those who were there in the Stadio Delle Alpi that night consider his display the finest individual performance they have ever witnessed.

It is the custom of most football teams to fly straight back home after an away tie in Europe rather than stay another night in the hotel in the host city. Keane kept himself apart from the rest of the team when they got to the airport in Turin. He sat alone on the flight in the early hours, too. Nobody was stupid enough to disturb him. No journalist even thought about approaching him. All he had were dark thoughts for company. Now, he allowed the enormity of what had happened to sink in. He had yearned all his career to lead out a side in the European Cup Final but his dream was to be denied him.

'When Andy Cole scored our third,' Keane wrote, 'I knew there would be a final to miss. I didn't care at that point (although later I would). I was proud of our team that night. I was, for once, proud of myself, content that I had justified my existence and honoured my debts to the manager who'd placed so much trust in me. The Champions League final was where I believed Manchester United should be. I genuinely felt that was so much more important than whether or not I would be there. When that euphoric feeling evaporated . . . I was gutted.'

Keane flew to Barcelona with the rest of the United squad on Concorde. He said he felt like an extra in a movie. He talked about how it was as if a glass partition descended between him and the players who would be playing. When United got their equalizer, Keane's overwhelming emotion was pleasure for the manager. That night, as the party raged at the Hotel Arts, he thought about how Ferguson had achieved his lifetime's ambition.

'There was a real sense of achievement shared by everyone belonging to the club Sir Alex Ferguson had created,' Keane said. 'Europe was the acid test and we had passed. Ultimately, this was his achievement. I could easily lay aside my personal disappointment at missing the final for in truth it was an honour to captain the team that delivered for a great manager and a great club.'

The next day, United returned to Manchester. The crowd that met them on the streets of the city was estimated at almost one million. Ferguson was the focal point of it all. He felt fulfilled. 'The celebrations begun by Ole Gunnar's goal will never really stop,' Ferguson said. 'Just thinking about it can put me in a party mood. At the time, all of us associated with the team were blissfully demented. Gary Newbon tried to interview me for television and, I am sure, got a flood of gibberish for his pains. I didn't mind sounding like an idiot. There was no happier idiot on the planet.'

25: Shankly and the Escape from Underground

When Bill Shankly was a boy growing up in the 1920s in a spartan, tough, wind-blown community 30 miles inland from Ayr, he watched his village team, the Glenbuck Cherrypickers, play a grudge match against a side from a neighbouring district. The opposition hired a special train with a couple of carriage-loads of supporters intent on causing trouble and walked the 4 miles from the station to the pitch.

The Cherrypickers were a famous side, renowned for producing a string of players who went on to be professional footballers. The opposition wanted to unsettle them in any way they could. Soon enough, a fight broke out that turned into a mass brawl, and Shankly watched as one of his four older brothers, Sandy, grappled with an opponent next to a barbed-wire fence. 'Oh, what a brawl it was,' Shankly said. 'There were a few broken noses that day.'

Football was a hard game in Ayrshire, both physical and unforgiving. The Cherrypickers played in the Ayrshire League and they rejected Shankly when he was seventeen because they knew only more experienced men could cope with the challenges that would be thrown at them on the pitch. Shankly was hardly a timid fellow himself, particularly when it came to tackling.

'As a player, I specialised in tackling which is an art,' Shankly said. 'I was never sent off the field or had my name in a referee's book. I played it hard but fair. No cheating. I'd have broken somebody's leg, maybe, with a hard tackle, with a bit of spirit, but that's a different story from cheating. Cheats will always be caught in the finish even if punishment is sometimes a long time coming.'

But even though it was a hard game, it was still an escape route for Shankly and his brothers, just as it has come to be for generations of working-class men. Theirs was not an inner city ghetto of tenements and shipyards like Ferguson's, but a decaying mining community in a rural wasteland, a community where unemployment was growing and growing at a remove from the rest of civilization.

Shankly was a child of the Depression. He was unemployed for the six months before he became a professional footballer. He did not have a bath until he moved away from Glenbuck. There was no hot water. No indoor toilet. People from the village walked 6 miles to work and 6 miles back as a matter of routine. Through rain and through snow. His father was a tailor in a community where there was no money to pay for fripperies. And fine clothes were fripperies. Most of the money was to be made in mending and sewing and it was not profitable work.

Perhaps that was why Shankly was so obsessive about football and why he pursued it with such ferocity. The alternative to football was so bleak. Life down the mine at a time when even that job was laced with uncertainties and the prospect of deprivation.

Football took all of the Shankly brothers – Bill was the youngest of five – away from the pits into new lives. Bob, Jimmy and Bill never went back but the mines sucked Sandy and John back below ground when their careers finished. John Shankly, in fact, went back down the pit but he didn't let it claim him. He died following his first love and watching football. He collapsed with a massive heart attack at the 1960 European Cup Final between the great Real Madrid and Eintracht Frankfurt at Hampden Park.

Jimmy played for Portsmouth, Halifax, Sheffield United, Southend and Barrow and sent money home to Glenbuck that allowed his parents and the remaining nine children to get along.

Bob played with Alloa and Falkirk and became a successful manager at Dundee, where he led them to a Scottish title and into the European Cup in 1962–63, where they put eight goals past FC Cologne and beat Sporting Lisbon and Anderlecht before AC Milan knocked them out in the semi-finals.

Shankly felt the family bond closely. He named one of his daughters after his mother, Barbara, who he said unashamedly was his greatest inspiration. To Shankly, the way his mother held their family of ten together was 'a miracle of dedication'. He spent the rest of his life trying to emulate it. 'I try, but mine is nothing compared to hers,' he said. His other daughter was named after his youngest sister, Jean.

It was a wrench when he left home, even though his older brothers had already made the break. Shankly spent a few months playing for Cronberry Eglinton, a team named after a castle that had fallen into ruin, in the Cumnock and District League in the 1931–32 season before he was spotted by a Carlisle United scout, Peter Carruthers, and invited for a trial with the Third Division North club. It may or may not have been significant that Shankly's uncle, Billy Blyth, was a director at Brunton Park.

Shankly was defensive about any suggestion of nepotism but his mother's family was unusually well connected in English football. Billy was at Carlisle and another brother, Robert, was the chairman of Portsmouth. Coincidentally, Shankly's brother, Jimmy, also began his career at Carlisle and his brother, John, got his first break at Portsmouth. When Shankly travelled south to try to take his first step on the ladder, it was the first time he had ever been out of Scotland.

Shankly scoffed at the importance of the family connection but Carlisle offered him a one-year contract worth £4.12 shillings a week in the summer of 1932, even though his solitary trial game for the reserves was a 6–0 humiliation by Middlesbrough reserves. Shankly accepted. Carlisle was close enough to Glenbuck that he could travel home by train every other weekend after the game on a Saturday, but he was adamant that Brunton Park was merely the first step on a journey to greater things.

'I was ambitious,' Shankly said, 'or impatient if you like because ambition is a form of impatience. You want to get at something before it's there. You want to burst the balloon before it's blown up.' Still, he made a good start. He was eighteen years old when he began to earn his living by playing football.

Shankly played the rest of the year in the reserves. He made his first-team debut at home to Rochdale in a 2–2 draw. Before the end of the season, he had made 16 first-team appearances. It was hardly a successful year for the club. They finished 19th in the 22-team division, separated from the bottom of the table only by York, New Brighton and Darlington.

But even though they scored fewer goals than any other side, they also conceded fewer than anyone else in the lower half of the table. That was something that reflected well on Shankly, who played at half-back and avoided being transfer-listed at the end of the season. He enjoyed his nine months in Carlisle and particularly his working relationship with the coach, Tom Curry. Curry went on to work with Matt Busby at Manchester United and died in the Munich Air Crash.

Half an hour after the final whistle of the last game of the season, Shankly was on his way back to Glenbuck for the summer. A week later he was playing brag with some friends, sitting on the pitch where the Cherrypickers had once played, when one of his sisters came rushing over from their house with a telegram for her brother. Telegrams were a rarity in Glenbuck. There was quite a fuss.

Shankly read it. 'TRAVEL TO CARLISLE TOMORROW STOP CARLISLE UNITED,' it said. He was puzzled. Eventually, he managed to find a telephone and make contact with the club. They told him another club had made a significant offer for him and that they wanted him at Brunton Park the next day to discuss terms. But they would not tell him the name of his suitor over the phone.

It was Preston North End, who had just finished the previous season in ninth place in Division Two but who were one of the biggest clubs in the country. They had offered Carlisle £500 for Shankly, a significant fee for a club of Carlisle's size, but Shankly was not impressed with the terms.

He and his brother Sandy listened to the Preston trainer, Bill Scott, tell him that he would be paid £5 a week, plus a £40 share of the transfer fee and a £10 signing-on fee. Shankly was worried that he might end up losing money if the standard of living was more expensive in Preston and it cost more to travel the longer distances back home to Glenbuck. He was also concerned that he would be consigned once more to long spells of reserve-team football just when he had established himself in the first team at Carlisle.

So Shankly turned Scott down. He told him he could earn the £40 in one hand of pontoon back in Glenbuck. The wage rise was so small it wasn't worth the leap into the unknown, he said. Scott left for the train station. He said he was going to catch a train to Newcastle where he would offer what he had just offered Shankly to his second-choice player.

When Scott had gone, Sandy told Shankly he was a fool. He told him that the money wasn't the issue. It was the opportunity of higher-grade football that Preston were offering him that mattered. He told him the money would come later when he made a success of the move. The speech, in fact, sounded remarkably similar to the one Shankly would deliver to Kevin Keegan when Keegan quibbled about the money Shankly was offering him to move from Scunthorpe United.

Shankly realized almost at once he had made a mistake. The two brothers raced to the station and arrived just as the Newcastle train was pulling in. They spotted Scott climbing into a carriage and Shankly chased after him and leapt on board. As the locomotive pulled away, steam billowing furiously from its chimney, Scott and Shankly began to talk about the terms again. After about half an hour, a third of the way to Newcastle, Scott laid the contract out on a table in the compartment and Shankly signed it. A couple of minutes later, the train pulled into the station at Haltwhistle, a small town near Hadrian's Wall, and Shankly said his goodbyes and jumped out.

He had almost blown it. Carlisle didn't make it out of the bottom division for another thirty years. They were stuck in the sidings of English football, and if Shankly had turned his back on Preston, he might have been stuck there with them. He'd changed his mind just in time. He got out of the train, crossed over the tracks to the other side and waited for the next train back to Carlisle.

26: Ferguson – The Rock and a Hard Place

Sir Alex Ferguson came under enormous pressure to settle his agreement with Magnier. People had been trying to tell him for more than a year that he was a fool to take on the might of Magnier and the Coolmore Mafia, the richest and most powerful men in Ireland. But somehow Ferguson had never detected the iron fist in the velvet glove and now he had made an enemy of his friend. This enemy was formidable and articles began appearing questioning the role of Ferguson's son Jason; questions were put to the board and the blue chip private investigators Kroll were instructed to prepare a report of their investigation into Ferguson's affairs and his dealings as Manchester United manager. Whether it was this pressure, or whether Ferguson just revised what he wanted, only Ferguson and his advisors know, but Ferguson settled the dispute. Ferguson's attempt to secure a fortune had failed.

He had contended that he was entitled to half the breeding rights to the wonder horse Rock of Gibraltar. He had been given a half-share in the horse by Magnier in the summer of 2001 as a favour and a plaything. He did not pay £120,000 for that share, as some reports have suggested. He did not pay anything. But because of the largesse and the generosity of Magnier, who considered him a friend, Ferguson shared in Rock of Gibraltar's record-breaking glories over the next fourteen months.

Ferguson's part-ownership of the horse helped to its feats and advertise the excellence of Magnier's Coolmore publicize

Stud. Ferguson was used extensively in Coolmore's publicity video. He brought them prestige and cachet. He advertised their excellence to a wider market. But Ferguson did not pay the horse's training fees. He did not pay its insurance fees. He did not pay its jockey fees. He did not pay its transportation fees. He did not pay its race entry fees. Together, those costs came to close to £200,000 in the fourteen months Ferguson was involved. Rock of Gibraltar did not live cheaply.

Rock of Gibraltar did not, for instance, fly cattle class to races. He flew by private jet. As far as Magnier was concerned the tacit agreement between him and Ferguson was that Ferguson was involved in the ownership of the horse in an honorary capacity and that Magnier would grant him a small but profitable share of the stud rights when the horse's racing career was over. As far as Magnier was concerned Ferguson never challenged that idea. Not when it came to him contributing to the upkeep of the horse, anyway.

But suddenly, when Rock of Gibraltar was retired after it had come second in the Breeders' Cup Mile at Arlington Park near Chicago at the end of October 2002, Ferguson seemed seduced by the thought of the dizzying riches he felt were so close.

Ferguson was already a millionaire several times over, but maybe it seemed like the buried treasure he'd dreamed of his whole life. Deafened by the siren songs of other greedy men lulling him into danger, his judgement failed him. In the instant he decided to sue Magnier for his half-share of the breeding rights to Rock of Gibraltar, he ruined a host of priceless friendships and destroyed his reputation in a new world that could have been his life after football.

Ferguson had always liked to gamble. The tenement building in Govan where he grew up with his family in the 1940s and 50s was surrounded by bars and illegal bookmakers. He went to dog tracks in Glasgow, too, when he was older. He gave it up when he was immersing himself in his job in Aberdeen in the early Eighties, but when he moved to Old Trafford he started betting again.

By the mid-1990s, he was starting to think about retirement. He had weathered the crisis of his early years at Old Trafford and established United as the leading force in English football again. He did not feel quite the same ferocious need to prove himself any more. He still had a great appetite for work, still lusted after the thought of winning the European Cup, but he was looking for ways to relax, too. The sadness of Shankly's last years had made Ferguson keenly aware of the need to begin to replace football with new challenges to dull the shock of retirement.

And so, as a gift to his wife, Cathy, on the occasion of their thirty-first wedding anniversary, Ferguson arranged tickets for them both to go to the Cheltenham Festival on Gold Cup day in March 1997. They had their own box, next to Lord and Lady Lloyd Webber. They all got on famously, at least until the Lloyd Webbers' horse, Uncle Ernie, a 20–1 outsider, won the Grand Annual Chase. Ferguson pretended to be annoyed his new friends hadn't given him a tip. 'That's the last fucking musical I ever go to,' he said.

But Ferguson enjoyed his day enormously. So did his wife. He was thrilled. He had found something they could enjoy together away from football. He wanted to take things further. He wanted to immerse himself in racing. Ferguson throws himself wholeheartedly into anything that pricks his interest. Football, cooking, piano-playing, red wine. And now horse-racing. Now he wanted to buy a horse.

Some of his friends advised him against it. They told how expensive it was, and the surest way of seeing money going up in smoke. He ignored them. He and some of his pals from Aberdeen formed a syndicate called the Right Angle Club and paid 17,000 guineas for a yearling. He named it Queensland Star after a ship his father had helped to build when he worked at the Freshfields yard on the Clyde.

On 16 April 1998 it ran for the first time in the 4.45 at Newmarket, the European Breeders Fund Stuntney Maiden Stakes. It won. The prize money was £4,191. Then it won again at Chester a month later. It ran on Derby Day at Epsom, too, and finished fourth in the Woodcote Stakes. Ferguson loved it. He got a thrill that was at least an approximation of the rush he got out of football. He was hooked.

He invested in another horse, Caledonian Colours, in partnership with the Hong Kong champion trainer Ivan Allan. It was trained in England by Sir Michael Stoute. When it ran at Haydock Park, Stoute chose to go to the NatWest Trophy Final at Lord's to watch Derbyshire v Lancashire as a guest of his friend, the former West Indies fast bowler Michael Holding. Most of the day was rained off. Up at Haydock, Caledonian Star won. Ferguson called Stoute and teased him about his absence. 'Serves you right,' he said. 'You should have been here.'

The acquisitions continued. The Right Angle Club bought another horse in October 1998. Ferguson called it Candleriggs, after an area of Glasgow. It was trained by Ed Dunlop at Newmarket. Ferguson was in deep and getting deeper. United chairman Martin Edwards, who had urged him to find a hobby, was suddenly alarmed that Ferguson was spending too much time away from the training ground.

At his second Cheltenham Festival, in 1998, Ferguson was introduced to Magnier and J. P. McManus by a mutual friend, Mike Dillon, the PR director for Ladbrokes, Britain's largest bookmakers. Now Fergie was playing with the big boys. In 2005, Magnier was ranked eighth in the 2005 *Sunday Times* Rich List and McManus was twelfth. Between them, the business partners are worth almost £1 billion. They are the leading lights in a group of racing giants known as the Coolmore Mafia.

Magnier is especially well connected. He is an Irish aristocrat who was appointed to the Irish Senate by his friend, the late Taoiseach, Charles Haughey, in 1987. He served for three years. Haughey, who shared Magnier's passion for horse-racing, later introduced legislation that exempted the Irish stud industry from tax, and when Magnier formed a partnership with the brilliant Irish trainer Vincent O'Brien, Magnier's talent for analysing equine bloodlines and O'Brien's clever training established Magnier's Coolmore stud farm in County Tipperary as the world's leading stud.

Magnier married O'Brien's daughter, Sue, and alongside associates like top owner Robert Sangster he made daring raids into the US bloodstock market. They wanted to bring back home thoroughbreds with gilt-edged pedigrees that would first race, and then act as stallions, attracting the very best mares to Ireland. The winners began to roll in. Magnier was a major shareholder in 2001 Derby winner Galileo. His fortune grew and grew.

McManus took a different route to wealth. He became an on-course bookmaker when he was twenty and soon earned a reputation as a fearless gambler. People called him The Sundance Kid, and in 1982 he won £250,000 with a single bet on Mister Donovan in the Sun Alliance Hurdle at Cheltenham. In 1997, he and fellow Irishman Dermot Desmond bought the Sandy Lane resort in Barbados for £38 million and his most famous horse, Istabraq, won three Champion Hurdles. Tax-exiled in Geneva, he has increased his wealth with astute currency dealing.

While Magnier's horses run on the flat, McManus's area of dominance is National Hunt racing. The row that was to explode over Rock of Gibraltar, therefore, did not involve McManus. It was between Ferguson and Magnier.

Ferguson hit it off with Magnier and McManus. They liked him for his frankness and his freshness and they knew that his growing involvement in their sport could only improve racing's profile and its popularity. Ferguson liked them, too. He admired their easy charm and was dazzled by their wealth. He had coveted wealth all his life and these men seemed like kings to him.

'When you meet someone like John who is successful,' Ferguson said, 'you want to know more about them and what makes them successful. There's an ordinariness about John that makes you think there must be more than this. But he's so humble, with his feet on the ground, and you realize that's it.'

His association with Magnier and McManus intoxicated Ferguson. He could feel their power as well as their money. He threw himself more and more into racing. He met Coolmore's favourite trainer, Aidan O'Brien, at the Ballydoyle yard a few miles from Coolmore where so many of Coolmore's sires of the future are nurtured as racing champions before being put out to stud.

The world's best yearlings are bought by Coolmore and sent to Ballydoyle to be developed into racing champions. The real profit in the horses is not in the prize money that they might win. Much of that is eaten up by the expense of running them. The real money is in their stud value. Stud fees for a leading horse might amount to £10 million a year.

At Ballydoyle, Ferguson compared notes with Aidan O'Brien. They talked about footballers and horses and the ways of getting the best out of the thoroughbreds in their care. They talked about warm-downs and warm-ups, diet and hydration. They talked about the pre-match, or pre-race, routine.

Ferguson quickly began to fancy himself as something of a bloodstock expert, although he was prone to making embarrassing mistakes that marked him out as a novice. Some racing people winced when he pronounced on a particular bloodline and talked about a horse being 'out of Mill Reef'. Mill Reef was a sire, not a dam. It should have been 'by Mill Reef'.

The friendship between Ferguson and Magnier grew. They often met at Les Ambassadeurs gaming club in London. Magnier started giving him a share in various horses – Zentsov Street, Heritage Hall – none of which Ferguson ever paid for. Magnier considered it a gesture of friendship and he was intrigued by being in the company of one of the most famous sporting figures in the world. Nor did it harm Coolmore's prestige to be associated with the manager of the world's most famous football club.

Magnier and McManus were, after all, part-owners of United. Through their investment vehicle, a company called Cubic Expression, they had bought a 2.9 per cent stake in the club. Their new friendship with Ferguson gave Magnier and McManus a kick. It added a bit of spice to their investment. They took to watching United games on a live feed in the cinema at Laughing Waters, Magnier's sprawling mansion in Barbados, where they spent the winter months.

The relationship between Ferguson and Magnier and McManus seemed like the perfect power friendship. It joined two different sporting worlds and brought mutual benefits. Ferguson thrived on branching out into another sport and often left his coach at United, Steve McClaren, to take training while he flew down to Newmarket to watch his horses on the gallops.

In August 1999, three months after Manchester United had sealed the Treble by winning the European Cup against Bayern Munich in Barcelona, Magnier's horse Mull of Kintyre won the Gimcrack Stakes at the Ebor meeting at York. The winning owner has the right to make the Gimcrack Speech the following December. The speech is flat racing's state of the nation address and a great honour. Magnier eschews public speaking and decided he would nominate Ferguson to take his place.

Magnier felt that the speech (and the sport) would attract widespread attention if Ferguson made it. After United's heroics, his stock had never been higher. John Smith, the managing director of York racecourse, was enthusiastic when he heard the plan and agreed that racing could only benefit from Ferguson's presence.

But Lord Manton, once the chairman of the York race committee and then still a powerful figure, vetoed the plan outright. Magnier was incensed. He regarded the decision as an affront and a short-sighted and snobbish snub to Ferguson. He was determined to make York bend to his will and decided he would put Ferguson's colours on his top horse each year just before the Gimcrack until Ferguson won it. That way, the committee would be powerless to blackball Ferguson, who would qualify as a winning owner, not just a nominated speaker. So in August 2000, a week before the Gimcrack, Magnier put Ferguson's colours on his leading entry for the race, Juniper. The plan failed. Juniper was beaten by a head and a neck into third place.

Magnier brushed off the setback. He waited a year. In August 2001 he did the same again. This time his leading entry in the Gimcrack was Rock of Gibraltar, a promising two-year-old running its fourth race. Magnier festooned it with Ferguson's red and white colours and listed Ferguson as the horse's co-owner with his wife, Sue. Ridden by Mick Kinane, it won by 3 lengths.

And so, on 11 December 2001, beaming from ear to ear and dressed in black tie, Sir Alex Ferguson rose to address the 231st Annual Gimcrack Dinner in the members' restaurant at York Racecourse. There were 120 people there, hanging on his every word. They sat at a giant horseshoe-shaped table. The speech was a triumph. It marked Ferguson's graduation to the racing establishment.

By now, the friendship was looking like a truly formidable alliance. During the course of 12 and 13 July 2001, Magnier and McManus bought another 10 million shares in Manchester United. It gave them a 6.77 per cent stake in the club which was worth about £30 million. They now owned the second-largest shareholding after Rupert Murdoch's NewsCorp.

Their spending only strengthened Ferguson's position at Old Trafford. When Ferguson found out later in the year that Cubic Expression was a vehicle for Magnier and McManus, he was buoyed by the news. Analysts started to speculate about how much his position would be bolstered if his friends staged a takeover of the club.

Some envisaged a golden age of massive spending on player transfers and a situation where the manager wrote himself a massive pay cheque. With his friends in charge, it seemed certain that Ferguson would be elevated to a position of prestige and standing like club president when he stepped down as manager.

On that same 12 July, Ferguson made Juan Sebastián Verón Britain's most expensive footballer by paying Lazio £28 million to secure his services. United had never spent anything like that sum of money on a player before. Ferguson felt it was a statement of intent that United could compete for the very best players in the world, the players who could bring him another European Cup triumph.

They were heady times for the United manager. He was surrounded on all sides by big money. It felt to him as though he and Magnier and McManus had formed a triumvirate to take over the sporting universe. When Rock of Gibraltar started accelerating through the racing firmament in the autumn of 2001, it was as if it was Ferguson, not Mick Kinane, who was riding it into a new world.

Rock of Gibraltar lost his first race after the Gimcrack when he was beaten into second place by Dubai Destination, owned by Coolmore's bitter rivals Godolphin, at Doncaster in September. But then he won the Grand Criterium at Longchamp in October. That was a Group One race, horse-racing's equivalent of a Formula One grand prix. He won the Dewhurst Stakes at Newmarket two weeks later, which made him the champion two-year-old. He won the 2000 Guineas at Newmarket in May 2002 as Chelsea were beating Arsenal in the FA Cup Final in Cardiff. Ferguson didn't care about the Cup Final that year. He won the Irish 2000 Guineas at the Curragh three weeks later. He won the St James's Palace Stakes at Ascot three weeks after that. He won the Sussex Stakes at Goodwood at the end of July. And he won the Prix du Moulin at Longchamp in September.

Rock of Gibraltar's victory in the Prix du Moulin was his seventh consecutive Group One victory, which broke the previous record of six, held by the great Mill Reef for thirty-one years. That put Rock of Gibraltar's status into context.

Seven weeks later, Rock of Gibraltar completed the final part of his racing career when he came second in the Breeders' Cup Mile at Arlington Park, near Chicago. Ferguson could not be there. He was at Old Trafford watching United play out a colourless draw with Aston Villa notable only for the fact that Diego Forlan, his expensive misfit striker, who was later to enjoy great success with Villarreal, scored his first goal in open play after 35 appearances for the club.

The time difference meant Ferguson could watch the race from Arlington at home in Wilmslow. He had a party and invited some friends round. For the second time in a day, it was not the result he wanted. He was pensive. His thoughts were beginning to turn to the money. It had been good while it lasted but now Ferguson was about to blow it.

Some observers had begun to sense his mood changing in the past six months. A sense of entitlement had started to replace the happy innocence of his initial involvement in racing. His eldest son, Mark, had taken to accompanying him to races and asked endless questions about how much various horses might be worth. But the alarm bells didn't really start ringing until December 2002.

Rock of Gibraltar had been retired after the Breeders' Cup Mile and put out to stud. Out of the blue, Ferguson called Ballydoyle and informed officials there that he wanted to arrange an appointment so he could travel over with his accountants and discuss how he might best invest the half-share of the monies he would be owed from the breeding rights to Rock of Gibraltar. Magnier and McManus were both in Barbados for the winter by then. When they were told about the call, they were stunned. Most of all they were puzzled.

Ferguson had a half-share in Rock of Gibraltar, but the arrangement had been made on a handshake. That was how Magnier worked. He believed he had made it plain that Ferguson's involvement was as a figurehead. That was why he was happy to pick up all the bills for Rock of Gibraltar. If it had been a more conventional arrangement, Ferguson would have picked up half the tab for the astronomical fees the horse accrued.

More importantly, Magnier also believed he had made it plain that Ferguson would be handsomely remunerated when it came to dividing up the stud rights to Rock of Gibraltar. There was no plan to carve him out of anything. It is traditional to divide the rights into fortieths. Mick Kinane was due a share because he had ridden six of the horse's seven Group One wins. For raising the profile of the horse, Ferguson was due a share, too. Magnier expected Ferguson would make £250,000 a year, probably for the next ten years, out of his share. For many it could seem like money for nothing. But Ferguson wanted more.

The United manager let things slide until April, when Magnier returned to Europe after their winter in the Caribbean. Magnier arranged to meet Ferguson at the Dorchester Hotel in Park Lane, London. Mark Ferguson turned up as well and Magnier told him that his presence was not required. Mark Ferguson left. The meeting did not go well. Ferguson stuck to his guns. Magnier was horrified. Most of all, he felt that his integrity was being impugned. He felt Ferguson was accusing him of going back on his word. An impasse developed. Ferguson said he was going to sue. Both men engaged lawyers.

Even now, it is hard to grasp how Ferguson so underestimated the man he was taking on. Maybe his undoing was the resentment he felt about being undervalued, maybe he just genuinely felt that he was entitled to the share he sought. He nearly made it with Magnier and McManus, but as Mark

McGhee said, it always ends in tears with Ferguson. 'No one's friends with Alex Ferguson,' McGhee said. 'He falls out with everyone eventually.' And this was no different.

Except in one way it was very different. Usually, when there was an argument, Ferguson was the bully. He did it with Brian Kidd and David Beckham. He did it with McGhee and Gordon Strachan. He was pretty good at dishing it out, but this time he had misjudged his enemy. The consequences almost destroyed him.

He thought he was a powerful man, but he soon began to find out what real power was like. He thought he was a wealthy man but he soon realized what havoc real wealth could wreak. He may have thought his position at Manchester United was impregnable after he had led them to the Treble four years earlier, but he wasn't impregnable at all.

The fact had been camouflaged by domestic success, but Ferguson had failed to capitalize on the Treble success of 1999. United had won the league again in 1999–2000, this time finishing 18 points ahead of an Arsenal side still devastated by their near-misses of the previous campaign. United were also helped by being freed from their obligations in the FA Cup. They had won the competition in 1999 but the government and the FA encouraged them to pull out of it the following season so they could play in the inaugural World Club Championship in Brazil in January 2000. The tournament was the brainchild of Sepp Blatter, the Fifa president, and it was felt that if United did not compete it would damage England's chances of hosting the 2006 World Cup.

United were reluctant but they bowed to the pressure and did not play in the FA Cup. For that they were roundly criticized. They were accused of destroying the world's most famous football competition. The tournament in Brazil was a mess. United managed to turn it into a PR disaster by demanding absurd levels of secrecy around their training sessions. They were knocked out in the group phase.

But at least the tournament acted as a winter break in the sunshine. They came back feeling refreshed. They moved steadily further away from Arsenal and cantered to the title. They won it for a third time in a row the season after. This time, they were 10 points clear of Arsène Wenger's side. Domestically, Ferguson had them running like a smooth machine.

But the signing of Verón was a colossal mistake. Ferguson had envisaged that the capture of the Argentine playmaker would elevate United to a new level in European football and establish them as a club capable of signing the very best talents in world football. He wanted a team of galacticos at Old Trafford and he thought that Verón would light the way.

But Verón could not adapt to the pace of English football. His passing range deserted him. He didn't work hard enough for the English game. He was overshadowed by Keane and Beckham. He unbalanced the side. Ferguson tried desperately to defend the purchase and grew furious with anyone who attempted to suggest he was anything less than a magnificent signing, but it soon became painfully apparent that Verón wasn't worth his place in the side.

Verón was like a test case. United never paid that amount of money for a foreign player again. Ferguson had had one shot at that kind of signing and he had made the wrong choice. And he was starting to make other errors of judgement. United's triumph in 2000–01 meant they had won the league seven times in the last nine years, but many felt that the manager's increasing irascibility and his growing tendency to engage in feuds with players was starting to do some damage to the club.

At the start of the 2001–02 season, he sold Jaap Stam, his towering central defender who had been brilliant since his arrival from PSV Eindhoven, because the Dutchman had written an honest, colourful account of his time so far at United in an autobiography called *Head to Head*. Among his dispatches, he mentioned that Ferguson had tapped him up when he was at

PSV Eindhoven. The book generated several days of headlines in the *Daily Mirror*.

Ferguson was furious. He dropped Stam and then sold him to Lazio, although Ferguson denied this was because of the book or its revelations. United's supporters were dismayed. Ferguson compounded his error by signing the veteran Laurent Blanc as Stam's replacement. Blanc had been a magnificent defender once, up there with Franco Baresi for his elegance and his ability to read the game. But he was thirty-five now and his legs had gone. Blanc for Stam was a desperately bad swap.

By now, United were going backwards in Europe. Ferguson's dream of creating a dynasty of champions, of building United into a team that could win the trophy regularly like AC Milan, Juventus and Real Madrid, was receding. In 2000, Ferguson's side had surrendered its crown when it lost to Madrid in the second leg of the teams' quarter-final at Old Trafford. The following season, they lost at home and away to Bayern Munich, again in the quarter-finals.

Part of the problem by now was that Ferguson had become distracted by his impending retirement, scheduled for the summer of 2002, and by the host of resentments and unrequited ambitions that swirled around his projected departure from the club. It all came back to his recurring feeling that he was being undervalued and disrespected by his paymasters.

By May 2001, negotiations had been going on for several months about what post-managerial role Ferguson would have at Old Trafford. Ferguson had stated clearly that he wanted to retire at sixty – his sixtieth birthday was 31 December 2001, so in effect that meant the end of the 2001–02 season – but he wanted to stay on in another role. The negotiations, though, had been complicated by the obstreperous presence of one of his twin sons, Jason, who had recently become a sports agent and had quickly slipped into an antagonistic relationship with the United chief executive, Peter Kenyon, and his deputy, David Gill.

A lack of appreciation of Ferguson's contribution to the club was the constant subtext of the conversations. He had been fretting for much of the season about the fact that some of the players at Old Trafford, notably Roy Keane, were paid much more than he was. It was an habitual gripe. Jason Ferguson even claimed that Kenyon had dismissed his father's achievements with a sweeping put-down. 'He may be a good manager,' Kenyon is supposed to have said, 'but he doesn't exactly sell the strips, does he?'

Ferguson wanted £1 million a year to work as a roving ambassador for United. The club was offering closer to £100,000. It was also worried about replicating the messy situation that developed when their last great manager, Sir Matt Busby, had failed to make a clean break with the club when he relinquished the post of manager in 1969. Liverpool avoided that fate by severing their ties with Shankly more cleanly, but Busby moved upstairs at United and blighted the fledgling career of Wilf McGuinness by acting as a sounding board for discontented players. Busby came back as manager in 1970 and then stepped down again in 1971. Frank O'Farrell was appointed manager, then Tommy Docherty, but the damage had been done, and in 1974 United were relegated.

Ferguson was exasperated that the United chairman, Martin Edwards, seemed so preoccupied with the precedent of Busby. He insisted that he wouldn't interfere the way Busby had. He said there was so much more for a manager to cope with now that he felt sure he could be of assistance. Edwards was right, though. When United appointed a successor to Ferguson, he would have to be a strong man to cope with the pressure, and a strong man would not need Ferguson hovering around in the background.

So in May 2001, Ferguson's patience snapped. When United refused to improve their offer, Ferguson threatened to leave the club altogether and the information was leaked to the *Daily Mail*. Then, on the penultimate day of the season, Ferguson told

MUTV he was going to abandon the idea of being a United ambassador and would sever all ties with the club at the end of the following campaign. 'All talks on that subject are now dead,' he said. 'I'm very disappointed with what's happened, to say the least.'

There were some suggestions that Ferguson might even quit after the final game of the season. United fans were horrified. This was, after all, the man who had just led them to their third successive Premiership title and who had given them the glory of the Treble in 1999. When the United share price plunged over the next couple of days, Sir Roland Smith, chairman of the plc board, and Peter Kenyon urged the board to meet Ferguson's demands.

They caved in and Ferguson was given nearly £50 million to buy Verón and Ruud Van Nistelrooy, who had cost £19 million when he arrived from PSV Eindhoven in April. Then his final year's salary was increased by £10,000 a week. And on 13 July he agreed a five-year, £1 million a year contract as a roving ambassador for United. It was a spectacular triumph for Ferguson.

But still something gnawed in his mind. It is both Ferguson's gift and his curse never to be satisfied, and as what was supposed to be his final season approached its halfway point he grew more and more restless. He was starting to think that he might have made a mistake, that maybe he didn't want to quit at sixty after all. He looked at Sir Bobby Robson, in his sixty-ninth year and still going strong at Newcastle, and thought again about Shankly walking away before he should have done.

Around the turn of the year, Ferguson not only heard that United had approached England manager Sven-Goran Eriksson to be his successor but he also discovered what the United board were said to be offering him. It was considerably more than the £3 million that Ferguson was earning. Ferguson, who was no admirer of Eriksson, found it hard to contemplate the idea of the Swede inheriting his empire.

He also knew that the 2002 Champions League Final was to be played at Hampden Park in Glasgow and the 2003 Final at Old Trafford. If United could win the trophy he valued more than any other in his home city and take him above Busby in the United pantheon at the same time, that would be a night of such emotion that it would top Barcelona. If they could win at Old Trafford, it would be perfect. That, for him, would be the equivalent of his film hero, John Wayne, riding off into the sunset.

When his wife and his sons told him during the Christmas holiday that they felt he was too young to retire, Ferguson made up his mind that he was going to stay. Till then he had felt that his family had made enough sacrifices for him already, that he had missed too much of the childhoods of his three sons, for him to suggest to them that he might stay on. But when they took the initiative, he snatched their hands off.

He had begun to realize that he could not bear the thought of someone else taking over his team and perhaps going on to even greater success in Europe than he had achieved. Again he thought of Shankly and the way he had bequeathed a side in its prime to Bob Paisley. Paisley went on to win his first European Cup with half of Shankly's side, and Ferguson knew he would find that difficult to countenance, especially if his successor was Eriksson. 'What if I wanted back in after a year out?' he said. 'That would be the worst thing that could happen. You couldn't just walk back into a job like this.'

If Ferguson had quit in the summer of 2002, it is reasonable to speculate that the rest of his life would have been clouded with regret. He would have become a carbon copy of Shankly in retirement. He confided in the United director Maurice Watkins about his change of mind and then told the rest of the board of his decision after United's 4–1 victory over Sunderland on Saturday, 2 February. Kenyon was delighted and dropped his plans to recruit Eriksson. Ferguson was offered a new three-year deal. He took it. A few days later, Roy Keane agreed a new deal worth £100,000 a week.

The players were pleased when Ferguson gathered them together at Carrington to tell them the news. Most of them anyway. Dwight Yorke was devastated. Ferguson had frozen him out and had tried to sell him to Middlesbrough so that he could bring in Paolo di Canio from West Ham. Yorke had refused to move and had been telling friends he would be at Old Trafford long after Ferguson had gone. 'That's you fucked, Yorkie,' one of his teammates shouted out as soon as Ferguson left the changing room. Yorke laughed, too, even though it was true.

The theory was that now the uncertainty about the future of the manager had been dispelled, United would go on and win a fourth title on the trot. They had gone top of the table in mid-December and Van Nistelrooy set a new club record by scoring in eight consecutive league games. But Arsenal hadn't read the script. They put together a magnificent run in the league and United began to falter. They did progress to the Champions League semi-finals for the first time since 1999, and even though they drew 2–2 against Bayer Leverkusen at Old Trafford in the first leg, Ferguson was optimistic they would get the result they needed in Germany.

At the team hotel in Cologne, Ferguson found out on the day of the match that Magnier and McManus had flown in from their base in Geneva to watch it. This would be the first time Magnier had ever seen the team play live. Ferguson was excited. He invited the two men to the hotel and was particularly keen for them to meet Van Nistelrooy and Ole Gunnar Solskjaer because Magnier and McManus had named horses after them. (The horses did not enjoy quite the same success in their field as the footballers did in theirs.)

Ferguson was with the two Irishmen in the hotel foyer when Keane came down the stairs and began to walk towards the restaurant for the team's pre-match meal. Ferguson beckoned him over to meet his friends. He thought Keane would be pleased to meet two of his countrymen. Keane glared at the scene for a split second, waved Ferguson away with a flash of his hand and kept walking towards the restaurant. A few hours before such an important game, the United captain felt Ferguson was wrong to be letting his focus waver. Ferguson was embarrassed.

United could only draw the second leg 1–1. It was not enough. Keane, who had missed the 1999 Final through suspension, was distraught. He had scored United's goal but could not drag his teammates with him all the way to Glasgow. He sensed that his last chance of winning the European Cup had just disappeared. He was disgusted with some of his colleagues, too. 'We had failed to take the next step towards greatness,' he said. 'We've settled for the now reflected glory of the treble year. The complacency that comes with the kind of success we've enjoyed has caught up with us.

'As we stood for the Uefa anthem before the second leg of the Leverkusen game, one of our players was fucking shaking. He was afraid. Played for his country, won championships, big star, fucking afraid of taking the big step up. Afterwards, in the dressing room, I looked around. It wasn't hurting some of them enough.'

That was the theme of much of the latter part of Keane's excellent autobiography. It was the idea that too many of the United players had lost their hunger after the 1999 European Cup Final triumph and had begun to coast. His impression was confirmed eight days after the Leverkusen defeat when United lost at home to Arsenal and handed their title to Arsène Wenger's side. Sylvain Wiltord got the winner, and in the corner of Old Trafford where the visiting fans stood, a banner was unfurled. 'Champions Enclosure,' it said.

Keane's argument was that United were being lulled into a false sense of security and a debilitating complacency by the ease of domestic competition. 'We were gone,' Keane said, 'beating nothing in the Premiership. The Arsenals, Liverpools, Chelseas, Leeds just weren't doing it. It deceived us into thinking we were better than we really were.'

The 2002–03 season provided more evidence of that. Ferguson strengthened the side in the summer with the lavish purchase of Rio Ferdinand from Leeds for £30 million, still the British transfer record. There is no disputing the fact that Ferdinand was a superb, footballing defender. At that time, he seemed to be the most accomplished, smooth centre half England had produced since Bobby Moore. He had been outstanding alongside Sol Campbell at the 2002 World Cup and he was still only twenty-three. But he didn't quite fit with Ferguson's early policy of buying a player for his character as much as his ability. Ferdinand was often pictured in London nightclubs and had something of a reputation as an enthusiastic party-goer well before he forgot to take his routine drugs test in the autumn of the following season.

In his early days at the club, Ferguson would never have tolerated the nocturnal habits of Ferdinand. Now, he seemed powerless to influence him, and that impotence ate away at him and at the fabric of the club. There could be no more damning comment on the dilution of Ferguson's autocracy than the fact that the missed drugs test cost United the title the following season.

Ferdinand did not settle well to begin with, but he found his form at the start of 2003 and United revived. They lost 3–1 at Middlesbrough on Boxing Day and trailed Arsenal, who seemed as though they were going to retain the title for the first time. But after the defeat at the Riverside, United embarked on a remarkable domestic run, going unbeaten for eighteen matches and winning nine of their last ten.

It is a tribute to the players and to Ferguson that they were not distracted by the increasing tension that scarred the relationship between the manager and David Beckham. After Ferguson had kicked the boot in February and cut Beckham above the eye, the England captain was increasingly marginalized at Old Trafford. But Ole Gunnar Solskjaer played well when he deputized for him and United pressed on.

United were still 8 points behind Arsenal at the beginning of March but they were relentless in their pursuit. Arsenal began to wilt, and when United drew 2–2 at Highbury on 16 April, Ferguson marched on to the pitch at the final whistle and saluted the visiting fans as they celebrated in their enclosure behind the goal at the Clock End. Ferguson punched the air with a clenched fist. Even though United and Arsenal were still neck and neck, he knew that the impetus lay with his side. He was right.

But Keane was right, too. A week before the draw at Highbury, United had been utterly outplayed by Real Madrid in the Bernabeu in the first leg of their Champions League quarter-final. Madrid gave them a masterclass. Zinédine Zidane and Luis Figo were untouchable, particularly in the first half. United were outclassed and embarrassed, men chasing shadows. They lost 3–1 and they were lucky.

A week after the draw at Highbury, United played the second leg of the Madrid game. Once again, they were easy meat for the Spanish giants. This time, Ronaldo scored a stunning hat-trick inside an hour and, with the tie out of United's reach, Madrid substituted him. The Old Trafford fans gave the Brazilian striker a rare standing ovation as he left the pitch.

By then, Ferguson had substituted Verón and brought Beckham off the bench. His decision to play Verón was the first of what was to become a steady stream of selection errors that often seemed to be based on his personal agenda rather than the merits of the players involved. Ferguson was on a mission to prove that Verón was a success, but no amount of playing time could prove that. Not at Old Trafford, anyway.

Verón was coming back from a long-term injury when

Ferguson decided to use a game as crucial as the second leg against Madrid to throw him back into the fray. Beckham was flabbergasted when he was told of the manager's decision. He would have been upset at being dropped anyway. He admitted that. But he could not understand the logic of being dropped for Verón.

Beckham played with fury and industry and scored a couple of goals, but by the time he came on, the match was a lost cause. United were on their way out in the quarter-finals, heading downhill in Europe again. And for a prime example of Keane's theory, Ferdinand was majestic in the second half of that Premiership season but was ripped apart like a novice by Ronaldo in the Champions League.

In the Premiership, Arsenal folded after the draw at Highbury. Campbell was sent off during the game for hitting Solskjaer with a trailing elbow. The red card was harsh. Arsenal felt they had been cheated and their form collapsed. They drew with Bolton at the Reebok and then handed United the title by losing 3–2 at home to Leeds. United won the league by 5 points.

And then the screaming started. Really started, Manchester United went into decline. Ferguson's eighth Premiership title was a remarkable and unprecedented achievement but it marked the end of the club's long period of dominance under his management. The problems started crowding in on him, and this time he couldn't fix them.

Too many players were allowed to get old together, Roman Abramovich turned up at Chelsea, Beckham left and was not replaced, Ferdinand missed his drugs test, Arsenal achieved what everybody thought was impossible by going an entire season unbeaten, Ferguson bought two more mediocre goalkeepers and more and more mediocre outfielders. The slide Keane had detected burst out into the open. The major trophies went elsewhere.

Off the field, Ferguson was still insisting he would pursue the case against them through the Irish courts, so Magnier and

McManus began to formulate their response. They began to probe for weaknesses in Ferguson's armour. They found some. They were particularly interested in the role that Jason Ferguson had been playing in Manchester United's affairs. In 2000, Alex Ferguson's son had become a football agent. Until then, the United manager had always professed to despise the profession. In the 1980s he had described them as 'rats' and identified them as the biggest problem in football. But now he encouraged Jason to join a Manchester-based agency called L'Attitude.

L'Attitude had been founded in 1997 by two of Ferguson's friends, Andy Dodd, whom he had met through Simply Red singer Mick Hucknall, and Kieran Toal, a former United youth team player who had moved out of football and trained to be a barrister. Dodd and Toal forged a good relationship with United, and it seems clear they felt it would be wise to take Jason on if they wanted that relationship to continue and prosper.

Jason began to work for L'Attitude in 1999. He was not a universally popular figure in the English football world, partly because it was perceived that he owed any success he had to his father's patronage. In his favour, anyone who abandons a job in television and heads for Bucharest to help Romanian orphans, as he did in his youth, cannot be the one-dimensional daddy's boy that many people seek to suggest.

Some felt his role at L'Attitude, though, did leave his father vulnerable to media accusations of nepotism and worse. For some it was one thing for the agency to conduct transfer work for United before the son of the manager jumped on board, it was quite another to take their share of fees once Jason Ferguson was working there. It was thought by some that United was suddenly turning into a family business. Ferguson's brother, Martin, had been recruited as the club's chief foreign scout at the start of 1999.

Jason and L'Attitude were involved in the transfer of Massimo Taibi to Reggina and received a modest fee of about £25,000 for their services.

L'Attitude also organized Alex Ferguson's testimonial year in 1999–2000. Testimonials had become an anachronism by then because men like Ferguson were already multimillionaires, but Ferguson pressed on with his anyway. His testimonial fund raised more than £1.3 million. Ferguson gave more than £100,000 to charity. Other men, like Niall Quinn and Alan Shearer, have chosen to donate their entire testimonial fund to charity.

Jason left L'Attitude at the end of 2000 and in the spring of 2001 he became a director of a new agency, Elite Sports Group. Elite played a role in the £17 million transfer of Jaap Stam from United to Lazio in August 2001. The deal was done by the agents Mike Morris, who was close to Elite's Dave Gardner, and Bruno Pasquale, but Elite got a piece of it too. They billed Lazio, not United, for their share.

Elite also organized the transfer of Roy Carroll from Wigan Athletic to United in 2001 for £2.5 million, and promising young players already on United's books, like Jonathan Greening and Mark Wilson, were encouraged to sign on for the agency. Greening and Wilson both refused. Ferguson, once again, was livid that they had chosen Mel Stein, probably because of his dislike of Stein who had also acted for Paul Gascoigne.

The dispute developed into something like a feud. In the end, Stein threatened Ferguson with legal action and United began to grow worried about the potential for adverse publicity. Agreement was reached, both players were transferred to Middlesbrough for £3.5 million.

The father-and-son involvement was not unique. Darren Dein, son of the Arsenal vice-chairman, David Dein, has worked for Jerome Anderson, Arsenal's favourite agent, and was even best man at the wedding of his client, Thierry Henry. Craig

Allardyce, son of Sam, has an involvement with an agent who regularly conducts transfers in and out of Bolton Wanderers. Ferguson insisted, through Hugh McIlvanney, that there was nothing untoward about the deal involving Elite and that he was 'Content in the certainty that, far from risking a conflict of interest, the transactions were straightforward and honourable and blatantly to United's benefit.'

But Jason's position at Elite still damaged Ferguson's reputation. The BBC put together a programme called *Fergie and Son* which was billed as a hard-hitting investigation into Jason Ferguson's business dealings with United. Ferguson was disgusted with the BBC when the programme was broadcast in May 2004. He has refused to speak to the corporation ever since, which continues to be a huge embarrassment for the club.

The investigative journalist Tom Bower also discussed the issue in his book, *Broken Dreams: Vanity, Greed and the Souring of British Football*. 'Protests about Sir Alex's apparent nepotism were ignored,' Bower wrote. Magnier didn't ignore it, though. He was way too sharp to do that. Instead, as the row over Rock of Gibraltar grew more and more acrimonious, and Ferguson pressed on with his preparations to sue Magnier in the Irish courts for a half-share of the stud fees, Magnier and McManus started increasing their stake in Manchester United, turning up the heat on Ferguson in ways that seemed to surprise him.

At one time, Ferguson had been thrilled at the growing involvement of the Irishmen in the club. Now, it only filled him and the rest of the United board with foreboding. Ferguson's dispute over Rock of Gibraltar was destabilizing the club. United supporters took Ferguson's side and issued threats of their own to Magnier and McManus. There was talk of sabotaging their horses or disrupting race meetings where they had horses running. In the autumn of 2003, Magnier and McManus engaged

Kroll to investigate Ferguson and United's finances. The situation started to spiral out of control.

At the end of January 2004, a letter and a list of 99 Questions posed to the Manchester United plc board chairman, Sir Roy Gardner, by Magnier and McManus was leaked to the *Daily Mail* and printed in full. By then, Cubic Expression owned 25.49 per cent of the club and speculation about Magnier and McManus launching a takeover was rife. Most of the questions were aimed at United's transfer dealings and the club's use of agents.

In the letter, Magnier and McManus called for 'the prohibition of payments for player transfers to agents or agencies whose members or directors have a close personal connection with the Company or any officer or employee of the Company'. It seems to many that this could only be a reference to Jason Ferguson. They also demanded 'the prevention of the possibility that any officer or employee of the Company might persuade or seek to persuade any player to engage as their football agent an individual, firm or company which is associated directly or indirectly with that officer or employee'.

Amid The 99 Questions, they demanded to know more information about a range of transfers. Significantly, those included the sales of Greening, Wilson, Stam, Taibi and Carroll. They wanted to know about commissions paid to agents. They wanted to know about the ethics of dealing with agents, whether the buying club or the selling club paid the agent, or whether the player paid him. In short, they were threatening to smash open the Pandora's Box of football's secrets. United blanched.

The day after The 99 Questions appeared, Ferguson gave a press conference. The reporters who cover United regularly were surprised to see him so disconcerted by what was happening. Ferguson made it plain he was distressed about the turn of events and that he had had no idea he was unleashing a whirlwind when he decided to sue Magnier and McManus.

Most people were surprised that he was surprised. It should have been obvious to him that he wasn't dealing with Andy Pandy and his pals when he took on the might of Coolmore. Magnier and McManus were serious men.

In the press conference, Ferguson appeared to accuse Magnier and McManus of taking the dispute beyond the law and mentioned a campaign of sustained harassment which had led to Jason making an official complaint. 'He's had to call in the police,' Ferguson said. 'They have been stealing his mail, his bin-bags, hiding in bushes outside his house. It's been a distressing week for the Ferguson family but Jason, in particular, has taken a real battering. The police have a registration number and they're investigating now.

'It is all a result of what we are reading about in terms of the transfer stuff. It's very distressing when it starts affecting your family like this. This is the kind of thing we have had to put up with and it is not easy. You have to wonder why they're attacking my family.'

Simultaneously, Gardai in Cork were investigating a complaint from Magnier's brother David that vandals had spray-painted 'Hands off Fergie' on the wall of his property. Magnier and his associates were appalled by Ferguson's allegations and there was speculation that Ferguson might have made himself the target of more legal proceedings if lawyers for Magnier and McManus considered his comments to be defamatory.

It was the first time Ferguson had spoken out against his former friends, but he was also keen to defend his reputation against the inferences made in The 99 Questions. 'It is inconceivable I would ever abuse my position,' he said, 'absolutely out of the question. I've been at this club for seventeen years and I've never had anyone questioning my propriety. Then all of a sudden, because of a private issue regarding a racehorse, all these things are happening.

'The club has declared its policy quite clearly. I have nothing to do with agents. I never talk to agents. I don't pick them, I don't employ them and I don't pay them. It's the chief executive's department and that's been the case since 1990. Since the club became a plc, it has always been that way.

'My conscience is clear about how we operate. We're a well-run club. Christ, you get clubs going into administration left, right and centre but we're making profits, winning trophies and we're a "badly run club"?'

Even so, Magnier and McManus had forced United to announce an internal review of their transfer policy and, by making plain their opposition to awarding Ferguson a new long-term contract, had ensured that he was only offered a one-year rolling deal when his existing contract ran out in June 2005.

Ferguson did his best to put a brave face on that. He denied it was a victory for Magnier. 'Not at all,' he said. 'The most important thing for me is that a four-year contract is a hell of a time. I might well decide in two years that I'm coming up to sixty-five and it's time to go. With this deal I'm in control.'

Ferguson wasn't in control of his struggle with Magnier, though. At last he was starting to realize how grave was the error he had made. He had always insisted privately that he would pursue his case until the bitter end, but suddenly, at the beginning of March 2004, as Arsenal closed in on the title and United headed for third place, it was announced that Ferguson had reached an out-of-court settlement.

It was rumoured he was given a £2.5m pay-off, but it was still a climbdown. He must have realized then that he had lost so much more than money. He had lost a gilded future in horse-racing, lost two very powerful friends and lost the respect of the racing community. 'The view of him, basically, was that he had killed the fatted calf,' one respected racing figure said.

Magnier and McManus are estimated to have made a £70 million profit when they sold their Manchester United shares to Malcolm Glazer in May 2005. Alex Ferguson has a much more limited involvement in racing now. He still has an interest in a few horses but he is not part of the golden circle any more. Another horse, as yet unnamed, is registered to Lady Ferguson. It's a two-year-old colt, the progeny of a sire that was once a racehorse called Rock of Gibraltar.

27: Shankly – Man from a Dead Town

The narrow road that winds its gentle way up the hillside from the busy A70 just outside Muirkirk is lined with ghosts. It's a road to nowhere. Glenbuck, the place of Bill Shankly's birth, has been wiped off the map. The King's dragoons hunted down Covenanters there in the seventeenth century and for a while the lands in that part of the west of Scotland were known as the Martyr Districts. When the mines on the edge of the Ayrshire coalfield closed down in the 1920s and 1930s, people moved away in search of work and the village began to die.

Thirty years ago, John Roberts, the journalist who was the ghost-writer for Shankly's autobiography, travelled to Glenbuck and saw the remnants of the community before it was razed to the ground. There were only twelve people living in a place that had been home to nearly 2,000 residents at the turn of the century. The village was in ruins. The grey stone church was derelict and covered with slabs of moss. Sheep grazed by its door.

There was an empty space where Auchenstilloch Cottages once stood. The locals called it Monkey Row and Shankly was born there on 2 September 1913, the ninth child of ten, a family of five sons and five daughters. Sometimes they slept six to a room, although things improved when Shankly's father, John, once a postman but a tailor for as long as Shankly could remember him, acquired the house next door too.

But five years before Shankly was born the pits had already begun to close, and by 1922 the population had shrunk to 700.

There was still a Co-op general store, the heart of the village, a fish and chip shop, a couple of sweet shops and the Royal Arms pub. Glenbuck struggled on for a few decades. Small industries like knitwear and finishing factories established a foothold and then slithered away. By 1951 there were still 320 inhabitants but 86 of the 107 houses were condemned.

In 1952 the railway to Coalburn 4 miles away was closed. The remains of the bridges crossing the phantom tracks can still be seen from the A70 that runs from Ayr through Muirkirk and on towards the A74. Some of the villagers who had left Glenbuck used to hold reunions in the village, but by the mid-Fifties these stopped too, and Glenbuck faded away.

It is an isolated place, tucked away in the folds of the hills. Shankly used to have to walk to Muirkirk 5 miles away if he wanted to go and watch the gangster films he adored at the local picture house. The winters were cold and bitter with four months of snow. Even in summer, there always seemed to be an icy wind blowing. 'No disrespect to Glenbuck,' Shankly said, 'but you would have been as far away from civilization in Outer Mongolia.'

In the Seventies, the remains of the Viaduct Mine and the Grasshill Mine where Shankly started his working life by emptying trucks and sorting coal at the surface were still visible. Grasshill closed in 1933 and the pits had been filled in but the rusting hulks of disused machinery still lay on the hillside. There were a couple of derelict phone boxes and a small row of ugly 1930s council houses. That was all that was left of old Glenbuck.

Thirty years on and even that has disappeared. The road still takes you to where it used to be but it's called something different now. A sign says it's Spireslack Open Cast Coal Site and at the top of the hill, where the church and the Auchenstilloch Cottages were, there is a small cluster of green Portakabins and a car park pockmarked with puddles.

A few hundred yards away, giant yellow trucks trundle up

and down roads obscured by mud. Below, in a little gulch, a small herd of longhorn cattle mope by a brook. There's a plateau just above the stream which used to be the pitch where the famous Glenbuck Cherrypickers used to play. Shankly had a trial for them once, but by the time he was old enough to make the team, they had been disbanded as the population dwindled.

So Glenbuck now is just a giant black scar on a beautiful, wild, Ayrshire landscape. There's one brick wall by the side of the road as you begin to climb to where the village once was. There are some sheep here and there, their coats stained with a red mark as if they have been shot. And a few stark trees, the kind you still see on the blasted battlefields of the Somme. A mile or so away, up on the hillside above Glenbuck Loch, where the countryside is still pristine, there is a clump of pine trees where Shankly and some of the local lads used to go and play cards.

Gambling was the only one of life's traditional vices to which Shankly subscribed. He was never a serious gambler, probably because he never had enough money in his early days to finance an addiction. But he was a regular at clandestine gatherings among the pines where a group of ten or fifteen local youths would congregate for games of brag away from the gaze of the village policeman.

Shankly's family was so poor during his childhood that he and his brothers often stole potatoes, turnips and cabbages from the fields of local farms just so that all the children could eat. They also pilfered food from a wagon that used to come to the village, laden down with goods to sell. On other occasions, they would go to the pit top and spirit away a bag of coal from the hundreds of tonnes that lay waiting to be collected. Those were the first flourishings of Shankly's idea of socialism.

'We knew we were doing wrong,' Shankly said, 'but we did not think of it as stealing really. It was devilment more than badness. When we had nothing and took something, we did not call it stealing. We were hungry. Our parents were too proud even to think we were poor and they would never imagine their children had been pilfering. If we had owed a millionaire a penny, we would have been told "pay him" '.

Shankly left the village school at fourteen. He had been a mischievous pupil. Once, he climbed a set of stepladders to wind the classroom clock half an hour forward to try to trick the teacher into sending everybody home early. He was caught in the act by the headmaster, who made him sit at the top of the steps for the rest of the lesson while the other kids giggled at him.

More often, the punishment that was administered was physical, a clip round the ear or a cane across the palm. 'We always put a cocky look on our faces like little gangsters when he told us to put our hands out,' Shankly said. 'We wouldn't show pain even though it was killing us.'

At school, he was brought up on tales of Robert the Bruce, William Wallace and Robert Burns. His father was a fierce Scottish nationalist who hated the English. 'The English were vilified,' Shankly said. 'We thought England was our enemy and the English were poison.

'Our conception of an Englishman was of someone who spoke differently from us, with a fancy dialect, plums in his mouth – "I say old chap" and all that kind of stuff – with his coloured blazer and a white hankie in the breast pocket and his old school tie and straw hat and maybe some powder on his face. All Oxford and Noel Coward. We seemed to forget about the miners on Tyneside and in Yorkshire who were just like us.'

His lack of a further education rarely betrayed itself. Eddie Boot, the Huddersfield trainer, noticed that it took him a painfully long time to sign his name. Watching him reminded him of a child concentrating very hard, Boot said. But if Shankly was short on formal education, he made up for it in natural intelligence and quick wits. In verbal exchanges, he was a match for anyone.

After he left school, he worked at the pit top for six months. And then he went underground. He did eight-hour shifts, loading trucks and pushing them to the point where they were sent up in cages. The pits were the first places to get electricity and Shankly thought it looked like Piccadilly Circus down there. He worked alongside the pit ponies, who still spent much of their lives in darkness.

For a while, he worked at the back of the pit, not hewing coal but transporting it to the trucks. He was too young to dig. He breathed the foul air, damp and dank and clogged with dust because of poor ventilation. He drank his tea an hour after he got to the pit bottom before it could go cold. He ate his food and saw men with rats sitting on their knee as they ate theirs.

'I saw the firing of shots to bring down the coal,' Shankly said. 'Men boring the big holes, stabbing them up with powder or gelignite and then . . . whoof. And men putting up props before they could go in and waiting for the smoke to clear. A lot of men went in before the smoke had cleared and they would get severe headaches.

'There were a lot of accidents in the pits when the coal-cutting machines came. At first, the men did not know how to work them properly. Those machines made a lot of noise and vibrated. I was lucky not to see any tragedies because men were being killed all the time.'

Shankly worked for two years in the pit. Then it closed and he was unemployed. Redundant, just like he was when he sat on the Blackpool promenade outside the Norbreck Castle Hotel in the last days of his life, beckoning the elements on. Back in Glenbuck, he and his mates had dared nature to do its worst, too. 'We would stand outside the pub or the chip shop talking until the early hours of the morning,' he said. 'Anybody who had a coat was a foreigner or a snob. We had jackets and open-neck shirts, even in the depths of winter.'

The seeds of Shankly's own talents as a raconteur and a master of the one-liner were sown in those days. Shankly stood on the street corners with local characters with nicknames that sounded as if they came out of the film *The Hustler*. There was no Minnesota Fats but there was a Barlinnie Swell, a Corry-Hughie, a Snibs, a Snooks, a Lots, a Pimp, a Bird, a Cob and a Bomber Brown.

Shankly was known as Willie, or Wullie, as it was pronounced in Glenbuck. 'I listened to these men and their wonderful humour and their exaggerated yarns,' he said, 'and this is where I picked up a lot of what I am. Where did Burns and Shakespeare and Wordsworth and men like those get their expressions from? From mixing with people.'

Shankly signed on the dole for a short time but he did not stay much longer in Glenbuck. He knew there was nothing for him there, that he was only killing time until he became a footballer. 'It was all worked out in my mind,' he said. 'I knew I had something to offer and I have always been an optimist. If I'd had to wait for a few years, it is possible that I might have lost my enthusiasm. But I was young and I felt that somewhere along the line, I was being guided. I believed I had a destiny.'

So Shankly left Glenbuck. He left like everybody else did, until soon there was no one left to leave. Just a few green huts and a black scar on a hillside and yellow trucks puffing and chugging up and down, up and down.

Only one thing remains now. A plaque on a wall by the road to nowhere, back down towards the A70. It's a memorial, dedicated back in 1997, a tribute to Glenbuck and its most famous old boy. Written in letters of gold the inscription reads:

'Seldom in the history of sport can a village the size of Glenbuck have produced so many who reached the pinnacle of achievement in their chosen sport. This monument is dedicated to their memory and to the memory of one man in particular, Bill Shankly. The Legend, The Genius, The Man. Born Glenbuck 2nd September 1913. Died Liverpool 29th September 1981. From Anfield with love. Thanks Shanks.'

28: Ferguson, Beckham and Things that End in Tears

Early in their estrangement, the two dominant figures of the last twenty years in English football brushed past each other at a funeral. As the mourners milled around outside a hilltop chapel perched high above the green fields of the Worcestershire countryside, Sir Alex Ferguson muttered a few words to David Beckham. Beckham heard them and moved on. It was all too late and anyway, Beckham thought, this was not the time or the place.

A sadness overtakes Beckham as he thinks about that day at Redditch Crematorium when he and Ferguson joined the grieving for Jimmy Davis, the young Manchester United striker who was killed in a car crash on the M40 in August 2003. There is grief for the memory of Davis but there is also an unmistakable sorrow for the loss of his relationship with a man he regarded as a father-figure.

Even as he sits in his company's office in the Calle Serrano in Madrid city centre, nearly three years since Ferguson forced him out of Old Trafford, the sadness grips Beckham and makes him choke on his words. He is still trying to come to terms with what happened, still trying to make sense of why Ferguson turned on him so suddenly and so ferociously and cast him out without a word.

There is a strange mix of wistfulness and simmering anger in Beckham when he talks about Ferguson now. A battle rages between two sets of memories: those of the kindnesses Ferguson showed him, and those of the backlash that followed, when it seemed as if the United manager had come to actively despise the man who was once his favourite son. Even now, Ferguson finds it hard to mention Beckham's name in public, such is the level of the antagonism he came to feel towards him.

Beckham still insists that Ferguson was the most important influence on his football life. He has only fond memories of how the United manager nurtured him and spoilt him when Beckham was in his early teens and Ferguson was trying to persuade him he should commit his future to the club. He remembers the first time they met, back in the late Eighties. United were in London, preparing for a game against Crystal Palace, and the twelve-year-old Beckham was taken to the Travelodge where they were staying.

Ferguson introduced Beckham to United icons Bryan Robson and Steve Bruce. He let him help the United kit-man, Norman Davies, clear up in the United dressing room after a game. He took him to a pre-match meal with the players and watched in amusement as the schoolboy ordered a salmon steak, thinking it was just a variety of steak, like fillet or sirloin, never imagining it was fish.

Ferguson knew Beckham's name. He telephoned his parents, Ted and Sandra, regularly. He even allowed him to sit on the bench during a game against West Ham United at Upton Park. Ferguson was everything to Beckham. He was the pathway to the dream. He looked after him when he moved into digs in Manchester when he was fifteen, he oversaw his rise through the great United youth team of 1992 and he gave him his chance on the right wing when he sold Andrei Kanchelskis in the summer of 1995 and resisted the temptation to buy a big name to play in the position.

His guidance, influence and patronage brought Beckham an England call-up. It got him to the World Cup. Ferguson threw a protective shield around him, too, when he returned from France 1998 as a pariah. Back then, he saved Beckham's career. He was responsible for the high point of his days at United when the club beat Bayern Munich to win the European Cup in May 1999. Beckham hasn't forgotten any of that. He knows how much he owes to Ferguson. He just wishes it had not ended the way it did.

It ended in the summer of 2003 when United announced they had accepted an offer from Barcelona for Beckham and Beckham's agent then negotiated a move to Real Madrid. It ended because Ferguson thought he had lost the last semblance of the control he had once exerted over his protégé. The boy had become an independent man, probably more ready to stand up for himself than any of his United teammates. He moved in a world that was strange and unfamiliar to Ferguson, a world of fashion and pop music and style magazines and cover shoots.

Ferguson hated that loss of control. He blamed Beckham's wife, Victoria, for showing him that new world and luring him into it. It was almost as if Ferguson was jealous of Victoria Beckham, as if he resented her for taking his boy away from him. Ferguson felt that somehow she had compromised the integrity of the footballing machine he had moulded.

And so he started to criticize him relentlessly. He imposed no sanction on Rio Ferdinand for something as fundamental as missing a drugs test and yet he left Beckham out of a crucial game against Leeds United in February 2000 for missing a day's training to look after his son Brooklyn, who was ill. Ferguson grew more and more exasperated by Beckham in the next couple of years. He accused him of neglecting the club for attending a Buckingham Palace reception for the 2002 England World Cup squad in November of that year when Ferguson felt he should have been recuperating from a rib injury. 'When I saw you turn up there, I questioned your loyalty to Manchester United,' Ferguson told Beckham.

Ferguson's anger and resentment towards the man he had made a superstar reached its apogee on 15 February 2003, when United lost 2–0 at home to Arsenal in the FA Cup fifth round. It may or may not be a coincidence that his friendship with John

Magnier was about to founder over a bitter row about the racehorse Rock of Gibraltar and turn into a feud that was to wreak havoc on Ferguson's hopes of building a life in racing after he retired from football.

In the dressing room after the Arsenal defeat, Ferguson rounded on Beckham and blamed him for the second Arsenal goal, scored by Sylvain Wiltord. Beckham answered him back and said he wasn't going to take the blame. 'No,' Ferguson said, 'take the blame is what you're going to do.' Beckham swore at him and Ferguson was so furious he kicked out at a boot that was lying on the floor. It hit Beckham above the left eye and cut him.

Ferguson apologized and, after his own fury had abated, Beckham released a statement to say that he wanted to put the matter behind him. But by now their relationship was failing. Ferguson began to leave Beckham out for important matches, most notably the second leg of a Champions League quarter-final with Real Madrid. United were destroyed by a Ronaldo hat-trick but Beckham came off the bench to score twice and give United a 4–3 win on the night, which wasn't enough to get them through to the semi-finals.

It was such a mesmerizing game that it persuaded the watching Roman Abramovich that he wanted to buy into football, but nothing could change Ferguson's mind about Beckham. He seemed to feel betrayed by how Beckham had branched out. He saw pictures of Beckham in a sarong or on the front cover of *Time Out*, arms spread out like Jesus Christ, and he heard about him becoming a gay icon, and it was sheer anathema to him. Ferguson could not reconcile the world he thought Victoria Beckham inhabited with football. He thought the two worlds were mutually incompatible and that Beckham's talent and his commitment would ebb away under its influence.

He was wrong about that, and United have paid for his mistake ever since – paid both on the pitch and off it. Early in 2006, the accountancy firm Deloitte & Touche released an annual report which showed that after eight years as the highest-earning football club in the world, United were no longer at the top. They had been overtaken by Real Madrid, whose revenues had risen by 17 per cent. And the biggest reason for Madrid's marketing surge? David Beckham.

Ferguson has never spoken to Beckham about the transfer. He never told him he wanted to sell him. Partly, that is just the way football is: brutally unsentimental, no time for fond farewells. But in Beckham's case it seemed particularly perverse and callous that there should be no contact from Ferguson. Beckham had been at the club for more than a decade, he had been one of the European Cup Final team, and yet Ferguson did not make even a cursory attempt to phone him and wish him good luck. Like Mark McGhee said, Ferguson moves on.

'I can't really trace a moment when things changed,' Beckham said. 'There was the odd occasion when things were said. When I first got an agent, an agent he didn't like, there was a frostiness for a while. The manager always liked to have that control. As much as he might think he did, he never lost control of me as a footballer. I still thought of him as a father-figure right up until the time I left the club. I was a man, I was twenty-eight years old and I still thought of him as a father-figure.

'He struggled with some of the things that happened outside of my career, some of the fashion magazine shoots I used to do. I enjoyed doing it but I would never have let it get in the way of the football. I realized he wasn't happy with me at those times and I think that was one of the main reasons why he wanted me to leave in the end. I'm sure, if you asked him, he would say it was football reasons but I think it was the control. He felt he had lost control of me as a person.

'What he probably still doesn't realise is that he never did lose control of me. I had too much respect for him to think about anything other than football when I was at the club. That was why it hurt so much when I left and the way I left. I had been there for so many years and he had been a father-figure to me and for it to end to like that was poor. I said that when I left and I got criticised by a journalist who said "What do you want him to do, do you want him to give you a kiss?" But he meant so much to me when I was at Manchester United. For it to go the way it went, I was gutted.

'I still feel a sadness about the way it deteriorated. I wish it could have been different. The one thing I wish I had done is try to get in touch with him that summer when the chief executive, Peter Kenyon, said that I should go. I wish I had spoken to the manager even if he had said he thought it was time for me to leave. That would have been fine. I would have liked a phone call from him just to say "Good luck and thanks for everything."

'I haven't spoken to him since. We were both at the funeral of Jimmy Davis. It wasn't the right place to talk about things. I had been at Real Madrid for a few months by then. He hadn't rung me or sent me a message or anything prior to that. At the funeral, he said "How are things over there?" To be honest, I wasn't in the right frame of mind because of Jimmy's funeral but that is the only thing that has ever been said.

'I didn't really think that was his way of trying to start things again. But I don't know. I just wish it had been done the day after I signed for Real Madrid. I would have liked confirmation that I wouldn't be playing for him again. From him. The last game I played for him at Goodison Park against Everton, we had won the league and everyone was celebrating. I was part of that midfield of Beckham, Keane, Scholes, Giggs, that worked so well together and I scored one of United's goals that day. I never thought for one minute that I wouldn't be playing for Man United the year after.

'But I don't think he could handle the loss of control. I was in my car once, near the Trafford Centre on the outskirts of Manchester, when he rang me on my mobile phone. He was shouting at me and asking why I was in Barcelona. I told him I was in Manchester. He said a friend had just phoned him to say that I was sitting opposite him in Barcelona airport. I told him I was outside the Trafford Centre. He shouted "Don't fucking lie to me" down the phone. I said "I am on the M60 outside the Trafford Centre in Manchester in my car." He said "Right, okay" and put the phone down.

'But, you know, I wouldn't have any problem playing for him again because he was such a big influence on my career, he was a father-figure to me and he is a person and a manager that I respect enormously. I don't think that will ever happen but I would like to think there might come a time when we are on friendlier terms, when there might be a dialogue between us. I had so many happy times there that I could never forget them. It would be great to be like that but he is stubborn and I am stubborn and that's life.

'Maybe that's just the way the manager has always been. I know he was like that with other players. But I still can't help wishing that it could have ended differently. It seemed needless to do it like that. I was a kid when I joined Manchester United. Perhaps that's why I felt it should have been different with me. But I suppose everyone has got their ways of moving on and that's Sir Alex's.'

The way the relationship between Britain's best manager and the world's most famous player fractured so bitterly for some is the most powerful symbol of a failure of judgement that has crept into Ferguson's management of Manchester United in the winter of his time in charge. It was also a worrying sign that Ferguson's methods of man-management were in danger of becoming outmoded. 'Ferguson's personality clash with Beckham,' the award-winning journalist Martin Samuel wrote in *The Times*, 'was the first sign that the newly empowered modern footballer and the patriarchal manager were no longer travelling the same path.'

Since the summer of 2003, when Manchester United won their last Premiership title, things have started to slip at Old Trafford and moral confusion has contaminated the once unyielding regime that Ferguson built. Others things, too, have contributed to the slow but gradual decline that has gripped United since then. Ferguson has made several calamitous forays into the transfer market that have crippled the club's ability to exert pressure on Jose Mourinho's Chelsea. The list of failures is long and painful. Eric Djemba Djemba, Kleberson, Liam Miller, Ji-Sung Park, David Bellion, Alan Smith and, of course, Juan Sebastián Verón, have all failed to make the grade.

The result is that in the 2005–06 season, while United may have had the best attacking line in the Premiership and a defence held together by the mental strength of the new captain, Gary Neville, plus the returning skill of Rio Ferdinand, it had one of the weakest midfields in the division. At one point in January 2006, Ferguson was playing Smith, a centre forward, and Ferdinand, a centre back, in the heart of midfield. Both were willing workhorses. Both were also out of their depth.

Later, as United fashioned an unlikely tilt at the title and put Chelsea under modest pressure, Ferguson played Ryan Giggs and John O'Shea in the heart of the team. They did better than Smith and Ferdinand. Giggs, in particular, was a revelation in the position. But they were still no match for established midfielders like Frank Lampard and Claude Makelele.

Wayne Rooney has been an outstanding success in attack and Ferguson deserves credit for bringing him to Old Trafford and harnessing his wonderful abilities. Ruud Van Nistelrooy is still the best goalscorer in the league, and even if Cristiano Ronaldo was overpriced when Ferguson paid £12.6 million for him from Sporting Lisbon, he has produced enough moments of bewitching brilliance to vindicate his purchase. The problem is that Ferguson fell out spectacularly with Van Nistelrooy in the second half of the 2005–06 season and the rest of the United team cannot give its all-star attack the service it needs to express its talents.

For that, the blame must lie at Ferguson's door. Part of the problem was that he neglected the dictum he was first taught by the former Notts County manager Jimmy Sirrell when he attended a coaching course at Lilleshall in the mid-Seventies. Sirrell told the group of young hopefuls never to let a team grow old together, and yet that is exactly what happened to United.

At the start of the 2005–06 season, the United midfield comprised Ryan Giggs, Roy Keane, Paul Scholes and Ronaldo. Scholes turned thirty-one that autumn, Giggs thirty-two and Keane thirty-four. To varying degrees, each player, each a magnificent servant to the club and each now past his prime, was beginning to rust. Djemba Djemba and Kleberson both represented halting attempts to inject new blood. So did Smith. None of them worked.

Perhaps it was because Ferguson took his eye off the ball when he became obsessed with horse-racing in general and his share in Rock of Gibraltar in particular. Perhaps it was because he grew distracted by the bitter and debilitating battle he waged with John Magnier over his claim to 50 per cent of the horse's stud rights. But Ferguson has conspicuously failed to prepare the team for the ageing of the graduates of the famous 1992 FA Youth Cup-winning side.

Of those great players, David Beckham, Nicky Butt and Phil Neville have all been moved on, Scholes has suffered protracted bouts of injury and loss of form and Giggs's influence has begun to wane. Only Gary Neville has maintained his effectiveness and worth to the team. As those players have been phased out, Ferguson has largely tried to replace them with foreign imports and the result has been that the team has lost much of its cohesion as well as the unique spirit and hunger that once bound it together.

The suggestion infuriates Ferguson, but it is clear now that Beckham's departure represented the beginning of the end for Manchester United's greatest manager. It is not just that United have not been the same team since. It is not just that Ferguson has never found an adequate replacement for Beckham in three years of trying. It is not just that Van Nistelrooy has never enjoyed the same kind of service he did when Beckham was supplying crosses. It is more than all that.

The reality is that Ferguson has allowed the codes of loyalty, comradeship and togetherness that he created at Old Trafford to be diluted. He has allowed personal dislikes to accelerate into bitter feuds and take precedence over football logic. Some feel that he rid himself of Beckham because of what he perceived to be a dissolute lifestyle and yet when Ferdinand, his £30 million record signing, missed his drugs test in September 2003, offering the excuse that he had forgotten because he was going shopping and moving house, Ferguson, supported by a supine board, backed him to the hilt.

Those two attitudes do not marry. Ferdinand's excesses make Beckham look like a monk in comparison, and yet Ferdinand has never suffered the same kind of censure that Beckham experienced. Ferdinand's a party animal, often nightclubbing in London, often getting into scrapes, and yet Ferguson tolerates his behaviour without a word. More damagingly, the energy the club expended on fighting Ferdinand's drugs case seemed to exhaust the players and deprive United of the moral compass that, under Ferguson, had always been its guiding force.

The battle on Ferdinand's behalf made the club look stupid. Worse, it made it look as if it was compromising sport's desperate war on doping. Ferdinand may never have tested positive but what Ferguson and the club seemed incapable of grasping was that driving away from drugs testers has to be treated with the same sanction as a positive test. If a Chinese runner or a Bulgarian weightlifter had done what Ferdinand did, he would have been laughed out of town if he tried to claim that he was innocent.

So when Ferguson and the club railed against Ferdinand's treatment it left them wide open to yet more accusations that they thought they were above the law. Ferguson, in particular, seemed to be attempting to bully his way out of the situation by casting aspersions on the modus operandi of the drugs testers.

Maurice Watkins, a club director who was Ferdinand's legal representative when the FA tribunal convened in December 2003 to decide what his punishment should be, described the player's eight-month ban as 'a particularly savage and unprecedented sentence'. Again, that hysterical reaction just made United look stupid. The reality is that Ferdinand got off lightly. 'The sentence is a third of the theoretical maximum he could have got,' Dick Pound, the president of the World Anti-Doping Agency, said, 'so he's done pretty well from that perspective.'

Ferdinand played his last game before his suspension in a 1–0 defeat by Wolves at Molineux on 17 January 2004. United lost five Premiership matches between then and the end of the season, including a 4–1 drubbing by Manchester City at the City of Manchester Stadium in March, and could only finish a distant third in the table, 15 points behind champions Arsenal and 4 adrift of Claudio Ranieri's Chelsea. They were eliminated from the Champions League in the second round by Jose Mourinho's FC Porto, who went on to win the competition.

United did celebrate a one-sided FA Cup Final victory over Millwall but there was a poignancy about the joy that a relatively meaningless triumph brought them. There was a time when United did not care about the FA Cup, when it came way down their list of priorities. Still, it was better than what lay ahead.

The following season, United were third again. This time they trailed in 18 points behind champions Chelsea and 6 behind Arsenal. Chelsea beat them on the opening day with a goal by Eidur Gudjohnsen but everyone could read the runes of their season in the mediocrity of the side they fielded that day. The starting line-up contained Quinton Fortune, Djemba Djemba, Liam Miller and Alan Smith. When Ferguson turned to the bench, he brought on Bellion, Kieran Richardson and Diego Forlan. Needless to say, that trio did nothing to change the game.

United's season was humdrum. They took most satisfaction from finally ending Arsenal's unbeaten run of 49 matches in October. Arsenal imploded after that defeat and lost their dignity, too. One Arsenal player marked the defeat by throwing pizza at Ferguson in the Old Trafford tunnel and Ferguson claimed that Arsène Wenger ran at him with his fists raised. But it was a pyrrhic victory for United. They lost 2–0 at Portsmouth six days later and drew too many games to be a real threat to Chelsea's dominance.

There was embarrassment when they drew 0–0 with non-league Exeter City at Old Trafford in the FA Cup third round in January, and in March they were eased gently out of the Champions League in the second round again, losing home and away to AC Milan. They had the better of the FA Cup Final against a cautious, negative Arsenal side but lost on penalties. They ended the season with nothing. Strip away the rhetoric and United were heading backwards.

Ferguson couldn't stop the rot in the 2005–06 season either. If anything, the rot grew more corrosive. In fact, before United's futile late-season rally, the campaign seemed to lurch from setback to disaster to controversy to embarrassment. At times, the club looked like a fighter jet in a death spiral. Ferguson was still at the controls, but all he seemed capable of doing was to accelerate towards the moment of impact. The deeper United slid into trouble in the middle of the season, the more combative and sour he became.

It didn't take long in the season for Ferguson's antipathy towards the press, for instance, to plumb new depths of farce. A couple of days after Wayne Rooney had been sent off in a Wednesday night Champions League tie away to Villarreal in September for clapping his hands in the face of the Danish referee, Kim Milton-Nielsen, Ferguson turned up for his regular Friday press conference with the daily newspaper reporters at Carrington.

Neil Custis, from *The Sun*, searched desperately for a euphemistic way of broaching the subject without causing Ferguson to explode. 'Any more thoughts on Wednesday, Alex?' Custis said. Ferguson glared at him. 'Aye,' he said. 'I've got plenty of thoughts but I won't be fucking sharing them with you.' So much for the softly-softly approach.

Custis, like most journalists under the age of sixty, had been in trouble with Ferguson before. Soon after he had become the *Sun*'s chief football writer in the north, the United manager had assailed him with a particularly vicious outburst about a piece he had written in the *Daily Express*. Custis pointed out that the piece in question had actually been written by his brother, Shaun. Ferguson swore again. 'Ach,' he said. 'Too many Custises.'

By now, Ferguson's problems with the written press were heading for meltdown. They had been less than cordial for many years, but there had been pockets of civility and humour. Now even those were beginning to disappear as Ferguson grew more and more sullen. One broadsheet writer who attended a Ferguson Friday press conference in the autumn of 2005 was struck by the change in him and appalled at how rude he had become even to those who might once have had the semblance of a relationship with him.

Most of the time, the journalists who had to suffer his barbs and his sneers chose to protect Ferguson as part of a kind of unwritten code. They chose not to report his profanities and his threats and the slanders he aimed at referees and rival managers. In that way, they showed him a respect that he failed to show to them. In the end, though, they grew bored of being treated like naughty boys and bit back. In May 2002, when Ferguson bawled at them for having the temerity to criticize Juan Sebastián Verón after the Argentinian had produced yet another stinking performance in the United midfield, they reported his outburst word for word. 'On you go,' Ferguson screamed at them. 'I'm no fucking talking to you. Verón's a great fucking player. Youse are all fucking idiots.'

Examples of Ferguson's foul-mouthed tirades against journalists are legion. One tabloid reporter fell victim to him when he was trying to get a shirt signed by some players for a child who was dying of cancer. The reporter had been ushered through the gates of The Cliff, United's former training ground, by a steward who knew him. He was waiting to get a player's signature. Ferguson came round the corner helping to support an injured Roy Keane, who was leaning on his shoulder.

Ferguson turned puce instantly. He dropped Keane, who yelped in agony, and stormed towards the reporter who had already started trying to explain why he was carrying the shirt. 'I don't care,' Ferguson kept saying, 'you're just a fucking snoop.' Another time, he shooed a startled journalist out of The Cliff with a volley of foul-mouthed abuse and then realized there was a crowd of kids with their parents looking on. 'I'm sorry about that,' he said to one of the parents, 'but it's the only language these cunts understand.'

A couple of years ago, Matt Lawton, the chief football writer of the *Daily Mail*, asked Ferguson a reasonable question. Even Ferguson thought it was reasonable. 'That's a good question,' Ferguson said, 'but it would take a whole interview to answer it and that's an interview you're never going to fucking get.'

More recently, Matt Dickinson, the Chief Football Correspondent of *The Times*, was brought down from the Old Trafford press box after a game by the Arsenal press officer, Amanda Docherty, to speak to Arsenal players after a match. Ferguson spotted Dickinson, broke off from an interview he was doing and started running towards him. 'Get that cunt out of my tunnel,' he screamed as he ran, veins popping and eyes bulging.

Sometimes his behaviour beggars belief. When the sports editor of the *Daily Mirror*, Dean Morse, asked Ferguson, at a lunch to celebrate his 1,000th game as a manager, if there was anything he could do to improve the relationship between the paper and the club, which had deteriorated when *The Mirror* criticized United for pulling out of the FA Cup in 1999–2000,

Ferguson sneered at him. 'Yes,' the manager of the self-styled greatest club in the world, said, 'you can fuck off and die.'

Before United played Benfica in Lisbon in their final group match in the Champions League, a *Daily Mirror* reporter asked Ferguson in a press conference if his own position as manager would be under pressure if United did not qualify for the knock-out phase. Ferguson said he would not answer the question. The reporter pressed him and Ferguson again refused to answer. A couple of seconds later, he turned to his assistant, Carlos Queiroz, who was sitting next to him. 'We've got some right fucking pricks in here today,' Ferguson said. Queiroz laughed obediently.

That's why when Ferguson used his match-day programme notes for a game against Everton in December 2005 to accuse the media of making it personal, a couple of dozen reporters in the Old Trafford press room fell down on the floor and died laughing. Because the truth is that when it comes to making it personal, Ferguson wrote the book.

In some respects, Ferguson's abusive behaviour towards journalists is of little interest to the public. Certainly, Manchester United supporters do not see it as a fault in their manager. In fact, they are inclined to laud him for his habits. But if you join the dots of Ferguson's expletive-ridden attacks on journalists over the years, there is a wider issue to consider. The more aggressive, angry, paranoid and unpleasant Ferguson becomes, the more likely it is that the legacy of a brilliant manager and a fiercely intelligent, fascinating man will be poisoned by the bile that threatens to consume him.

He appears to hold grudges against most people not of pensionable age, the entire BBC, every national newspaper, multimillionaires who give him a free horse, every referee who ever lived, anybody who isn't Scottish and everyone who ever crossed him or stood up to him. But when he shouts and bawls and sneers now, fewer people no longer cower.

The worse he gets, the more it seems that he will be re-membered as a great manager but not a great man. He will be respected for what he achieved and the statistics will say that he was the best manager United ever had. But he will never be remembered with the same affection as Sir Matt Busby at the club. And because of his demeanour and his increasing sullen-ness, many feel he will never be held in the same esteem as Shankly, Sir Bobby Robson, Bob Paisley, Brian Clough or Bill Nicholson.

In some ways, the last five years of his time in charge at Old Trafford almost seem like a wilful attempt by Ferguson to stain his own reputation. Following all his magnificent achievements and the style with which he won, his dispute over Rock of Gibraltar, his son Jason's involvement in United deals, his acceptance of the Glazers, his treatment of Beckham, his indul-gence of Ferdinand, his relentless rudeness and, finally, his seemingly ruthless banishing of Roy Keane are like a gulp of hemlock after a cup of nectar.

After United had won their home Champions League game against Benfica in 2005, Ferguson attended the post-match Uefa press conference because Uefa rules, unlike Premiership ones, decree that he has to. Again, he was sour and little more than monosyllabic. Oliver Kay, from *The Times*, asked him if he could explain his thinking in pushing Paul Scholes further forward than he had been used in recent matches. Ferguson bristled. 'Why should I explain anything to you?' he said. 'I don't want to blunt your imagination.' Another one for the scrapbook.

By then, though, Ferguson was coming under extreme press-ure. He was booed by sections of the Old Trafford crowd after United lost at home to Blackburn on 24 September and fell 10 points behind Chelsea after seven games. The problems were mounting up. Circumstances were ganging up on him. Still, during the Benfica match, the United fans, chastened by the criticism they had received for jeering him a few days earlier, started a chant of 'Stand Up if You Love Fergie' and all around the stadium people gradually rose to their feet and started cheering.

But the problems did not cease. They came in a torrent now. At the end of September 2005, Roy Keane announced on MUTV that it was unlikely he would be at the club the following season because the club had not offered him a new contract. Ferguson promptly banned MUTV. Rio Ferdinand, unpopular because he was stalling on the signing of a new contract, was booed by the United supporters during the match against Fulham at Craven Cottage when he was handed the captain's armband. Queiroz labelled the United fans 'stupid' for questioning tactics against Blackburn and Cristiano Ronaldo was arrested in connection with the alleged rape of two women at the Sanderson Hotel in central London. The allegations were later dropped.

It felt in those dark days as if Ferguson was facing the last great crisis of his United reign. At the end of October, United were thrashed 4–1 by Middlesbrough at the Riverside. It was pointed out that it was a 4–1 defeat at Southampton that had spelled the end for his predecessor, Ron Atkinson. Two days later, Keane, who was injured, filmed an interview for an MUTV show called *Plays the Pundit* in which he was critical of the performances of several of the United players. MUTV got nervous and told chief executive David Gill about the content. Gill told Ferguson. Ferguson pulled the plug on *Plays the Pundit*. It never went out.

The *Daily Mirror* published the transcript of Keane's comments soon afterwards. Keane picked out Ferdinand, John O'Shea, Darren Fletcher, Kieran Richardson and Alan Smith for harsh criticism. But the way Keane had been gagged provoked much more criticism and comment than anything he could ever have said. Ferguson might fancy himself as a media manipulator but he had just made another critical error of judgement.

'Keane clearly never studied the Soviet propaganda model,' the *Daily Mail's* highly respected columnist Paul Hayward wrote. 'He obviously doesn't know that the organs of the state exist to promote an image of serenity, unity and success. Keane is so off-message that they're going to need the Red Army to shut him up. When Keane was gagged, MUTV must have been tempted to play martial music and switch to a documentary about shirt sales in Mongolia and monogrammed duvet production in United's licensed factories.'

United fans sang Keane's name as a rallying cry when United lost a Champions League tie 1–0 to Lille on a filthy night at the Stade de France at the beginning of November. Some journalists and fans who had been watching United for more than thirty years agreed it was the worst performance by the team that they could remember. When the United players trudged forlornly over to the fans after the final whistle, they were greeted with a wall of two-fingered salutes and a chorus of boos. 'There's only one Keano,' the fans sang, as if it were a reproach to the players who the United captain had lambasted.

United were now third in Champions League Group D and the unthinkable was suddenly thinkable. United were struggling even to make it beyond the group stage into the second round. A joke started doing the rounds on the internet. 'Sir Alex is queuing in his local building society when a gunman bursts in through the door demanding money,' it goes. 'Ferguson attempts to tackle the raider but gets knocked over and as he falls, his head smashes against the counter and he is knocked out cold. The robber escapes and the cashier tries to revive Ferguson. After a few minutes, he comes round and looks bewildered. "Where the hell am I?" he says. "You're in the Nationwide," the cashier tells him. "Fuck me," says Ferguson, "is it May already?"'

But on 18 November the joking stopped. On 18 November Ferguson got rid of Roy Keane. Keane had been growing increasingly exasperated with United's performances on the field. He was openly scornful of the attitude of many of his teammates and robustly critical of some of Ferguson's moves in the transfer market. Keane had turned into the conscience of

United, the one man who dared to say what nobody else would. He cut through the propaganda and the dissembling. He told the truth about the state United were in and the legacy Ferguson was bequeathing. He was the child who shouted out that the emperor had no clothes.

Keane had had a bitter argument with Ferguson in the summer over the arrangements made for the players' families on a pre-season bonding trip to Portugal. He felt that the hotel facilities were not suitable for kids, and when he pointed this out to Ferguson the two men soon became locked in a shouting match. The result was that Keane was left behind when United went on their pre-season tour of the Far East.

The problems did not abate when the season started. Keane had lost respect for Queiroz and told him on several occasions that he should not have come back to the club after his short reign as Real Madrid boss had ended in ignominy. Keane's outbursts were nothing new, but things had changed. In the past, his criticisms had been levelled at a team that was in a position of strength, but now they were merely pointing out the weaknesses of a side on the slide. Secondly, Keane's age meant that Ferguson thought he was expendable.

Ferguson was furious about Keane's criticisms on *Plays the Pundit*. He was seething when he heard the United fans singing Keane's name in the Stade de France during the match against Lille, using the captain's comments as a stick with which to beat the players. Keane was given the chance to explain his comments to his teammates, and at the time United officials used the usual glib words like 'constructive' and 'positive' to describe the atmosphere.

In fact, the meeting was more like Saipan Mark II. Out in Saipan, Keane had told Ireland manager Mick McCarthy to 'stick it up your bollocks' in an out-of-control rant about the squad's chaotic preparations for the 2002 World Cup. His clear-the-air performance at Carrington was not dissimilar, and Ferguson decided then that he had to rid himself of his captain and the man who had been his incarnation on the field of play for so many years, the man who had shared his hunger and his hatred of losing.

On 18 November he met with Keane and his lawyer, Michael Kennedy, at Carrington and the decision was made. There was more sadness than anger. Shortly before 10 a.m., Ferguson pushed open the swing doors to the players' canteen and walked in looking lost and shattered. 'This is a sad day for Manchester United,' he announced to no one in particular and wandered over to sit with a bemused Cristiano Ronaldo, who had just signed a new contract.

At 11.30 a.m., Ferguson walked into his regular Friday press conference and behaved as if nothing had happened. He was asked about Keane's contractual situation. He shook his head. 'Nothing to report,' he said. 'There hasn't been any decision about his contract. It's just like I told you a few weeks ago.' No one sensed anything was wrong. Keane had been at Old Trafford for twelve years but his departure was swift and brutal. The manager was moving on again. The lesson was this: many things may change at Manchester United but there is one constant, no one takes on Ferguson and wins. After United had beaten Charlton Athletic at The Valley the next day, Ferguson sat and chatted with Alan Curbishley for half an hour. Curbishley said Keane's name was not mentioned once. The Irishman was like the elephant in the corner. 'Players get older,' Ferguson said later. 'This is the horrible part when you are a manager of one club for a long time.'

Keane left but the problems at United remained. On 7 December, a couple of weeks after the death of George Best, United played Benfica in the Stadium of Light, the venue of Best's most memorable performance in a 5–1 victory in 1966. This time was memorable, too. But for different reasons. United needed to win to be sure of progressing to the knock-out phase of the Champions League. But they never looked like winning, not even when Scholes gave them an early lead. Benfica scored twice, United lost and finished rock-bottom of the group. They didn't even qualify for the Uefa Cup. It was a humiliation.

The sense that Ferguson's United regime was imploding increased six days later when he staged what was to be his final Friday press conference for the written media. It was the last privilege the daily newspapers received from Ferguson after his long-term refusal to attend Premiership post-match press conferences. Ferguson began this time by saying he would be very brief. He was. The press conference lasted 74 seconds. He just about had time to forget Paul Jewell's name. Then he walked out. 'See you later boys,' he said as he marched through the door.

Earlier, he had told the broadcast press conference that the newspapers had a 'hatred' of United. It was an old trick that he had been using ever since his first managerial job at East Stirlingshire. He told his players there that the papers favoured their local rivals, Falkirk. At Aberdeen, he told the players all the Glasgow journalists hated going up to the northeast and were rooting for Celtic and Rangers. By now, it had become a transparent manoeuvre to try to deflect attention away from United's desperately underachieving season. It was a tired ploy. It didn't work. The problems United had couldn't be fixed by making monsters out of the media.

In *The Times*, Martin Samuel drew a comparison between United's fall from grace and the end of Liverpool's great empire at the start of the 1990s. 'Liverpool were overtaken by wealthier rivals as United have been and key players grew old together, as is happening at United,' he wrote. 'Liverpool could clearly not adequately replicate the talents of Ian Rush, Graeme Souness, Kenny Dalglish, Steve Nicol, Alan Hansen and Mark Lawrenson just as Ferguson is labouring to find the heirs to Keane, Beckham, Schmeichel, Giggs and Scholes.'

In January, United drew 0–0 at non-league Burton Albion in the FA Cup third round and then lost 3–1 away at Manchester City. Ferguson threw his new £4.5 million left back

Patrice Evra in for his debut. He looked like a frightened rabbit. Ferguson had to substitute him at half-time. It was only the fourth time Ferguson had been in charge of the losing side in all his Manchester derbies.

In the middle of February, another record went. United lost an FA Cup tie to Liverpool for the first time in eighty-five years. Ferguson picked a particularly eccentric five-man midfield with Ryan Giggs in a holding role. United were appalling. Liverpool won 1–0 but it should have been more. United's misery was completed when Alan Smith suffered an horrific injury near the end when he blocked a free kick from John Arne Riise. He broke his leg and dislocated his ankle.

The weight of evidence was growing and growing. Everything about Ferguson seemed suggestive of a man who had realized that he could not live without the game or the club and was silently pleading for more time. Plenty of journalists were at pains to point that out, of course, but the words of one of them may have given Ferguson cause for reflection.

Hugh McIlvanney is that rare thing: a journalist Ferguson admires. McIlvanney, one of the best sports journalists Britain has ever produced, helped him write his autobiography, *Managing My Life*, and has stayed with him at his home in Wilmslow. The two men have been friends for decades. It must have taken a good deal of courage for him to write the following words of advice to Ferguson in *The Sunday Times* as United stumbled on without direction into the new year.

'Ferguson's warrior spirit abhors the thought of ending his managerial career in any way but on the crest of a triumph,' McIlvanney wrote, 'but his achievements are already so monumental that recent events could not conceivably cast a shadow on them and a personally choreographed exit would be bathed in the dignity and the honour that are his due. He must never run the risk of being dispatched by remote control from Florida. Eventually, there comes a moment when the best and bravest of fighters shouldn't answer the bell.'

That moment is upon us. But it seems as if Ferguson can't even hear the bell, let alone think about not answering it. His rifts and feuds are so many and so various, it is hard to keep track of them. He even managed to part company with the United team doctor, Mike Stone, in the summer of 2006, allegedly because of a row over the treatment of Wayne Rooney's foot injury. Perhaps Ferguson doesn't need a doctor any more. What he really needs is a healer, someone to bind up all the wounds he is causing. He's turning into one of his Western heroes, leaving a trail of dead men in his wake. But there are new gunslingers in town now. It's time for him to put away his gun before McIlvanney's prophecy comes true and someone shoots him down.

Bibliography

Two sources have been particularly useful in researching this book – Michael Crick's *The Boss* (London, 2002) and Alex Ferguson's autobiography, *Managing My Life* (London, 1999). Others are:

Beckham, David, with Watt, Tom *David Beckham: My Side* (London, 2003)

Bower, Tom *Broken Dreams* (London, 2003)

Dalglish, Kenny *Dalglish: My Autobiography* (London, 1996)

Eade, Paul *Workington Association Football Club* (Stroud, 2003)

Keane, Roy, with Dunphy, Eamon *Keane: The Autobiography* (London, 2002)

Keegan, Kevin *Kevin Keegan: My Autobiography* (London, 1997)

Keith, John *The Essential Shankly: Revealing the Kop Legend who Launched a Thousand Quips* (London, 2001)

Kelly, Stephen F. *Fergie* (London, 1997)

Kelly, Stephen F. *Bill Shankly: It's Much More Important Than That: A Biography* (London, 1996)

Law, Dennis *The Lawman: an autobiography* (London, 1999)

Leighton, Jim, with Robertson, Ken *In the Firing Line* (Edinburgh, 2000)

McLintock, Frank, with Bagchi, Rob *True Grit: The Autobiography* (London, 2005)

McGrath, Paul *Ooh Aah Paul McGrath* (Edinburgh, 1994)

McIlvanney, Hugh *McIlvanney on Football* (Edinburgh, 1994)

Miller, Willie, with Macdonald, Alastair *The Miller's Tale* (Edinburgh, 1989)

Pettigrew, David *Old Muirkirk and Stenlock* (Camnock, 1996)

Rollin, Jack *Soccer at War 1939–45* (London, 1985)

Shankly, Bill *Shankly* (London, 1976)

Stam, Jaap, with Butler, Jeremy *Head to Head* (London, 2001)

St John, Ian, with Lawton, James *The Saint: My Autobiography* (London, 2005)

Thompson, Phil, with Rogers, Ken *Stand up Pinocchio: From the Kop to the Top – My Life Inside Anfield* (Liverpool, 2005)

Index

Aberdeen 140, 155–68, 186–98
    Ferguson approaches 136, 137
    Ferguson leaves 227
    League Cup 159, 161, 197
    league titles 168, 187, 193, 196,
        197
Abramovich, Roman 380
A'Court, Alan 180
Adams, Tony 279, 327, 331
Agustin 192
Ajax 101–2
Allan, Ivan 345
Allardyce, Craig 366
Allison, Malcolm 69
Allison, Willie 86–7, 88, 91–2
Allodi, Italo 129
America, Liverpool tour 169, 182
Anderlecht 183–4
Anderson, Chris 155, 161
Anderson, Jerome 365
Anelka, Nicolas 326
Archibald, Steve 157, 164, 167, 187,
        226, 227, 319–20
Arges Pitesti 163, 187
Arrowsmith, Alf 181
Arsenal 75–6, 77, 78–9, 181, 182,
        285–6, 289, 301–2, 309,
        310–11, 316, 359, 360, 362,
        363, 379–80, 387–8
    FA Cup Final 73
    Liverpool struggle 325–31
    point docking 274
Asprilla, Faustino 297

Aston Villa 277, 278, 297, 351
Atkinson, Ron 194, 238–9, 240, 277,
        393
L'Attitude 364–5
Augenthaler, Klaus 189
Ayr United 96, 135–6, 138

Ball, Alan 100
Banks, Gordon 127, 180
Barcelona 267, 274, 331, 334
Barnes, Peter 238
Barthez, Fabien 269
Basler, Mario 320
Bastin 310
Batista, Jose 227
Bayern Munich 188, 189–90,
        319–24, 331, 379
Beattie, Andy 66, 67, 229, 230–2,
        263, 310, 312–13
Beckenbauer, Franz 226
Beckford, Darren 237
Beckham, David 3, 5, 290, 297, 303,
        328, 385–6
    European Cup 320, 322–3, 333,
        379
    FA Cup 299, 330
    Ferguson tension 361–2, 363,
        377–99
Beckham, Victoria 379, 380
Bell, John 90
Benfica 130, 131, 391, 392–3, 396–7
Benitez, Rafael 62, 131

Bennett, Reuben 29, 49, 66, 70–1,
110, 208–9, 210–12, 214
Bergkamp, Dennis 326, 330
Best, George 68, 103, 127, 131, 150,
171, 250, 305, 321
Bett, Jim 226
Bishop, Ian 236
Black, Eric 189, 191, 195
Blackburn Rovers 289, 292–3, 327
Blanc, Laurent 269, 355
Blatter, Sepp 353
Blomqvist, Jesper 320, 321
Blyth, Billy 282, 338
Blyth, Bob 318, 338
Bonhof, Rainer 80
Boot, Eddie 229, 231, 235, 374
Boot Room 29, 49, 208–20
Boreland, Johnny 37
Borras, Omar 227
Bosnich, Mark 297
Botsford, Keith 128–9
Bower, Tom 366
Bremner, Billy 50, 146, 149
Brennan, Eddie 228, 232
Brightwell, Ian 237
Broadis, Ivor 318
Brondby 331
Brown, Bobby 62
Bruce, Steve 264, 271, 277
Burton Albion 397
Busby, Matt 42, 43, 103, 171, 215,
230, 234, 323, 356
Busquets 274
Butt, Nicky 9, 290, 297, 320, 329,
385
Byrne, Gerry 71, 100, 147, 149, 152,
178, 215

Caledonian Colours 345
Callaghan, Ian 48, 55, 71, 100, 106,
111, 180, 208
debut 215
European Cup 127, 153–4
FA Cup Final 84, 148, 149
Shankly's funeral 28

signing 200–2
Sixties 219–20
Candleriggs 345
Cantona, Eric 242, 267, 268, 270,
271, 274–7, 279, 280, 289,
290–2, 293–4, 297–8, 299–301
Cardiff City game 214
Carling Cup, Manchester United 6–7,
56
Carlisle United 15, 16, 282–6, 318,
338–41
Carragher, Jamie 326
Carroll, Roy 365, 367
Carruthers, Peter 338
Case, Jimmy 206
Cass, Bob 300
catenaccio system 126
Catterick, Harry 99, 171, 172, 212
Celtic 89–90, 102, 156, 167, 187–8
European Cup 89, 102, 128, 191,
221
Scottish Cup 93
Uefa Cup 192–3
Chalmers, Steve 93
Champions League
Liverpool 23–4, 123
Manchester United 267, 358,
359–60, 362, 380, 387, 388,
391, 392–3, 394, 396–7
Chapman, Herbert 309
Charity Shield, Liverpool 50
Charlton 233
Charlton, Bobby 240
Charlton, Jack 11, 49–50, 146, 215
Chelsea 6, 9–11, 100, 147, 171, 173,
174–5, 280, 387
Clemence, Ray 21–2, 48, 55, 67, 71,
76, 104–5, 106, 111, 186
Clough, Brian 20, 73, 136–7
Cole, Andy 292, 299, 321, 328–9,
333–4
Collins, Bobby 146, 149
Collymore, Stan 206, 299
Cologne game 184
Considine, Dougie 166–7

Coolmore *see* Magnier, John
Cooper, Davie 223
Copland, Jackie 133, 135, 158
Copping, Wilf 310
Corrieri, Johnny 283
Corso, Mario 126
Crick, Michael 57, 136, 137–8, 239, 248
Cronberry Eglinton 338
Cruyff, Johan 102
Crystal Palace game 251–2, 291
Cumberland Cup Final 283
Cunningham, Willie 57–9, 94, 95, 119
Cup Winners' Cup
    Aberdeen 188–95
    Manchester United 274
Curbishley, Alan 11, 396
Currie, Harold 119, 120, 135
Curry, Tom 234, 339
Custis, Neil 388–9

Dalglish, Kenny 21, 50, 124, 156, 186, 225, 289, 292
Davids, Edgar 332, 333
Davies, Norman 378
Davies, Simon 107
Davio, Jimmy 377, 382
Dein, Darren 365
Dein, David 365
Deloitte & Touce 380–1
Derby County 75, 76
Desert Island Discs 142–3
Desmond, Dermot 346
di Canio, Paolo 359
di Stefano, Alfredo 190, 191
Dickinson, Matt 390
Dillon, Mike 345
Dixon, Lee 330, 331
Docherty, Amanda 390
Docherty, Tommy 171, 356
Dodd, Andy 364
Dodds, Jock 13, 143
Doherty 309–10
Donachie, John 134

Donald, Dick 155, 157, 161, 194, 195, 239
Donnelly, Tom 120
Dortmund 101
Douglas, Fred 161
Drake, Ted 310
Drumchapel Amateurs 63
Drury, Reg 254–6, 263
Dublin, Dion 275
Dunfermline 56–60, 62
Dunlop, Ed 345

East Stirlingshire 113–21
Ed Sullivan Show 169
Edelson, Mike 239, 240
Edwards, Edward 345
Edwards, Martin 239–40, 246, 247, 250, 275, 292, 295, 296, 302–3, 327, 356
Elite Sports Group 365, 366
Elleray, David 330
England, Mike 222, 224
Eriksson, Sven-Goran 357, 358
Essaoulenko, Grigory 295, 296
Etherington, Matthew 107
European Cup 128–31
    50th anniversary 124
    Aberdeen 186
    Celtic 89, 102, 128, 191, 221
    Liverpool 21, 50, 55, 81, 101–2, 122, 123–31, 152–4, 174–5, 182–5, 186–7, 212
    Manchester United 103, 130, 131, 299–300, 319–25, 331–5, 379
    Nottingham Forest 136–7
European Cup Winners Cup
    Aberdeen 163
    Liverpool 101
European Super Cup 193
Evans, Alun 73, 74, 105
Evans, Roy 213
Everton 19, 52, 72–3, 99, 100, 171, 172, 179–80, 182, 295, 317, 382

Everton (*cont.*)
  Shankly's funeral 27–8
  Whiteside 248, 249
Evra, Patrice 398
Exeter City 388

FA Cup
  Carlisle 285–6
  charity match 280
  Liverpool 41, 68, 71, 73–4, 77,
    81–5, 108, 122, 124,
    142–53, 180, 185
  Manchester United 238, 250–2,
    280, 295, 299, 329–31, 353,
    379–80, 387, 388, 397–8
  Preston 310–13
  Shankly as player 316
  Workington 262
FA Youth Cup 289
Fachetti, Giacinto 127
Fagan, Joe 29, 49, 66, 76, 111,
    208–9, 212–13, 214
Fairs Cup 93, 103
Falkirk 94–6, 113, 117–19
Ferdinand, Les 328
Ferdinand, Rio 6, 145, 361, 363, 379,
    384, 386–7, 393
Fergie's 95, 96, 114
Ferguson, Sir Alex 1–11, 56–63,
    132–41, 221–7, 264–81,
    319–35, 342–70
  Aberdeen 155–68, 186–98
  alcohol 240–6
  and Beckham 361–2, 363, 377–99
  card games 264–5
  childhood 31–40, 87
  European Cup 130
  fans 168, 192
  foreign players 108
  management beginnings 113–21
  money 177
  peak 289–303
  press 10–11, 300–1, 324, 388–91,
    392, 397
  purge 236–53

  Rangers 86–93
  Shankly meeting 186
  temper 134, 159, 162–5, 266–9,
    380
  transitional years 72
Ferguson, Alex (father) 32–3, 34–5,
    37, 59, 60, 140, 155, 159–60
Ferguson, Cathy (wife) 35, 59–60,
    86–8, 90–1, 157, 194, 293,
    344, 358
Ferguson, Elizabeth (mother) 160
Ferguson, Jason (son) 280, 291, 342,
    356, 364–5, 366, 367, 368
Ferguson, Mark (son) 91, 278, 351,
    352
Ferguson, Martin (brother) 31, 32–3,
    34, 37, 134, 168, 240, 364
Figo, Luis 362
Fink, Thorsten 322
Finney, Tom 20, 170, 230, 305–7,
    316, 317, 318
Firs Park 113, 119–20
Fitton, Peter 218, 300–1
Fitzpatrick, Tony 135
Fletcher, Darren 393
Forfar game 115–16
Forlan, Diego 351
Fotherby, Bill 275
Francis, Trevor 275
Furnell, Jim 180

Gallacher, Ken 91
Gardner, Dave 365
Gardner, Sir Roy 367
Garner, Willie 198
Gascoigne, Paul 242–3, 259, 333
Gatti, Arturo "Thunder" 272
George, Charlie 73, 144
Germany game 226
Gerrard, Steven 24, 30
Giggs, Ryan 5, 9, 265–6, 270, 271–3,
    276, 277, 290, 320, 322, 330,
    384, 385, 398
Giles, Johnny 27, 146
Gill, David 7, 355, 393

Gillespie, Keith 264
Gillies, Mark 94
Gimrack speech 348–9
Glanville, Brian 128–9
Glazer, Malcolm 6, 7, 369
Glenbuck 15, 24–5, 336–8, 339,
    371–5
Glenbuck Cherrypickers 336, 373
Goslin, Harry 313
Goss, Jeremy 279
Gothenburg 190–3
Gourlay, Tom 115
Govan 31–9, 87
Graham, Bobby 71, 100, 108
Greening, Jonathan 365, 367
Greig, John 91–2, 194
Grimsby Town 286–7
Gudjohnsen, Eidur 387

Halifax game 261
Hall, Brian 46–8, 70–1, 73, 74, 75,
    80, 98, 110–11, 273
    and Bennett 211–12
    degree 72
    FA Cup Final 83, 84
    signing 105–6
Hamburg 187, 193, 196–7
Hammer, Armand 319
Hansen, Alan 112, 186, 222, 225,
    297
Hapgood, Eddie 307, 310
Hardman, Harold 234
Harford, Ray 213
Harmony Row 39, 63
Harper, Joe 157, 164
Hartson, John 302, 327
Harvey, Colin 248
Harvey, Joe 64, 82
Hasselbaink, Jimmy Floyd 327
Hateley, Tony 67, 105
Haughey, Charles 345
Hayward, Jonathan 4
Hayward, Paul 394
Heighway, Steve 14, 55, 72, 73
    FA Cup Final 83, 84

signing 105, 106
Henry, Thierry 365
Herrera, Helenio 89, 126, 152, 154
Hewitt, John 189, 192
Heynckes, Jupp 80
Heysel Disaster 212
Hibs 92–3, 95, 159, 168
Hickson, Dave 233
Hilditch, John 277
Hill, Jimmy 250
Hillsborough Disaster 25, 174, 247
Hinchcliffe, Andy 236, 237
Hitzfeld, Ottmar 321
Hodgson, Roy 254
Hogan, Billy 285
Holding, Michael 345
Houllier, Gérard 29, 46, 203, 275
Hucknall, Mick 364
Huddersfield 214, 215, 229–35, 263,
    312
Hughes, Emlyn 14, 55, 67, 71, 75,
    76, 81, 98
    Shankly's funeral 28
    signing 103–4, 106
Hughes, Mark 222, 250, 251, 273–4,
    275, 279, 280, 289, 294, 295
Hulston, Billy 115
Hungary 262
Hunt, Roger 100, 101, 171, 179, 181,
    215, 219
    dropped 108
    and Eric Sykes 98
    European Cup 153–4, 183, 184
    FA Cup Final 148, 149
    leaves 71
Hunter, Norman 146

Ibrox Stadium disaster 32–3
Ince, Paul 237, 247, 267, 271, 277,
    279, 280, 289, 294–5, 326
Inter Milan 89, 101, 102, 122, 123,
    124–31, 152–4, 170, 184, 185,
    331–2
Inzaghi, Filippo 332
Ipswich Town 187

Irwin, Denis 264, 271, 275, 279, 297, 326

Jackson, Jimmy 285
James, David 299
Jarvie, Drew 157
Jewell, Paul 210
Johnson, Bert 64
Johnston, Mo 194, 225
Juanito 192
Juventus 212, 331, 332–3

Kahn, Oliver 323
Kanchelskis, Andrei 271, 276, 289, 294, 295–6, 378
Kay, Oliver 392
Keane, Roy 4, 9, 145, 200, 221, 271, 275, 279, 280, 289–90, 297, 356, 385
    Champions League 359–60
    cruciate injury 301
    drinking 243
    European Cup 130, 320, 332–4
    FA Cup 330
    leaves 393, 394–6
    new deal 359
    Plays the Plundit 393–4, 395
    shoulder injury 390
    United's complacency 360–1
Keegan, Kevin 14, 21, 27–9, 50, 53, 55, 70, 72, 74–5, 76–7, 81, 109, 273, 340
    FA Cup Final 73–4, 83, 84
    Newcastle 290, 297–9
    signing 67–8, 106
    Uefa Cup Final 80
Keith, John 55
Kelly, Eddie 73
Kelly, Stephen F. 50
Kendall, Howard 41, 238
Kennedy, Michael 396
Kennedy, Ray 55, 186
Kennedy, Stuart 157, 189, 190
Kenyon, Peter 356, 357, 358, 382
Kidd, Brian 3, 267, 277–8, 302, 327

Kilmarnock 156, 162
Kinane, Mick 349, 352
Knighton, Michael 249
Knox, Archie 186, 191, 198, 251
Koeman, Ronald 274
The Kop 174–5, 176
Kuffour, Sammy 321

Labone, Brian 60, 100
Lake, Paul 237
Latham, Harry 235
Law, Denis 60, 215, 229–30, 232–3, 234–5
Lawler, Chris 71, 106, 147, 152, 154, 178, 184
Lawrence, John 88, 90
Lawrence, Tommy 101, 105, 111, 112, 126–7, 180
    FA Cup Final 147
    leaves club 71
Lawton, James 109
Lawton, Matt 390
Lawton, Tommy 304
Leeds 124, 142–54, 165, 171, 275, 298, 327
    Championship title 269–70
    FA Cup 142, 144, 146–9
Leicester 77, 108, 180
Leighton, Jim 157, 167, 192, 195, 221, 222–3, 227, 236, 251–2
Leighton, Linda 252, 253
Lennox, Bobby 60, 93
Leverkusen 359, 360
Lewis, Kevin 215
Leyton Orient game 262
Libuda, Reinhard 101
Liddell, Billy 214
Life Boys 37
Lindsay, Alec 67, 71, 73, 84, 105, 106
Lindsay, Jack 285
Linke, Thomas 321
Liverpool 14, 234, 267, 270, 294, 299, 325, 326, 329, 398

see also European Cup; Shankly,
Bill
boards 206–7
Boot Room 29, 49, 208–20
Championship title 77, 99–100,
181–2, 269–70
drugs rumours 124
Ferguson's research 186
promotion to First Div. 219–20
staff v apprentices 72
Lloyd, Larry 67, 71, 72, 80, 105, 106
Luton game 263

McAllister, David 138–9
McCall, Walter 162–3
McCann, Jim 66
McCarthy, Mick 395
McClair, Brian 280, 297
McClaren, Steve 322, 326, 348
McCreadie, Eddie 147
McCulley, Bobby 116, 118
McDermott, Terry 186
Macdonald, Malcolm 64, 82, 83
McDougall, Frank 197
McFaul, Willie 83
McGarvey, Frank 133, 135
McGhee, Mark 4–5, 9, 156, 157,
162–3, 164, 165–7, 168, 353
Cup Winners' Cup 191, 192
transfer 196–7
McGrath, Paul 238, 240, 241, 242,
243–4, 245–6, 247
McGregor, Jim 264
McGuinness, Wilf 42, 356
McHale, Kevin 230, 232
Machin, Mel 236
McIlvanney, Hugh 237–8, 305, 366,
398
McInnes, Jimmy 122–3
Mackay, Calum 57
McKeever, Frank 31
McKeever, Madge 31
McKimmie, Stewart 197
McLaren, Ian 87–8
McLaughlin, John 59

McLeish, Alex 157, 189, 192, 195
MacLeod, Ally 96, 114, 136
McLintock, Frank 218–19
McManaman, Steve 272
McManus, J. P. 3, 345, 346–7, 348,
349–50, 351–2, 359–60, 364,
366–9
McMaster, John 157, 189
McNally, Bernard 32
McNeill, Billy 50, 61, 93, 137, 156
McQueen, Gordon 165
McQueen, Tommy 197
Magnier, John 3, 4, 6, 342–3,
345–53, 359–60, 363–4,
366–9, 380, 385
Manchester City 236–7, 249, 279,
387, 397–8
Manchester United
see also Ferguson, Sir Alex
card games 264–5
European Cup 103, 130, 131,
299–300, 319–25, 331–5,
379
Ferguson appointment 227
Ferguson's peak 289–303
league title 278–9
Munich Air Disaster 233–4
Premiership titles 290, 299, 353,
354, 363
purge 236–53
Manton, Lord 348–9
Martin, Lee 252
Matthäus, Lothar 321
Matthews, Sir Stanley 143, 304
May, David 323
Mazzola 153
Meakin, Jim 116
Mee, Bertie 73
Melia, Jimmy 179, 215
Melling, Joe 300
Melrose, Harry 59
Melwood 203–7
Mercer, Joe 75, 147, 183
Methven, Colin 97
Middlesbrough 326, 393

Milburn, Jackie 109
Miller, Willie 157, 158, 160, 186,
    195
Milne, Gordon 50, 71, 108, 147, 152,
    181, 183
Milne, Jimmy 310
Milton-Nielsen, Kim 388
Moenchengladbach 55, 80
Moncur, John 279
Montgomerie, Jim 144
Moore, Bobby 70
Moores, John 172, 216
Moran, Kevin 238
Moran, Ronnie 29–30, 46, 48, 49,
    51, 66, 78–9, 129, 147, 178–9,
    204, 207, 213–14, 215
Moratti, Angelo 129
Morris, Mike 365
Morrissey, Johnny 179–80
Morse, Dean 390–1
Mortensen, Stan 263
Morton game 166–7
Mourinho, Jose 10, 62, 108, 173, 185
Muirhead, Tom 310
Muirhead, Willie 114, 116–17, 120
Mullen, Jimmy 115
Munich Air Disaster 171, 215,
    233–4, 339
Mutch, George 312
Myers, Canon Arnold 23

National Sports Centre 114
Neal, Phil 124, 186
Neil, James 138
Neville, Gary 9, 242, 290, 293, 297,
    324, 328–9, 331, 384, 385
Neville, Phil 242, 290, 297–8, 329,
    385
Newbon, Gary 335
Newcastle 82–4, 109–10, 165, 290,
    297–9, 329
Newton, Denis 200
Nicholson, Bill 171
Nottingham Forest 93–4, 136–7, 250
Notts County game 232

O'Brien, Aidan 347
O'Brien, Vincent 346
O'Farrell, Frank 356
O'Kane, John 297
O'Neill, Martin 20, 66, 192
Ortiz de Mendibil, Jose Maria 127,
    128, 131
O'Shea, John 384, 393
Overmars, Marc 301, 325, 330
Oxford United 240, 241

Paisley, Bob 48–50, 66, 76, 81, 110
    award 124
    Boot Room 29, 208–10
    European Cup 2, 124–5, 152
    FA Cup Final 149
    as manager 2, 16, 18–19, 23,
        51–5, 124–5, 152, 209–10
    one-liners 69
    war 314
Pallister, Gary 236, 237, 247, 249,
    250, 264, 265, 267–9, 271, 277,
    278, 281, 297
Parker, Paul 271, 297
Parlour, Ray 330
Pasquale, Bruno 365
Peck, Michael 277
Peiro, Joaquin 127, 153
Petit, Emmanuel 325–6
Pfluger, Hans 189
Phelan, Mike 237, 247
Pires, Robert 130
Pound, Dick 387
Prentice, John 95, 96, 118
Preston North End 16, 283, 304–14,
    316, 317–18, 340–1

Queen's Park 61, 62–3, 114
Queensland Star 33–4, 344–5
Queiroz, Carlos 391, 393, 395

Radio City 20, 24
Ramsden, Ken 324
Rangers 156, 188, 195
    Cup Winners' Cup 191

Ferguson as child 36–7
Ferguson management offer 193–4
Ferguson as player 61, 62, 86–93
Reade, Brian 24
Reakes, Sid 217
Real Madrid 188, 190–2, 362, 380
    Beckham 379, 381, 382
Red Star Belgrade 81
Redmond, Steve 237
Remington Rand 57
Revie, Don 45, 49, 72–3, 146, 171
Reykjavik game 182
Richardson, Kieran 200, 393
Rideout, Paul 295
Right Angle Club 344 5
Riise, John Arne 398
Riley, Bert 203
Risman, Gus 257
Ritchie, Jimmy 133–4
Roberts, John 371
Robins, Mark 250, 251, 276
Robinson, Peter 14, 41, 42–3, 44,
    45–6, 50, 54–5, 172, 176, 178
Robson, Bobby 109, 187
Robson, Bryan 238, 240, 242, 247,
    264, 267, 269, 271, 279, 280
Rock of Gibraltar 6, 342-, 349,
    350–2, 366, 385
Rohde, Shelley 18, 24, 25, 27, 102
Rollin, Jack 316
Ronaldo 331–2, 362, 363, 380, 384,
    385, 393, 396
Rooney, Wayne 264, 384, 388, 399
Rougvie, Doug 157, 189, 196
Roxburgh, Andy 94
Rush, Ian 222

Saha, Louis 56
St John, Betsy 217
St John, Ian 50, 68, 100, 147, 171,
    180, 181, 205, 218, 219
    America 169–70
    Anfield mafia 179
    dropped 71, 109–10
    and Eric Sykes 98

European Cup 129–30, 153, 154,
    183
FA Cup Final 148, 149
and Fagan 212–13
fans 145
Huddersfield 235
league title 181
and McInnes 122
Shankly's funeral 28
signing 67, 173, 200, 216–17
soccer school 20–1
St Johnstone 61–2, 96
St Mirren 119–21, 132–40, 160–1
    Ferguson sacking 137, 139
    First Division championship 133
    industrial tribunal 136, 137–40,
        155, 159
Samuel, Martin 383, 397
Santillana 192
Sarti, Giuliano 153, 154
Saunders, Tom 29–30
Sawyer, Eric 172–3, 178, 216–17
Scanlon, Ian 160
Schmeichel, Peter 267, 268, 279, 290,
    297, 328
    European Cup 320, 321, 322, 323,
        332
    FA Cup 330
    signing 271
Scholes, Paul 29, 290, 297, 320, 329,
    385, 392
Scholl, Mehmet 321
Scotland
    Ferguson 60–1, 198, 221–7
    Shankly 304, 313, 316
Scott, Bill 310, 340–1
Scottish Cup
    Aberdeen 187–8, 193, 195, 197
    Dunfermline 56, 58–9
    Rangers 93
    St Mirren 135
Scottish League Cup 115–16
    Aberdeen 159, 161, 197
Scottish Professional Footballers'
    Association 95

Sealey, Les 251, 252
Seaman, David 330
Sexton, Dave 73
Shankly, Agnes (wife) 317
Shankly, Barbara (daughter) 26, 317, 338
Shankly, Barbara (mother) 338
Shankly, Bill 1–3, 5–6, 11, 64–85, 93, 199–220, 273, 304–18, 336–41, 371–5
  Big Idea 169–85
  Carlisle United 282–6, 318, 338–41
  fans 7–8, 22, 77, 144–5, 146, 149, 151, 176–7
  Ferguson meeting 186
  football chant 65
  funeral 23, 27–8
  greatest day 142–54
  Grimsby Town 286–7
  immortality 228–35
  kit change 1, 117
  minework 375
  new breed 98–112
  new kit 183, 284
  Preston 304–14, 316, 317–18, 340–1
  retirement 2–3, 13–30, 41–55, 84–5
  vision of hell 122–31
  war 307–8, 313–17
  Workington 254–63, 287–8
  xenophobia 107, 170
Shankly, Bob (brother) 92–3, 337, 338
Shankly, Jeanette (daughter) 26, 338
Shankly, Jimmy (brother) 337, 338
Shankly, John (brother) 337, 338
Shankly, John (father) 371, 374
Shankly, Nessie (wife) 13–14, 17, 21, 26, 27, 46, 50, 214–15, 257
Shankly, Sandy (brother) 336, 337, 340
Sharp, Graeme 226–7

Sharpe, Lee 242, 243, 246, 265–7, 271, 274, 276, 280, 291, 297
Shaw, Bob 114, 116, 120
Shaw, Richard 291
Shearer, Alan 94
Sheffield Wednesday 277
Sheridan, John 277
Sheringham, Teddy 321, 322, 323, 328, 329–30
Simmons, Matthew 291
Simpson, Gordon 118
Simpson, Neil 189
Sirrell, Jimmy 114, 384–5
Smith, Alan 327, 384, 385, 393, 398
Smith, Dave 92
Smith, E. D. 254
Smith, John 18, 43–4, 50, 54, 348
Smith, Professor Sir Roland 292, 302, 357
Smith, Tommy 14, 16, 46, 47, 55, 71, 72, 76, 81, 127, 146–7, 313
  Anderlecht game 183
  FA Cup Final 83, 84
  Shankly's funeral 28
Solskjaer, Ole Gunnar 321, 323, 329, 359, 362, 363
Souness, Graeme 46, 158, 186, 194, 224, 226
Spencer, Charlie 286
Sprake, Gary 149
Spurs 171, 328–9
Stam, Jaap 218, 330, 332, 354–5, 365, 367
Stark, Billy 133, 135, 197
Stead, Jonathan 107
Stein, Colin 92, 93
Stein, Jock 57, 89–90, 102, 119–20, 128, 130, 190, 198, 221–4, 292
Stein, Mel 365
Stepney, Alec 78
Stevenson, Willie 67, 71, 102, 108, 153–4, 180
Stockport County 185
Stone, Mike 399
Stoute, Sir Michael 345

Strachan, Gordon 5, 157, 158, 162, 163, 167, 189, 191
    and Atkinson 239, 240
    boredom 198
    leaves club 195, 196, 270–1
    Scotland 223
    World Cup 226, 227
Stringfellow, Mike 180
Strong, Geoff 148, 153
Stuart, Graham 295
Suarez, Luis 127
Sullivan, June 136, 138
Sunderland game 310
Sykes, Eric 98
Symon, Scot 89

Taibi, Massimo 365, 367
Tarbuck, Jimmy 146
Taylor, Graham 247
Taylor, James 311
Taylor, Phil 207, 214
Terry, John 175
Thomas, Geoff 252, 280
Thompson, Peter 67, 68, 72, 171
    FA Cup final 148
    signing 173, 180
Thompson, Phil 20, 51, 52–3, 72, 76, 81, 82–3, 110, 210
    debut 78–9
    European Cup 153
Thomson, Elizabeth 35–6, 39
Thornley, Ben 324
Toal, Kieran 364
Todd, Willie 132, 135–6, 137, 140
Toshack, John 67, 72, 73, 74, 75–7, 80, 81
    FA Cup Final 83, 84
    Shankly's funeral 28
    signing 106
    Uefa Cup 80
Toxteth 199–202
Trautmann, Bert 144
Tweedy, George 286–7
Twentyman, Geoff 66, 285

Uefa, European Cup celebrations 124
Uefa Cup
    Aberdeen 187
    Celtic 192–3
    Liverpool 19, 79–80
Ure, Ian 121
Uruguay game 226–7

Vadas, Gyorgy 129
Van Himst, Paul 183
Van Nistelrooy, Ruud 56, 130, 357, 359, 384, 385
Vaughan, Frankie 146
Venables, Terry 243
Verón, Juan Sebastián 269, 350, 354, 357, 362–3, 389
Vieira, Patrick 326, 330
Vitty, Jack 261

Waddell, Willie 94
Waddle, Chris 277
Wales 222–4
Walker, Ian 328, 329
Wall, Sir Frederick 313
Wallace, Willie 60
Watford game 108
Watkins, Maurice 240, 292, 296, 358, 386–7
Watson, Billy 257, 260
Watson, Russell 328, 329
Watt, Colin 177
Webb, Neil 247, 252
Weir, Peter 192
Weller, Keith 77
Wenger, Arsène 10, 62, 182, 256, 289, 301–2, 325–6, 388
West Ham 70, 175, 179, 270, 292
White, David 61, 89, 92, 94, 236, 237
Whiteside, Norman 238, 240, 241, 242, 243–6, 247–9
Whittle, Ernie 261
Wilkinson, Howard 269, 275
Williams, Tom 214, 219, 235
Wilson, Bob 73

Wilson, Harold 24, 25, 27, 171
Wilson, Mark 365, 367
Wilson, Ray 100, 230
Wilson, Tony 48
Wiltord, Sylvain 360, 380
Wimbledon 279, 303
Workington 254–63, 287–8
World Cup 303, 378
　England win 100
　Scotland 222–7
World Cup Championship 353–4
Wright, Ian 251

Yeats, Ron 18, 20–1, 50, 98, 100,
　101, 179
　and Eric Sykes 98

European Cup 152, 153, 183–4
FA Cup Final 147, 148, 150
fans 145
Huddersfield 235
leaves club 71
new kit 183
Shankly's funeral 28
signing 67, 173, 216, 217–18
Yorke, Dwight 302–3, 321, 322,
　326–7, 329, 333, 359
'You'll Never Walk Alone' 143,
　175–6
Young, Alf 312, 313
Young, Willie 95

Zidane, Zinédine 332, 333, 362

Visit www.panmacmillan.com to read more about all our books and to buy them. You will also find features, author interviews and news of any author events, and you can sign up for e-newsletters so that you're always first to hear about our new releases.